Retail Design

The late twentieth century saw rapid growth in consumption and the expansion of retailing and services. This was reflected in the number and type of stores and locations, from regional shopping malls and out-of-town superstores to concept and flagship stores. Retail design became an essential part of its success by creating distinctive brands and formats. However, the economic recession in the developed world and competition for consumer goods from the developing world has led to a re-assessment of the growth-led conventions of the retail industry. In addition, the rapid advance of e-commerce and online shopping has created new challenges for physical stores and the communication and distribution of retail brands. The book will provide students, researchers and practitioners a detailed assessment of retail design, taking a distinctive global approach to place design practice and theory in context. Chapters are devoted to key issues in the visual and structural contribution of design to retail brands and format development, and to the role of design in communication. In the course of the book, the authors engage with problems of convergence between retailing and other services and between the physical and virtual worlds, and also changing patterns of use, re-use and ownership of retail spaces and buildings. *Retail Design* concerns designers and organisations but also defines its broader contribution to society, culture and economy.

Ann Petermans holds a PhD in Architecture and is affiliated to the Faculty of Architecture and Arts of Hasselt University (Belgium). Her PhD focused on the translation and investigation of the principles and practices of the 'experience economy' within the discipline of interior architecture in general, and retail design in particular. Her current research is on experience, well-being and happiness in architecture and interior architecture. Ann also teaches on these subjects in the Master's in Architecture and Interior Architecture at Hasselt University.

Anthony Kent is Professor of Fashion Marketing at Nottingham Trent University. He completed a PhD from the University of the Arts London for his research into the locational contexts of fashion retail stores, their built environments and interior design. He is a Member of the Chartered Institute of Marketing, Fellow of the Royal Society of Arts and Fellow of the Higher Education Institute, and he is Chair of the Marketing Special Interest Group of the British Academy of Management.

Retail Design

Theoretical Perspectives

**Edited by
Ann Petermans and Anthony Kent**

Routledge
Taylor & Francis Group

LONDON AND NEW YORK

First published in paperback 2024

First published 2017
by Routledge
4 Park Square, Milton Park, Abingdon, Oxon OX14 4RN

and by Routledge
605 Third Avenue, New York, NY 10158

Routledge is an imprint of the Taylor & Francis Group, an informa business

Publisher's Note
The publisher has gone to great lengths to ensure the quality of this reprint but
points out that some imperfections in the original copies may be apparent.

British Library Cataloguing in Publication Data
A catalogue record for this book is available from the British Library

Every effort has been made to contact copyright holders for their permission
to reprint material in this book. The publishers would be grateful to hear
from any copyright holder who is not here acknowledged and will undertake
to rectify any errors or omissions in future editions of this book.

Library of Congress Cataloging in Publication Data
Names: Petermans, Ann, editor. | Kent, Anthony (Professor of fashion
    marketing), editor.
Title: Retail design : theoretical perspectives / edited by Ann Petermans and
    Anthony Kent.
Description: Abingdon, Oxon ; New York, NY : Routledge, 2017.
Identifiers: LCCN 2016025530 | ISBN 9781472467836 (hardback) |
    ISBN 9781315605920 (ebook)
Subjects: LCSH: Stores, Retail. | Design. | Display of merchandise.
Classification: LCC NA6220 .R48 2017 | DDC 745.4—dc23
LC record available at https://lccn.loc.gov/2016025530

ISBN: 978-1-4724-6783-6 (hbk)
ISBN: 978-1-03-283725-3 (pbk)
ISBN: 978-1-315-60592-0 (ebk)

DOI: 10.4324/9781315605920

Typeset in Bembo
by Apex CoVantage, LLC

Contents

Figures

Tables

1 Introduction

Anthony Kent and Ann Petermans

Retail design is concerned with the environments in which people shop, in which 'design is a means of communicating a message to people, and "good design" . . . must be a comprehensive and co-ordinated approach to everything the shopper sees' (Mitchell 1986). It should add value to retail strategy by improving the quality of the shopping environment and influencing consumer decision-making and loyalty. Design should be practical too, in searching for and providing solutions to practical consumer needs, and it has an important role in the efficient use of materials and space to maximise profitability and the return on investment in the project (Kent and Omar 2003).

The visual identity of the retailer, its image and its distinctive branding is fundamentally created through design; it must attract and keep customers, support a brand or store's image, showcase the product, and work as a functional shopping environment. Design should define but also re-define brand identity because 'few solutions have an effective time span of more than five years' (Plunkett and Reid 2012: 5). Retail design has to address the conflicting requirements of maintaining brand consistency and shorter-term objectives inherent in retailing. Fierce competition, innovations and fashions mean that store interiors have to change too, as a visible symbol of improvement and a demonstration of the retail brand's contemporary appeal.

As the retail industry has become more significant, both economically and socially, so the design of retail outlets, shops and stores has increasingly become the focus of design attention. Early shops combined both making and trading activities, where workshops and commerce were both found on the same site. The two activities were split, as the functions became more specialised, and shops became distributors of producers' merchandise. Their spatial requirement was twofold, for the shopkeeper's stock, both on display and in storage, and for circulation areas in which staff could sell to customers. However, the nineteenth century saw the appearance of department stores and a more conscious approach to store design. New types of store architecture, the development of advertising, and improvements in window display stimulated competition. The street scene was transformed by multiple or chain stores which expanded across countries, identified through their owners' names and effectively branded them.

The twentieth century saw the expansion of retail formats to meet the demands of economic growth, increasing personal income, wealth and consumption. The locations of retailing expanded as well, as out-of-town superstores, shopping malls and centres spread from the United States to Europe and later found global recognition. As retailers internationalised, so their formats and distinctive designs became increasingly evident as a global manifestation of consumption, in particular as a sign of a post-industrial movement from production to consumption. American and European at its outset, retailing – by the twenty-first century, through many its many forms, sites and locations – had become well established as a global industry. Reflecting its origins, it has been dominated by Western-centric approaches to design. However, with its global reach and new centres of wealth, retail and the design of its shops and stores has required a more balanced approach.

Retail Design has been researched and discussed from both academic and practice-based perspectives, providing a number of disciplinary perspectives. The fullest accounts are commonly found in texts about designing for the store, its requirements and its features, and, more partially, in accounts by practitioners of their work and contribution to the field. These tend to describe design rather than more fully engage in the theoretical frameworks that contribute to its realisation: consumer culture and consumption, symbolism and meaning, ownership and commercial value. The aim of this volume is to bring these elements together, with researchers and practitioners presenting an international dimension to retail design's evolution and future direction. The chapters are organised around key themes, rather than specific disciplinary perspectives. In what follows, *retail design* emerges as a more complex and nuanced field of design, which holds important implications for designers, retailers and consumers.

Retail design literature

Prior to the late 1990s there were relatively few general studies in the history of retail design (Adburgham 1967; Davies 1991). Those specialising in the architecture of shops tended to be distinguished by a periodisation approach, primarily modern and post-modern, and categorisation of architectural design (Pevsner 1976; Jencks 1979; Papadakis 1990; Watkin 1996; Morrison 2003). A common thread has been their concern with historical and contextual development, and the creative integration of store concepts through their exteriors and interiors, their visual identity and their spatial footprints. In these historical accounts, the post-war period tends to form a watershed in the development of shops and shopping. In the early years, shortages of products and materials constrained retail development and shop design. As new consumer markets emerged in the 1950s, the retail industry responded with new typically American-inspired formats and new challenges for designers. Retail store identity was typically affirmed through window displays; new and more varied merchandise influenced interior layouts. The new medium of television communicated their accessibility. However, windows and shop interiors continued to be organized separately until a more coherent and integrated approach to store design emerged in the 1960s. Lifestyle retailing saw product and store design brought together, to create a visually harmonious and distinctive brand (Ind 1997).

The subsequent ascendency of services and shopping in particular led to the convergence of transactional retailing with social and leisure activities. The store as a sociable 'third place' (Oldenburg 1997; Mikunda 2004) began to create opportunities for more memorable and experiential environments. Their contribution to simulation and reality, and more generally the growth of consumerism, provided a major strand of postmodern theoretical development (Baudrillard 1994). From an anthropological perspective, they contributed to the formation of identity and identities of individuals and social groups (Miller et al. 1998). In these conditions, the signature architect and designer identified by Din (2000) found new communicative and meaning-laden opportunities.

The scope for retailing and its design extended at this time as managerial and commercial approaches were adopted in the public sector. In these ways, retailing, and its store environments, became more hybrid, transforming such disparate places as bookshops, museums and airports. Through them, retailing became more concerned with services and experiences and further transformation through the emergence of the digital world and e-retail in the twenty-first century.

Situating retail design in design

Design

Retail design is characterised by its visibility, accessibility and commerciality, but nevertheless reflects changes evident in the broader development of design. Design itself refers to both the process and the outcome (Walsh 1996), although designers are not always engaged in design activities. There are possibilities for 'silent design' in the absence of the designer (Gorb and Dumas 1987). Nevertheless, the processes and outcomes themselves are subject to change both in activity and in interpretation. Buchanan (2001), reflecting on the evolution and future development of design, describes places or placements as areas of discovery and invention that characterise the practice of design. Consequently, design enters into new 'orders' of practice and research as a way to answer new project and society demands. Its trajectory is from 'signs' (graphic and communication design) to 'objects' (product design), 'interactions' (interaction design) and finally 'systems' (environment and system design). These orders are not rigidly fixed or separated but represent the growing scale and complexity of design interventions.

Design, as form and function in contexts, sees products as objects. Buchanan's third order in the trajectory of design moves from object to interaction, an approach that embraces human-centred design. In these accounts the user is a resource, and design is focused on understanding and delivering what users want. It sees designers as part of a wider group of agents in the process of co-production or co-creation. It also accounts for changes in understanding the process of designing, suggesting that we are constituted in relation to the world not only as thinking subjects but as bodily beings (Schön 1983).

Design for services fits into this interaction order, where human beings relate to other human beings through the mediating influence of products; in this mode of design, product is defined more broadly as not only physical artefacts but also experiences, activities or services (Meroni and Sangiorgi 2011). Meroni and Sangiorgi (2011), distinguish twenty-first-century design from the previous century by its complexity, movement away from the design of simple objects. The designing process and outcomes now hinge on unpredictable factors, characterised by a social economy with a variety of actors and motivations and the dynamics of social innovation. The designing process is something that occurs over time, and an activity to achieve results. It designs entities in the making, whose final characteristics will emerge only in the complex dynamics of the real world.

Buchanan's 'orders' demonstrate the expansion of the concept of design, its engagement and its application – not least, because he himself explained design as a problem-solving activity suited to complex, non-linear 'wicked' problems, by contrast to more sequential 'tame' problems. The expansion of the design world into a broader problem-solving activity (Brown 2008) was reflected in the possibilities of design as meaning. Objects are shaped by human intentionality, and human-made things are dependent on intention to exist; this is part of the language that a design can create and shape.

Meaning not only signifies a product's basic functions and aesthetics; it also carries an emotional and symbolic value, bringing a product message to the user (Krippendorff

2006). It is concerned with making sense of things: people and very personal items, relating them to who gave them and whom it reminds them of. In this mode, designers manipulate form, gesture, materials, texture, interaction and other design elements to convey a message to the consumer, consciously or unconsciously (Buchner 2003). Thus, meaning is mostly in the consumer's mind. Things people use and surround theirselves with reflect the owner's personality; their things are signs and part of the process that constitutes consciousness in a person. Signs, symbols and objects have another function too, as expressions of differentiation that stress unique qualities of the owner and skills or superiority over others.

Elements of these 'orders' or approaches to design are, and have the potential to be, evident in retail design and the designer's relationship with the client and consumers. Of particular concern to designers as they move between closure and adaptation in each project is the extent to which design can ever be said to be complete, and how businesses can adapt to change and continuity concurrently. Great designs are typified by simplicity and emotional engagement, combining the new and familiar (Liedtka and Mintzberg 2006). The extent to which this summary can be applied to retail design is examined in the next section.

Retail design

General viewpoint

The retail designer may have to prioritise specific roles, as a navigator of complexity, a negotiator of value (how design can increase margins by reducing costs or enhancing price points), and a mediator of stakeholders. At a project level, designers orchestrate their development by producing drawings, setting out dimensions and specifying materials and the provision of information for other specialists involved in the detailed specification and implementation of the project. For Plunkett and Reid (2012: 6) the retail designer has to balance the client's objectives and preferences with new solutions, to 'identify, adopt and adapt the aesthetic preferences of target customers but always obliged to innovate, to present something that, while unfamiliar, excites as it communicates the recognised, or redefined brand values to an extended family of old and new customers'. In multiple retail businesses, emphasis is placed on the relationship between design team and client, and the need to engage with a wide range of stakeholders, directors, managers and staff, in the design process. The process here must meet strategic and operational objectives that balance the costs of construction with the store brand identity and experience, and that balance efficiency with profitability.

More challenging views on retail design and the designer appeared when architects became involved in prestigious retail projects. For a long time, buildings have been acknowledged as symbols of good taste, power and status through the attention paid to the identity of the architect (Berg and Kreiner 1990). However, in the 1980s and 1990s, the combination of commercial interests with architecture gave new prominence to the architect (Glendinning 2004). Design for meaning and symbolism led to unique, sometimes iconic, buildings that were defended for a sense of heightened experience. Their ambiguity, combined with at least some consistency in meaning, provoked and invited decoding; they achieved an endless and superfluous variety through the liberated imagination of their consumer (Jencks 2005). Consequently, the retail brand could now be defined by discourses drawing on the elements of distinctive design: the celebrity (signature) architect and media engagement (Sklair 2006).

These perspectives define the scope of retail design. The external details, the frontage of the store, are important as first impressions can form a lasting image in the mind of the consumer (Fitch and Knobel 1990). The way the store presents itself and attracts people to it first arises from how it is seen at a distance, and second from how the edge of the store forms a liminal aspect – the threshold – through its windows and doors. A fundamental question is how to encourage people to enter the store. Its signage has to be visible from both the front and the side. Stores tend to utilise a fully glazed façade and consequently need to account for views of the interior and its displays onto the street. The external aspect requires the designer to work on the coherence of its visual properties and identity, and, in the homogenised shopping street or centre, these elements have to distinguish each retailer. Prestigious, iconic buildings and distinctive façades have been used successfully by luxury brands. However, cost-conscious market entrants have successfully used a more edgy approach in their buildings. Boxpark in London's Shoreditch, for instance, is an agglomeration of small retailers each occupying a shipping container.

Interiors form the more detailed part of the design. They should 'signal' the positioning of the retail brand: from low-cost stores with modest finishes and utilitarian displays, to expensive luxury brands as showcases. Inside the store, planning and circulation are influenced by the size of the store, number of staff, variety of merchandise, building regulations, and flow of customers. The rate of flow again depends on the positioning of the brand and its objectives: supermarkets will generally require quick and efficient throughput; fashion stores may require customers to linger, to engage with the sensory environment and to try on the clothes. The transferability of retail design into other services and leisure and cultural institutions, including museums, restaurants, hotels, airports and hospitals, has led to different conceptualisations and organisations of internal spaces. They contribute to an understanding in other ways of wayfinding, routing and navigation to the customer journey. Moreover, this has been a two-way process with the concept of curation and showcasing the presentation of merchandise entering the fashion designer store.

Related to these planning considerations is the location of the merchandise, determined by the retailer's priorities and plans for visual merchandising and display. The merchandise itself requires fixturing and fittings, flooring and lighting; and the selection of materials and structures help to convey the store's identity. At times these have created particular points of difference. Habitat's originality and initial success depended on a store stocked with furniture and household goods, and the idea of instant availability. Smaller items were displayed as in a warehouse or market stall stacked up, and larger ones in room settings: the 'tension between the two forms of display created a buzz of excitement in the stores which proved to be irresistible' (Conran 1996: 20). New interpretations of space and its finishes contribute to the Universal Design Group's success; textured space is created through the use of pattern in a variety of materials and scales. This has been applied to great effect in smaller retail spaces, but also to break up the large spaces of a department store (Watson 2007). These elements form the 'front of shop' design, but the 'back office' exists as working areas to be organised around ergonomic and human factors and compliance with regulations for fire protection, emergency exits, security, heating and ventilation. Plunkett and Reid (2012) argue that most retail interiors have a comparatively short life and that economic realities will necessarily influence choice of materials and methods of construction. But style or a sense of luxury requires close attention to the detail of interiors, and that perception of quality and exclusivity must be evident in the selection and detailed assembly of finishes and fittings.

Retail design and retail branding

Design plays a significant role in the development of a brand. This is evident from the visual elements within a successful brand – its name, symbol or design (or a combination of all three) (Doyle 1995). Retail design has an important role in turning retail stores into brand names that simplify shopping, guarantee a specific level of quality and allow degrees of self-expression. The retail brand is highly visible and carries with it a strong image of the retailer to the consumers and can also prove difficult to change. The concept of branding is inextricably linked to advertising and marketing (Mesher 2010). In retail terms, the store is built around the concept of the brand and the products sold within it. 'The interior emulates the aspirations of the brand values and qualities to enhance the relationships between the space and the message' (Mesher 2010: 12–13). Consistency makes the message stronger and re-affirms the brand's worth.

The design of shop exteriors and their signage has clearly become more consistent, creative and adventurous over time. Yet earlier frontages were frequently used to advertise the retailer, in some cases almost as a billboard. Photographic records of nineteenth-century shops displayed prominent signage in affluent areas with very large lettering repeated wherever space allowed: above and below the window area, and on fascia boards, gas lamps and mosaic entrance doors (Mathias 1967). The extent of large and opulent company signage dominated the street. This style of architectural design is well documented in Sainsbury's (Williams 1994) and appears to have remained popular until the end of the Second World War. Williams describes the architecture of Sainsbury's high street shops where the interiors were richly decorated with Minton tiles and mahogany screens, mosaic floors and marble-topped counters (Williams 1994; Kirby 2009). The rise of branding may partially account for growing interdisciplinarity of design as clients' demands and designers seek greater integration of product, graphic and interior design to create coherent and fulsome design solutions (Julier 2008).

Visual identity forms an important strand of store design research, which acknowledges the seminal influence of Olins (1978, 1989, and 2003) on corporate design to convey the shape and nature of organisations. Olins (2003) came to regard retailers as brand innovators, replacing FMCG companies with their emotional appeal and providing more comprehensive engagement with consumers through 'brand temples'. Changes to comprehensive store design practices drew on accounts of lifestyle retailing from the 1960s but more commonly from the 1980s onwards, through narratives and histories, often biographical, of designers and their retail branding initiatives (Fitch and Knobel 1990; Conran 1996; Olins 2003). The three approaches – categorisation of building styles, visual identity and designer accounts – made a distinctive contribution to the re-conceptualisation of a marketing-led perspective on store environments and retail branding.

Research into branded retail spaces is a relatively new field; one which this book aims to extend. The role of atmosphere, the influence of sensory perception on affect, in service environments was introduced by Kotler in 1973 as an extension of the marketing concept. Studies in brand and corporate identity from management and design perspectives with varying degrees of emphasis explain the significance of visual integrity to communicate the brand. Retail design studies have increasingly observed and used a holistic approach to store design, in which interiors and exteriors integrate into a single concept.

Store design became an integral part of clothing retailers' strategies during the 1980s, leading towards more creative interiors and exteriors. The concentration of food retailing into fewer and more powerful multiples and the transformation of store distribution and product ranges expanded branded activity in this sector. The 'store as brand' came to relate appearance and identity to core brand values (Magrath 2005) as consumer experiences reflected the development of retail branding and store design, and their engagement with emotions and physical contact (Kent 2003).

Retail design: A source of creativity and inspiration

For consumers, the store can provide a source of inspiration, for new spatial ideas as well as new merchandise and its arrangement. How things are organised, co-ordinated and presented can contribute to individual identity, social identity as well as individual problem-solving.

Fundamentally, retailing both sustains creative design and also enables consumers to be creative. This may be the very act of creation in DIY stores, and increasingly food can be understood as fashion – for example, by creating fusion meals with eclectic ingredients. Bookstores provide social spaces for creative thinking, of a more philosophical realm of concepts and for art, dreaming and an internalised sensory embodiment of possible worlds. Clothing retailers offer creativity at a local level. Retail design has to be multi-faceted by linking together art, instinct and business in a problem-solving and planning process (Kent 2007).

Interactivity and experimentation present further creative challenges. Static spatial configurations can create 'product museums', while flexibility enables stores to adapt and change to meet commercial and social needs (Kent 2007). Concept stores demonstrate this approach; the Colette store, in Paris, focuses on distinctive fashion style, beyond the clothes themselves. It describes itself as 'an inimitable mix and match, modelled after its customers . . . in the spirit of the moment' (Colette 2014). The store design features neither postmodern deconstructive or eclectic elements, nor particularly distinctive modernist 'white cube' tendencies. It remains monochromatic so that the lighting focuses attention on the products and gallery-like presentation of artwork and wall displays. The hard surfaces of the floor, tables and glass cabinets further contribute to this effect consistently throughout the store. In a sense, the store itself is an exhibition. An alternative route to interaction with products and services is found in the large, open-plan internal spaces of Apple stores. Curation and a new approach to minimalism has role models in Hermes, Swarovski, Puma and Jeanswest that have more things to demonstrate, and more stories to tell, than other stores (Punk 2011). These spaces combine human contact and personal communication and, through their in-store technologies, enable a 'richness' of personal encounters to extend to online communities (Lindstrom 2003; Lammiman and Syrett 2004).

Organisation of the chapters

The aim of the book is to provide a comprehensive assessment of retail design, through different design and contextual lenses, taking a distinctive global approach, to place design practice and theory in context. As retailing has expanded, so concepts of the shop and its spaces, meanings, ownership and uses have become more complex. Explanation of retail design in terms of stores has to be qualified by the profusion of places that perform a retail function. Distribution of goods forms only part of their function, as leisure, socialization and experiential uses account for sometimes a considerable part of the retail space. These are reflected in the broader discussion of the contribution of society, culture and economy to retail design.

The chapters are devoted to key themes in the contribution of design to retail brands and format development, and to the role of design in communication. These engage with the evolution of retail and its design from a transactional product-led world to a more multi-faceted one of transient, yet memorable, experiences. Throughout there are distinct challenges: to map boundaries and chart convergence between retailing and other services and between the physical and virtual worlds. These are evident in the changing patterns of use, re-use and ownership of retail spaces and buildings that contribute to the complexity of the designed physical world. Technological advances in devices, software and networks and their integration underpin the complexity of the digital world.

Chapter 2 introduces theoretical perspectives on retail design, because how it is seen, used and experienced in everyday life can be understood by examining its contexts. As Papanek (1995: 236) observes, 'new directions in design and architecture don't occur accidentally, but always arise out of real changes in society, cultures and concepts'. In particular, retail design has been profoundly influenced by the opportunities created through economic growth and consumption since the mid-twentieth century. These are reflected in social change where individualism, personal independence and mobility distinguish consumers from previous generations. New products and services, increased leisure time for many and personal wealth have created both opportunities to choose and the time to use and enjoy. While these contexts shape the possibilities for retail design, modernist and postmodern approaches have a direct bearing on retail projects, their conceptualization and their delivery.

These lead into Chapter 3 and the historical development of retail design. While experiential design appears to be a very late twentieth-century concept, the remarkable detail in the design of department stores some one hundred years earlier provides a different perspective on the trajectory of retail design. A more enduring source of design innovation is found in the technological developments over this period. In some instances, their application has been profound, as in the creation of entirely new retail formats. The expansion of the retail industry led to a more distinctive profession in the late twentieth century, and the emergence of new roles and organisation of retail designers and consultancies and the characteristics that emerged. The new opportunities for design contributed to a plurality of design interests and debates discussed in the subsequent chapters of this book.

In parallel with these developments, the retail industry saw the emergence of different retail formats, functions and locations and the implications for retail design. The definitions of retailing and store formats are themselves problematic, as they encompass economic, marketing, governmental and industrial approaches and classifications. From this, the dynamic nature of retailing is evident in the rapidly changing product mixes, promotions and communication, the transferability of design concepts, the emergence of new and temporary forms of retailing, and the decline of others – for example, American shopping malls. In Chapter 4, the modelling of retail store typologies provides insights into store design from the perspective of the consumer's shopping experience. This approach integrates stores, store visit intention and types of consumption experience, and it provides a foundation for designers to understand consumer behaviour in a retail context.

Within this contextual and definitional framework, the retail environment can be understood from a focus on retail as place and its space. The mapped, geographical certainty of these locational aspects of design are challenged by meaning-led, social and individual definitions of spaces. These concepts extend to the store and development of new places and spaces of retailing in commercial, cultural and leisure space. The concept of retail space serving a more abstract *social* usage concerns the use and design of retail spaces in the store itself, and its extension into the wider shopping environment, typically the street, mall or centre. These reflections are key topics in Chapter 5. Such spaces are used for the consumption of products and services for different purposes. Gender, ideology and modern consumer culture have their place in the creation of shopping space (Lowe and Wrigley 1996). Shopping can be understood as a social activity, an important medium for communication and interaction. New forms of social space emerged in developments of the 'third place' and later virtual 'third places'. Such hybrid spaces and the influence of virtual environments demonstrate new directions for retail design, with a focus on the evolution and design of experiential stores.

A key theme throughout the book is the globalisation of retailing and its design through international brands, consultancies, products and services. Their replication, as with many service industries, is relatively straightforward with low locational and infrastructural costs and risk. In Chapter 6, the authors examine retail globalization through the lens of retailing in China and Hong Kong, and they focus on the stability of the relationship between brand and design. In the light of multiple global retailers' brand strategies and their icons, identities and images projected through sensory – primarily visual – engagement with consumers, they ask whether retail design is still significant. East Asia with its rapidly growing cities, constrained space, increased consumption and expectations appears to provide a new environment for designers to integrate the virtual world with a profusion of media and its images.

Chapter 7 examines regeneration and re-use in retail design. Government policy on planning issues, guidance to local authorities on the operation of the planning system and their application by retailers has influenced retail design particularly in Europe. Phases of liberalisation towards the location, size and appearance of buildings have enabled designers to adapt and create new formats and styles. More restrictive policies too have contributed to the adoption of new sites, features and spaces. In part, this has led to the regeneration of inner cities within a broader context of sustainability, and an appreciation of re-using industrial, commercial and domestic architecture. Government support and the anxiety of local government bodies to keep retailing alive in towns and cities are also an important consideration in store development and design (Kirby 2009). Increasingly there is a need to re-think the use of stores themselves, from redundant shopping malls to superstores both in and out of town. The chapter examines design issues in re-developing older buildings for retail use, questions of authenticity and new possibilities for branding.

The preceding chapters address key elements in the contextualization of the physical retail environment and its design with a focus on its theoretical dimensions. In this, the role of the designer has been implicit. Therefore, in the next chapter, Chapter 8, the book turns to retail design from a designer perspective, with a reflexive assessment of the designer's own design activity and process. In keeping with the complex issues introduced earlier, the author explains the multi-faceted role of the designer as a facilitator, curator and guide, rather than a simple creator of spaces. More than this the designer has to interpret the culture of the client and navigate the project to market. Fundamentally, this chapter engages with what the designer does, while advancing perspectives on the designer as a force for social change. Nevertheless, in retailing, the designer must also be a negotiator to implement government policy and be a communicator with the client and external stakeholders. The designer has to consider the ways by which the message or promise is not only communicated but also received, adopted and embedded.

Chapter 9 develops this theme of communication, and the communicative power of design. Retail and retail design can be examined formally through advertising and promotion and examined informally – for example, via word of mouth and coolhunting. The chapter examines the role of consumers in the store and explores current and emerging issues in 'co-creation'. Tesco in the UK, for example, has insisted that its supermarket design and facilities are led by customer demand which is tested in depth for both new and established stores (Kirby 2009). It also extends beyond consumers to discuss the role of stakeholders in determining the location and design of stores. Increasingly, customers share with designers an understanding of the interaction between social and design conventions and can interpret the languages and dialects of commercial interior design which they have assimilated while shopping (Plunkett and Reid 2012).

The physical store has been the traditional channel for the distribution and communication of goods in which producer-led transactions have been paramount. The digital channel has challenged this primacy and led to new ways of communicating and interacting. Co-creation of relationships and brands has become an established part of this world, and more generally the Internet and e-commerce have been the focus of wide-reaching academic interest and research. The Internet raises important new possibilities in terms of mobility, temporality and subjectivity. It reveals how the retail sector is increasingly operating through a range of collectivities and hybrid representational networks that are both, at the same time, physical and virtual, social and solitary, aesthetic and transactional (Crewe 2013). This virtual remediation generates additional effects and forms, and it demands new knowledge, space and the making of markets.

For store-based retailers, the rapid growth of information gathering and shopping on the Internet is a major challenge. Less well understood are the design elements of online retail sites and the visual relationship between the physical and virtual worlds. Chapter 10 examines online retail site design and its technologies, functionality and consumer interfaces; and it demonstrates interactional approaches to e-commercial design and specifically key issues in human-computer interaction design and gamification. It concludes by examining the potential of merged worlds – for example, the application and combinations of Augmented Reality, personalised services and geo-positioning, and the opportunities they present in spatial, visual and sensory design.

The last two chapters broaden the scope of retail design. Chapter 11 examines issues of globalisation and localization to provide a more detailed assessment of global, regional and national markets and how design communicates across boundaries. By contrast, localisation draws on the locale a sense of place and sensitivity to local culture and society. The author explores the contradictions between globalisation and localisation with a focus on luxury and designer fashion retailing. A significant aspect of globalization is the need to balance a consistent brand message with the requirements of local conditions. 'Glocalisation' has been popularly applied to this effect, while brand asymmetry techniques can measure the points at which the international retail business diverges from its original domestic form. In this respect, fashion flagship stores are an important medium to develop a local approach to the business, through their engagement with the arts and local artists. The case of Louis Vuitton demonstrates how retail design has a prominent role in market-entry strategies through the identity it creates for its flagship stores. In this case, the store becomes the setting for local experiences.

The final chapter examines the future of retail design and turns to the forces for change in consuming – the media of consumption and consumers themselves. Digital and mobile connectedness contribute to impulsiveness and the need for entertainment, immediacy and surprise. Sustainability, use and re-use of resources appear to take the retailer in another more planned and reflective direction. In these, retail design faces new conditions of temporality and permanence and their application to formats, spaces and content. A formative dimension of these conditions will be the convergence between the physical world, the virtual world and other services. Barron (2015) pertinently questions how retailers can commit to the long term when there is little certainty about what the future looks like. This may be the dawn of the 'beta brandscape' era, where the world is constantly in flux, one lacking predictability and stability: a future of shape-shifting for stores and retail design.

References

Adburgham, A. (1967). *Shops and Shopping 1800–1914 – Where and in What Manner the Well-Dressed Englishwoman Bought Her Clothes.* London: George Allen and Unwin Ltd.

Barron, K. (2015). *Being Human Today: Re-imagine Agenda.* Presentation, 16th October. London: University of the Arts London.

Baudrillard, J. (1994). *Simulacra and Simulation.* Ann Arbor: University of Michigan Press.

Berg, P.O. and Kreiner, K. (1990). Corporate Architecture: Turning Physical Settings into Symbolic Resources. In P. Gagliardi (Ed.), *Symbols and Artifacts: Views of the Corporate Landscape.* New York: Aldine de Gruyter, pp. 41–68..

Brown, T. (2008). Design thinking. *Harvard Business Review, 86*(6), 84–92.

Buchanan, R. (2001). Designing research and the new learning. *Design Issues, 17*(4), 3–23.

Buchner, D. (2003). The role of meaning and intent. *Innovation, 22*(1), 16–18.

Colette. (2014). *About Colette.* Accessed online at http://en.colette.fr/about, 5th December 2014.

Conran, T. (1996). *Terence Conran on Design.* London: Conran Octopus.

Crewe, L. (2013). When virtual and material worlds collide: Democratic fashion in the digital age. *Environment and Planning A, 45*(4), 760–780.

Davies, C. (1991). *High-Tech Architecture.* London: Thames and Hudson Ltd.

Din, R. (2000). *New Retail.* London: Conran Octopus.

Doyle, P. (1995). Marketing in the new millennium. *European Journal of Marketing, 29*(13), 23–41.

Fitch, R. and Knobel, L. (1990). *Fitch on Retail Design.* London: Phaidon.

Glendinning, M. (2004). *The Last Icons: The Lighthouse Scottish Architectural and Design Series 1.* Glasgow: Graven Images.

Gorb, P. and Dumas, A. (1987). Silent design. *Design Studies, 8,* 150–156.

Ind, N. (1997). *The Corporate Brand.* London: Macmillan Business.

Jencks, C. (1979). *Bizarre Architecture.* London: Academy Editions.

Jencks, C. (2005). *The Iconic Building.* London: Francis Lincoln.

Julier, G. (2008). *The Culture of Design* (2nd ed.). London: Sage.

Kent, A.M. (2003). 2D23D: Management and design perspectives on retail branding. *International Journal of Retail Distribution and Management, 31*(3), 131–142.

Kent, A.M. (2007). Creative space: Design and the retail environment. *International Journal of Retail and Distribution Management, 35*(9), 734–745.

Kent, A.M. and Omar, O.E. (2003). *Retailing.* Basingstoke: Palgrave.

Kirby, A.E. (2009). *The Architectural Design of UK Supermarkets: 1950–2006.* Unpublished PhD Thesis, University of the Arts, London.

Kotler, P. (1973). Atmospherics as a marketing tool. *Journal of Retailing, 49*(Winter), 48–64.

Krippendorff, K. (2006). *The Semantic Turn: A New Foundation for Design.* Boca Raton, FL: CRC Press.

Lammiman, J. and Syrett, M. (2004). *Coolsearch: Keeping Your Organisation in Touch and on the Edge.* Chichester: Capstone.

Liedtka, J. and Mintzberg, H. (2006). Time for design. *Design Management Review, 17*(2), 10–18.

Lindstrom, M. (2003). *Brandchild.* London: Kogan Page.

Lowe, M. and Wrigley, N. (1996). *Retailing, Consumption and Capital*. Harlow: Longman.

Magrath, A.J. (2005). Managing in the age of design. *Across the Board*, 42(5), 18–27.

Mathias, P. (1967). *Retailing Revolutions*. Harlow: Longmans.

Meroni, A. and Sangiorgi, D. (2011). *Design for Services*. London: Gower.

Mesher, L. (2010). *Retail Design*. Lausanne: AVA.

Mikunda, C. (2004). *Brand Lands, Hot Spots and Cool Spaces*. London: Kogan Page.

Miller, D., Jackson, P., Thrift, N., Holbrook, B. and Rowland, M. (1998). *Shopping, Place and Identity*. London: Routledge.

Mitchell, G. (1986). *Design in the High Street*. London: The Architectural Press.

Morrison, K.A. (2003). *English Shops and Shopping*. London: Yale.

Oldenburg, R. (1997). *The Great Good Place* (2nd ed.). Philadelphia, PA: Da Capo.

Olins, W. (1978). *The Corporate Personality*. London: The Design Council.

Olins, W. (1989). *Corporate Identity, Making Business Strategy Visible through Design*. London: Thames and Hudson.

Olins, W. (2003). *Wally Olins: On Brand*. London: Thames and Hudson.

Papadakis, A. (1990). *The Question of New Modernism: The New Modern Aesthetic, Architectural Design*. London: The Academy Group.

Papanek, V. (1995). *The Green Imperative-Ecology and Ethics in Design and Architecture*. London: Thames and Hudson.

Pevsner, N. (1976). *A History of Building Types*. London: Thames and Hudson.

Plunkett, D. and Reid, O. (2012). *Detail in Contemporary Retail Design*. London: Laurence King.

Punk, E. (2011). *Curated: A New Experience in Retail Design*. Barcelona: Promopress.

Schön, D. (1983). *The Reflective Practitioner: How Professionals Think in Action*. Aldershot: Ashgate Press.

Sklair, L. (2006). Iconic architecture and capitalist globalization. *City*, 1(1), 21–48.

Walsh, V. (1996). Design, innovation and the boundaries of the firm. *Research Policy*, 25(4), 502–529.

Watkin, D. (1996). *A History of Modern Architecture* (2nd ed.). London: Laurence King Publishing.

Watson, H. (2007). Seoul's interior landscapes. *Architectural Journal*, 77(2), 114–119. Chichester: Wiley.

Williams, B. (1994). *The Best Butter in the World – A History of Sainsbury's*. London: Ebury Press.

2 Retail design

A contextual lens

Ann Petermans and Anthony Kent

Introduction

While the practices of retail design have been discussed and illustrated in some detail, the theoretical perspectives of retail design deserve fuller consideration. The efficiency and functionality of modernism in retailing have been challenged by postmodernist design, and both continue to make distinctive contributions to the industry, consumers and society. In addition they are moderated and adapted as other influences, notably sustainable and participatory design practices, become more prominent. This chapter discusses how retail design reflects the time or decade in which it is created. In particular, the authors focus on the importance of *context* as a driver for the development of retail design.

Retail design fundamentally concerns the physical space in which goods are sold and increasingly requires a broad understanding of what creates a unique retailing experience. For brands in particular, retail provides one of the most challenging encounters producers will have with their consumers. The retail outlet is where brand promises and myths are realised, and where brand relationships and brand ambassadors are won and lost. It presents a significant if not quite final challenge at the end of a sometimes long and expensive route of consumer seduction.

Like architecture, retail design is situated as part of a larger whole, taking shape in a wider context of demographic, social and cultural changes; economic development; and technological advances. The urban environment is a product of these conditions, and its commercial spaces are inevitably subject to continued redefinition by the contexts wherein they exist (Lefebvre 1991). Consequently, the transitions between economic, social and cultural contexts usher in new architectural styles and typologies. The same approach can be applied to retail design in order to understand consumer needs and shopping experiences. To be able to do so, architects, interior architects and retail designers need to develop a thorough understanding of the contexts wherein people live and function in order to include these issues into their design processes. It is the 'people and places [that] are the most important inspiration for everything that is done in design. Only by understanding people's motivations can the status quo be challenged, which in turn can lead to the most exciting expressions of creativity' (Klingmann 2007: 318).

The chapter starts with an overview of the socio-economic, cultural and consumption contexts that influence the design of retail stores and contribute to the completion of retail projects. The second part examines the influence of modernism and postmodernism and the evolving relationship between architecture and retail design. The chapter concludes with an assessment of the drivers of change and the implications for the future of retail design, clarifying the macro-environmental themes and trends that will engage designers in retail projects.

The practice of retail design: Macro-environmental context as driver for change

Towards the end of the twentieth century, Western societies, cultures and economies experienced major changes, including fragmentation, secularisation, pluralism and the ascendency of capitalist forms of consumerism. These brought to light many insecurities for individuals, not least an on-going search for personal and social identity. In response, retail design over this period began to address this feeling of insecurity, assisting people in the formation of their identity and the discovery of meaning. More generally, the interrelationship between contexts influenced key aspects of retail design projects. Every project starts with a retailer, active in a particular market, and the project is always an interpretation of a particular socio-economic, political and cultural context. These conditions inevitably influence the range of actions that a retailer and designer can undertake in the process of interior and exterior retail design. For example, although the political context appears distant from individual projects, it determines national policy towards retail development, its jurisdiction, and the specific rules and regulations that can establish a list of 'demands' to which a particular design strictly needs to adhere. In this respect, regulations with regards to heritage or accessibility issues can influence how a particular retail design project is developed commercially, functionally and aesthetically. However, it is the socio-economic, cultural and consumption contexts that form the focus of this contextual analysis: the drivers behind the structural trends in a macro-environment that inevitably impact on the practice of retail design.

Socio-economic context

The development of retail design and its 'manifestation' has been profoundly affected by changing economic and societal circumstances. From an economic perspective, companies in industrialised countries continuously compete with others from all over the world and respond to the development of technologically equivalent products and services (Pine and Gilmore 1999; van der Loo 2004). From a societal viewpoint, changes in fertility and mortality rates, improved healthcare, changed perceptions concerning the work/life balance, rising affluence and changes in households' expenditure patterns are important factors which have influenced the 'openness' of people towards the economy (Pine and Gilmore 1999, 2008) in which they currently live. The outlook for the design of retail environments can therefore be considered as an exponent of these developments.

The influence of the economy on retailing and its design in developed countries has shifted as it has changed from a focus on production to consumption over the past fifty years. More specifically, these countries have moved from economies of commodities to economies of goods, services and (by the end of the century) experiences (Pine and Gilmore 1999). In the decades following the Second World War, the economies of developed countries grew exponentially in a number of dimensions, fuelled by post-war regeneration, population growth, and investment and employment strategies. Increasing personal wealth from the 1950s onwards was reflected in the rise in consumer goods (Sparke 2013).

These developments had a fundamental influence on design as the proliferation of new products and brands appearing in retail stores required novel approaches to packaging, communications and advertising. Stores and their locations began to change, from a market dominated by many small-scale retailers, to one in which larger multi-location, or chain stores, flourished. Increased affluence and widespread car ownership led to the design of parking lots, canopies, and signs, altering building layout and orientation (Jakle and Sculle 1999). These economic growth factors more than doubled the demand for energy sources, consequently contributing to the oil crises of the 1970s which had enormous economic and social repercussions continually felt into the 1980s. Combined with the effects of economic cyclicality, public debts increased, unemployment escalated and numerous companies encountered serious market challenges.

In response, during the 1980s, some Western countries sought to overcome their economic problems through market-led policies, which resulted in de-regulation of financial markets, encouragement of competition, and emphasis on personal wealth creation. These led to a resurgence in consumption, which was reflected in retail and services developments as evidenced by the creation of new malls and out-of-town shopping centres. Concurrently, advances in information technologies provided the first signs of home computing, while providing businesses the processing power of larger mainframe computers. Arguments for efficiencies in production and distribution became all the more important, with increasingly sophisticated analysis of company success ratios and profitability. In the retail economy, these changes were apparent in the success of large multiple stores and in particular food retailers, where mass production and consumption enabled economies of scale and cost advantages.

In 1989 the socialist East European bloc began to dissolve, most evocatively in the tearing down of the Berlin Wall, which presented new opportunities for capitalist Western industries in a united Europe. The effects were felt more widely because of the acceleration of economic globalisation, with the resulting interconnectedness between countries and industries fuelling further investment and growth. Technological advances accompanied these developments with the enormous success of the Internet, the World Wide Web and early initiatives with mobile communications. In these conditions, retail and the contribution of retail design continued to attract attention by focusing on differentiation strategies and initiatives to counter the effects of global homogenisation: the effect of retail branded 'sameness' throughout the urbanised world.

This trend was strengthened from 2000 onwards, with the ever-growing possibilities of digital devices and online connectedness. E-retail has come to the fore, with the development of diverse small-scale e-initiatives, often in very specialised domains, such as children's clothing and other niche markets. However, digitisation also brought about problems for various small-scale retailers who could not compete with larger competitors, 'big' data and the challenges of dominant internet portals, notably Amazon. Along with the pervasiveness of digital media came increasing concern about the future of physical retail design. Yet recent insights show that the creation of attractive physical store environments (store as places of destination and escape) is highly valued by consumers, offering reassurance to some retailers about the continuing importance of investment in physical retail design.

Societies and economies have thus experienced a transition from a material to a post-material value orientation (van der Loo 2004; Kilian 2009; Boswijk et al. 2012): when individuals' material needs have been fulfilled, their focus shifts, and they aim for the completion of immaterial needs and wants. The era of rationality has evolved into an era of desire, in which society has transitioned from a focus on the object to an emphasis on subjectivity and experience. The effects of economic globalisation have extended the reach of these characteristics. Developing countries through a rapid phase of industrial growth have demonstrated the same transitions in their major cities. In the future uncertainty and instability must continue to be managed in new and different ways. Additionally, these developments, which were summarised here, have also influenced the 'cultural' context, creating another important driver of retail design.

Cultural context

The influence of culture on shaping retail design arises from different visual and material cultural strands that interact with design that needs to face increasing complexity. The growth in consumption expanded the dimensions of popular culture and its possibilities for research. Popular culture focuses on the culture of daily life, and retail is very much part of this popular everyday world.

Visual culture

Vision defines and is defined by modernity, which is partially a consequence of mass consumer markets and urbanisation following the industrial revolution. The rise of the department store and catalogue shopping were dependent on the mediation of the visual experience. Commodities needed to be made more visual in order to appeal to a wider, anonymised audience. Production and reproduction of cultural items that included architecture and advertising provided focus for a broader set of concepts of visual culture (Julier 2008). By the end of the twentieth century, vision could be seen as (almost) entirely divested of its originality, illustrated by rapidly changing and infinitely replaceable images and representations (Jenks 1995). The expansion of mobile technologies has provided a further dimension to the instability of image, allowing viewing to be seen as a series of activities (Johnson 2014) that empower the individual to create visual 'mashups'. In all this, design has had a central role in image creation and transformation, 'as visual information has become more ephemeral and immediate, so . . . the ubiquity of design as a self-consciously distinguishing feature of everyday life expands the grounds on which visual values lie' (Julier 2008: 9). The contribution of retail design is less well documented in visual culture. Nevertheless, the design of store windows creates an advertising billboard of displays and marketing communications for consumers. Packaging, point of sale, posters and screens, and their design and location with merchandise in the store demonstrate a complex relationship between things, images and their reproduction.

The primacy of the visual has been challenged by a more three-dimensional view of culture where design is not just the creation of visual images but a structuring of systems of encounter in the visual and material world. The experience of design is not engulfed by its multiplication of artefacts but can be organised into an architectonic structure, serially produced through a range of media. Julier (2008: 12) provides an example of a system of branding using retail spaces, reception areas, website and 'other points of corporate and consumer interface to turn information into an all around us architectonic form'. In retailing, this is supported by the design of retail brands: an architectonic form consisting of store buildings, frontages, logos, windows, interior design, fittings, promotional materials and colours through multiple stores.

This perspective has implications for design and its contribution to this structure of encountering through the shop's accessibility and ubiquity; it is part of a system that is defined by the economy, the individual, and social identity creation and maintenance. By being specifically three-dimensional-as a shop and shop interior-retail design is a self-consciously distinguishing feature of everyday life through its windows, interiors and product displays of increasingly designed products. Conran's (1996) dictum that 'there's only one lowest price, everything else must be distinguished by design' appears to have intensified the awareness and application of design.

The production of many more products and opportunities for possession has led to an increasing concern for things themselves in addition to their visual representation and image. Material culture is concerned with the popular and 'every day' world of things and 'how people have used objects to cope with and interpret their physical world' (Massey 2000: 4). It has its roots in two distinct disciplinary traditions, sociology and social anthropology, with a focus on the social life of 'things' or – to avoid their objectification – 'stuff'. The importance of materials and objects themselves, while not strange to designers, has been asserted in response to a study of material culture that remains restricted to the symbolic register (Ingold 2007) and a view of culture that downplays 'things' (Olsen 2010). Further, integrity can be found in the interweaving of material and social domains (Küchler and Miller 2005).

Material culture can provide a different focus for design through a re-engagement with materials and things with which consumers can interact. It is an approach that reconnects with craft and making skills. These qualities are demonstrated in the fashion sector, where 'slow fashion' has its focus on the materiality of objects, while image dominates the prevailing 'fast fashion' system. In this context, it raises questions about the role of fashion stores, the place of individual and community enterprises, and facilitating and sharing skills. More generally, it turns attention back to the earliest forms of retailing when premises combined workshop and selling functions. It points to the design of new places that combine commerce with learning new skills, the tactile experience of materials, and leisure activities.

Consumption context

A third context of consumer consumption draws on both socio-economic and cultural developments. In general, consumer goods communicate cultural meaning through social rituals, including acquisition, possession and exchange. The display of status symbols is as important as their possession. Distinctions can be made through not just buying more goods but playing with an existing vocabulary of signs, and through the rhetoric of use. Consuming goods highlights the role of strategies of distinction in allowing ever more subtle variations of taste to be articulated.

Consumer culture in the developed world is defined through consumption being intrinsically a cultural process: consumption concerns economic exchange in part, but also the exercise of taste as part of a self-identifying act (Julier 2008 citing Slater 1997). In the balance between the quest for achieving a meaningful life and the resources available to achieve it, consuming led to a world defined by 'having rather than being'. The changing context of consumption is evident from the post-war period onwards, with the different phases distinctively impacting the relationship between consumers' lives and personal identities, retail and design.

1950s–1960s

The contribution of this formative period of consumption to retail design was evident in the influence of new goods and images but also the temporal aspect of consumption. These twenty years distinctively identified the times and places of consideration and deliberation of purchases, highlighting desire before consumption, and determining the times and places of product display and enactment through use of post-purchase occupation. In retailing, these dimensions of time changed perceptions of shopping and were reflected in new retail formats and brands. Increasingly, consumption of, and participation in, the fashion cycle became a formative part of self-identification (Sparke 2013). Fashion became more gendered and fragmented, evident in emergent youth identities and, for the first time, new male sub-cultural groups. As Sparke (2013) observed, consumption, in part, required educated taste to inform consumer choice not only in clothes but also in household products and home furnishing. Consumers – in particular new consumers – were increasingly introduced to modern and, especially, 'good' modern design as 'good taste'. Thus, the purchasing of modern goods and images required necessary visualising skills from designers to create appropriate forms of presentation. Many retailers made efforts to display the modern character of their goods. The popularity of home-shopping catalogues broadened the appeal and accessibility of ownership of goods. Department stores welcomed less affluent customers, encouraging the use of credit facilities. Collectively, these developments formed the basis for new design approaches that were realised over subsequent decades.

The 1960s saw a significant shift in design interest towards popular culture, in which age rather than gender became the dominant cultural category. Freedom of choice and independence contributed to 'lifestyles' that defined modes and attitudes of consumption, by referring to the ways in which people sought to display their individuality and sense of style through the choice of particular products (Lury 1996). Additionally, consumers' confidence in the future, but also a popular interest in the past, created a new form of second-hand retailing for the young that valued objects that were quirky, unique and not well established in design hierarchies. This freedom fuelled designers, so 'their work was characterised by spontaneity, impermanence and references to popular culture' (Pimlott 2007: 7), framed by mass communication and enabled by a technological revolution.

1970s to 2000s

The 1970s onwards demonstrated greater eclecticism in the emergence of interest in the past, the recycling of styles, and heritage. The Craft Revival of groups of makers working outside mass-production contributed to this pluralism. In these decades, design and designers played a central role in the construction of multiple consumers' identities and lifestyles, aided by mass and increasingly specialised media. These factors enabled retail designers to create many more fashion stores, branded by lifestyle from the 1980s onwards. The success of Top Shop in the UK is a notable example of how the store itself could become a brand.

During the 1980s and 1990s, design became all the more part of a process dependent on advertising and marketing. The combination of these three elements created identities to be consumed through images, goods and spaces, both visually and functionally. Retailers were the frame of reference and decided what consumers would experience in their store environments. The entwining of images, identities and design became a component of branding in which the material object – the building – contributed to the manifestation of the brand. The expansion of consumption explains the commodification of architecture, to promote corporate identity seen in flagship stores, and the use of logos and posters to brand the basic structure.

Democratisation of design created multiple fragmented markets for goods, including products that depended heavily on the signatures and identities of the designers who had conceived them. By the 1980s and 1990s, both established and new designers – including Armani, Calvin Klein, Ralph Lauren, Tommy Hilfiger and Donna Karan – successfully expanded their businesses in this way. The extension of designers into retail provided opportunities for the expansion of retail design, to be more creative, or at least distinctive, at a high level which also reflected the distinctive and original qualities of the fashion-designer brand. In this period, the culture of consumption with design at its centre embraced many areas of everyday life, including shopping centres, museums and resorts. It became increasingly difficult to separate the real from the designed experience, as the design of the shopping centre included not only its spatial shell but also its contents, general interior and directional signage (Sparke 2013).

From the 1990s, businesses started to be aware of the more active role of consumers in the company, and the marketing and management of these relationships. Senses and emotions were recognised as important elements of retailing. Even more, companies recognised that affect and emotion played a significant role in consumer behaviour and decision making. The implications for the twenty-first century are that retail designers have to get closer to consumers, researching and understanding who they are and their functional needs, emotional and experiential wants and desires.

By the end of this period, retail design visualised specific places of consumption that contribute to the categorisation of goods. Shops are identified by their different assortments of goods and services, offering a degree of stability to categories as a shorthand for specific goods. They facilitate social meaning by their location, consistency and homogeneity, defining the identities of both the retail brand and the provided goods and services. In this way, the retail environment aids intelligibility through design. Retailers contribute to making and sustaining social relationships through their accessible locations and the opportunity to share product interests in an effort to seek and share new ideas and knowledge.

In Veblen's view (in Corrigan 1997), the desire for social status is demonstrated through wealth. Bourdieu (1984) advances this visibility when he states that designers can act as 'cultural intermediaries' who construct value by framing how others – end consumers, as well as other market actors – engage with goods, affecting and effecting others' orientations towards those goods as legitimate. In this context, 'goods' are understood to include services, ideas and behaviours as well as material products. Examining retail design through this lens, the designers of retail environments can be considered to be cultural intermediaries, because they frame how consumers, suppliers and advertisers engage with goods through the commercially designed environment of the shop. The style, functionality, communications and spatial organisation of such environments determine the affect of different types of consumers to the shop itself and to the immateriality of the brand.

Modernism and postmodernism as drivers for change in retail design

The macro-environmental contextual drivers create conditions for change, in which retail design is held between commercial, social and cultural forces, and the vernacular world of material objects and images. More specifically, retail design drew from design thinking, practices and solutions, following the evolution of the wider design community. As a discipline closely connected with architecture and interior architecture, retail design is evidently influenced by major shifts that came to the fore in these disciplines. In this section, we elaborate in particular about the characteristics of modern and postmodern theories and their application to design, architecture and retail design.

Modernism

At the turn of the twentieth century, the contextual drivers advanced significant and enduring change in design in general and architecture in particular. Modernism came to the fore in an effort to reconcile principles and practices of architectural design with rapid technological advancements and the modernisation of society. The processes and outputs of modernist design were inspired by the economic principles of Fordism, and its application to architecture implied, first, that it focused on the spatial optimisation of the distribution of functions and, second, that efforts were taken to standardise production and labour processes. Modernity thus saw a move from a bodily, practical relationship with the world to a more abstract and intellectual one. These approaches were subsequently critiqued by Marxist theorists for their routinisation of labour and rationalisation. Learning from and refining these techniques, fast food chains came to typify over-rationalisation, efficiency and control and to define the 'McDonaldisation' of society (Ritzer 2000; Julier 2008). By this time, modernist principles determined some of the most significant retail formats, brands and designs that emerged from America and their global acceptance.

Form and function

Efficient commercial practices in retailing require close attention to store operations and the functionality of the store and its fittings, merchandising and displays. Functionalism was first recognised during the industrialisation of mid-nineteenth-century America but gained its modernist significance in the Bauhaus philosophy of the 1920s (Benton et al. 1975). Bauhaus developed the principle of functional aesthetics that emphasized geometry, precision, simplicity and economy in the design of products. Design should be from the 'inside out', with form following function. This is an approach later summarised by Mies van der Rohe as 'less is more'. For Alexander (1964), the ultimate object of design was specifically form and its context. Context is anything in the world that makes demands on the form, and good fit is a desired property of the ensemble, divided in some particular way into form and context. By contrast, modernist product design in America until the 1960s emphasised the product's external styling in response to commercial demands for the creation of product appeal. A leading proponent, Raymond Loewy, famously pronounced that 'ugliness does not sell' and set about streamlining, using non-functional aero-dynamic shapes (Ulrich and Eppinger 2012). Both of these approaches influenced the architecture of mid-century stores and their internal design and visual contribution to the shopping street and mall.

Ergonomics and aesthetics of industrial design

In the practices of industrial design and new product development (NPD), good design came to be explicitly stated in another way. Of enduring influence in this respect are Dreyfus's (1967) five critical goals: to achieve utility, appearance, ease of maintenance, low costs, and communication, by which he meant the visual quality of products to communicate corporate design philosophy and mission. In this way, industrial product design came to be considered in two important dimensions: first, ergonomics, which encompasses all aspects of a product that relate to its human interfaces, and includes novelty of interaction needs, maintenance and safety issues; second, aesthetics and considerations of whether visual product differentiation is required, and the importance of pride of ownership, image and fashion (Ulrich and Eppinger 2012). This approach shifted the focus of design of products to the users and their needs, albeit defined by the designer and the organisational environment.

Modernist architecture

Modernist architecture was a reflection of modern society. The modern movement initially emphasised the functional aspect of architectural design above that of appearance (Kirby 2009). In architectural design, sober, clear and unpretentious geometrical forms, glass and transparency, flat roofs and the use of 'modern materials' such as reinforced concrete defined modernist buildings from earlier styles and the use of decoration and ornamentation. Skyscrapers became the archetype of modernist buildings. The principles of mass production were applied to building projects, which brought about time and cost efficiency, but also standardisation (Klingmann 2007). In a modernist commercial world, the architect took on the functions of coordinator and site planner as much as creator (Smiley 2013). Retailers adopted the efficient use of space inherent in the single-floor, box shapes of supermarkets, hypermarkets and retail warehouses. Watkin's (1996) history of modern architecture cites examples of modernist buildings that display elements found in the designs of post-war supermarket architecture. The use of concrete, steel and large areas of glass used from the early 1950s and in more contemporary supermarket buildings echo these developments (Kirby 2009).

Discussing retail design, Miller et al. (1998) examine the example of London's Brent Cross shopping centre and suggest that the modernist sheet glass used to up-date this project was already out-of-date. They state that supermarkets were giving up 'glass boxes' and constructing buildings with gabled tile roofs and clock towers, which they describe as having 'their own version of nature' (Miller et al. 1998: 116). Nevertheless, most purpose-built supermarket structures, in common with many post-war buildings in the UK, are constructed largely from prefabricated units. After the Second World War, the materials and approaches of modernism were embraced by local authorities required to produce large quantities of low-cost housing and functional buildings. Williams (1994) reported Sainsbury's first out-of-town store in Coldhams Lane showing large glass windows reminiscent of Mies' Farnsworth House. In the case of this store, the purpose of the glass was not only to allow natural light into the building but also to allow people to see inside.

A high-tech architectural style was later evident in supermarket design, evidence of a different aspect of Modernism – that is, 'technology transfer', a process in which techniques or processes used in one field of industry are used in other industries or fields (Pawley 1998). From this, a serious analysis of technology transfer in the field of architectural design would provide a base from which to compare pre-Modernism, Modernism and postmodern architecture.

Postmodernism

From the end of the 1960s, the production-oriented concept of modernist design and architecture began to be supplemented by a new approach characterised by the use of free and playful forms, the use of details, full of fantasy elements and references to the past.

Definitions of the subject included the collapse of boundaries between art and everyday life, the distinctions between high and popular culture, eclecticism, parody, pastiche, irony and the suggestion that art can be only repetition (Featherstone 1991). Postmodernism was inspired by the changing relationship between design and culture. As a consequence, postmodernists and postmodern architects increasingly also took aspects such as consumption, advertising, marketing, branding and identity creation into account (Sparke 2013). As Klingmann (2007: 5) stated, 'for architecture to succeed in a consumer market, it had to cater to the diverse tastes and demands of a postmodern society, pairing a stylistic variety with instant recognisability'. So while in modernist times, the operation of the object was key, in the postmodern era the experience of the subject has become essential.

The influence of postmodernism on design generally has been profound. It came to be defined by three themes (Adamson and Pavitt 2011). Adhocism and bricolage exemplified the piecing together and creation by 'cut and paste' of something new, playful and vibrant. It allowed for the confiscation and appropriation of existing things, the assembly of elements and a tendency to bypass technical drawing. The radical possibilities of bricolage led to a different understanding of time, to think in new ways about the past and the future, a compression of past and present, time and space. A second theme concerned mediation and how radical ideas were interpreted by a wider population and the extension of the concept of bricolage into the concept of performance space. Even everyday things could contribute to the 'hyper-real life of the postmodern subject: a life lived as if always on a stage' (Adamson and Pavitt 2011: 50). For retailers, the visual language of postmodern design in such artefacts provided more opportunities to create new, as well as refresh, their existing merchandise ranges. Homeware, furniture and fast fashion could be launched onto the display and visual merchandising stage. The third theme concerns commercialisation. One of the most influential postmodern design groups, namely Memphis, was itself overtaken by commercial exploitation. Designers in different fields – from Jeff Koons, Karl Lagerfeld to Philip Johnson – influenced extravagant shopping centres and the subversion of the material world. Postmodern places demonstrated a greater interest in the surface, evident in the mirrored surface of the Bonaventure Hotel, creating an illusion of illusion.

Postmodern architecture

A critical moment in the development of postmodern architecture was Robert Venturi and Denise Scott Brown's (1972) study of the architecture of Las Vegas, and an awareness of the city defined by its signs rather than its buildings. With the rise of consumption and the demands of spectacle, buildings for the first time 'began to be looked on purely as images or marketing objects' (Glendinning 2004: 10). Venturi and Brown's (1972) work contributed to architects (re)thinking what architecture is or should be about. Together with Aldo Rossi and Charles Jencks, they developed various positions with regard to postmodern architecture. In 2000, Jencks discussed the competitive pluralism of the twentieth century, with four to five movements at any one time, and a new movement or trend every five years which functions as the engine of continual revolution. Between 1945 and 1970, Jencks argued that a bureaucratic International Style was dominant. It became the style of the state and for commerce, especially big business. Described as faceless pragmatism, the architectural reaction was seen in late modernism's faceted provocative box; high-tech architecture's skeletal and tubular forms; and Postmodernists' hybrid collage. By sheer numbers alone, mainstream modernism dwarfed every other approach. Jencks (2000: 98) claimed that 'dominant practice is constantly attracted back to both stripped out classicism and degree-zero Modernism', because the corporate forces of modernist production and patronage favour an impersonal, abstract, semi-classical sobriety. In Jencks' view (2000), postmodernism declined in the last part of the twentieth century to be partially replaced by minimalism, New Modernism and Deconstruction.

Postmodernism and retail design

The origins of a designed organisational identity are found in a formalised and commercial approach introduced by the Wolf Olins consultancy in the 1970s (Olins 1995). The seminal influence of Olins (1978, 1989, 2003) conveyed the shape and nature of organisations as corporate design. Olins (2003) came to regard retailers as brand innovators, replacing fast-moving consumer goods (FMCG) companies with their emotional appeal and providing more comprehensive engagement with consumers through 'brand temples'. Changes to comprehensive store design practices drew on accounts of lifestyle retailing from the 1960s, but more commonly from the 1980s onwards, through narratives and histories (Fitch and Knobel 1990; Conran 1996; Olins 2003).

The changing socio-economic, cultural and consumption context not only resulted in postmodern architecture but also provided a major strand of postmodern theoretical development about reality and simulation (Baudrillard 2000). Designers and theorists responded to the creation of simulated leisure phenomena, typified by Disneyland, which were part of the move to re-create the past. This presented a new challenge, as neo-buildings in a neo-classical style emerged. There was a need for imaginative skills in the creation of 'theatres of memory' (Samuel 1994). As Sparke summarises (2013: 116), 'the landscapes of Disneyland and Las Vegas permeated the environments of shopping malls and city centres worldwide: blurring the boundaries of shopping and leisure'. Products and buildings now emerge from the continuing desires and identity requirements of consumers, rather than resting with architects.

Towards the end of the 1980s, and certainly in the 1990s, the retail design landscape breathed a postmodern eclecticism, with classical references, pediments and a few distinctive architectural designs, such as Sainsbury's supermarkets in the 1990s and Prada's epicentres.

Indeed, towards the end of the 1990s, different retailers opted to set up collaboration with renowned architects or 'star architects', such as Koolhaas, Hadid, or Herzog and De Meuron. They developed flagship store architecture and, in the case of Koolhaas, the epicentre concept which helped brands to distinguish themselves from competitor brands through architecture. The rise of flagship stores marked retailers' and designers' efforts to develop branded retail contexts wherein consumers could be immersed (Carù and Cova 2007). Flagship brand stores as store concepts were at the forefront of experiential retail contexts (Kozinets et al. 2002), an issue which would even become much more important in the years to come, at that time. These branded stores are set up to (re)build, reinforce and represent a brand rather than to function as a particular point-of-contact with consumers where brand products can be sold at a profit (Kozinets et al. 2002; Klingmann 2007; Mesher 2010). The use of 'star architects' has positioned architecture as a strategic tool in a highly competitive marketplace (Klingmann 2007; Petermans 2012).

Designers thus have developed the concept of 'brandscape', in which the architecture and design of the building communicate the retail brand identity (Brauer 2002; Riewoldt 2002). In postmodern retail design, they became increasingly engaged with the visual identity of the retailer as a totality of store and products. As a result, the focus was on the store environment. In this respect, Rendell (2000) indicated that by providing a memorable place, architecture enhanced product identity.

Drivers for retail design

Framing the evolution of retail design in the socio-economic, cultural and consumption context has highlighted how the macro-environment stimulated retail design to change over time. These underlying conditions influenced retail architecture and interior design thinking and practice. These demonstrate a movement towards greater engagement with consumers, the built and wider environment, and their contribution to distinctive and memorable places. Consequently, the future of retail design lies in its ability to adapt to and deliver projects in one or more areas of experience, services, sustainability and authenticity.

Retail design and experience

As indicated earlier, retail design originates in an era where consumers were considered to be passive partakers in the company-consumer relationship. Companies decided what consumers could experience in a retail environment without taking into account consumers' needs, wants, perceptions or experiences. Over time, insights have changed. From the 1980s onwards, first signals became apparent that consumers were not purely rational decision-makers; emotions seemed to be important as well. Pine and Gilmore's (1999) book *The Experience Economy* established a focus on consumers' search for experiences, and increasingly the value of good service, participation, facilitation and interaction.

In the retail industry, experience therefore is continuously 'being used' as a tool for differentiation in a sector which is being typified by homogenisation. Different store typologies are being developed and implemented in an effort to work on differentiation. In the years to come, these typologies will continue to be subject to societal, economic and cultural changes. Retail(ers) and retail design(ers) thus not only will, but also will need to, continue to follow upcoming trends in the societies wherein they function (Petermans 2012). Moreover, retail designers will need to continue translating these trends into ways that appeal to the brands for which they work in their physical as well as online retail environments, while taking into account that what counts today is not so much how buildings and retail interiors exactly look like, but how they are experienced by people (Klingmann 2007).

Stores can become all the more places for festivals, image, illusion and representation. Increasingly there is a cross-over between cultural places and retail stores: between museums, arts and cultural institutions. Steiner (2000) explains that the drive to sell consumables will render the architecture of cultural monuments, galleries and department stores almost indistinguishable. In other words, in the future, people will be wondering if it is a cathedral, a museum or a shop. At the same time, fashion retail continually seems to be inspired by commercial art galleries, as they emulate their design and their location in cities, and incorporate exhibitions into their shop floors (Merkel in Battista 1999). Creating an appropriate and appealing in-store atmosphere continuously is important, and triggering consumers' senses is key in this respect. As Klingmann (2007: 2) states, 'while form and function in architecture remain important criteria, personal identity and personal growth have become even more crucial in the assessment of architecture's value'. In her view, architecture in general (and in our view, retail design in particular) has evolved from emphasising ' "what it has" and "what it does" to "what you feel" and "who you are" – the key concepts in what is increasingly referred to as the "experience economy"' (Klingmann 2007: 1). This shift towards experience has enormous repercussions for all designers who are interested in developing retail design projects.

Retail design and service design

As retailing forms a major part of the services industry sector, retail design and service design are highly connected. Customer participation in services requires an essential understanding of human factors, and, in service design, the designer must conceive and give shape to brand identities, interior spaces, buildings and consumer products (Sanders and Stappers 2008). The intentional design of services records and monitors the process of service delivery (Shostack 1982; Kimbell 2011). In considering the design of services, the first point of distinction is their perishability, that unlike goods they cannot be stored. As a result, communication and information design are important elements in their delivery, and the intangible can be made tangible through brand identity, logos, exterior fascia and in-store communications. A second characteristic in the design of services, which is of particular importance in multiple retailing, is the problem of heterogeneity and standardisation in service quality. Problems of variation to the branded service offer can be overcome by designing a standardised interior space (Lee, Nam and Chung 2011). However, services may be anticipated and the experience of the service can endure after the service encounter through customer relationship management (CRM) and communications. Consequently, service design has both spatial and temporal elements that transcend the boundaries of the store.

Shostack's (1982) solution for a systematic way of describing a service was to devise the blueprint. Using a flow-chart style, service blueprints demonstrate interdependence among activities, people and products. They define services through a line of visibility dividing the customer-facing areas of engagement, from the supported service delivery, which the customer does not see. 'Front office', or front-of-house, and 'back office' explain a similar division in the design of retail environments. A second element of blueprinting is to identify fail-points, the parts of the service that are most sensitive to errors (Gummesson 1990), and the importance of the service encounter and interfaces between providers and users. Visual representation is central to blueprinting not only to communicate but to create dialogue. It can be further extended to be a means of processing information and understanding context, and provide a substantial narrative to the relationships that exist within the context (Prendiville 2012).

As services and service environments vary, from the functionality of kiosks and self-service outlets to complex, luxury department stores, so they are reflected in their designed elements. Touch-points are a defining characteristic in the delivery of service to users, taking shape in the form of virtual interfaces and physical interfaces, where employees and users interact. They make up the obvious parts of the service interface but are often connected in sequences and chains (Holmlid 2008). The possibilities for extending both individual touch-points and networks increases with the integration of the digital and physical worlds within the store, and their ubiquitous possibilities as these channels converge.

Generally, service design concerns human-centred frameworks, in which designers can simplify and unify design opportunities in order to conceive possible futures (Coughlan and Prokopoff 2004). The future of service design may see further development of participative design practices through interdisciplinary understanding of anthropology, societies and social change. These will expand the opportunities for retail design to develop existing spaces and stores, while also creating new formats to meet broader societal challenges, such as for an ageing population, or for more explicitly taking into account users' health and wellbeing.

Retail design and sustainability

The ever-increasing consumption of goods has made system-wide solutions a necessity for achieving a sustainable future (Mont 2002). During the 2000s, more ecologically conscious consumers have come to the fore, with a more critical attitude towards consuming, production and the production of waste. Recycling and up-cycling by consumers and enterprises has created an awareness of materials, and presents new opportunities for design. These range from experiments with new forms of retailing, to the creation of places for the collection and recycling of consumer goods. Sustainable building design itself has emerged as an integrated approach towards social, economic and environmental aspects directed towards the use of natural resources, energy consumption and environmental performance. Buildings can be understood as complex 'products' with significant capital and operating costs, which consume energy and water and produce waste, while indoor air-quality issues and thermal comfort standards need to be achieved. Consequently, fundamental design decisions need to be 'future-proofed' from the early lifecycle stages against long-term social, technological, economic, environmental and regulatory impacts (Georgiadou et al. 2011). This will not be easy, taking into account that building solutions cannot be easily revised because when just 1 per cent of a project's design and construction upfront costs are spent, up to 70 per cent of its lifecycle costs may already be committed (Hawken et al. 1999). Hence, the earliest design decisions if anything become even more important.

In the short term, recycling and energy-saving systems have become significant elements in the design of new stores. In the future it is likely that the use of more sustainable materials in store construction will radically change the look, at least of supermarket buildings (Kirby 2009). A more sustainable approach has to find a place alongside the use of low-cost, temporary materials, such as cardboard in store design, as is reflected in the limited temporality of pop-up and guerrilla stores. Indeed, some formats appear to have come to the end of their lifecycles. For example, out-of-town hypermarket formats in Europe and some shopping malls in the United States demonstrate signs of redundancy. Design solutions are sought to re-conceptualise and develop them.

However, when focusing on store interiors, there is relatively little research in sustainability that specifically addresses consumer attitudes to store atmospherics in environmentally responsible retail environments (Hyllegard et al. 2006). In some retail sectors, wasteful practices are integrated into the distribution system. Fast fashion contributes to sustainability problems through short-product lifecycles, reflected by the in-store merchandising and communication materials. As demolition and construction are by far the largest producers of waste – in the UK for instance, demolition and construction account for 24 per cent of the total waste material (Clark 2008) – reducing waste is vital for creating environmentally responsible buildings and interiors. Here lies an important role and challenge for retailers who can try to reuse existing buildings, as it is clear that reusing existing buildings is intrinsically humble towards the environment. In addition, working on sustainability through the reuse of existing buildings can answer another current concern – namely, that consumers increasingly seem to value a 'local connection' in their consumption activities.

Revaluation of authenticity and originality

The globalisation of the retail industry has led to a worldwide presence of various retailers, which has also resulted in homogenisation. Consumers strolling around in a mainstream shopping street in Mexico City today encounter a similar shopping street image when passing a mainstream shopping street in Antwerp, Belgium. However, all the more, consumers in Western economies want something unique, authentic, original – something 'real'.

Indeed, people currently search for authenticity and co-creative activities, wherein they are no longer considered to be passive partakers in the company–consumer relationship, but wherein they now take a more active role. Indeed, in the second-generation experience economy (Petermans 2012) wherein co-creation has become important, the needs and wants of the customer have taken a central place. At the beginning of the twenty-first century, consumers no longer want to be considered mere 'customers'; instead, they want to achieve life goals, realise ideals and contribute to issues they value to be important. They want to go back to what is essential in their lives and re-value issues such as authenticity and originality. Retailers and retail design should take such insights and considerations into account when working on retail interiors in the (near) future, as these trends hold good as illustrations of the spirit of our times.

In Europe, as in many countries worldwide, economic growth is uncertain and at times recessionary. This sets an agenda wherein people currently live and function, and this also helps to explain the manifestation and success (or failure) of some concepts in the retail landscape. Retailers and retail designers thus certainly need to take the audiences for whom they work into account when developing store concepts. In addition, consumers in Western Europe have started to protest against what Manzini (2001, paraphrased in Carù and Cova 2003) labelled as 'the disappearance of the contemplative time'. Manzini (2001) linked this idea to the lifestyle of consumers today, which in his view is being nourished by the experience economy and by experiential marketing. Carù and Cova (2003: 272) paraphrase Manzini's work when they write:

> currently . . . every minute is saturated with activity: we 'need' to do something, and ever more quickly, in order to have the impression, or illusion, of doing more. The experiences proposed by the market do no more than compensate this loss; they are remedies offered by the market to treat the illness that it itself has caused: the disappearance of the contemplative time.

Reading Carù and Cova's notes on Manzini's (2001) work reminded the authors of Aldous Huxley's famous book *Brave New World* (1932). Huxley wrote this novel immediately after the famous Wall Street crash of October 1929, in a period wherein almost all Western industrialised countries became subject to an economic depression ('the Great Depression'). In *Brave New World*, Huxley aimed to sketch a frightening vision of the future, and he used the setting and characteristics in his now seminal work to express opinions that were widespread at the beginning of the 1930s, such as the fear of Americanisation in Europe, and the fear of losing personal identity in the (at that moment) still-upcoming future with all its technological changes and evolutions. Huxley's ideas, expressed in his novel almost eighty years ago, are still very much alive and subject of debate today. Indeed, according to Carù and Cova (2003), consumers are progressively reacting against the 'disappearance of contemplative time' as they tend to re-appreciate simpler and more common experiences, such as for instance taking a walk or reading a book at ease at home.

Conclusion

This chapter has shown how socio-economic, cultural and consumption contexts have been instrumental in the development of retail design. Retail design is always part of a 'larger whole' and thus only comes into being in a wider context of socio-economic developments, technological advances and demographic and cultural changes. This has resulted in retail design which continuously needs to re-shape its focus over the course of time. In order to be able to adapt to changing conditions, architects, interior architects and retail designers need to keep track of the changing contexts within which individuals live and function. In time, additional drivers for retail design have come to the forefront. As a consequence, the future of retail design lies in designers' capacities and abilities to adapt, while taking into account the wider contexts wherein retail design will operate. Retail design projects need to continue to answer calls for experience, services, sustainability, authenticity and originality. Further development of these issues in theory and practice will help to advance retail design in academia but will also be to the benefit of industry and society in general.

References

Adamson, G. and Pavitt, J. (2011). *Postmodernism*. London: V&A Publications.

Alexander, C. (1964). *Notes on the Synthesis of Form*. Cambridge, MA: Harvard.

Battista, K. (1999). The art of shopping, Salon 3 and Saks 5th Avenue: A place between. *Public Art Journal*, 2(October), 34–35.

Baudrillard, J. (2000). *Simulacra and Simulation*. Ann Arbor: University of Michigan Press.

Benton, T., Benson, C. and Sharp, D. (Eds.) (1975). *Form and Function*. London: Granada.

Boswijk, A., Peelen, E. and Olthof, S. (2012). *Economy of Experiences*. Amsterdam: European Centre for the Experience and Transformation Economy BV.

Bourdieu, P. (1984). *Distinction: A Social Critique of the Judgement of Taste*. London: Routledge & Kegan Paul.

Brauer, G. (2002). *Architecture as Brand Communication*. Basel: Birkhauser.

Carù, A. and Cova, B. (2003). Revisiting consumption experience: A more humble but complete view of the concept. *Marketing Theory*, 3(2), 259–278.

Carù, A. and Cova, B. (2007). *Consuming Experience*. London: Routledge.

Clark, K. (2008). Only connect-sustainable development and cultural heritage. In G. Fairclough, R. Harrison, J. Schofield and J.H. Jameson (Eds.), *The Heritage Reader* (pp. 82–98). Abingdon: Routledge.

Conran, T. (1996). *Terence Conran on Design*. London: Conran Octopus.

Corrigan, P. (1997). *The Sociology of Consumption: An Introduction*. London: Sage.

Coughlan, P. and Prokopoff, I. (2004). Managing change by Design. In R. Boland and F. Collopy (Eds.), *Managing as Designing* (pp. 188–192). Stanford: Stanford University Press.

Dreyfus, H. (1967). *Designing for People*. New York: Paragraphic Books.

Featherstone, M. (1991). *Consumer Culture and Postmodernism*. London: Sage.

Fitch, R. and Knobel, L. (1990). *Fitch on Retail Design*. London: Phaidon.

Georgiadou, M., Hacking, T. and Guthrie, P. (2011). The role of future-proofing in achieving sustainable building design. In the Proceedings of the *Cambridge Academic Design Management Conference*. Cambridge: University of Cambridge.

Glendinning, M. (2004). *The Last Icons: The Lighthouse Scottish Architectural and Design Series, 1.* Glasgow: Graven Images.

Gummesson, E. (1990). Service design. *The TQM Magazine, 2*(2), 97–101.

Hawken, P., Lovins, A. and Lovins, L.H. (1999). *Natural Capitalism: Creating the Next Industrial Revolution.* London: Earthscan.

Holmlid, S. (2008). *Towards an Understanding of the Challenges for Design Management and Service Design.* International DMI Education Conference, Design Thinking: New Challenges for Designers, Managers and Organizations, 14–15 April 2008, ESSEC Business School, Cergy-Ponitoise, France.

Huxley, A. (1932). *Brave New World.* London: Chatto and Windus.

Hyllegard, K., Ogle, J. and Dunbar, B. (2006). The influence of consumer identity on perceptions of store atmospherics and store patronage at a spectacular and sustainable retail site. *Clothing & Textiles Research Journal, 24*, 316–334.

Ingold, T. (2007). *Lines: A Brief History.* Abingdon: Routledge.

Jakle, J.A. and Sculle, K.A. (1999). *Fast Food.* London: The Johns Hopkins University Press.

Jencks, C. (2000). Critical modernism in the twentieth century. *Architectural Design, 70*, 94–99.

Jenks, C. (1995). *Visual Culture.* London: Routledge.

Johnson, L. (2014). *Mobility and Fantasy in Visual Culture.* London: Routledge.

Julier, G. (2008). *The Culture of Design* (2nd ed.). London: Sage.

Kilian, K. (2009). Experiential marketing and brand experiences: A conceptual framework. In Lindgreen, A., Vanhamme, J. and Beverland, M. (Eds.), *Memorable Customer Experiences: A Research Anthology* (pp. 25–44). Surrey: Gower Publishing Limited.

Kimbell, L. (2011). Designing for service as one way of designing services. *International Journal of Design, 5*(2), 41–52.

Kirby, A.E. (2009). *The Architectural Design of UK Supermarkets: 1950–2006.* Unpublished PhD Thesis. London: University of the Arts London.

Klingmann, A. (2007). *Brandscapes: Architecture in the Experience Economy.* Cambridge: MIT Press.

Kozinets, R., Sherry, J., DeBerry-Spence, G., Duhachek, A., Nuttavuthisit, K. and Storm, D. (2002). Themed flagship brand stores in the new millennium: Theory, practice, prospects. *Journal of Retailing, 78*, 17–29.

Küchler, S. and Miller, D. (Eds.) (2005). *Clothing as Material Culture.* Oxford: Berg.

Lee, K., Nam, K. and Chung, K. (2011). A typology of services for managing touchpoint design. In the Proceedings of the *Cambridge Academic Design Management Conference,* University of Cambridge.

Lefebvre, H. (1991). *The Production of Space* (transl. by D. Nicholson-Smith). Oxford: Basil Blackwell.

Lury, C. (1996). *Consumer Culture.* Cambridge: Polity Press.

Manzini, E. (2001) 'Ideas of Wellbeing: Beyond the Rebound Effect', paper presented at the *Conference on Sustainable Services & Systems: Transition towards Sustainability,* Amsterdam, October.

Massey, A. (2000). *Hollywood beyond the Screen.* Oxford: Berg.

Mesher, L. (2010). *Retail Design.* Lausanne: AVA Publishings SA.

Miller, D., Jackson, P., Thrift, N., Holbrook, B. and Rowland, M. (1998). *Shopping, Place and Identity.* London: Routledge.

Mont, O.K. (2002). Clarifying the concept of product-service system. *Journal of Cleaner Production, 10*(3), 237–245.

Olins, W. (1978). *The Corporate Personality.* London: The Design Council.

Olins, W. (1989). *Corporate Identity: Making Business Strategy Visible through Design.* London: Thames and Hudson.

Olins, W. (1995). *The New Guide to Identity – Wolff Olins'.* Aldershot: Gower.

Olins, W. (2003). *Wally Olins: On Brand.* London: Thames and Hudson.

Olsen, B. (2010). *In Defence of Things.* Plymouth: Altamira Press.

Pawley, M. (1998). *Terminal Architecture.* London: Reaktion Books.

Petermans, A. (2012). *Retail Design in the Experience Economy: Conceptualizing and 'Measuring' Customer Experiences in Retail Environments* (PhD thesis). Hasselt: Hasselt University Press.

Pimlott, M. (2007). The boutique and the mass market. In L. de Wit and D. Vernet (Eds.), *Boutiques and Other Retail Spaces* (pp. 1–15). Abingdon: Routledge.

Pine, J. and Gilmore, J. (1999). *The Experience Economy – Work Is Theatre and Every Business a Stage*. Boston: Harvard Business School Press.

Pine, J. and Gilmore, J. (2008). *Authenticiteit: Wat Consumenten Echt Willen*. Den Haag: Academic Service.

Prendiville, A. (2012) *Strategic Systemic Design: Working with the Private and Public Sector*. Presentation. MDMN Network Workshop. January. London: London College of Fashion.

Rendell, J. (2000). Between architecture, fashion and identity. *Architectural Design*, 70(6), 8–11.

Riewoldt, O. (2002). *Brandscaping: Worlds of Experience in Retail Design*. Basel: Birkhäuser.

Ritzer, G. (2000). *The McDonaldization of Society*. London: Pine Forge Press.

Samuel, R. (1994). *Theatres of Memory*. London: Verso.

Sanders, E. and Stappers, P.J. (2008). Co-creation and the new landscape of design. *CoDesign*, 4(1), 5–18.

Shostack, G.L. (1982). How to design a service. *European Journal of Marketing*, 16(1), 49–63.

Slater, D. (1997). *Consumer Culture and Modernity*. Cambridge: Polity.

Smiley, D.J. (2013). *Pedestrian Modern: Shopping and American Architecture, 1925–1956*. Minneapolis: University of Minnesota Press.

Sparke, P. (2013). *An Introduction to Design and Culture, 1900 to the Present*. Abingdon: Routledge.

Steiner, D. (2000). Promotional architecture. In M. Pawley (Ed.), *Fashion + Architecture*, Architectural Design, 70(6), December, 6–92. London: John Wiley and Sons.

Ulrich, K.T. and Eppinger, S.D. (2012). *Product Design and Development* (5th ed.). New York: McGraw Hill.

van der Loo, H. (2004). Shopping experiences: Kathedralen van de 21ste eeuw. In R. van Amerongen and H. Christiaans (Eds.), *Retail & Interior Design* (pp. 89–120). Rotterdam: Episode Publishers.

Venturi, R., Scott Brown, D. and Izenour, S. (1972). *Learning from Las Vegas: The Forgotten Symbolism of Architectural Form*. London: MIT Press.

Watkin, D. (1996). *A History of Modern Architecture*. London: Laurence King Publishing.

Williams, B. (1994). *The Best Butter in the World – A History of Sainsbury's*. London: Ebury Press.

3   Retail design

What's in the name?

Katelijn Quartier

Learning from the late nineteenth- and early twentieth-century stores

Retail today has arisen from the developments that occurred in the past. By reflecting on that past and comparing it to the present state of retailing, we should understand better what is happening in retail design and the retail design profession today and what might emerge in retail design practices of the future. Therefore, this chapter expands on two significant developments which originated in the past, and it offers insights or inspiration to anyone involved in the retail design discipline: how retailers strived to seduce their clientele on many different levels and how different senses were a focus of design many years ago, and, second, how stores have always been at the forefront of new technical developments. By understanding its history, we can more easily relate to what constitutes retail design and the profession of retail designer.

Progressive retail institutions

Trying to trigger unique experiences to engage the consumer is not something retail has invented today. At any time, from the moment competitors entered the field, retailers have been obliged to differentiate themselves from others. The triggering of experiences is not the only possibility for differentiation, but it is a valuable one. What is seen today, and what will be explained later in this chapter, is the retailer's choice of path towards trying to create multi-sensory experiences. It may seem that an experiential approach is typical of contemporary retailing, but the department store and boutique had already appealed to the public's imagination, in a very sophisticated manner, integrating atmospheric aspects into the store. The department store and boutique 'microcosms' offered their customers advice, service, warmth and exclusivity. Boutiques opted to offer something unique, in terms of products as well as in terms of store design. First founded in the nineteenth-century arcades of metropolitan cities, boutiques were small, independent outlets with carefully crafted interiors selling specialised merchandise (Vernet and de Wit, 2007). The boutique reflected the particularities and uniqueness of its creator – that is, the fashion designer. At that time, customers identified with the products that were sold in boutiques, the interior spaces of the boutiques themselves and their owners (Pimlott, 2007).

Department stores were the most distinctive form of retailing in the nineteenth century. No other commercial building type better captured the public's imagination (Henderson-Smith, 2002). Moreover, no other single building type succeeded in fulfilling economic and cultural expression so effectively. While other more typical shops emphasised functionality and formality (Kent, 2007), department stores offered novel shopping experiences, seducing their clientele by appealing to the senses. As many historical essays observe (for example, Grunenberg, 2002; Rappaport, 1996), the department stores of the late nineteenth and early twentieth centuries – starting from the first new build department store Au Bon Marché in 1872, until the end of the art nouveau period around 1910 – were 'halls of temptation'. They are described as monuments of seduction of the senses through colour, material, sound and form (Grunenberg, 2002; Henderson-Smith, 2002). Like no other store, they adapted quickly to the buying tastes of the wealthy. Samson (1981, p. 27) writes that to the average person, large department stores have long been more than just rational business enterprises: 'A particular store can be, like a home town baseball team, a civic institution: we follow its advertising in the daily newspapers, and we are interested in its every peculiarity and nuance'. Also, Émile Zola's 'The Ladies' Paradise' (*Au Bonheur des Dames*, 1883) is a tribute to this phenomenon. He writes:

> The architect was a young man in love with modernity . . . the store was a cathedral of modern business, strong and yet light. Inside, the lifts were clad with velvet, but the main route to the upper floor was the iron staircase with double spirals in bold curves. Bridges ran across high up, and the detail of the ironwork is compared with lace. The summing up is a temple to Woman, making a legion of shop assistants burn incense before her.

From this description, it is only possible to imagine what kind of 'experience' the department stores in the nineteenth and early twentieth centuries offered to their audiences, at first to the wealthy and later to 'everybody', and, second, how their focus on offering an excellent service enriched consumers' experience.

In what follows, it will become clearer how progressive department stores have been, as I elaborate about their typical design features.

Efforts to impress and attract people

There are different architectural and interior architectural features that Western department stores have used in order to attract people and seduce them into entering and strolling around the store. First, the exterior of a department store was designed to attract consumers, and the interior was designed to impress them and to keep them close to the products for as long as possible (Clausen, 1985). Clausen (1985) also demonstrates that the building was designed as a stage set, or an elegant theatre, for the public. Indeed, the large public entrances were designed to communicate free access. Second, different department stores' designs were inspired by architectural or interior architectural elements of renowned public buildings to elicit associations with the values of those buildings. For example, when Louis-Auguste Boileau (1812–1896) extended Bon Marché in 1876 with the help of engineer Gustave Eiffel (1832–1923), the Paris Opéra was used as an inspiration, leading to the design of a majestic staircase connecting each floor. Third, there is the use of daylight. Daylight has always been an important design aspect in department stores, even after electricity was invented. More specifically, light courts – a glass roof, most often round or oval rather than rectangular – over a central gallery flooded the interior with natural light. These galleries were transitional spaces that directed the customers' movements and attention to strategically placed displays in a sequential way (Henderson-Smith, 2002).

The art of visual merchandise

To increase consumers' impulse buying, defined as purchases that are unplanned and happen on the spur of the moment, department stores first placed products that had a high demand rate, such as children's clothes and everyday objects, upstairs or at the back of a store environment which drew customers up and around the store, passing as many display counters as possible (Clausen, 1985). Goods were categorised and themed, based on the living spaces of people's homes. Carpets, drapes, light fittings, sofas and decoration were placed in one department, resembling the sitting room, while other goods, such as kitchen and kitchen-related goods, were grouped together in another department, preferably next to the department with dining-related products. The idea of 'departmentalisation' not only helped customers to orientate, but it tempted them also to buy more than they initially intended (Henderson-Smith, 2002). This evolution would also create the concept of 'customer routing', which describes the route that customers choose to take, are stimulated to take, or are forced to take in a store. The way of presenting products stimulated customers to buy more. While the techniques that were previously used, or used by other sectors and smaller stores, had a more functional purpose, presenting a selection of goods sold inside (Kent, 2007), the visual merchandising techniques that the department stores applied were more elaborate.

The use of such elaborate shop window displays can be traced back to the end of the eighteenth century in London (Henderson-Smith, 2002). Although the term as such was not yet in use, 'display' or 'visual merchandising' products were meant to sell themselves, instead of being personally sold by the salesperson, as before. Department stores went one step further and used elaborate presentation techniques as an important factor in a store's spatial design, making it a true art which became very popular by the end of the nineteenth century. They showed extravagant mock-ups of products: showing the way in which products should be used. They used lifelike mannequins, model rooms in the home furnishing departments, a mock-up of a railway coach to present travel accessories and so on, giving the customers information about products on which they might know nothing. The displays elicited sensory and tactile interactions between customer and product (Donellan, 1996). Moreover, the products were lavishly displayed with all sorts of possible accessories, in a way that was sometimes even educational (Henderson-Smith, 2002). This concept of display created a 'narrative' that involves the consumer more actively with the presented article. The element of fantasy, showing the customer the pleasure that can be derived from possessing such goods, resulted in higher purchasing levels (Wanamaker, 1906, cited in Henderson-Smith, 2002, p. 61). So the dialogue (oral culture) between the seller and the customer was partly exchanged for visual marketing strategies (visual culture) (McLuhan, 1994; Reekie, 1993, cited in Kooijman, 1999, p. 39).

Integration of entertainment

Increasing competition between department stores at the beginning of the twentieth century stimulated innovation. As a consequence, they added hybrid functions, such as restaurants, reading rooms containing newspapers and journals, and parlours where art exhibitions could be organised. Also, concerts and fashion shows were staged to change the department stores into places where social behaviour could be mixed with commercial activities. 'Seeing' and 'being seen' became the new hobby of the general public. During events that were organised at department stores, which were often themed events, the stores were decorated spectacularly. Huge advertising campaigns were used to attract customers to the stores. This was the start of an evolution in sensory experience, which has a long, but inconsistent, tradition (Kent, 2003). In the early days, the late nineteenth century, in the origins of 'display' and 'visual merchandising' consumers were mainly tempted by visual means. Lavishly displayed goods, the use of rich materials, daylight through filtered – coloured – glass roofs, richly ornamented façades and exuberant decorated displays appealed to the eye. Next to the visual sense, touch was already a part of the department stores' way of selling from the early days; sales clerks cleverly praised selected products to the clientele, which encouraged them to touch the product. But also different textures and surfaces were chosen to add to the tactile experience. At the end of the nineteenth century, department stores first introduced sound and music by organising small concerts in-store to enrich the experience. With this multi-sensory approach, the department store became a real theatre for the public. Selfridges, for example, provided the most complete sensual experience of its time: a hidden string orchestra and banks of flowers contributed to an ultimate sense of opulence (Pound, 1960, cited in Kent, 2003, p. 135), also introducing the sense of smell. It is only during the second half of the twentieth century, that the sense of smell – with the arrival of fresh products – became indispensable. The architecture and interior architecture (designed by architects), the skills of the retailers who managed the department stores, and the art of visual merchandise formed the powerbase of department stores. In a way, department stores might actually be considered as the forefathers of the interdisciplinary design approach that we recognize in current retail design.

Innovations and store design

In the history of retailing, certain innovations have had a profound impact on the advance of various store typologies. Though technical innovations and improvements – in glass and iron, for example – have always influenced retail architecture, it is argued that two particular technical innovations caused a shift in store design. The first was the development of the escalator. The first department store to install an escalator was the Siegel Cooper Department store in New York, in 1896. By 1898, Harrods had installed an alternative model, and other commercial enterprises rapidly adopted the escalator in the early twentieth century. While they were not invented on the shop floor, escalators eliminated the drawback found in elevators: that only a limited number of people can be transported. Escalators, however, allowed a continuous flow of customers, blurring the distinction between separate floors (Weiss and Leong, 2001) and, in that way, contributing to customers' in-store experiences. Escalators became a symbol of quick and efficient shopping (Van den Broek, 1946). The success and vast expansion of the physical store space of the department store would not have been possible without the accessibility afforded by the escalator. In turn, the escalator would not have become so popular and commercialised without the success of department stores.

A second innovation was the development of the Universal Product Code (UPC) in the 1950s. By the end of the 1950s, the growth in size of a supermarket had reached its limits due to difficulties with managing the store and tracing the many products in-store. For instance, an average American supermarket offered three thousand products in 1946. The UPC made it possible to increase the size of the supermarket (Hosoya and Schaefer, 2001), leading to new superstore and hypermarket designs. As the code is actually a thumbprint of a product it enabled the retailer to globally orchestrate the flow of all coded goods, improving supply chain efficiencies and enabling a wider range of products to be displayed. In the spring of 1973, the UPC was formally adopted in food retailing worldwide (Hosoya and Schaefer, 2001).

Other innovations originated in the operations of a specific store format but eventually influenced the entire retail industry. A first shift in store design occurred with the introduction of the self-service concept. Originating in the supermarket, it influenced the pattern of shopping in other sectors as well. The self-service concept was introduced in America, shortly after the Great War, by progressive grocers. One of the proponents was Clarence Saunders, who started a grocery shop in Memphis around 1917. Until then, it was common practice that the grocer took the product from behind the counter; personal service and the sales 'talk' were one of the main features. Many commodities, such as oats and sugar, needed to be weighed and packed since they were delivered to the grocer in large sacks. Saunders chose to give the customers the liberty to take the products they wanted from the shelves and then make their purchases. This way of working revolutionised the relationship between grocer and client (Du Gay, 2004). The grocer's sales talk now became a shopping experience enriched with the ability to touch the products. In the next stage, as a result of the revolution in the packaging industry, products were delivered perfectly weighed in a closed package, a clear expiration date was printed on it and the packaging provided at least an assurance of food quality and hygiene.

This innovation was beneficial for the breakthrough of the self-service concept (Kooijman, 1999). Self-service decreased prices significantly, and low prices became the most preferred benefit for customers during the first phase of its implementation (Regan, 1960). Only later, in a second phase, customers started to value the freedom to browse and the increase with regards to shopping efficiency (Regan, 1960). Further, self-service led to higher turnovers due to an increase in impulse purchases (Kooijman, 1999). Both phases of development had a major influence on store layouts and supplier and retailer communications. From the early 1950s, grocers in Western Europe took the first step in introducing the self-service concept, and other store typologies such as department stores and chain stores quickly followed suit. Department stores adopted the self-service system in response to mass consumption and the demand for increasing staff remuneration. This required a new type of shop furniture, which changed the store interior completely (Kooijman, 1999; Miellet, 2001). Shelving and other types of furniture that support self-service started to replace the counters. Only jewellery, perfumes, new foods and other luxurious products remained staff-serviced. Payment was made at separate cash registers. Customers were now encouraged to browse throughout the store, so the route through the store had to be carefully designed. Some typical plan strategies were developed, such as the open plan, the loop plan and the centre-core plan (Israel, 1994).

A later development in department store design, arising from the integration of self-service, was the launch of 'Gallerias' and superstores in Western Europe in the early 1970s (Kooijman, 1999). The 'Galleria' was a new type of department store that followed the trend of consumers, who now bought products as an extension of their lifestyles (Miellet, 2001). A 'Galleria' subdivides its departments based on target groups by creating certain atmospheres that appeal to them. The importance of brands increased, resulting in department stores' introduction of the shop-in-shop concept. Consequently, there were fewer uniform interiors because the brands were allowed to design their own mini-shop within the store.

Superstores, also known as 'hypermarkets', combined the product range of a department store with a large variety of food products. Because these large stores – between five thousand and ten thousand square meters – needed a large amount of space, they moved to the edges of towns where they found lower land values. The design of the superstore remained the same as a supermarket from the 1950s, but was larger and aimed to be more efficient. Already in the 1970s the use of colour, the importance of atmospheric elements and the level of service were acknowledged as quality characteristics (Kooijman, 1999). Further, the size of the superstore enabled the integration of the shop-in-shop concept. This resulted in a strip of small stores/kiosks – such as a news stand, a wine kiosk, a flower shop or a music store offering additional services – occupying the entrance/exit zone.

A second shift in design occurred in shopping centre development halfway through the twentieth century, with the integration of entertainment and shopping: a combination that quickly became a mainstream in shopping mall design (Gruen, 2005). Around the same time, destination stores like Ikea adopted this concept as well by offering a coffee corner or restaurant to serve their customers. Adding leisure activities to a store eventually led to the current hybrid stores with multiple functions.

The opening of Niketown in New York in 1996, which abandoned the idea that stores mainly needed to serve to sell products and generate high turnovers, caused a third shift. In addition to the complete product range, the new store offered the chance to experience the product: a small basketball court in a cage and a soccer cage took up a large amount of the store space. The focus of this store was selling the brand, not the product (see flagship stores). Niketown blurs the boundaries between promotional, sales and educational spaces (Penaloza, 1999). Customers were triggered to spend time with the brand as a pleasure activity (Penaloza, 1999). Moreover, while Nike is promoting an 'active store' that is more about brand identity than bottom-line sales, it succeeds in engaging its visitors and in building fans (Hensler, 1997). The Samsung Experience store in the Time Warner Center in New York for instance takes the selling of brand strategy one step further. By showing and letting customers experience the latest development of Samsung's digital vision, Samsung hopes to build up a relationship with the user. The store is designed only for customers to get to know the brand since no purchases can be made. Customers who do want to buy a Samsung product are referred to the nearest Samsung retail outlet or the outlet in the customers' hometown.

Following the same ethos but applying it to the luxury sector, Prada launched a store with their Soho flagship store, designed by Rem Koolhaas in 2001. The half-pipe–shaped wooden curve that connects the two floors visually is a strong architectural statement, even to the extent that the architecture of the store is more important than the products, which are sold in the basement in a rather cramped environment. With this design, Koolhaas aimed at creating an epicentre rather than a flagship store. Koolhaas has put the Prada brand literally on a pedestal and a stage, elevating the merchandise to the level of art objects. Although opinions on whether this is a good store differ, it is an archetype that marks a change in store design. Along the same line, one of the first brands to approach a product as 'art object' is the Calvin Klein store in New York, designed by John Pawson in 1993. Pawson's minimal sensibility and Calvin Klein's modern tailoring resulted in a perfect fit. These shifts in store design through the second half of the twentieth century demonstrate how the designer of a store played an increasingly important role in the evolution of the retail design discipline. The next section elaborates about this evolution.

Retail design as a discipline

Designing retail interiors was only recognised as a design discipline in its own right very recently (Christiaans and Almendra, 2012; Murialdo, 2014; Quartier, 2011). Earlier, it was understood as an intuitive expression of commercial acumen (Fitch and Knobel, 1990).

Great retailers of the nineteenth century (for example the department stores) were primarily commercial entrepreneurs. A first sign of the increasing attention given to specifically designed commercial interiors can be traced back to 1912 when De Bijenkorf, formerly known as 'Magasin de Bijenkorf', hired two different architects to design their new store, architect Van Straaten Jr. (1862–1920) for the exterior, and architect Schlöndorf for the interior. The store building, though, was still considered as an economic unit, with a particular cost per square foot and consequently space considerations as layout and departmentalisation to be considered purely from the standpoint of sales per square foot (Markin et al., 1976). As discussed earlier, this idea lasted until the end of the previous century. When the value of store design increased, retail design gradually evolved into a design discipline in its own right.

Evolution of the discipline

Tracing a recognisable identity through store design is a recent development (van Tongeren, 2003). First, graphics such as logos and fascia were used as the primary identity communicator for a retailer and a store (Fitch and Knobel, 1990). The design of the logo was at that time critical. Also, the shopping window display was used as a creative way to express the retailers' identities. During the 1960s there was still a difference between the design of the shop window and the interior of the store. In the store interior, design took a functional role in creating sales-driven environments. Also, many fixtures were sent from manufacturers to promote their products, not taking the store environment into account (Offenhartz, 1968, cited in Kent, 2003, p. 136). Gradually, the development of communicating retailers' identities continued into the design of the store interiors. Boutiques, for example, often provided inspiring cases to gain insight into how retailers created identity in-store. However, it is only with the emergence of modern chain stores, during the interwar period, that retail branding began to take its form (Kent, 2003). To create a coherent image, the store façade, the signing, displays, packaging and ticketing were designed with the same graphic elements as the company logo. Via retail branding, a store could become considered as a brand, relating store appearance and identity to its key brand values (Magrath, 2005). Design, however, also played a functional role, as it needed to display merchandise effectively and create an image of consistency and quality (Kent, 2003).

By the end of the 1960s, the design of a retail store was approached more artistically than functionally (Din, 2000). The start of the retail design discipline emerged when design companies and retailers jointly developed a type of shop that established appropriate perceptions with the retailer's targeted customers (Kent, 2003). Terence Conran, for example, was one of the first proponents of this approach with his design of the interior of the '21 shop' in Woolworths department store in 1961 (Parsons, 2001, cited in Kent, 2003, p. 136). Between the 1960s and the 1980s, retail design has been viewed as a discrete activity in the store development process, though with its very own practice (Israel, 1976, cited in Kent, 2007, p. 739).

In the 1980s, the profession of an interior designer became emancipated, and interior architecture / interior design became a discipline in its own right. This had implications for retail design as well, which started to lose its artistic dimensions (van Amerongen and Christiaans, 2004). At that time, retail design became increasingly claimed as a domain within interior architecture, with furniture makers and interior decorators often leading the way (Howe, 1994). Store design came to relate consumer behavioural needs to functionality and branding (Kent, 2003).

During the last two decades of the twentieth century, retail design evolved to a professional design discipline where knowledge of influencing customer behaviour by gaining attention, provoking emotional responses and communicating messages through environmental signalling and brand cues are key. Several steps led to the growth of the discipline, its definitions and its methodology. The first step is the increasing need for differentiation. In the 1980s, products were key, and a design only needed to be complementary and never eclipsing the products on offer (Din, 2000). During the last decades, however, this has changed. Kent (2003), for example, argues that instead of functioning as a background to products, retail spaces have taken on their own properties. Indeed, in today's global market it has become difficult for retailers and brands to be perceived as 'different' from competitors. One of the key roles for design has thus become to 'make the difference': while being aware of the merchandise carried by competitive retailers, the design of a store becomes more important when the merchandise itself is increasingly perceived as similar. Creating a unique retail environment thus almost has become a necessity for customer binding (Quartier, 2011).

A second step concerns a shift in Western economies between producers and consumers which made the consumer the focus of attention. In the current experience economy, consumers are no longer seen as solely buyers of products; they are also seen as consumers with proper personalities, feelings and longings. This perspective requires different, more sophisticated (marketing) approaches and new retail concepts with more attention to the designed environment (Pine and Gilmore, 2007). Third, today's society is one where shopping and looking for new experiences are essential aspects (Petermans et al., 2013; van der Loo, 2004). Pine and Gilmore (1999) referred to this phenomenon as the Experience Economy. Shopping has become a leisure activity as part of our daily lives. Some would even argue that it is becoming the principal source of public activity (Leong, 2001). As experiences have become more important, the store environment has changed into a place where you can buy products into a space where interactivity, socialisation and communication are key (Kent, 2007). Designing such places requires knowledgeable designs, in terms of both quality and a holistic approach. Fourth, the consumer's shopping behaviour has changed. With the arrival of Web 2.0 and Web 3.0 technologies in the early twenty-first century, consumers spend more time shopping on the Internet, searching information in order to compare products and prices, or making real purchases. This changed the consumer from a passive, unaware partaker to an informed, active participant (Wuyts et al., 2010). Finally, design agencies themselves played a role in the emancipation of the discipline, as will be explained in the following section.

The role of design agencies

While in the previous section the history and development of the discipline is described from an outside-in perspective – that is, while studying external factors that impacted on the evolution of the discipline – from an inside-out perspective, designers and design agencies also caused the discipline to evolve and become more professional. Terence Conran and Rodney Fitch (1938–2014), both at the forefront of retail design and both British, are discussed as innovators to illustrate this point.

Conran started his own design practice 'Terence Conran Design' in 1956, designing a shop for Mary Quant. Though he sold his design company to continue with his homeware chain Habitat, founded in 1964, he continued to reshape thinking about retail design and the high street in the 1970s and 1980s (Glancey, 2001). His designs for Habitat saw a fundamental translation of the retail brand in the design of the exterior and interior. Focusing on young marrieds and singles, products and store design were brought together (Kent, 2003). With great passion, he was selling not needs but wants, and Habitat stores offered a place where shopping for homeware was as pleasurable as shopping for clothes (Glancey, 2001; O'Sullivan, 2014).

Rodney Fitch, mentored by Conran, founded his own design company, Fitch and Company Design Consultants, in the 1970s by buying the design side of Conran Design (Bayley, 2014). Fitch was distinguished by his lively interiors in the 1980s, with Topshop and Marks & Spencer as prime examples. Though the economic boom of the 1980s played a role in the rapid expansion of the Fitch company, Fitch's designs had been well placed in the late seventies to shape the coming zeitgeist of 1980s consumerism (Times, 2014). It has been argued that Fitch practically invented the *business* of retail design – making money out of designing stores (Holdsworth, 2001) – and giving it credibility (Hocking, 2015). However, there are three changes in the perception of the role of retail design, instigated by Fitch, that were crucial for the development of the discipline.

The first change was the shift towards the idea of retailers not merely being distribution channels for third-party brands but being brands in and of themselves (Hocking, 2015). Approaching a retailer as a brand and designing the store as a whole changed the British High Street in the 1980s (Times, 2014). As the function of a store evolved from a necessity to becoming a place that should facilitate buying experiences in a rather innovative or creative way, the role of the designer changed profoundly. The designer, and his/her skills, became increasingly important. When consumers started to buy products as an extension of their lifestyle, increasing the importance of brands and image, target-group-oriented strategies proved to be profitable. Knowing the target group, what they want and how they were best approached was the primary knowledge necessary for a designer to design a matching store. Both Fitch (with Topshop) and Conran (with Habitat) were designing stores where product and store came together to create a lifestyle offer.

A second change was re-thinking, in an analytical way, about how merchandise needed to be presented and lit and how customers would flow through the stores. Fitch always aimed at designing better places to shop for ordinary people (Times, 2014), which was reflected in his book *Fitch on Retail Design* (1990). This influential book provided other designers with the design tools to create 'good' retail environments while at the same time promoting Fitch's own perspective. Third, Fitch believed that 'shopping is the purpose of life' (Fitch, 2012). His belief shifted the way all stakeholders in retail thought about what retail and retail design should be about. In his view, shopping, being one of the most important cultural indicators of the modern age, should be fun, rewarding and entertaining.

By recognising that retail design is more than just designing a store's interior, Fitch set the tone in creating a business that crossed over various disciplines, and he incorporated retail design and architecture, alongside product and packaging design, to offer his clientele a particular design service. This idea of a multidisciplinary design agency became the norm during the first decade of the twenty-first century, mediated by the impact of the digital (r)evolution around 2005. This (r)evolution caused a holistic turn in retail design (Teufel and Zimmerman, 2015). By 2005, it became widely known that retailing, as a multichannel business, had to integrate a whole range of distribution channels. Because the number of different designers or agencies working on a project can cause problems of dissonance, design agencies started to combine forces offering once more the entire service to their clientele. So, instead of separate specialists such as interior architects, visual merchandisers, graphic designers, web designers and so on, each designing their proper part of the retail experience, the retail business has evolved into the design of a customer holistic experience for which specialists from diverse disciplines need to work together (Teufel and Zimmerman, 2015).

The merger generates an opportunity to create physical and digital spaces that are consistent, coherent and, above all, complementary. The challenge though is integrating the human, digital and physical contexts seamlessly (WPP, 2013): the consumer, as a social human being, is the key point of attention, having the world in his/her hand (mobile device); is connected at all times; yet also wants to physically interact – with a retailer, with the brand, with other consumers, in a physical store space which facilitates the creation of an engaging sensory experience. Technology can assist in making the store experience personal, enabling the retailer to communicate on a one-to-one level with the consumer, making him/her feel important and valued. Next to employing many different trained designers to be as complementary as possible, design agencies also employ psychologists and sociologists to understand better the people for whom they are designing. Because of the importance of such a customer-oriented approach, product design offices and service design firms are moving their services into the retail design industry, designing stores with a more user-centred approach. In an omnichannel age, the merger of both worlds, being product design and (interior) architecture, might offer the opportunity to come up with store designs that answer better to the needs and wants of today's consumers.

This is also reflected in retail design education. Over the last fifteen years, retail design education has come to the fore at a university level. Before, only retail management had its own curriculum (Christiaans and Almendra, 2012), but now retail design education is evident in different design disciplines ranging from interior, product or industrial design to architecture, leading to specific training, each with their own accent. Precisely because of its trans-disciplinary approach, as stated in our definition, this is beneficial to the field.

In sum, retail can be explained in three phases: in Retail 1.0, the manufacturer was in charge, and no designer was needed; Retail 2.0 was a phase where the retailer was in charge but hired an architect or interior architect to design the store following the brands' or retailers' ideas. By 2016, the industry finds itself in Retail 3.0, a time where the consumer is more and more in charge (van Tongeren, 2013). This asks for much more than a designer to translate a retailer's identity into a store design and goes beyond mere functionality and efficiency – even more so now that a commodification of products, brands and retail is occurring. The ever-changing expectations and aspirations of the consumer, that are above all paramount, have made retail design a fast-emerging discipline with a sophisticated design approach. Store design is now emphasised in retailer differentiation strategies (Doyle and Broadbridge, 1999) and retail positioning (McGoldrick and Greenland, 1994; van Tongeren, 2013). Creating a competitive, strongly differentiated retail store asks for designers with an in-depth understanding of retail's contexts and parameters (Teufel and Zimmerman, 2015). In respect of the contexts, Teufel and Zimmerman (2015) define five key factors: the history of retail; art as a role model for innovation and unique experiences; the market as a dynamic pluralistic and competitive system of supply and demand; consumers' wants and needs; and evolution in technology. Of these I have elaborated on three key factors, explaining the history and role of department stores, focusing on innovations and unique experiences that occurred on the shop floor, and, finally, focusing on the role of society as design agencies tried to answer to the new consumer. In what follows I will examine the fourth factor of 'what consumers want and need' since that is the key driver in current retail design, as space precludes a more detailed discussion of the fifth factor, on technology.

Describing the discipline in the twenty-first century

The word 'retail' refers to the selling of goods to consumers (businessdictionary.com). So retail design should be about designing spaces to facilitate the selling of these goods. This also includes the selling of services (Skjulstad, 2014). What might sound simple has become increasingly complex since the concept of 'space' has changed in the early twenty-first century. Whereas 'space' used to refer to a physical store environment, nowadays 'space' has become a broader concept with the development of e-tailing. Space no longer concerns solely a physical space but also includes virtual spaces, web shops and also Facebook, Instagram and other platforms that retailers and consumers continuously use to buy and sell products. Due to this development, being a retailer or a retail designer has become increasingly complex and interdisciplinary since there are many channels where a consumer can be reached and that, as a consequence, should be designed properly. From my point of view, it is for this reason that the retail design discipline is still lacking a clear definition. In addition, retail design is still evolving rapidly. Evolutions in technology and society cause the rules of the game to change at an increasing pace, contributing to the growing complexity of the retail discipline (Maatman, 2009), and making it difficult to accurately define and remain truly up to date. Earlier definitions did not take the aspect of e-tailing into consideration. To explain how retail design has progressed and to arrive at a definition of the contemporary discipline requires a summary of both academic and practitioner perspectives.

Though retail design with all its aspects has been described before, a meaningful definition of retail design was first developed by Kindleysides (2006). His definition shows the different aspects that a retail designer needs to be aware of when designing commercial spaces. In Kindleysides's view, retail design is 'an understanding not only of what will work aesthetically within the space, but how it will perform functionally and commercially, and how it can be built to budget and meet all of the regulations governing the use of a public space'. Kindleysides indicates that designing commercially and for public spaces requires more skills than interior design alone. Furthermore, on the one hand, as a semi-public space, a store needs to be inclusive to different people with different social, personal and even cultural backgrounds, each experiencing a store differently. Peek (1999, cited in de Châtel and Hunt, 2003, p. 101) means the same when saying: 'it is not the amount of design that makes a successful shopping environment, but knowing of the effect of it on the consumer'. Note that although Kindleysides uses the term 'space' to define the physical store space, 'space' can also relate to the virtual store space. On the other hand, designing commercially is about designing spaces that eventually generate or increase turnover. In that case, building to budget is part of commercial design.

In order to design a commercially effective store, an understanding of the retailer and the brand is necessary. Van Tongeren (2003) confirms this by describing the design of a store as 'a creative representation of the interplay of the rational and emotional elements of the brand and its formula' (p. 12). According to van Tongeren, design shapes thoughts. So thinking is and should be the primary action when designing stores. He continues by explaining the necessity for a deep understanding of how brands work and how formats are organised and established. This needs to be related to what consumers expect from a brand. So a retail designer designs for the retailer and the consumer and must place himself/herself in the aura of those two groups.

Din (2000, p. 10) emphasises this brand perspective in a second definition, depicting retail design through its role linking

> instinct, art and commerce . . . to come to efficient (in terms of space, flexibility and cost) and effective (to communicate the retailer's brand values and encourage consumer activity) retail environments that meet the ever-tougher consumer demands. It incorporates the management of people and space to meet up to the most essential characteristic of retail: change. Therefore a designer's task is to combine his expertise and the retailer's knowledge of the market with elements of psychology, technology and ergonomics.

Din continues by stating that of the major industrial sectors, retail is the most susceptible to the ever-changing demands of consumers, the economy and public policy. With this description, he considers design at a strategic level and applies it to every aspect of retail space. He also indicates that retail design is multi-disciplinary as it is a result of contemporary design processes drawing the consumerist, psychological and aesthetic elements together.

Both descriptions present essential aspects of retail design; however, they fail to answer one question: what is the purpose of retail design? Although price, brands, quality and location are important choice determinants and, for some stores, the most important ones, the answer seems to lie beyond. What Roberts (2005) says about products in his book *Lovemarks* can also be adopted by stores: it is about a relationship. To Roberts (2005), lovemarks are brands with which consumers have a special emotional connection, which generates loyalty beyond reason. Kapferer and Bastien (2009) mean something similar in explaining a relationship being created when a retail space ceases to be merely a merchandising outlet and instead becomes a place where passion is shared. David Kepron (2014) adds to this that the difference between a space and a place is exactly that emotional connection.

So defining the dynamic field of retail design is quite a challenge. Retail and society influence and change each other constantly, making it hard for retailers to stay relevant to our changing habits (Christiaans and Almendra, 2012). Although retailing as commerce is timeless, retail design is one of the most challenging new fields of design, embracing the disciplines of architecture, industrial design and communication design as well as social science disciplines such as environmental psychology, sociology, cultural anthropology, marketing and management (Christiaans and Almendra, 2012). These disciplinary perspectives make it difficult to describe or define what retail design actually is: any definition will fall short in including them all. Therefore, the aim should be to *describe* the retail design discipline as it is at this moment, rather than *defining* it:

> Retail design refers to designing spaces for selling products and/or services and/or a brand to consumers. It is interdisciplinary in its intention to create a sensory interpretation of brand values, through physical or virtual stores. A retail designer therefore tends to conceptualise the consumers' needs and wants into a spatial program.

Though this description says nothing about the emotional connection, which a store should try to make with its visitors, I strongly believe that this aspect will increase in attention in the years to come. What the spatial programme entails will be discussed in more detail in the next section.

Designing the physical store space

Despite the digitisation of retail, the physical store space remains the most important channel for retailers to communicate with their consumers (Stevens, 2013). This perspective on the design of physical store space and taking the previously mentioned definitions into account is visualised in Figure 3.1.

In most interior design assignments, understanding a building and its (future) occupants are the starting-point and subject of investigation. In retail design, however, the brand and its (future) consumers are the starting-point, and the building or site often comes later. This makes designing physical commercial store spaces very specific. Being a retail designer therefore involves on the one hand placing oneself in the retailer's position. 'Who

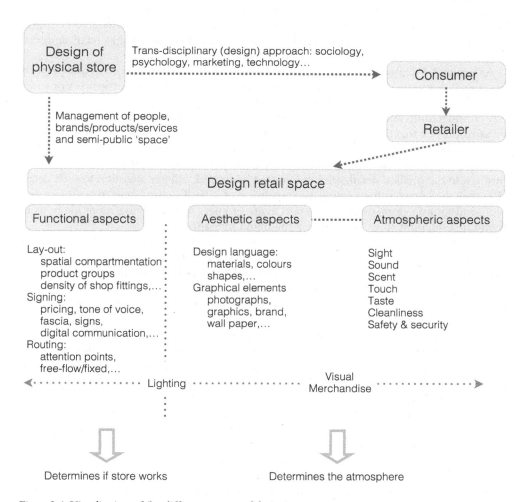

Figure 3.1 Visualisation of the different aspects of designing a store

am I? What image do I want? What am I selling, and to whom am I selling it?' are questions to consider, in order to find that unique thumbprint a retailer should have these days. On the other hand, it involves placing oneself in the position of the consumer. The first aim of a space is to make the consumer feel at ease, making him/her able to relate to the store and to find his/her way. Moreover, what the retailer wants to be and what the consumers expect of it need to be in balance. Translating the values of both, taking into account boundary conditions – such as budget, retail legislation and commercial policy, which have a huge impact on the proliferation of retail formats (Colla, 2004) into a feasible store design – implies finding a design language that fits both. Understanding the way in which retail space can affect and provoke, how people interact with it and how they behave are only a few of the aspects a retail designer should consider. While the traditional model of retail design shows three primary stakeholders (the designer, whether internal or external to the retail organisation; the retailer; and the customers), modern practice generally recognises that there is a complex network of stakeholder groups, situated at varying distances from the design briefing, development and implementation process (Kent, 2007). Retailers, marketers, retail designers, (digital) communication designers, product designers and so on all have to work together in an effort to create a holistic, consistent and congruent physical translation of the retailers' unique identity. Because of this, retail designers would benefit from the knowledge of other specialists.

As Figure 3.1 demonstrates, the interior of a store space can be clustered in three aspects: functional, aesthetic and atmospheric. Note that the division between them is not strict. Just as visual merchandising can function within all three aspects, so can concrete designerly considerations and choices, such as lighting. Moreover, these elements do not function in isolation but together generate the holistic experience of a retail space. This holistic aspect has become increasingly important and includes integrating every aspect very consciously and consistently. Thus, creating a consistent store environment should be carried through to the smallest detail, since committed customers will pay attention to such detail. Whether that detail is the non-visual suspension of a shelf, more likely to be found in a high-end fashion store, or the deliberate usage of cheap iron shelving more likely to be found in a discount store, both convey the brand message.

To achieve such an environment, not only the products and people need to be aligned with the brand, but also all functional and aesthetic aspects have to express the retailers' brand values and personality. When the store looks and feels consistent with the retailer's image – that is, the way the customer perceives the retailer and bases an expectation on that perception – the customer is immersed in the retailer's world. In other words, from A to Z the retailer should tell its story via all means that reach its customer. Since the start of the new millennium, retailers and designers increasingly emphasize atmospheric aspects since they are relatively easy to manipulate and since they can really make a difference (for example, see Turley and Milliman, 2000). Depending on the sector and price range, these atmospheric cues are implemented from a low level in discount stores to a higher presence in more upscale retailing.

So, once more and with reference to the earlier department store discussion, retail spaces have evolved from a three-dimensional place to a five-dimensional space, including the five senses (smell, sound, touch, taste and sight) and including an emotional connection. Compared to the stores of one hundred years ago, designing for all senses has become increasingly sophisticated but complex. There are many more materials and techniques available for design, making it both challenging and exciting to design for as much senses as possible. Creating an environment for the senses is a tactic to immerse the customer in a brand's world, not only by telling and visualising a brand's story, but also to create an atmosphere that offers a five-dimensional experience. For example, the tasting of products has reached another level since supermarkets installed cooking displays to offer freshly cooked snacks for the customer to taste, prepared with the products from the store to promote them. In addition, fashion brands started including taste. To appeal to more senses, Armani developed a chocolate line, which is presented in its latest New York store. The store in Milan also sells flowers. The stores in Milan and New York also have Armani restaurants where the designer's personality is projected onto the food. Also, the Armani hotel and spa in Milan enrol the visitors in a multi-sensorial experience. Scent is appealed to more often due to new technologies.

Supermarkets have been vaporising artificial odours of freshly baked bread for a long time, but other fragrances are being developed and studied for their impact on customer behaviour in a wide range of store typologies and product segments (for example, Doucé and Janssens, 2013). The sense of smell was added by the use of carefully chosen aromas (Kent, 2007). But, in addition to the scent of products, induced or not, the space or the materials used to design the store might also release an odour that determines the atmosphere in the space. A designer might even choose a specific material to release its scent into the store to complete a specific experience. At this point, touch is possibly the most under-appreciated sense in terms of store design. Currently, many of the touchpoints between the consumer and all elements of a store lack a consistent design approach. Think of touching the door handle when entering a store, touching the curtain of the fitting room before trying out an outfit, feeling the material of a cash desk when paying and so on. Designers have a wide range of materials at their disposal, which can be processed in many different ways in an effort to find the perfect material that fits the design of the store and identity of the retailer best. Together with the reason of choice for a specific material for its touchable qualities, there are its acoustic qualities. What we hear in a store is determined by much more than solely the music that plays in-store. Think of the sound of high heels on a floor, the sound of shopping trolleys, the hum of the ventilation system, the echo of voices, etc. They all determine the atmosphere of a store and should be carefully selected. Finally, we have what we see. Most visual aspects have some level of determining the atmosphere and the experience. Colours and materials are obvious visual aspects, but there are also shapes, aspects relating to lighting (colour, intensity, location, type), cleanliness and patterns. All have an impact on what we 'see'.

Ultimately, what determines the perception of a store is more than the architecture and its aesthetic, functional and atmospheric aspects alone. It is the preferably harmonious combination of architecture, its interior architecture and façade, the products, the service delivered, the staff and so on. Nevertheless, a retail designer focuses on staging the 'space' domain, and the design of a store does have an influence on how the staff feel and behave as a result (Underhill, 1999). For example, if a store lacks efficiency through bad design, this will determine the mood of staff and in turn their interaction with the customer. So, it actually lies within the responsibilities of the designer to design properly functioning stores.

Conclusion

The developments that occurred in the past help to understand retail and retail design today. In sum, the crux of designing a physical store space has not changed that much over time, but there has occurred a shift towards increased attention for personalized sensory design facilitating emotional connections with the customer. The design of environments that are able to trigger an experience will become a critical factor in making stores relevant in a world of omnipresent access and abundant choice. In addition the seamless integration of the still developing digital world is today's challenge, which inevitably also challenges the role of the retail designer. But as stores have always been on the forefront of new (technical) developments, they can once more take up that role.

References

Bayley, S. (2014). Rodney Fitch obituary. *The Guardian* [online] 10 Nov. Available at: http://www.theguardian.com/artanddesign/2014/nov/10/rodney-fitch [Accessed 11 December 2015].

Christiaans, H. and Almendra, R.A. (2012). Retail design: a new discipline. In: *Design 2012, 12th International design conference.* Dubrovnik, Croatia, 21–24 May 2012.

Clausen, M.L. (1985). The department store: the development of the type. *Journal of Architectural Education,* 39(1), pp. 20–29.

Colla, E. (2004). The outlook for European grocery retailing: competition and format development. *International Review of Retail, Distribution and Consumer Research,* 14(1), pp. 47–69.

de Châtel, F. and Hunt, R. (2003). *Retailisation: the here, there and everywhere of retail.* London: Europa Publications.

Din, R. (2000). *New retail.* London: Conran Octopus Limited.

Donnellan, J. (1996). *Merchandise Buying and Management.* New York: Fairchild.

Doucé, L. and Janssens, W. (2013). The presence of a pleasant ambient scent in a fashion store: the moderating role of shopping motivation and affect intensity. *Environment and Behavior,* 45(2), pp. 215–238.

Doyle, S.A. and Broadbridge, A. (1999). Differentiation by design: the importance of design. *International Journal of Retail and Distribution Management,* 27(2), pp. 72–83.

Du Gay, P. (2004). Self–service: retail, shopping and personhood. *Consumption, Markets and Culture,* 7(2), pp. 149–163.

Fitch, R. (2012). *Shopping is the purpose of life.* Inaugural speech at TU Delft, 22 May 2012.

Fitch, R. and Knobel, L. (1990). *Fitch on retail design.* Oxford: Phaidon Press Limited.

Glancey, J. (2001). Old habitats die hard. *The Guardian* [online] 22 Dec. Available at: http://www.theguardian.com/culture/2001/dec/22/artsfeatures2 [Accessed 2 November 2015].

Gruen, V. (2005). *From urban shop to new city.* Barcelona: Actar.

Grunenberg, C. (2002). Wonderland: spectacles of display from the Bon Marché to Prada. In: C. Grunenberg and M. Hollein (Eds.), *Shopping: a century of art and consumer culture.* Ostfildern: Hatje Cantz Publishers, pp. 17–25.

Henderson-Smith, B. (2002). *From booth to shop to shopping mall: continuities in consumer spaces from 1650 to 2000.* Ph. D. dissertation, Griffith University, Nathan, Queensland, Australia.

Hensler, K. (1997). NikeTown New York City. *Interiors,* 156(4), pp. 60–65.

Hocking, R. (2015). Remembering Rodney. *Block Display & Design Ideas,* 27(3), p. 44.

Holdsworth, P. (2001). Fitch and the designer's itch. *Brand Strategy,* 152, pp. 9–11.

Hosoya, H. and Schaefer, M. (2001). Brand zone. In: R. Koolhaas, C.J. Chung, J. Inaba and S.T. Leong (Eds.), *Project on the city 2: Harvard design school guide to shopping.* Köln: Taschen, pp. 165–171.

Howe, K.S. (1994). *Herter brothers: furniture and interiors for a gilded age.* New York: Harry N. Abrams in association with the Museum of Fine Arts, Houston.

Israel, L.J. (1994). *Store planning/design: a history, theory, process.* New York: John Wiley & Sons. Inc.

Kapferer, J.-N. and Bastien, V. (2009). *The luxury strategy: break the rules of marketing to build luxury brands.* London: Kogan Page.

Kent, T. (2003). 2D3D: management and design perspectives on retail branding. *International Journal of Retail & Distribution Management,* 31(3), pp. 131–142.

Kent, T. (2007). Creative space: design and the retail environment. *International Journal of Retail & Distribution Management,* 35(9), pp. 734–745.

Kepron, D. (2014). *Retail (r)evolution.* Cincinnati, OH: ST books.

Kindleysides, J. (2006). About: retail design. *Designcouncil* [online]. Available at: www.designcouncil.org [Accessed 7 November 2006].

Kooijman, D. (1999). *Machine en theater.* Rotterdam: Uitgeverij 010.

Leong, S.T. (2001) . . . And then there was shopping. In: R. Koolhaas, C. J. Chung, J. Inaba and S.T. Leong (Eds.), *Project on the city 2: Harvard design school guide to shopping.* Köln: Taschen, pp. 129–156.

Maatman, J. (2009). Retail: a reflection of society. In: M. Russem-Willems and S. Shultz (Eds.), *Powershop II: new retail design.* Berlin: Frame, pp. 36–40.

Magrath, A. J. (2005). Managing in the age of design. *Across the Board,* 42(5), pp. 18–27.

Markin, R. J., Lillis, C.M. and Narayana, C.L. (1976). Social–psychological significance of store space. *Journal of Retailing,* 52(1), pp. 43–54.

McGoldrick, P. J. and Greenland, S. J. (1994). Modelling the impact of designed space: atmospherics, attitudes and behaviour. *International Review of Retail, Distribution & Consumer Research,* 4(1), pp. 1–16.

McLuhan, M. (1994). *Understanding media: the extensions of man.* Cambridge: The MIT Press.

Miellet, R. (2001). *Winkelen in weelde.* Zutphen: Walburg Pers.

Murialdo, F. (2014). *The practice of consumption and spaces for goods.* Amazon Digital Services.

Offenhartz, H. (1968). *Point of Purchase Design.* New York: Reinhold.

O'Sullivan, J. (2014). Habitat at 50: a new way of living. *The Guardian* [online] 4 May. Available at: http://www.theguardian.com/culture/2014/may/04/habitat-50-year-anniversary-terence-conran [Accessed 29 October 2015].

Parsons, A. (2001). *The branding of Burton menswear.* Paper presented at the CHORD conference. Wolverhampton: University of Wolverhampton.

Penaloza, L. (1999). Just doing it: a visual ethnographic study of spectacular consumption at Niketown. *Consumption, Markets and Culture,* 2(4), pp. 337–465.

Petermans, A., Janssens, W. and Van Cleempoel, K. (2013). A holistic framework for conceptualizing customer experiences in retail environments. *International Journal of Design,* 7(2), 1–18.

Pimlott, M. (2007). The boutique and the mass market. In: D. Vernet and L. de Wit (Eds.), *Boutiques and other retail spaces.* Abingdon: Routledge, pp. 1–15.

Pine, J. and Gilmore, J. (1999). *The experience economy: work is theatre and every business a stage.* Boston: Harvard Business School Press.

Pine, J. and Gilmore, J. (2007). *Authenticity: what consumers really want.* Boston: Harvard Business School Press.

Pound, R. (1960). *Selfridge.* Portsmouth, NH: Heinemann.

Quartier, K. (2011). *Retail design: lighting as a design tool for the retail environment.* Ph. D. dissertation, Hasselt University, Hasselt, Belgium.

Rappaport, E. (1996). The halls of temptation: gender, politics, and the construction of the department store in late Victorian London. *The Journal of British Studies,* 35(1), pp. 58–83.

Regan, W. J. (1960). Self-service in retailing. *Journal of Marketing,* 24(4), pp. 43–48.

Reekie, G. (1993). *Temptation: sex, selling and the department store.* St. Leonards: Allen & Unwin.

Roberts, K. (2005). *Lovemarks.* Second edition, New York: PowerHouse Books.

Samson, P. (1981). The department store, its past and its future: a review article. *The Business History Review,* 55(1), pp. 26–34.

Skjulstad, S. (2014). What's on in retail design? A transdisciplinary approach to a bachelor programme in retail design. In: *Cumulus Aveiro,* At Aveiro, Portugal, May 2014.

Stevens, D. (2013). *The retail revival.* New York: Wiley.

Teufel, P. and Zimmerman, R. (2015). *Holistic retail design, reshaping shopping for the digital era.* Amsterdam: Frame Publishers.

Times (2014). Rodney Fitch: obituaries – retail designer whose company shaped the distinctive look of the 1980s shopping boom. *The Times* [online] 15 Nov. Available at: http://search.proquest.com.bib–proxy.uhasselt.be/docview/1625102516?pq–origsite=summon [Accessed 29 October 2015].

Turley, L.W. and Milliman, R.E. (2000). Atmospheric effects on shopping behaviour: a review of the experimental evidence. *Journal of Business Research,* 49, pp. 193–211.

Underhill, P. (1999). *Why we buy, the science of shopping*. New York: Simon & Schuster.

van Amerongen, R. and Christiaans, H. (2004). *Retail & interior design*. Rotterdam: Episode.

Van den Broek, J.H. (1946). Het wonen in de stad. *Bouw*, 10, pp. 666–669.

van der Loo, H. (2004). Shopping experiences: 21st century cathedrals. In: R. van Amerongen and H. Christiaans (Eds.), *Retail & interior design*. Rotterdam: Episode, pp. 90–120.

van Tongeren, M. (2003). *Retail branding: from stopping power to shopping power*. Amsterdam: BIS Publishers.

van Tongeren, M. (2013). *1: 1 de essentie van retail branding en design*. Amsterdam: BIS Publishers.

Vernet, L. and de Wit, L. (2007). *Boutiques and other retail spaces*. Abingdon: Routledge.

Wanamaker, J. (1906). *The Wanamaker Diary 1906*. Philadelphia: John Wanamaker.

Weiss, S.J. and Leong, S.T. (2001). Escalator. In: R. Koolhaas, C.J. Chung, J. Inaba and S.T. Leong (Eds.), *Project on the city 2: Harvard Design School guide to shopping*. Köln: Taschen, pp. 337–365.

WPP (2013). *Brand Z: top 100 most valuable brands 2013*. [pdf] New York: Millward Brown. Available at: http://www.millwardbrown.com/brandz/2013/Top100/Docs/2013_BrandZ_Top100_Report.pdf [Accessed 28 October 2015].

Wuyts, S., Dekimpe, M., Gijsbrechts, E. and Pieters, R. (2010). *The connected customer: the changing nature of consumer and business markets*. New York: Taylor & Francis Group.

Zola, É. (1883). *Au Bonheur des Dames*, translated as The Ladies' Paradise by Brian Nelson (1995). New York: Oxford University Press.

4 Retail formats

*Filipe Campelo Xavier da Costa, Gabriel Gallina
and Marcelo Halpern*

Introduction

This chapter aims at presenting and discussing a set of models employed to classify retail operation formats. Throughout time, several efforts have been made to define criteria and systems in order to classify business activities focused on end consumers (Gilbert, 2003; Guy, 1998; Kozinets et al., 2002). Fields such as business management, economics, architecture, and more recently design share an interest in this topic, leading to an increasing number of studies and research about how to organize typologies for retail.

From a managerial point of view, establishing typologies for retail structures is relevant because understanding different types of retail operations allows assessing the competitive impact they have on the retail industry, as well as identifying competitive strategies adopted by leading companies and competitors in the segment. Therefore, it is possible to build retail business strategies that are likely to be more efficient and more successful. From a retail design perspective, a broad and rich understanding of store format alternatives, and the different elements of store and retail management variables, will enable the development of better point-of-sale projects. Innovative in-store customer experiences and enhanced business performances can be designed using a knowledge platform built from retail store typologies and its usage according to company strategies and resources. Information about the diversity of store formats should be a relevant resource for designing meaningful shopping experiences and successful retail strategies, mainly considering different types of variables of point-of-sale structure. This chapter aims to analyze tools and models that help designers to deal with retail store alternatives in design projects.

Typologies of store formats

One of the first initiatives identified was developed by Louis Bucklin, published in 1963 in *Journal of Marketing*. This paper's purpose was to define types of retail strategies that might be used, based on the classification of the merchandise available in the stores. The starting point was the nature of the available goods related to buying occasion. Products could be organised into three categories: convenience goods, comparison buying goods and specialty goods, on the premise of the level of involvement the consumer experiences when searching and purchasing these goods. 'Convenience goods' are classified by the effort made in comparing product alternatives, where a low level of time and resource is required from the consumer. Products requiring an intermediate level of involvement were seen as 'comparison buying goods', and those requiring great efforts by the consumer when buying them were 'specialty goods'. According to Bucklin, the product type would be the decisive element in order to classify the retail strategy to be adopted – that is, the store profile best suited to the nature of the corresponding merchandise.

One of the most usual ways of classifying retail activities is associated with the type of products being sold at a particular type of business. Classification frameworks employed by governments such as in the United Kingdom and the United States are based on classifying businesses by product type or activity segment. In the British case, businesses are divided into predominantly food stores, non-predominantly food stores, non-store retailing, and automotive fuel (Office for National Statistics, 2010). The first category encompasses all stores specialized in selling food (butcher's, greengrocer's, bakery, fish market), supermarkets, and liquor and tobacco specialty shops. The second category includes department stores, apparel, homeware, and pharmaceutical and cosmetics, among others. Non-store retailing corresponds to any form of remote shopping, such as through catalog and mail order. Finally, automotive fuel focuses exclusively on the sale of fuel at vehicle gas stations.

The American system, managed by the U.S. Census Bureau and denominated North American Industry Classification System (NAICS) (U.S. Census Bureau, 2015), classifies retailing activities according to a logic similar to Great Britain's, with a broad division into food and non-food retailing; however, it presents a more detailed subdivision of business categories, such as motor vehicle and parts dealers, electronics and appliance stores, and sporting and hobby goods, for example. Both systems are much applied by agencies responsible for domestic economy statistics and information, yet they have less applied relevance in fields such as business management, design, and urban policies.

Classification of retail: Business strategy, consumer behavior, and urban space

From the perspective of other fields of knowledge such as geography, Clifford Guy developed an analysis of the methods used to classify stores and spaces dedicated to retailing practices (1998). A set of criteria was identified to categorize retail outlets and malls which may be organized in three dimensions: retailer business strategy, consumer behavior, and aspects of urban space.

The classification criteria of the retailer business dimension are store size, type of goods sold, and the nature of operation ownership, as Figure 4.1 demonstrates. Store size is usually measured by indicators such as square footage, number of checkouts, or even stock size as assessed by number of items of SKUs (stock keeping units).

The nature of the goods sold may be represented by the classification utilized by official agencies, such as food, cosmetics, furniture, etc. This criterion, however, is greatly limited because many retailing businesses work with large-sized assortments, as is the case of hypermarkets, that may sell food, home appliances, and clothes in the same store. The hybrid categories used by official sources, such as *mass merchandisers* or *variety store*, which do not allow a clear identification of the type of merchandise sold, highlight their deficiency as classification criteria. A simplified manner of approaching the topic is to assume as classification criterion the depth of the merchandise assortment – i.e. the variety and level of specialty a retailing operation has in a certain product category. Thus, points-of-sale can be classified according to their function: generalists (large assortment of product ranges and categories) or specialized (reduced number of categories, but great variety of items).

The type of retail operation ownership represents a criterion of easy understanding and application. The distinction between independent operations, store chains, or even

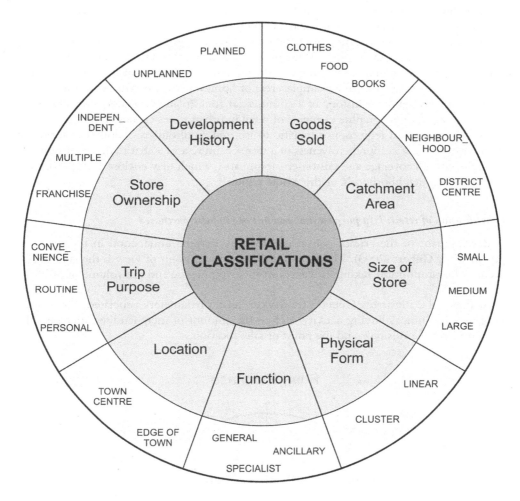

Figure 4.1 Retail categorization framework
Source: Guy, 1998

franchising systems is an established, shared notion among all stakeholders (Guy, 1998). This is an extremely useful dimension to comprehend the competitive scenario and the size of retail organizations.

As to consumer behavior, the criterion identified by Guy is associated to the trip purpose, or shopping occasion, of the buyer. Within this concept, an individual could shop by convenience or by comparison, in an analogous fashion to the classification proposed by Bucklin (1963). Convenience buying is then more associated to frequent, immediate purchases involving minimum effort, featuring routine characteristics and less consumer involvement. Comparison buying is more related to personal indulging, is more seldom, and features greater time commitment by the consumer. Items of greater economic/personal value are included in this kind of consumption, where the retail environment is designed to create more elaborated and less automatic experiences. Guy (1998) also makes a distinction between household shopping (i.e. purchases related to the household) and personal/fashion shopping (more associated to individual consumption with a strong hedonistic content).

The last dimension this author approaches is related to criteria associated to retail geography in urban spaces. As Figure 4.1 demonstrates, aspects related to the central or peripheral (suburban) location in an urban space, the existence of a cluster of stores belonging to a certain product category (for example, areas of homeware or electrical hardware stores), or even the development history of a commercial zone (planned or not) that allows the characterization of geographic elements of retail in urban zones creates classification variables for commercial regions, not specific to isolated retail outlets. Another criterion of spatial nature is the comprehensiveness of a store's capture area – that is, the extension of a retail operation's coverage and customer capture area, which may enclose a neighborhood (local), several neighborhoods, or the whole region.

Classification of retail: Trip purpose and amount of products purchased

A development of the criteria set created by Guy may be understood in the typology presented by Gilbert (2003). The focus on the consumer point of view is the central element of his proposition, taking into account the trip purpose and the volume of products purchased.

As Figure 4.2 illustrates, Gilbert's framework relates parameters associated to the planning of a consumer's buying activity, such as the amount of merchandise purchased, the time available for this task, and the point of sales location.

Figure 4.2 Retail formats' framework by trip purpose
Source: Gilbert, 2003, p. 292

Products are placed on the horizontal axis according to their buying involvement level; the axis ends are purchases with greater research and evaluation intensity (comparison) and purchases made more quickly and automatically (convenience). On the vertical axis, the amount of merchandise purchased or the item size (furniture, home appliances) of each purchase are related; at one end there are large-sized purchases, and at the opposing end there are purchases with a lesser amount of items (portable purchase).

Convenience products are naturally purchased through a more immediate buying process, and thus must be physically located in stores easily accessed by the consumer (for example, near to his or her residence or workplace). On the other hand, products requiring comparison to confirm a buying decision – which demands involvement of time – may be located in places far from the consumer's daily life, such as downtown or even shopping facilities located in distant areas, such as malls. It is usual to find store clusters or commercial zones concentrated mainly on one type of product, allowing greater research and evaluation intensity by the consumer and a more immersive consumption experience.

As to the amount or size of merchandise purchased (bulky purchase), the consumer may carry out buying tasks with a more automatic and extended decision-making process, which leads to distinctive store format and location strategies by the retailer. Monthly supermarket purchases (food, personal care, cleaning supplies) undertaken by consumers looking for convenience and less involvement are appropriated to geographically accessible stores with large parking lots ('solus' in Figure 4.2). Similarly, large purchases may occur involving individuals with a greater involvement with their decision-making process who wish greater variety in product options, which suggests the existence of large-sized stores in areas concentrated with competing companies ('retail parks' in Figure 4.2).

For smaller-sized or personal use items, stores located in the vicinity of the consumer's residence or work may be interesting point of sales sizing or locating strategies, such as drugstores or grocery stores with a limited assortment of products (local shops). At the other extreme, for less frequent purchases such as clothing and jewelry, stores located in central commercial zones or the high street allow comparison behavior between products and stores in the same area.

The framework proposed by Gilbert does not constitute a typical taxonomy for retail formats, but it contributes to a broader understanding of the strategic possibilities of setting up a retail space from the perspective of the consumer's buying activity. According to time availability and perceived risk associated to the planned purchase, the very same individual may choose completely distinct store structures (from a small business around the corner to a mall that is very distant from his or her home) in order to purchase the same product. The distinct behavior variations that the consumer may present offers greater obstacles to defining a unique retailer's business strategy. This framework allows identifying and defining work quadrants and visualizing possible scenarios in order to establish the most appropriate retail format.

Classification of retail: Strategy business and consumption experience

Other models are able to offer a more specific approach to retail classification, like a typology developed by Kozinets et al. (2002) that is based on the diversity of strategic options a particular business can adopt. It is based on different levels of store and service that can be incorporated for the sale of similar products. This typology proposes four store formats. *Flagship stores* are defined as stores built to create, reinforce, and represent an organization's brand, not necessarily as a point of contact and sales between consumers and products

(Kozinets et al., 2002). The main objective of this type of space is not generating economic or sales results, such as greater profitability or sales productivity per square foot, but providing the consumer with a relevant brand experience. Thus, facilities, service, and location are carefully planned to provide that experience.

Less sophisticated than flagship stores, *premium stores* are characterized by superior service in comparison with the standard and pop categories, offering a broad assortment and higher perceived quality. Different from the previous, it has more explicit sales and profit purposes, and yet it provides a sales experience of high perceived value (Kozinets et al., 2002).

Standard stores are a company's regular stores, with standard assortment, dimensions, facilities set-up, and service. Its performance is assessed by its sales productivity and profitability, and it is responsible for the greater part of the organization's turnover.

Pop stores are point-of-sales structures located in regions of high flows of people, with simplified dimensions and set-up and reduced product assortment, having as objective to provide convenience and a lower-complexity consumption experience.

This framework-related store profile classification has parameters according to the type of experience sought by the consumer. On the vertical axis we find the customer's orientation in his or her buying activity, which may be more focused on a set of benefits from the purchase and the shopping experience or, at the opposing end, a cost-optimizing disposition, either related to the prices found in the stores or the interest in investing time in this particular buying mission. On the horizontal axis, the typology of transactions that the consumer establishes with each type of retail structure is presented, from the occurrence of a single, immediate sale to repeated, continued sales at the same point-of-sales. The dimension of each store-type circle indicates how relevant the corresponding format is to the company in terms of sales.

A flagship store pretends to allure and entertain a trendsetting consumer who is keen on novelties and values. For this kind of store, an architectural component translating this brand experience is key, aiming at a unique environment. At the other extreme, in a popular store, where the client seeks a mix of low price and quick sale, the architectural standard allows reduced scale and simpler standards.

The scheme presented presents distinct strategies regarding store format, correlated to the consumer behavior described by trip purpose and type of consumption experience. By mapping the retail outlets' possibilities, it is possible to identify distinct customer segmentation strategies for a company, as well as verify the relevance of each format in the organization's bottom line.

Integrating typologies and retail formats

Based on the selection of models and typologies exposed, we present a retail business classification framework integrating different elements that we identified in the retail literature. This framework features six axes summarizing the classification proposed by Guy, where we take into consideration the goods sold (whether daily or extraordinary), the function (whether the store is generalist or specialist regarding the mix offered), the format (whether its spatial configuration follows a simple or complex layout), the volume (whether the purchase is portable and can be carried by one person or bulky and demanding a car to be transported, for example), the location (how accessible it is), and the trip purpose (whether it is a purchase demanding more analysis and comparison time or a less time-consuming, more convenient purchase).

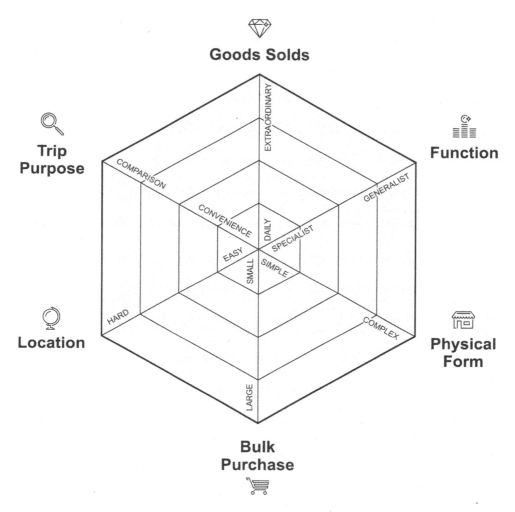

Figure 4.3 Typologies integrating matrix of retail formats
Source: Developed by the authors

The axes

Each axis is scaled from *two extremes*, where directly related parameters are taken into account. We next describe each axis.

Goods sold

This dimension corresponds to the level of user involvement as to the type and specific characteristics of the product retailed. Based on the consumer behavior logic and the purchase decision-making process, we believe that extraordinary products (those out of the ordinary consumption patterns, such as jewelry or a car) tend to a higher involvement by the user. Daily products, however, such as personal care or food, are acquired more frequently and thus demand less effort in the purchase decision-making.

The user-experience intensity may be gauged between these extremes from the combination of certain parameters related to it: risk (financial, psychological) associated to purchasing a certain product, where we perceive higher tension and decision involvement when extraordinary goods are at stake; financial investment (high, low) in the purchase, where we also perceive higher involvement with extraordinary goods, since they tend to be more expensive; comparative, where the set of attributes perceived in a product is more or less relevant when comparing options – this parameter is considerably important when acquiring extraordinary goods and less important for daily goods; occasion or product seasonality, where its availability may provoke a purchase opportunity and add a tension ingredient to the acquisition of extraordinary goods; and assessment and decision-making time, where there is higher involvement in extraordinary goods and lower in daily goods. As an example of retail formats we have supermarkets, convenience stores, and stationery stores for *daily goods*; and jeweler's shops, art objects stores, and car dealers for *extraordinary goods*.

Function/mix

The function/mix dimension involves issues related to how the variety of products in a retail environment or market segment may influence the level of involvement and user experience. For this, we consider a polarized axis ranging from specialist retailers (specific market niches with a smaller product mix – house brand, such as bicycle, cell phone, or feminine underwear) to generalist retailers (environments with more varied and plentiful products – competing brands in the same environment, such as family clothing, technology, or books).

The user experience intensity may be gauged between these extremes from the combination of certain parameters related to it: *variety*, where we see that a broader mix in several segments is related not only to more time spent browsing but also to the interference of unplanned purchases, which results in more involvement and a more diversified experience; *comparative*, where we have diverse options (brands) within the same product category, and the user's involvement is directly proportional to the amount of options at his disposal; and *offer*, where a special sale condition (promotion) enhances the value perceived by the customer in relation to a certain product, resulting in an experience of greater relevance/intensity when compared to normally priced merchandise. As an example of retail formats, we have extreme sports stores, technology flagship stores, and wine stores for *specialist function*; and department stores, music stores, and bookstores for *generalist function*.

Store format

This dimension refers to the involvement level related to physical aspects, size, and organization of the retail environment. Simple, familiar environments usually are thought to offer fewer barriers to the user, but they often do not break through traditional standards (such as footwear, photography, or medication). On the other hand, complex environments require more learning and more browsing effort to interact and find products (such as furniture and decoration, building material, or food).

The user experience intensity may be gauged between these extremes from the combination of certain parameters related to it: *area*, where larger square footage and considerably sized spatial perception bring more ingredients to the user experience and involvement with the environment; *layout*, where the space setup (circulation, checkout, product exposition, etc.) determines the perception of more or less complexity in reading the environment, thus requiring assisted browsing or not; *product exposition*, where sectorization and organization of the amount of SKUs offered are considered as influencing the environment reading, thus understood as more or less complex; and *familiarity*, considered as a composite related to a standard format followed by certain types of segment (providing quick spatial understanding) as a reducer of expectation and, consequently, involvement and experience. As an example of retail formats, we have shoe stores, greengrocers, and drugstores for *simple format*; and wholesale discount outlets and megastores for *complex format*.

Purchase volume

This dimension refers to physical aspects of the product (size, quantity, volume) and its direct relation to the user, where the gauging of his or her involvement and experience is directly subject to the practical portability of the merchandise bought. Small-sized and/ or low-quantity elements are more practical and simplify the user dynamics in the post-sales process (such as cosmetics, cell phones, or fruits), while large-sized, big-volume, or high-quantity elements (such as building material, furniture, or household appliances) result in greater involvement and organization, which brings complexity to the shopping experience.

The user experience intensity may be gauged between these extremes from the combination of certain parameters related to it: *product characteristics* (which takes into account its dimensions, volume, and weight) is related to an eventual necessity of assisted portability (that is, the more complex it is to take the purchased goods to its destiny, the more involvement is present); and *product mix*, where the variety available is often associated to the resulting purchased volume. As an example of retail formats we have kiosks, grocery stores, and optical stores for *small or portable volume*; and wholesale stores, hypermarkets, and megastores for *large volume or quantity*.

Location

Location is a dimension linked to user involvement in terms of access, transit, and geographic convenience. Retail environments with greater difficulty of access are believed to require more involvement, preparation, and organization by the user.

The user experience intensity may be gauged between these extremes from the combination of certain parameters related to it: *transit*, where we consider the effort the user makes to arrive at the location, determined according to the different access modalities (on foot, bicycle, automobile, subway, bus); *proximity*, that is, how convenient and practical the location is (distant locations result in an experience of greater complexity, involving a different organization by the user regarding the portability of the merchandise purchased, such as furniture or industrial equipment); and *surroundings*, where the urban (streets, neighborhoods, buildings, lighting) and social composite (areas of lower or higher safety) contributes with an important experience ingredient as the user approaches his or her destiny. As a consequence, as Figure 4.1 illustrates, we can differentiate between 'easy-to-access locations' and 'hard-to-access locations'. Drugstores, sidewalk stores, and kiosks can be considered as examples for *easy-access locations*; and factory outlets and wholesales for *hard-access locations*.

Trip purpose

Trip purpose, apart from having a direct relationship with the product type, is associated to the user's objectives and motivations (Kang, Herr & Page, 2003; Kim & Park, 1997). The search for a retail business may have different motivations: making a convenient purchase (such as grooming articles, hygiene products, beverages, or bread) or undertaking a process of knowing, learning, and comparing products (such as technology, automobile, or gourmet cooking). Daily products are usually less related to comparative trip purposes, while purchases requiring more involvement tend to relate to comparing and involvement.

The user experience intensity may be gauged between these extremes from the combination of certain parameters related to it: *comparison*, where attributes are weighed in order to choose a certain product or not, resulting in an important tension in the decision-making process; *time*, a factor corresponding to the depth of the buying decision-making, and consequently resulting in more or less user involvement until the action is performed; *product type*, where a product may be classified as possessing low-decision involvement (everyday purchase) or high-decision involvement (e.g., automobile), directly influencing the breadth of user involvement in the purchase process; and value, as either emotional, personal worth, or financial investment, where the experience is more elaborated and less automatic due to the involvement it entails. As an example of retail formats, we have kiosks, bakeries, and drugstores for *convenience*; and showrooms and car dealers for *comparison*.

The framework applied and the experience intensity

This framework integrating retail format typologies is organized as a radar-like scheme, where a geometric form is built resulting from the level of intensity/relevance of these predefined axes. In the authors' point-of-view, the framework allows us to define any given segment (clothing, food, bookstore, drugstore, etc.) and, based on the consumer expectation or experience, scale these axes according to their importance. The final geometric form represents the experience intensity as perceived by the user but offered by the store design. As the geometric figure grows larger, the user experience in that particular store becomes more intense and relevant, requiring higher involvement during the shopping task. Smaller geometric shapes indicate less impacting experiences, probably related to routine and repeated purchases, based on pragmatic criteria as location and convenience.

For a small neighborhood drugstore, for instance, the scaling of the axes results in a geometric form of small breadth, thus representing a low intensity or relevance of user experience (see Figure 4.4). Regarding the goods sold, this type of retailer meets a more routine consumption need, with low risk, comparison, and seasonality aspects. Its function is more appropriate to a specialist retail form, although a composite of products (grooming articles, hygiene goods) added to the medicine mix somewhat increases the scaling on this axis. As to its physical format, the prevailing characteristic is small size, small area, and a more simplified, traditional, and very familiar layout. On the purchase volume axis, as the product is small (bottles, medicine cartons, etc.), there is evident portability, and this practicality does not require great user involvement. With regard to location, a neighborhood drugstore presents great convenience because of its proximity and ease of access, and thus this axis presents low scaling due to the scarce user involvement required to reach the place. In the case of a drugstore, trip purpose is subject to the need for drugs and/or wellness products. These goods tend to demand low-decision involvement, since the user

Figure 4.4 Framework applied to a neighborhood drugstore, a jeweler's shop located in a mall, and a clothing discount outlet

Source: Developed by the authors

either has a doctor's prescription or has already a clear notion of the type of product he or she needs, without the need to compare much.

In the case of a mall jeweler's shop, for example, the geometric form has a more expanded area (Figure 4.4), where broader parameters represent a considerably intense user experience. In the goods sold dimension, there is great involvement as these are extraordinary items worlds removed from the general consumption routine, with high perceived psychological risk, investment, and time involved in the decision-making process. As to the function axis, this retail typology presents low scaling due to its depth in a specific product mix (jewelry), characterized by a strong specialist aspect. In the store format dimension, we usually see small size and low area, since the product dimension is minute and it has low space needs for exhibition or presentation. Also, the purchase volume axis is not significant thanks to its practicality. Regarding location, there is a small scaling increase on this axis since the store is located in a commercial center, a space requiring a certain complexity in terms of transit and access modalities. In the case of acquiring jewelry, a high-priced product, the urban surroundings represent an important composite due to its perceived safety. For this specific type of product, the trip purpose presents a high scaling due to the increased time for analysis (products, value, options), comparative involvement, and correlated risks.

In the case of a family clothing discount outlet, perceptions are different. The user experience has increased, as the situation requires a greater level of involvement and effort when compared to the other examples presented (Figure 4.4). The goods sold axis presents considerable scaling since clothes are not bought on a daily basis, and they demand great choice and decision involvement too, which is inherent to the nature of the product itself. In the function dimension, we see more generalist features, with a great variety of available options. The breadth of offer by competing brands generates a more complex choice experience. The format of this retail type generally presents massive square footage due to the quantity of SKUs available and exhibited, resulting in a spatial perception environment that may be complex and may demand learning and familiarization time. As to the volume axis, there is an increase due to post-purchase requirements, since it is often needed to use a vehicle in order to transport the content acquired. The presence of this last component (vehicle) is associated to the next axis – location. Factory outlets are usually located in the outskirts of town, since they need large physical space to be implemented (a rare luxury in urban centers). For these situations, transit and access modalities are critical in view of their importance; therefore, this axis is scaled higher. Finally, on the trip purpose axis, the nature of the product entails increased time (trip, choice, decision) and comparison (variety of options available), resulting in considerable scaling.

Visualization of this radar graphic scheme allows not only quick diagnostics but also identifying opportunities to enhance user experience. Consumer perception level can be scaled in relation to a specific retail typology. This contribution is relevant for retailers and designers as it makes reading this perception easier, and improvement strategies focused on each axis may be viewed as well.

Conclusion

The purpose of this chapter was to identify and discuss retail format typologies available in the literature from different areas of knowledge, such as administration, geography and marketing.

The intense transformation suffered by the retail industry in recent decades caused the diversification of store formats and typologies (Kumar, 1997). Most of the models identified in retail management literature are based on regular elements of store and trade activities, ranging from the nature of products, the physical size of the store (footage as metric), or its location. From the perspective of demand, store formats might be defined as broad, competing categories that provide benefits to match the needs of different types of consumers and/or different shopping situations. Many studies have attempted to identify the benefits sought by the motivations and demographic characteristics of customers of different store formats as appropriate tools to classify retail sites and build business strategies (Redondo, 1999; Reynolds, Ganesh & Luckett, 2002). The multiplicity of retail typologies has been more confusing than helpful for retailers, designers, managers, and policymakers (Dawson, 2000). The existence of classification models might contribute to managers and designers for building better retail strategies; however, relevant issues such as customer experience have been neglected by these models.

Therefore, the proposal of an integrative model of retail store typology, characterized by a consumer shopping experience perspective, aims to lead the retailer to reflect on the relationship between traditional decisions of retail management and consumer behavior. Elements such as trip purpose and user involvement represent the core variables a retailer needs to gain insight in, in order to understand the nature of consumer patronage building, which in turn is a key element that can contribute to business performance. Decisions on retail format often neglect such aspects, focusing on such tangible components as merchandise selection, store size, or location analysis.

This chapter presents distinct approaches for retail formats and typologies, contributing for a better understanding of their components. These elements have a strong impact on the experiences promoted in retail environments and, hence, on the shoppers. The proposed framework enables designers and retail practitioners to visualize and to assess an integrated set of variables, which are very often available but disposed separately. The combined presentation of different elements of retail design project decision allows planners to discover what category of customer experience can be developed and collaborate for the project discussion.

The proposed framework could be used as a design tool. Through the conjoint analysis of variables over the axes, it is possible to draw up a prognostic reasoning that contributes to the process of decision making concerning not only planning or project but also relating to relevant decisions about retail management issues such as location, store size, sales strategies, ambience, etc.

Available literature renders generally a more practical perspective, concerning mainly business and marketing variables. Including design and architecture elements for this reflection, retail designers can realize issues related to aesthetic trends, interior design, different layouts, and even new business models. Models or frameworks, as the one proposed in this chapter, intend to bridge the gap between two mental models for retail planning (that is, business and design approaches), qualifying the discussion about user experience and the relationship variables that shape a particular retail segment format.

The selection process of the systems of classification applied in this chapter did not aim to be exhaustive but intended to bring different perspectives for understanding the retailing industry together and classifying the retail market. The framework proposed, developed while being based on a theoretical basis, should be improved in order to be able to be used as a managerial tool in retail strategy building and for retail design purposes. Regarding its elements and its functioning, future research is recommended considering the framework use on different types of products and sectors (food, apparel, homeware, etc.), competitive marketplaces (less/more competitive), and company ownership (chains, independent stores, or franchising). The authors believe that further investigations and studies concerning the use and testing of the proposed framework, such as derivatives, could broaden the understanding and invoke interest in retail environments as complex canvases for design research.

References

Bucklin, L.P. (1963). Retail strategy and the classification of consumer goods. *Journal of Marketing*, 27, 1, pp. 50–55.

Dawson, J. (2000). Retailing at century end: some challenges for management and research. *The International Review of Retail, Distribution and Consumer Research*, 10(April), pp. 119–148.

Gilbert, D. (2003). *Retail marketing management*. 2nd ed. Harlow: Prentice-Hall.

Guy, C.M. (1998). Classifications of retail stores and shopping centres: Some methodological issues. *GeoJournal*, 45, 4, pp. 255–264.

Kang, Y., Herr, P., & Page, C. (2003). Time and distance: Asymmetries in consumer trip knowledge and judgments. *Journal of Consumer Research*, 30, 3, pp. 420–429.

Kim, B., & Park, K. (1997). Studying patterns of consumer grocery shopping trips. *Journal of Retailing*, 73, 4, pp. 501–517.

Kozinets, R., Sherry, J., DeBerry-Spence, G., Duhachek, A., Nuttavuthisit, K., & Storm, D. (2002). Themed flagship brand stores in the new millennium: Theory, practice, prospects. *Journal of Retailing*, 78, pp. 17–29.

Kumar, N. (1997). The revolution in retailing: From market driven to market driving. *Long Range Planning*, 30, 6, pp. 830–835.

North American Industry Classification System (NAICS). (2015). *U.S. Census Bureau* [online]. Available at: http://www.census.gov/epcd/www/naics.html [Accessed 25 July 2015].

Office for National Statistics (2010). *Information paper – Classification changes for retail sales* [online]. Available at: http://www.ons.gov.uk/ons/rel/rsi/retail-sales/february-2010/classificationchangesinretail sale_tcm77–232219%20(1).pdf [Accessed 25 July 2015].

Redondo, I. (1999). The relation between the characteristics of the shopper and the retail format. *Marketing and Research Today*, 28, 3, pp. 99–108.

Reynolds, K., Ganesh, J., & Luckett, M. (2002). Traditional malls vs. factory outlets: Comparing shopper typologies and implications for retail strategy. *Journal of Business Research*, 55, pp. 687–696.

5 Retail environments

Bethan Alexander and Anthony Kent

The changing relationship between producers and consumers, the growth of service industries, and the opportunities for shopping as a leisure activity have significantly influenced where retailing takes place through the use of internal and external spaces. The opportunities for consumption beyond the selling of products have embraced the development of the 'third place' and the design of explicitly experiential retail environments. The focus on consumer experience but also the convergence of commerce, service, leisure and culture has contributed to both the hybridity and the fluidity of the designed environment. Fluidity extends to the physical retail space itself, as it becomes permeated by online connectivity to the virtual environment.

The spatial theme is one of increasing complexity as the boundaries between transaction and leisure have become blurred; stores have a commercial, sales function but also showcase the brand, communicating its values and providing a sensory leisure experience. With its extension into cultural institutions, retailing has had to negotiate its commercial function with predominant educational and recreational functions. More generally, retail outlets have contested or enhanced public space. Their appearance at airports and railway stations, sports venues and tourist attractions provides further insights into the diversity of retail formats, sizes and purposes, and the temporality of space. This chapter commences with a more detailed exploration of the theoretical contexts of place and space, and their influence on the diversity of retail formats and their design. It continues by explaining how stores can be distinguished by their 'atmosphere' and experiential properties. The development of the 'third place' concepts leads to further consideration of the possibilities for more complex sensory environments in two contrasting formats: flagship (especially luxury) stores and pop-up stores. The final section of the chapter extends these environments into the online sphere and the ways in which digital technologies challenge notions of retail space. It concludes with the problem of stores as showrooms or showcases for online shopping. In so doing, the chapter reflects the dimensions of the retail environment from more bounded, visual places, focused on products and display, to the fluid, consumer-engaging spaces of experiential and sensory stores.

Perspectives on retail environments: Place and space

Retailing is a global activity, but one not necessarily requiring a global solution. Buildings and the streets and malls that contain them provide the contexts for the empty retail 'shell' (Plunkett and Reid 2012). Towns and cities offer both idiosyncrasies and less anonymous spaces but bring with them the homogeneity of multiple store brands. The environments of retailing, and their design, are determined by their relationship to concepts of place and space. These define the possibilities for design, through their location, the built environment, the size of store and its internal conceptualisation.

Retail places from a geographical perspective can be defined by the proximity of outlets to their customers and competitors together with other elements of their environment that have a spatial imprint (Murray 2001). The location of places can be planned, and governments have had varying degrees of influence on retail development of out of town as well as urban centres. Planning has both restricted but also created different retailing formats. Entire creative quarters in cities came to be identified as important contributors to vibrant and successful cities. As such, they created opportunities for small-scale retail, independent and often creator-owned shops, accompanied by cafes, bars and restaurants. These served the creative community and – through their association with design – a wider market.

However, places and spaces are not necessarily determined by plan, map and chart. Anthropological place first is geometric, defined by the line, the intersection of lines and the point of intersection (Augé 1995). However, in everyday terms they are really axes or paths that lead from one place to another and are traced by people. Second, places are invested with meaning and share at least three characteristics: identity, relations and history. By contrast, Augé (1995) defines a 'non-place' as an allusion to a negative quality of place devoid of the substance of these characteristics. Supermarkets, and other commercial centres, can demonstrate these transient non-place qualities, while evolving different sorts of opportunities for interpersonal communication (Jeffres et al. 2009).

In summarising anthropological and phenomenological geography, Sherry et al. (2007) explain the importance of managing the physical and tangible environment of a space. Thus, space is transformed into place through the incorporation and acknowledgement of cultural meaning of boundaries, rules, structures and paths which consumers interpret and use as journey-makers to find their own way. It is the individual's perception of the meaning of space and its uses that are important, rather than any meaning, which might be prescribed by others, or by the administrator of a given space (Lofland 1998).

The relationship between the human condition and tangible surroundings can be the result of 'insideness', and in a phenomenological account, where an environment generates a strong sense of belonging, then that environment becomes a meaningful place (Relph 1976; Laing and Royle 2013). The difference between a space and a place is its emotional connection, where emotion imbues an environment with personal meanings based on its 'lifeworlds' (Seamon 1979; Kepron 2014). Quartier (see chapter 3, citing Kapferer and Bastien 2009) provides a similar explanation of relationship creation describing how retail space is transformed beyond its transactional, product-led function into a place where a passion is shared.

The focus on consumers' transformative roles in defining space through meaning is found in sociological accounts of place and space and their concern with inhabitation. How people make use of and imagine space in their everyday lives is inherently social. Space is historically contingent, and socially produced space perpetuates society's values, culture, goals and ideologies: 'to know space is to understand the social world and ultimately to understand ourselves' (Zieleniec 2007: xiii). Boundaries concern the practical use of space divided by elements of boundedness, proximity and distance, and where mobility is related to fixity and 'the fixed spot become a pivot for the relationship and social context' (Frisby and Featherstone 1997: 47). This is significant for retail space because, in the city, social relations have come to be increasingly fragmented, fleeting and superficial. Everyday experiences underpin society in which everyday forms of sociation take place in the spaces of the city and lead to a self-preserving blasé, urban personality.

In these contexts, shopping centres, malls and galleries become spaces of albeit temporary distraction and escape (Harvey et al. 2005).

A more political position, the ownership of space, engagement with it and its meanings, is at the centre of Lefebvre's (1991) spatiology, which explains interdependent 'moments' of space as a generative process of social relations. His conceptualisation recognises that Cartesian space is calculable and controllable and that it consequently enables social and technological domination (Elden 2004). Instead, space expresses specific representations of the interaction between the social relations of production and reproduction, which serve to maintain social relations in a state of co-existence and cohesion. This gives rise to a 'conceptual triad' of conceived-perceived-lived space, defined as representations of space, representational spaces and spatial practice. Representations of space are official spaces codified by knowledge of experts, conceived by physicality and their architecture. Representational space is perceived through signs and images of its users and inhabitants. Spatial practice is enacted in the everyday lives of embodied actors. Moreover, as a moment of space, place is wherever everyday life is situated (Merrifield 1993).

Lefebvre's spatiology provides the basis to examine the spatial processes of the retail store itself, codified by the brand, and its representation: its perception by networks of users, suppliers, designers and commentators. Both are implicated in the continuing growth of fashion through online and social media and the opportunities to contest the role of the store as online connectivity, e-commerce and social interaction. The social processes of perceived moments of space are found in fashion brands located in stores and shopping centres. More specifically, a fashion event defines physical and social networks of fashion people that can include retailers, wholesalers, importers and manufacturers; designers; intellectual property lawyers, management consultants and accountants; marketing, events and media specialists; logistics; and distribution intermediaries (Weller 2013).

Ultimately, spaces in the landscape are never isolated and bounded, and everyday life is constituted by many different kinds of space: discursive, emotional, affiliational, physical, natural, organisational, technological and institutional (Gammon and Elkington 2015). As a result, places are never static and continually produced and reproduced in interaction with their spatial surroundings and thus may acquire new meanings over time. These perspectives contextualise retail stores, for while the store is bounded in one sense by the materiality of its windows, internal structures and floors, the spaces it creates are open to interpretation. Interior store design refers to spaces for selling and working, for circulation and storage of stock, and the 'back office' functions, but these are defined and re-defined over time. Periodic refits, seasonality, new products and services, communications and promotion contribute to a flow of spatial allocation.

More defined and controllable measures of the store environment are imposed by marketing and management theorists and practitioners, which reflect their economic and commercial focus on retailing. For marketers, distribution and communication are important elements of the marketing mix, in which place has, from the outset, been one of the essential four variables (McCarthy 1975). Retailing is fundamental to the channel of distribution of goods and services as a mediator between producer and consumer. In this context, design facilitates the efficient distribution of products to specific consumer markets and differentiates store formats with the aim of favourably influencing consumer behaviour. In the elaboration of the marketing mix to seven variables, the physical evidence dimension of the mix also finds strong support in the place, as retailers emphasise the store environment and its colours, themes, lighting and layout. In this commercial context, sales space is an important measure of retailer success: sales per square foot (metre) and like-for-like trading comparisons of outlets over one or more years. Store operational managers will define space allocation to specific products in precise detail through spatial planning systems, such as planograms. The influence of these measures on designers is evident in the need to provide objective evidence about the retail environment's place in the business plan and that it consistently demonstrates how the right interior has a positive impact on sales and investment (Plunkett and Reid 2012).

The location of stores continues to form a critical element of retail planning and opportunities for format development. The relaxation of out-of-town planning regulations in Europe led to the development of the out-of-town store, and the availability, often due to oversupply, of urban retail space contributed to pop-up stores. In brand management, places can provide instant associations for a corporate brand. They can have strong emotional or self-expressive associations and content that can be linked to the corporate brand and contribute to the emotional dimension of corporate reputation (Berens and Van Riel 2004; Uggla 2006). The concept of the brandscape (Sherry 1998; Kent 2003; von Borries 2003; Ponsonby-McCabe and Boyle 2006; Klingmann 2007) transforms the brand into a location (Riewoldt 2002) in which experimentation with creative ideas and innovative spatial concepts is crucial to adequately counter prevailing notions of place in the context of globalisation (Klingmann 2007). More explicitly in a retail design context, Riewoldt (2002: 79) proposes that store design merges with the brand image down to finest details to achieve expressiveness through the 'purposeful use of characteristic forms and calculated elements of surprise' to send out powerful signals, communicate images and promise new experiences.

The conceptualisation of space within the physical environment of the store can be extended in another direction to explain customer and employee behaviour and interactivity. The servicescape communicates service quality attributes, establishing customer expectations and creating the service experience (Bitner 1992; Zeithaml et al. 2009). These are achieved through environmental stimuli in three dimensions: ambient conditions, spatial layout and functionality, and signs, symbols and artefacts (Kotler 1973; Hightower et al. 2002). More broadly, the servicescape has an impact on brand equity as a 'material and symbolic environment that consumers build with marketplace products, images and messages, that they invest with local meaning, and whose totemic significance largely shapes the adaptation consumers make to the modern world' (Sherry 1998: 112). This symbolic environment with its visual and non-physical qualities is one that is co-created with consumers, rather than directed by retail marketers.

The implications for the retail store are the recognition that boundaries between images and material forms are unclear, and that images and material forms define the merging process between building and sign, decoration and architecture (Klingmann 2007). This approach foregrounds the significance of spaces and surfaces, which tend to be marginalised by their very intangibility in other definitions of the physical environment. Brandscapes are often artificial environments (Klingmann 2007), but they can also be real locations that enable the brand to be staged and encountered in its purest unusual and unique style (Riewoldt 2002). Both internal spaces and external design communicate distinctive brand values but also opportunities for consumers to co-create experiences with the brand. These are found in the re-use and interpretation of internal design features and spaces (evident in the attention to micro spaces and the sense of absence in the superstores), and in the museum the anticipation of learning more about the museum through the store, and the opportunity to reconfigure space for leisure and learning. In brandscape environments, experiences in the form of events as well as environments, including exteriors or interiors, become identical with the message of a given brand (von Borries 2003).

Reflecting the social definitions of space and the development of service industries, including retailing, a design agenda for services emerged, characterised by its intangibility, heterogeneity, inseparability of production and consumption, and perishability (Zeithaml et al. 1985). Design research and practice consequently approached services from two distinctive perspectives. The 'interaction paradigm' focused mainly on the interactivity of services, to improve the user experience in places and spaces where users and services interact. Second, the 'functional' paradigm is based on functional thinking and distinguishing between functions and products, and its application in sustainability strategies (Meroni and Sangiorgi 2011).

Service design acknowledges both users and providers – from the user perspective by being useful, usable and desirable, and from the provider perspective as efficient, effective and different. Co-creation is one of the driving forces, involving users, employees and other actors in order to integrate the expertise of those that are in the heart of the service experience and mobilising energies for change. Moreover, services are delivered and consumed over time, and, consequently, service design came to focus on the full customer journey, including the experiences before and after the service encounters (Mager 2008). These developments carry a number of implications for retail design: first, the use of designer insight tools to capture consumer experiences, including participant observation, storytelling and emotional mapping; second, and more literally, wayfinding and navigation have become important objectives to determine usage of the service environment; third, the development of touch-points between the retail brand and consumer have evolved to include both environmental and communication dimensions.

Retail formats and their design implications

The preceding perspectives demonstrate dimensions of place and space and the contexts of retail design that are realised in the diversity of retail formats. Retail brands and store designs evolved rapidly in the UK, specifically from the 1980s through new retail formats and new locations. Out-of-town development enabled the conceptualisation and design of new, large-scale shopping malls, outlet centres and subsequently shopping villages. In urban locations, lifestyle retailing transformed multiple retailers, primarily in the clothing sector, through marketing strategies typified by distinctive and co-ordinated store design. A further change in retail development saw the emergence of urban regeneration programmes that emphasised the mix of leisure and retail usage and inspired the design of new shopping areas (Jansen-Verbeke 1990).

Solus retail sites vary in size and have relatively restricted space. Some stores create memorable experiences through the intimate use of space. The cube-shaped Clube Chocolate in Sao Paulo was conceptualised as 'not so much a micro-department store phenomenon but a different – almost intimate – attitude to luxury shopping, one that serves fresh, unique products on every visit and a diverse shopping experience, all wrapped up in an aesthetically pleasing and social environment' (Harkin 2004: 9). Smaller spaces afford opportunities to create idealised room settings, drawing on positive emotions about home and leisure, personal identity and branding (Jeffres et al. 2009). On this small scale, the relationship between creativity and spaces, sensuality and homeliness, enables retail spaces to be perceived as personal habitats where the brand's 'core function is complemented by an emotional extra of almost equal value' (Mikunda 2007: 4). Such spaces afford retailers the opportunity to co-create experiences with consumers and stimulate peer-to-peer communication.

Department stores have always occupied larger spaces and multiple floors by definition and have offered more design possibilities. Although the sector has generally declined, Selfridges department store designed in Birmingham by Future Systems demonstrated a distinctive approach to the building itself. The interior of its London store, re-designed to reflect its position as a 'house of brands', has contributed to its success as an upmarket destination. Department stores have tended to open up their floors, creating galleries and flexible spaces for their extensive product assortments. While the breadth of offer has tended to decline, notably electrical goods and home furnishings, it has opened up space for a greater depth of assortment in clothing and accessories.

By contrast, food retailing through supermarkets, and out-of-town superstores, offers larger self-service spaces usually on one floor level. While supermarket design is largely functional, out-of-town stores provide more communal spaces where new kinds of consuming rituals can take place. These offer a very different experience from the restrictive, smaller urban locations, as the larger stores often involve family groups, and shopping can take place at all times of the day and night (Kirby 2009). On a larger scale still, shopping malls provide space for many retail stores and become increasingly concerned with the formal provision of leisure opportunities. The spaces of shopping malls became gradually more expansive and diverse, encouraging consumers to stay longer and to use more facilities. The Mall of America, one of the largest in the world, distinguished itself by strategically blended entertainment, food outlets and retail outlets, and it progressively updated by the addition of new attractions. Apart from shopping, it offers entertainment in nine nightclubs, a wide variety of restaurants, cinemas and virtual games.

Less extravagant, but rapidly gaining in popularity, shopping outlet centres were conceived as low-cost locations from which to sell end-of-line products at low prices. They were later re-defined as retail villages, an artificial, designed centre featuring an extensive range of outlet shops, usually outdoors, and differentiated by both low prices and an increased leisure element, with cafes and coffee shops. The opportunity to combine different activities has been further extended through 'micro villages', smaller-scale mergers of consumption and culture, incorporating hotels and restaurants alongside complementary retail stores and high-end services to offer a fully encompassed brand experience (Saunter 2015a). These village locations can be urban phenomena; the Ham Yard Hotel, in Soho London, opened in 2014 with the aim of creating such a hybrid shopping lifestyle destination, including boutiques and a hotel, spa, nail bar, florist, juice bar and bowling alley. Urban Outfitters is due to open the 'Devon Yard' in Philadelphia, USA, in 2016, a lifestyle experience incorporating Urban Outfitters and Anthropologie, together with a garden centre, cafe, restaurant, speciality food market, wellness centre and boutique hotel (Saunter 2015a). These villages are less driven by cost and more by their close focus on specific market segments and the creation of service propositions that showcase upmarket sociocultural and experiential consumption.

The range of retail formats provides contexts for design, and in different ways successful retail interiors should be memorable for the consumer. For Plunkett and Reid (2012), this points to the importance of detail in store design. Customers are necessarily in close proximity to the materials and the 'construction details that have redefined the walls, floor, ceiling and objects contained within them . . . the small-scale details of the building fabric are present in their peripheral vision to underpin, or undermine, their perception of a product's worth' (Plunkett and Reid 2012: 6). However, detail is evident both in the building and in display and Visual Merchandising plans and schemes that realize the presentation of products and their communication to customers. Until the 1980s display was limited to two largely uncoordinated activities: window dressing and the interior product presentation. Window displays had an important external perspective by linking shopfronts – including fascias, shop windows and upper floors and interiors – to the environment of the shopping street (Mitchell 1986). The display manager was required to be creative in much the same terms as today (even in the 1950s a sense of theatrical production was recommended), although this quality rarely extended to the shop interior.

However, the development of Visual Merchandising in the United States expanded the display function beyond the shop windows to include floor layouts, standardised merchandise presentation and signage. It became a more broadly based function contributing to the total impact of display, marketing advertising and publicity activities for retail businesses to succeed in a particular community (White and White 1996). As a consequence, it has come to integrate retail communications within the store, creating interest, encouraging comparisons as well as stimulating purchase decision-making, and reinforcing the market position of the company (Harris and Walters 1992). In addition, Visual Merchandising influences product selection processes as it provides a coordinating activity between effective merchandise selection and effective merchandise display.

The design of the store and its integration with product display and presentation attracted the attention of marketing researchers for its influence on consumer behaviour and its contribution to store 'atmospherics'. Kotler (1973) introduced the term, arguing that consumption spaces can be consciously designed to create certain emotional effects in buyers, thereby enhancing their likelihood to purchase. Since then retail environments and consumer behaviour have been widely explored, through Mehrabian and Russell's (1974) stimulus-organism-response model and later Donovan and Rossiter's (1982) work linking atmospheric cues with affective consumer responses. More detailed studies into isolated atmospheric cues – such as music, lighting, colour and crowding – demonstrate numerous outcomes in retail settings, such as affective response, shopping duration, merchandise evaluations, shopping satisfaction and purchase intention (Ballantine et al. 2015). These aspects of the store environment were summarized by Turley and Milliman (2000), who developed a systematic classification of atmospheric variables, identifying fifty-seven cues grouped into five categories (see Table 5.1). Each variable attempts to identify and tailor appropriate atmospheric elements that strongly impact consumer behaviour in store.

A recurrent theme across these studies is that store atmospherics encompasses a set of sensorial stimuli that range from tactile, sensory, gustatory, olfactory visual and social factors, capable of influencing internal states of shoppers (Kotler 1973; Bitner 1992; Skandrani et al. 2011). Moreover, the environmental cues should be considered as contributing to a holistic experience of the store (Ballantine et al. 2015). Thus, it can be reconceptualised as a multidimensional space comprising environmental stimuli capable of triggering emotional responses, which in turn necessitate consciously designed spaces that deliver excitement, entertainment and fun (Holbrook and Hirschman 1982; Baron et al. 2001; Kozinets et al. 2002). Indeed, Sachdeva and Goel (2015) argue that the innovative editing of atmospheric variables to create intriguing, ingenious, engaging retail environments has never been so significant. This evolution of retailing towards stores as multidimensional experience spaces continues to place new demands on retail design and the design process, to enable other stakeholders to co-create products, services and interactions that take place within the spatial configuration of the store and, in a wider context, mall and street. In other words, it moves the focus from a study of the objects of the creative process in the store – visual merchandising, branding and to a lesser extent its architecture – to their relationship with consumers.

Table 5.1 Store atmospheric variables

1. External variables	2. General interior variables	3. Layout and design variables	4. POP and decoration variables	5. Human variables
a. Exterior signage	a. Flooring & carpeting	a. Space design & allocation	a. Point of purchase displays	a. Employee characteristics
b. Entrances	b. Colour scheme	b. Placement of merchandise	b. Signs & cards	b. Employee uniforms
c. Exterior display windows	c. Lighting	c. Grouping of merchandise	c. Wall decorations	c. Crowding
d. Height of building	d. Music	d. Work station placement	d. Degrees & certificates	d. Customer characteristics
e. Size of building	e. P.A. usage	e. Placement of equipment	e. Pictures	e. Privacy
f. Colour of building	f. Scents	f. Placement of cash registers	f. Artwork	
g. Surrounding stores	g. Width of aisles	g. Waiting areas	g. Product displays	
h. Lawns & gardens	h. Wall composition	h. Waiting rooms	h. Usage instructions	
i. Address & location	i. Paint & wallpaper	i. Department locations	i. Price displays	
j. Architectural style	j. Ceiling composition	j. Traffic flow	j. Technology	
k. Surrounding area	k. Merchandise	k. Racks & cases		
l. Parking availability	l. Temperature	l. Waiting queues		
m. Congestion & traffic	m. Cleanliness	m. Furniture		
n. Exterior walls		n. Dead areas		

Source: Adapted by authors from Turley and Milliman (2000)

Beyond the retail store

The design opportunities arising from the diversity of store sizes, interiors and sensory environments have expanded through the merging of retail with other sectors of the economy, particularly the cultural and leisure sectors. As Andy Warhol observed, 'all department stores will become museums, and all museums will become department stores' (Harris 2006). Warhol's statement has been borne out by the changing purpose of museums since the 1980s, driven by a commercial imperative to increase the attractiveness and profitability of public space. Market-oriented ideology combined with an imperative for revenue generation and the introduction of new technologies gave rise to new and different expectations (McPherson 2006). Consequently, brand management and design of profitable retail operations came to be a function of museum management, and the museum shop was elevated to become an important element of the museum brand.

As the boundaries between commercial, educational and recreational orientations have become increasingly blurred (Rentschler and Potter 1996), so the purpose of many cultural institutions has turned to visitor experience. These perspectives imply that the shop environment, its products and its services have the possibility of extending the visitor experience to a wider range of people. However, the influence of the museum on retailing as 'curation' has also been felt, particularly for luxury retailing in its designed spaces and visual merchandising. This approach is evident in the design concept for the Lotte department store in Seoul, which aimed at creating 'a space that was much more about curation', and which involved the placement of potentially diverse objects together to create a unique, layered environment (Watson 2007: 119).

These uncertainties about the use of space draw on Bauman's (2007) 'liquid modernity' characterised by a lack of fixity and permanence, in which mobility and transience generate a preoccupation with novelty, and the possibilities for temporary spaces and stores (Surchi 2011; Pomodoro 2013). Consumers move from one experience to the next, seeking brief, pleasurable sensations, or what Maslow (1964) refers to as 'peak experiences': short, sudden, unique, immersive occurrences capable of generating ecstasy. They underlie Lipovetsky's 'carpe diem' within postmodern consumption, emphasising the urge to live in the moment in pursuit of immediate gratification (2004, cited in Pomodoro 2013). The culture of transience merged with immediacy is assimilated in flagships, temporary (pop-up) stores, and showrooms that collectively embody the shift from static, one-dimensional transactional spaces to multi-functional hybrid retail spaces.

Flexible store concepts offering creative opportunities for reinvention are becoming a priority for retailers, as they seek out ways to differentiate and motivate consumers to visit the physical store (Saunter 2015b). With the demand for experience, immersion and innovation from customers, stores have to work harder at providing space fluidity to flex and change with the trends and spatial demands; they become part shop, part cafe, part gallery, part event space and so on. This is manifest in versatile fixtures, modular and movable displays, adaptable hanging systems and playful temporary installations to create impact at minimal cost. New York retailer Story is a significant example of a retail concept that 'takes the point of view of a magazine, changes like a gallery and sells things like a store' (Story 2015). The result is that every four to eight weeks, the store reinvents itself, from the store design to the stock, to enable the creation of a new theme or story to be told. It embodies ephemeral retail and, for at least some commentators, has become a revolutionary model.

Increasing consumer demand for contextually relevant retail is evident in new forms of 'on-the-go' retail, expressed in transit hubs becoming retail destinations – for example, the personal shopping lounge at Heathrow airport terminal 2; London's Kings Cross and London Bridge train station retail regeneration; vending retail within airports, malls and transit hubs; and situationally relevant pop-ups, evident in Starbucks 'on wheels' commuter train carriages in Switzerland (Anon 2014). Thus, retail as a fixed, rigid entity, developed on the notion of the consumer journeying to it is being displaced, driven by consumer demand for flexibility, immediacy and experience, where retail goes to the consumer.

Experiential spaces

The hybridity of retailing has enhanced shopping experiences, and consumer expectations of experiences has led to more generalised insights into experiential design. Retailers create value not only through utilitarian and functional benefits of a purchase but also in the hedonic and experiential elements surrounding the product and service, and in the consumption experience itself, regardless of whether it leads to purchase or not (Kotler 1973; Holbrook and Hirschman 1982; Bitner 1992; Arnould and Price 2002; Carù and Cova

2003; Schmitt 2003; Carbone 2004; Gentile et al. 2007; Verhoef et al. 2009). Further, in an increasingly consumer-centric, globally competitive and digitally driven fashion retail landscape, the necessity to emotionally connect with consumers has never been greater (Brakus et al. 2009). Value is created through experiential consumer dimensions, in which the consumer is emotionally involved in the consumption process and where imagination, sensory perceptions, immersion and emotions are prevalent (Pine and Gilmore 1999; Schmitt 1999). From the retailer's perspective, entertainment is central to the experience in order to achieve pleasurable and stimulated consumer responses to the environment (Mehrabian and Russell 1974). Pine and Gilmore's authoritative text conceptualizes a 'Realms of Experience Model', in which experience is based on the level of customer involvement, with 'entertainment' and 'aesthetic' experiences requiring passive reception and 'educational' and 'escapist' experiences requiring active participation.

This focus on entertainment, which received criticism for its focus on the consumer as spectator, has led to the argument that experiences are not provided but rather co-created between retailers and customers (Gentile et al. 2007; Spena et al. 2012) – thus enshrining a collaborative rather than a producer-driven approach to experience. This supports empirical research, which suggests that Generation Z (post-millennial) consumers seek individualism in retail experiences. Therefore, retailers need to find ways to empower consumers, whether through product personalisation as in the Converse creative lab or the brand personalisation seen in Burberry's collaboration with Google for customers to personalise the 2015 Christmas campaign at its flagship Regent Street, London, store (Anon 2015b). This shift to an elevated customised experience is also evident in department stores and the concept of members clubs. Canadian Holt Renfew's new dedicated menswear space in Toronto is designed as a one-stop shop for the millennial male. Alongside the collections, they offer bespoke tailoring, suit alteration, valet service, shoe shining, cobbler for shoe repairs, on-site monogramming and a doorman. Selfridges London also recently launched a bespoke men's personal shopping space comprising three shopping sites, a reception area and a library-cum-gallery with work by Damien Hirst (Saunter 2015a).

The third place

The restless consumer, the emergence of new spaces for retailing in the public sector, and experiential spaces converge as an extension of the 'third place' concept. Oldenburg (1999) explained the third place as somewhere that is not home (the first place) or work (the second place) but a comfortable space to browse, relax and meet people. Defined as a 'public place that hosts the regular, voluntary, informal, and happily anticipated gatherings of individuals beyond the realm of home and work' (Oldenburg 1999: 16), it can include outdoor markets, bookstores, garden stores, gyms and pubs.

The character of third places is underpinned by their distinctiveness from other settings of daily life. They provide a neutral ground, acting as a leveller, an inclusive place for sociability rather than defined by roles found at work. The third place enables generations to still enjoy each other's company, and it is where conversation is the main activity. As Crick (2015) suggests, Oldenburg's third place becomes a third place because of the action of those who inhabit the location; they choose it, imbue it with meaning and decide what takes place there. Third places are accessible, keep long hours and serve people's need for sociability and relaxation, so proximate locations are important. Moreover, these places have a low profile, defined by plainness and homeliness, which has the additional effect of discouraging pretention.

The commercial third place is designed to proactively attract customers, understand their behaviour and increase their time, 'dwell-time', spent in store. Starbucks is often cited as exemplifying this typology, serving as a place for casual social interaction (Crick 2015). No longer relegated to the back of the stores with minimal space, the serving counter was prominently placed in all stores. The new format had the feel both of an espresso bar and a fine coffee purveyor, thereby serving customers seeking either or both product types (Seaford et al. 2012). More importantly, further studies highlighted the experience offered by Starbucks and what Skenasy (2007, cited in Crick 2015) refers to as an extension of the living room. Similarly, mainstream bookstores came to exemplify commercial third places. Barnes and Noble used this notion of community as a key brand differentiator, pioneering the concept of the store as 'community centre' in the 1990s. More broadly, Laing and Royle (2006) summarise bookstores' success in creating a 'lifestyle environment' with sofas and coffee shops, generating a more comfortable and less intimidating space to dwell, and in doing so promoting a sense of community.

The third place as a homely environment can be contrasted with more experiential, 'spectacular' spaces, temporary in nature, that stimulate customer emotions and trigger memories or 'brand scripts' (Mikunda 2007). Mikunda conceived four functions for this type of third place: landmarks, designed for malling, concept specific, or magnetic places that have the ability to attract and draw in consumers. He cites museums, concept stores and fairs as serving the new third place because they are places where people feel momentarily at home and where they can reconnect emotionally. More dramatic manifestations have been found in the Rainforest Cafe and Hard Rock Cafe.

Manifestations of Mikunda's (2007) spectacular and experiential hybrid retail spaces have had a global significance. Within a fashion context, retailers have experimented with new retail spaces that fuse art, culture and consumption collectively as a way of setting apart the physical from the online space and, in so doing, enriching the shopping experience. Artistic collaborations, immersive installations and gallery inspired curation have been some of the devices used to tap into this growing cultural economy (Saunter 2014). Diesel used an interactive Twitter-powered living art installation to celebrate the opening of its Rome flagship; Brazilian footwear brand Melissa's newly opened London flagship is designed like a gallery, with shoes displayed within perspex cubes and on pedestals, alongside modern sculptures and digital art installations. Following this gallery-infused design theme, French brand Sandro, in creating its New York menswear store called the 'Workshop', features monthly artist collaborations, whereby emerging artists are invited to craft installations using the 'Workshop' as their studio for a week with the remaining three weeks serving as a gallery to showcase the artworks (Saunter 2014). To promote the launch of its six-floor New York Fifth Avenue store, H&M collaborated with artist Jeff Koons, with the design of the store resembling an art museum. Within the luxury sphere, the long-standing connection between art and fashion is strengthened with brands acting as cultural facilitators by creating art foundations, funding new galleries and sponsoring cultural events. Fondazione Prada was one of the first, more recently followed by Louis Vuitton's Foundation gallery in Paris (Saunter 2014).

In a further classification of third places, Crick (2015) claimed that definitions of home and work have changed through the adoption of information technologies that facilitate working at any time and place, and Crick proposed commercial, spectacular, virtual and hybrid third places as new forms of space. Digital disruption gave rise to the virtual third place (Klang and Olsson 1999), where a network of like-minded individuals converge in a virtual environment to converse. Consequently, place shifts from being conceived through its physical dimensions to a virtual one. Social media – including Facebook, Twitter, blogs and virtual chat rooms – permit continuous interactions online, and the online gaming community is a virtual meeting place to play and be relational (Wellman and Haythornthwaite 2002). Used synergistically with other third places, Crick (2015) infers that virtual places could contribute additional dimension of perceptive value.

These trends have led to the convergence of third-place typologies and, as a result, conflicting functions. For example, coffee shops increasingly offer free Wi-Fi, allowing the customer to be with others without actively participating in community and social interaction, which would appear to conflict with Oldenburg's (1999) traditional perspective of the phenomenon. However, implicit within the evolving definition is a space with a social function to persuade consumers to linger for longer in the store, and in which it assumes an experiential hedonic role where selling is often relegated or even non-existent.

The fashion sector in particular reflects these developments. Fashion consumers have been shown to demand immersive, connected experiences that engage them on an emotional, physical, intellectual or even spiritual level (Pine and Gilmore 1999). In this context, Niketown, New York is a seminal example of this more complex third place, fusing commerce, culture and experience, and establishing itself as a landmark, museum and homage to the brand. The provision for consumption, culture and leisure within one retail environment, manifested as a third place, is therefore both desirable and practical for consumers (Nobbs 2014). Consequently, third places in fashion stores take the form of cafes, restaurants, galleries, cinemas and educational and grooming spaces, which are categorized in Table 5.2 according to Crick's (2015) third place and Pine and Gilmore's (1999) experience typologies.

Table 5.2 Fashion third places

Retailer	Third places manifested in-store	Third-place typology (Crick 2015)	Experience typology (Pine and Gilmore 1999)
Patagonia, NY	Cafe, yoga sessions, community work space, mending lessons	Traditional, commercial, spectacular	Educational, aesthetic, escapist
Nike Town, NY, London	Sports club/s, personal run analysis, museum (town square)	Commercial, spectacular	Entertainment, escapist, educational, aesthetic
Aubin & Wills, London	Cinema	Traditional, commercial	Entertainment
Alfred Dunhill, London	Screening room, barbers/male grooming, cafe	Traditional, commercial, spectacular	Entertainment, escapist, aesthetic
Rapha Cycle Club	Cafe, community hub	Traditional, commercial	Aesthetic, escapist
Thomas's (Burberry), London	Restaurant/cafe	Traditional, commercial	Aesthetic
Ralph's (Ralph Lauren) & Polo Bar, NY	Café and restaurant	Traditional, commercial	Aesthetic
Armani café, Milan	Cafe	Traditional, commercial	Aesthetic

(Continued)

Table 5.2 (Continued)

Retailer	Third places manifested in-store	Third-place typology (Crick 2015)	Experience typology (Pine and Gilmore 1999)
Sweaty Betty, London	Yoga/sports club	Traditional, commercial	Escapist, entertainment
Space Ninety 8 (Urban Outfitters), Brooklyn NY	Restaurant, two bars, gallery	Traditional, commercial	Aesthetic, escapist, entertainment
Colette, Paris	Restaurant, gallery	Traditional, commercial, spectacular	Aesthetic, escapist
Merci, Paris	Cafe, restaurant, bookstore	Traditional, commercial, spectacular	Aesthetic, escapist
10 Corso Como, Milan	Restaurant, gallery, bookstore	Traditional, commercial, spectacular	Aesthetic, escapist

Source: Developed by Alexander

However, while Crick's commercial and spectacular forms of place align with Pine and Gilmore's concept of retail theatre and staging in the experience economy, the latter's typology points to alternative characteristics of the fashion third place, suggesting that the most prevalent realm of experience utilised by retailers is aesthetic and escapist. In these environments, people can recharge their emotions, interact and socialise as well as spectate. They may reflect an increasing desire to disconnect from the permanence of being 'always on' and engage in analogue brand expressions, echoing Rosenbaum's (2009) and Laing and Royle's (2013) notion of restorative servicescapes. This aligns with the concept of 'stuffo-cation', the stifling of millennial consumers by excessive materiality, and their search for more authentic ways to (re)connect offline with their community. As a result, new hybrid retail environments have emerged to host supper clubs, community cafes (such as Good-Hood London's Commune café), repair stations, mending lessons, community workspaces and swapshops for garment exchanges – all housed in retail spaces and exemplified in the opening of Patagonia's New York store in 2015.

Store space and the senses

The discussion of consumption experience and store design has tended to focus on the visual sense, and, while touch is also an important element of apparel shopping, the remaining three senses have tended to be neglected (Lindstrom 2005; Elliott and Percy 2007). However, with the development of online shopping and virtual experiences, consumers need further motivation to visit brick-and-mortar stores. Experiential multi-sensory retailing is less easily replicable online and provides an opportunity to holistically engage with consumers using many or all the senses in the physical store. The strategy, reflected in the design, is to drive differentiation and create distinctive environments (Lindstrom 2005; Hultén 2011; Alexander and Nobbs 2016). Thus, research in the experiential field has extended spatial design with specific studies on the impact of sensory cues on consumer preferences, memories and choices (Krishna 2010); on their role in emotionally connecting customers with retail brands; and on consumers' affective response and holistic experience (Schmitt 2003; Hultén 2011).

London luxury department stores Harrods and Selfridges have both experimented with multi-sensory experiences. Harrods 'Senses' event saw each lift reimagined as one of the senses by a collaborating artist, with the final lift interpreting the sixth sense through 'cosmic ordering'. In 2014, Selfridges conceived its 'Fragrance Lab', where consumers, after providing personal information on an iPad, were taken on 'a voyage of personal discovery' through a series of sensory rooms until they popped out in Selfridges windows and were greeted by a lab technician who then escorted them to select a customised perfume attuned to their personal preferences. 'It's not about selling fragrance, it's about creating an experience and testing the boundaries' (Sanderson, CEO Future Laboratory, cited by Thomson 2014). The possibilities of sensory environments are summarised by Australian beauty business Aesop, who

> utilise all the senses to evoke memory . . . so that customers leave our space with a memory beyond the architecture and they talk about light, the way it evolves, smell, taste the tea, touch, feel and tactility, when touching the tap or the fabric of the store or the product itself.
>
> (Alexander and Nobbs 2016)

These sensory environments demonstrate ways in which the internal spaces of department stores and more generally luxury flagship stores can offer sensory experiences to differentiate themselves. The embodied extraordinary experience offered in a flagship is explained by it being a "larger than average speciality retail format in a prominent geographical location, offering the widest and deepest product range within the highest level of store environment and serving to showcase the brand's position, image and values" (Nobbs et al. 2012: 922). The foci on brand personification through the flagship store is incorporated in the form and function schema, depicted in Figure 5.1. From an experiential perspective, it is significant that emphasis is placed on the highest-quality store environment, where the language of the store is transparently communicated and

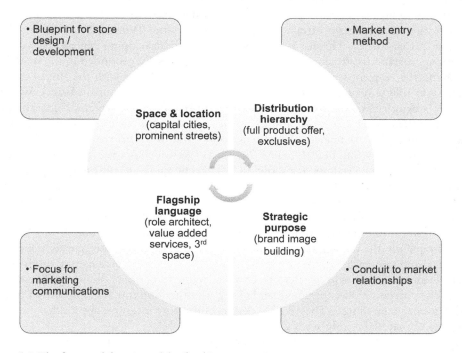

Figure 5.1 The form and function of the flagship store

Source: Alexander, adapted from Moore and Doherty (2007) and Nobbs et al. (2012)

serving to communicate the brand strategy. Functionally, it is important that a flagship serves as a prototype for store design and development, a place to experiment with new products, new services and new concepts of visual design (Moore et al. 2000). As a three-dimensional model, it becomes a place to realise innovation in store design and reiterate its central role in brand communication and design.

Within the last decade, collaborations between fashion brands, architects, set designers and artists have intensified the drive towards aesthetic differentiation of the flagship store (Manlow and Nobbs 2013). The elements of this brandscape, from architecture to merchandise, are utilised to create a multi-sensory consumer experience. Whilst collaborations are not new, Barreneche (2008) suggests architect John Pawson's collaboration with Calvin Klein in 1996 gave new momentum to the phenomenon by elevating the expression of the brand and its positioning, image and message. Second, flagship stores have advanced sensory experiences through added-value services and initiatives that are evident in a variety of formats, and which provide opportunities for the senses to be engaged in members clubs, cafes, bars, spas and barbers amongst others (Nobbs et al. 2012; Rumsey 2015; Saunter 2015a). Their role is partly transactional, as longer dwell times in store result in higher expenditures, but importantly these places within the store create an immersive emotional connection between the retail brand and consumer. Thus, flagships represent the melding together of consumption and social and cultural currency with experimentation and innovation to provide more complex experiences within one physical location.

The mix of brand and store environment in a prestigious location assumes a high level of investment and consequently implies a degree of permanence for a flagship store. The possibilities for sensory design can also be realized at the other extreme of retailer permanence, in the temporary locations and the uncertain environments of the pop-up store. Turning – again – to the fashion industry's dynamism, and the growth of digital and consumers' desire for novel experiences, retailers demonstrate the need to continuously rethink their retail spaces to attract consumers into the store (Pedroni 2011; Rumsey 2015; Saunter 2015a, 2015b). This has resulted in new ways of developing experiential yet temporary approaches to attract and retain customers. Originally, grounded in the marketing discipline, the concept was applied to the physical environment with the aim of creating spaces that fully engage customers (Carù and Cova 2003). A focus on brand awareness is often a priority, with sales performance a secondary function (Surchi 2011): the pop-up store offers novelty, surprise and excitement within and around a temporary space achieved through a spontaneous experience and sense of exclusivity (Pine and Gilmore 1999; Pedroni 2011; Surchi 2011; Spire 2013). As the store has a fleeting existence, it can alternatively be conceived not as a shop but as an event, rooted in the present, to engage all of the customers' senses (Pomodoro 2013). Moreover, it can be a manifestation of various forms of guerrilla marketing or unconventional promotions to generate 'buzz' around the retailer. With their ability to generate an exciting and immediate form of communication, retailers can capture the attention of a global audience (Forney et al. 2007).

Consequently, the pop-up store can be designed to engage the customer in memorable, theatrical and sensorial experiences. It can utilise a social fear of 'missing out' on the unrepeatable and, for those who participate, create a feeling of personal discovery. These stores present opportunities to experiment and play by another, and much smaller, set of rules to conventional store design. They enable designers to grow inventive approaches, concepts and uses of materiality (Holwich 2015).

The key forms, function and features of the pop-up store can be derived from extant literature to model its dimensions (Figure 5.2). It is clear that the pop-up provides the opportunity

Table 5.3 Fashion pop-up formats

Pop-up form	Pop-up function/feature	Example
Guerrilla store	Raise brand awareness, novelty, surprise, promote, exclusivity	Comme Des Garcon 'guerrilla stores', globally
Nomad store	Mobile store – van, truck, test market, go to market	Uniqlo 'truck shop', NYC
Temporary online store	Pop-out online, limited time, collaborate	Chanel fine jewelry popped out on Net-A-Porter
Temporary outdoor site	Reach target market, stationary location, exclusivity	Target outdoor pop up, Bryant Park, NY; Puma's twenty-four shipping containers, world tour
Concept brand store	Raise brand awareness / image, experiential	Louis Vuitton & Yayoi Kusama collaboration, popped out at Selfridges, London
Community store	Reinforce customer relationships, community building, hosts social events	Paul Frank, NYC, Oakley 'bike' community store, London
Test store	Test new market, test brand concept	Zalando popped out in Italy
Sustainable temporary store	Promote eco-friendly/sustainability, well-being	Monocle popped out, Siam Centre, Thailand

Source: Developed by Alexander

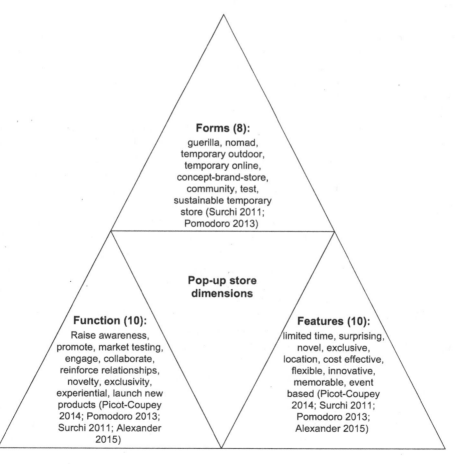

Figure 5.2 Pop-up store dimensions model

Source: Developed by Alexander

to engage, experience, interact and co-create with the brand, regardless of form (Spena et al. 2012). Whilst it has received criticism for its ubiquity, raising questions over its effectiveness as a provider of novelty, pop-ups present a viable approach not only to individual brands but also to the more complex retail environmental problems found in the regeneration of urban centres (Gallagher 2013; Townsend 2014). In a challenging economic climate, with unpredictable and often low store occupancy rates, the concept provides a commercial solution for both landlords and retailers. In particular, these spaces offer opportunities to small businesses that may have been previously limited due to financial and legal restrictions.

Digital expansion and new retail spaces

Digital disruption has created empowered consumers whose demands for convenience, speed, efficiency, flexibility and consistency across channels has created fundamental challenges for retailers (Blazquez 2014). Adoption of new technologies has changed shoppers' behaviour with the growth of smartphone ownership and mobile Internet use. This has contributed to the distinction between offline and online retailing becoming increasingly blurred due to the proliferation in enabling technologies, such as smart mobile devices, smartphones and tablets; software, including apps, mobile payments and location-based services; accessibility through big data and cloud based services; and increased availability of in-store technologies. These encompass both passive and interactive screens and devices from augmented reality, virtual mirrors and digital signage, to self-service kiosks and vending machines (Piotrowicz and Cuthbertson 2013). Consequently many retailers are utilising technology as the medium to deliver a convergent customer experience (Piotrowicz and Cuthbertson 2013; Alexander et al. 2014; Kent et al. 2014). The role of the physical store has thus been reconceptualised as the place to harness the best of both physical and digital worlds – that is, the multi-sensorial experience of the offline with the access, interactivity and convenience of the online (Alexander et al. 2014).

There is a growing body of research on the role and impact of technologies utilised in the physical store. Pantano and Naccarato (2010) assert how technology innovations can modify store appearance and directly impact consumer shopping behaviour. Blazquez (2014) links technology within the ambient cues of store atmospherics. They contribute to the servicescape, through the impact of technology on the retailer-customer relationship, enabling retailers to create more customised services, optimise logistics and better understand consumer preferences (Pantano 2010; Pantano and Naccarato 2010; Renko and Ficko 2010).

The role and impact of technology in fashion stores on the shopping experience demonstrates wide variations in the adoption of technology forms and their utilisation across retailers and inconsistencies in combining the physical, online and mobile stores into one seamless experience. Online access contributes to the prevalence of webrooming behaviours including search online and buy in-store and exposed many opportunities to enable integration at each stage of the buying process (Alexander et al. 2014). Kent et al. (2014) progresses this further by focusing on the role of mobile specifically in channel convergence with findings inferring that consumers engage with technology and mobile apps more on a utilitarian level than hedonic.

These developments raise questions regarding the usefulness of technology within physical stores and challenges retailers to think beyond, what has often been criticised as utilising 'gimmicky tech' to technology that interacts fully and synergises with the customer experience. Piotrowicz and Cuthbertson (2013) suggest the physical store could change its role to a 'hub', as the focal point which would integrate all sales channels – an opportunity to use the place to provide enhanced personal service, regardless of channel used. The role of the store in attracting customers depends, however, on the product characteristics and the level of customer experience provided or demanded. This re-imagining of the connected physical store, however, comes at a price, often requiring store re-design to fully embed technology within the store fabric rather than simply bolted on (ibid.).

Traditionally, brick-and-mortar retail stores uniquely allowed customers to touch, feel and try on product and provided instant gratification. Online retailers tried to attract consumers with wide product assortments, low prices and content such as reviews and ratings. As retailing evolves towards realising this seamless omnichannel experience – turning into, what Brynjolfsson et al. (2013) refer to as, 'a showroom without walls' – the physical store is being transformed. This shift from a transactional to a concierge model, focused on helping customers, is evident in the development of a suite of tailored service options available, including 'click and collect', 'buy in store, deliver to your door', 'order online, return to store', payment booths, web return centres, drive through collection services and 'showrooms' (Anon 2012; Brynjolfsson et al. 2013). This, in turn, has profoundly challenged the traditional notions of retail format, retail place and retail design.

Retail showrooms and showcases

The convergence of online and offline retail environments presents challenges and opportunities for retail designers, and one particular challenge is the practice of 'showrooming', viewing a product in store but buying it online. For some, the traditional physical store has been reduced to a showroom as more shoppers buy online. Early reports demonstrated that customer showrooming behaviours reduced the profitability of traditional retailers whilst benefiting online-only retailers. Possible responses are demonstrated by Target Corporation with demands to suppliers for exclusive products unavailable elsewhere, significant increases to its online product offer and initiation of many new cross-channel services, such as the 'endless aisle' to prevent customers from switching (Zimmerman 2012). Others, especially online pureplayers, have seized the opportunity to open physical showroom stores, designed as retail laboratories, where consumers can browse, try on and then buy online. Whilst they do not instantly gratify purchasers, the stores reduce the barriers to purchase associated with the communication of non-digital product attributes to customers (Bell et al. 2013). They enable online retailers to test physical store identities before committing to more formal formats whilst creating a valuable offline touch-point for consumers to engage with, build awareness and drive credibility (Anon 2015a; Bell et al. 2013).

A growing number of online-only retailers have recognised that uncertainty about offline product attributes is a barrier to purchase and therefore have experimented with free two-way shipping, pop-ups or showrooms to combat it. 'Guide shops' were opened by US retailer Bonobos in 2012 to enable its customers to try on clothing before buying, as they recognised fit was a significant purchase barrier. Bonobos's CEO referred to them as 'small, service-driven experiential stores where you have one-to-one service and where we keep out the complexity of a lot of inventory, but you can access this incredibly wide assortment' (Kansara 2013). A second approach extends the conception of retail showroom, by renting space from existing third-party independent retailers. US eyewear retailer Warby Parker practiced collaborative retailing by renting showroom spaces across the US before opening their own dedicated retail showrooms, consequently running their business from rented and owned space (Bell et al. 2013; Warby Parker 2015). The diversity of practices of display showrooms are demonstrated in Table 5.4. The offers, showrooms

Table 5.4 Showroom practices in fashion retail

Retailer	Product offer	Traditional channel	Display showroom	Function
Warby Parker (established 2010, USA)	Eyewear	Online	Four rented spaces in host independent stores; fifteen own stores; all showrooms (2015)	Try before buy online, product fit, brand awareness, credibility, enhance brand experience across channels
Bonobos (established 2007, USA)	Menswear	Online	Twenty guide shops (2015)	As above
Zappos (established 1999, USA)	Shoes and clothing	Online	One pop-up showroom shop in collaboration with Shopwithme (2014)	Integrate online and offline using Shopwithme technology solutions
Frank & Oak (established 2012, Canada)	Menswear	Online	Six showrooms in Canada; six pop-up showrooms in the US (2015)	Elevated brand experience, integrate online/offline
Finery, London (established 2014, UK)	Womenswear	Online	Pop-up showroom, London (2015)	View collection, try on, touch, feel
Sneakerboy (established 2013, Australia)	Footwear	Online	Three showrooms, Melbourne, Sydney, Victoria (2015)	Blend tactility of a physical store with the efficiencies of online
Everlane (established 2010, USA)	Womenswear and menswear	Online	NY pop up showroom (2014)	Try before buy online, integrate tech with tactility, called 'the non-store'
The Arrivals (established 2014, USA)	Womenswear and menswear	Online	Showroom within the NY studio, by appointment	Provide more tactile, personalised experience
Outdoor Voices (established 2012, USA)	Sportswear/ recreation wear	Online	Two showrooms (designed as third space)	Promote community, neighbourhood feel, provide home from home
Combatant Gentleman (established 2012, USA)	Men's suiting	Online	The Haberdashery showroom, within HQ	Educate consumers about its craftsmanship, quality, production
David Kind (established, USA)	Eyewear	Online	One showroom (April 2015)	By appointment only, personalised service, elevated customer service, destination for international customers
Desigual (established 1984, Spain)	Womenswear, menswear, children's	Multichannel (bricks and mortar first)	Shop-showroom (Barcelona, 2012)	No stock, just samples, full collection available, elevated brand experience, personal shoppers elevate customer service, space used for art exhibitions, catwalks, events

Source: Developed by Alexander

and functions highlight how they are operated by mainly pureplay fashion retailers, their role within channel strategy, and their ability to deliver an elevated, personalised customer experience a critical functional benefit for utilisation.

Conclusion

The places and spaces of the store environment are essential to retail design; they determine the possibilities for distinctive identities and balance commercial functions with leisure, recreation and learning. Their definitions alone provide insights into the complexity of retailing, with its diversity of sites, formats and sizes from urban centres to edge-of-town and sub-urban locations, from hypermarkets to temporary pop-up stores. Underlying this complexity is the recognition of stores as social and experiential places, sometimes clearly owned or directed by the retailer, but increasingly co-created with the consumer. These are further compounded as the physical store's boundaries are permeated by online world: interactive information screens and a merchandise collection area for online purchases are just two access points that may have to be designed into the store.

From a marketing perspective, retailers use store environments to bring together elements of the marketing mix, to have direct contact with the consumer through product, price and promotion in a place or, for multiple retailers, places. Traditionally, the store has had a well-defined commercial function, and its spaces contribute to precise measures of business success. These have been determined by merchandise and brands, concessions and services, front and back office functions and the efficient use of floor space for stock holding and display. Such formalized concepts and allocations of space exist alongside less defined commercial and leisure space: for circulation, for looking and sensing, socialising and entertainment. As commercial transactions have been supplemented by the provision of services and experiences, the retail environment has to facilitate the development of customer relationships, and the extension of engagement and interactivity between the retailer and the customer, and between customers. Social spaces, experiential spaces and temporary spaces are essential to defining but also re-defining the purpose and conceptualization of the store and its design.

The concept of the third place has been particularly influential in this respect as somewhere between work and home that specifically addresses these possibilities for social interaction. As consumers seek experiences from the retail store, so the demands on its designed environment require more responsiveness and openness to change, where interaction and engagement with consumers increases the scope for a multiplicity of meanings. The unifying themes of hybrid retail formats are the critical elements of transience, ephemerality, immediacy and multi-functionality. The retail store has the capacity to be more than a place for commercial transactions, by accommodating social, cultural and experiential consumption, which evolves with changing consumer and retailer demands.

The store but also retailing itself can be reinterpreted as facilitating multiple moments of interaction, which lead to impactful consumer memories. Transitory yet lasting impressions are constructed, which contribute to the retail brand and its associations. Thus retail design will include an eclectic mix of touchpoints that are evident in pop-ups, third places, flagships and showrooms. Here, elements of place, context, timing, services, staff, store design, atmospherics and bespoke (often co-created) experiences create distinctive environments. Developments in the digital, online environment are modifying consumers' expectations of how to use store space and to engage with the retailer. The implications for design are to adjust to, and create, new formats and concepts to showcase and curate merchandise, to create appropriate in-store atmosphere and experience, and to allow for social exchange. The acceptance of the 'Internet of things' will continue to define store design, and connecting with consumers through personal information and communication devices will continue to extend notions of retail space, place and the designed environment.

References

Alexander, B. and Nobbs, K. (2016) Multi-sensory fashion retail experiences: The impact of sound, smell, sight and touch on consumer based brand equity. In *Handbook of Research on Global Fashion Management and Merchandising*, pending publication Spring, 2016.

Alexander, B., Alvarado, D.O. and Nobbs, K. (2014) Online-offline integrated shopping experience: An exploration of effective implementations of advanced technologies in the physical store. In the proceedings of the *Oxford Retail Futures Conference: Innovation in Retail and Distribution, 8–9th Dec, 2014*.

Anon. (20 Dec, 2012) *Combatting showrooming*, WGSN.

Anon. (6 Jun, 2014) *Relocating retail: On-the-go selling and service*, WGSN.

Anon. (18 Jun, 2015a) *Top 5 – US showroom stores*, WGSN.

Anon. (12 Sep, 2015b) *10 ways retailers can service the Gen Z consumer*, WGSN.

Arnould, E.J. and Price, L.L. (2002) River magic: Extraordinary experiences and the extended service encounter. *Journal of Consumer Research*, Vol. 20, pp. 24–45.

Augé, M. (1995) *Non-Places, Introduction to an Anthropology of Supermodernity*. London: Verso.

Ballantine, P.W., Parsons, A. and Comeskey, K. (2015) A conceptual model of the holistic effects of atmospheric cues in fashion retailing. *International Journal of Retail & Distribution Management*, Vol. 43(6), pp. 503–517.

Baron, S., Harris, K. and Harris, R. (2001) Retail theater: The intended effect of the performance. *Journal of Service Research*, Vol. 4(2), pp. 102–117.

Barreneche, R.A. (2008) *New Retail*. London: Phaidon Press Inc.

Bauman, Z. (2007) *Liquid Times: Living in an Age of Uncertainty*. Cambridge: Polity Press.

Bell, D., Gallino, S. and Moreno, A. (2013) Inventory showrooms and customer migration in omnichannel retail: The effect of product information. Available at SSRN 2370535.

Berens, G. and Van Riel, C.B. (2004) Corporate associations in the academic literature: Three main streams of thought in the reputation measurement literature. *Corporate Reputation Review*, Vol. 7(2), pp. 161–178.

Bitner, M.J. (1992) The impact of physical surroundings on customers and employees. *Journal of Marketing*, Vol. 56, pp. 57–71.

Blazquez, M. (2014) Fashion shopping in multichannel retail: The role of technology in enhancing the customer experience. *International Journal of Electronic Commerce*, Vol. 18(4), pp. 97–116.

Brakus, J., Schmitt, B. and Zarantonello, L. (2009) Brand experience: What is it? How is it measured? Does it affect loyalty? *Journal of Marketing*, Vol. 73(3), pp. 52–68.

Brynjolfsson, E., Hu, Y.J. and Rahman, M.S. (2013) Competing in the age of omnichannel retailing. *MIT Sloan Review*, Vol. 54(4), pp. 23–29.

Carbone, L.P. (2004) *Clued in: How to Keep Customers Coming Back Again and Again*. New York, NY: Prentice Hall.

Carù, A. and Cova, B. (2003) Revisiting consumption experience: A more humble but complete view of the concept. *Marketing Theory*, Vol. 3(2), pp. 267–286.

Crick, A. (2015) New third places: Opportunities and challenges. In Woodside, A.G. (ed.) *Tourism Sensemaking: Strategies to Give Meaning to Experience (Advances in Culture, Tourism and Hospitality Research*, Vol. 5). Bradford: Emerald Group Publishing Limited, pp. 63–77.

Donovan, R.J. and Rossiter, J.R. (1982) Store atmosphere: An environmental psychology approach. *Journal of Retailing*, Vol. 58(1), pp. 34–57.

Elden, S. (2004) *Understanding Henri Lefebvre: Theory and the Possible*. London: Continuum.

Elliott, R. and Percy, L. (2007) *Strategic Brand Management*. Oxford: Oxford University Press.

Forney, J., Kim, Y.K. and Sullivan, P. (2007) *Experiential Retailing: Concepts and Strategies That Sell*. New York: Fairchild Publications.

Frisby, D. and Featherstone, M. (1997) *Simmel on Culture*. London: Sage.

Gallagher, V. (7 Sept, 2013) Property: Mapping out the retail horizon. *Drapers*.

Gammon, S. and Elkington, S. (2015) *Landscapes of Leisure: Space, Place and Identities*. Basingstoke: Palgrave Macmillan.

Gentile, C., Spiller, N. and Noci, G. (2007) How to sustain the customer experience: An overview of the experience components that co-create value with the consumer. *European Management Journal*, Vol. 25(5), pp. 395–410.

Harkin, F. (2004) Stores that trade on club style. *Financial Times, FT Weekend – Shopping*, Sept 18, p. 9.

Harris, J. (2006) Modernism in store, art monthly. Available from http://www.artmonthly.co.uk/magazine/site/article/modernisms-in-store-by-jonathan-harris-june-2006. Accessed 17 December 2015.

Harris, D. and Walters, D.W. (1992). *Retail Operations Management*. London: Prentice Hall.

Harvey, D., Low, S.M. and Smith, N. (2005) *The Political Economy of Public Space*. London: Routledge.

Hightower, R., Brady, M.K. and Baker, T.L. (2002) Investigating the role of the physical environment in hedonic service consumption: An exploratory study of sporting events. *Journal of Business Research*, Vol. 55(9), pp. 697–707.

Holbrook, M. and Hirschman, E.C. (1982) The experiential aspects of consumption: Consumer fantasies, feelings and fun. *Journal of Consumer Research*, Vol. 9, pp. 132–140.

Holwich, M. (2015) Lasting impressions: Pop-up culture by HWKN. *Architectural Design*, Vol. 85(3), pp. 124–129.

Hultén, B. (2011) Sensory marketing: The multi-sensory brand experience concept. *European Business Review*, Vol. 23(3), pp. 256–273.

Jansen-Verbeke, M. (1990) Leisure and shopping = tourism mix. In Ashworth, G. and Goodall, B. (eds.) *Marketing Tourism Places*. London: Routledge, pp. 128–137.

Jeffres, L.W., Bracken, C.C., Jian, G. and Casey, M.F. (2009) The impact of third places on community quality of life. *Applied Research in Quality of Life*, Vol. 4(4), pp. 333–345.

Kansara, V.A. (2013) Andy Dunn of Bonobos on building the Armani of the e-commerce era. *Business of Fashion*, July [Online]. Available from http://www.businessoffashion.com/articles/founder-stories/founder-stories-andy-dunn-on-building-the-giorgio-armani-of-the-e-commerce-era. Accessed 13 March 2016.

Kapferer, J.-N. and Bastien, V. (2009) *The Luxury Strategy: Break the Rules of Marketing to Build Luxury Brands*. London: Kogan Page.

Kent, A.M. (2003) 2D23D: Management and design perspectives on retail branding. *International Journal of Retail Distribution and Management*, Vol. 31(3), pp. 131–142.

Kent, A.M., Schwarz, E. and Blazquez Cano, M. (2014) Convergence of physical and virtual retail environment: Mobile phone use in-store. *2nd Colloquium on Design, Branding & Marketing, 9–10 Dec, 2014, Nottingham Trent University*.

Kepron, D. (2014) *Retail (r)evolution*. Cincinnati, OH: ST books.

Kirby, A.E. (2009) *The Architectural Design of UK Supermarkets: 1950–2006*. Unpublished PhD thesis. London: University of the Arts London.

Klang, M. and Olsson, S. (1999) Virtual communities. In *Proceedings of the 22nd Information Systems Conference*, Penn State University.

Klingmann, A. (2007) *Brandscapes*. Cambridge, MA: MIT Press.

Kotler, P. (1973) Atmospherics as a marketing tool. *Journal of Retailing*, Vol. 49(4), pp. 48–64.

Kozinets, R.V., Sherry, J.F., Deberry-Spence, B., Duhachek, A., Nuttavuthisit, K. and Storm, D. (2002). Themed flagship brand stores in the new millennium: Theory, practice, prospects. *Journal of Retailing*, Vol. 78(1), pp. 17–29.

Krishna, A. (2010) An introduction to sensory marketing. In Krishna, A. (ed.) *Sensory Marketing: Research on the Sensuality of Products*. New York: Taylor and Francis Group, pp. 1–13.

Laing, A. and Royle, J. (2006) Marketing and the bookselling brand: Current strategy and the manager's perspective. *International Journal of Retail & Distribution Management*, Vol. 34(3), pp. 198–211.

Laing, A. and Royle, J. (2013) Examining chain bookshops in the context of "third place." *International Journal of Retail & Distribution Management*, Vol. 41(1), pp. 27–44.

Lefebvre, H. (1991) *The Production of Space*, transl. by D. Nicholson-Smith. Oxford: Basil Blackwell.

Lindstrom, M. (2005) *Brand Senses: How to Build Powerful Brands through Touch, Taste, Smell, Sight & Sound*. London: Kogan Page.

Lofland, L.H. (1998) *The Public Realm*. New Brunswick, NJ: Aldine Transaction.

Mager, B. (2008) Service design. In Erlhoff, M. and Marshall, T. (eds.) *Design Dictionary: Perspectives on Design Terminology*, pp. 354–356. Basel: Birkhäuser.

Manlow, V. and Nobbs, K. (2013) Form and function of luxury flagships: An international exploratory study of the meaning of the flagship store for managers and customers. *Journal of Fashion Marketing and Management: An International Journal*, Vol. 17(1), pp. 49–64.

Maslow, A. (1964) *Religions, Values, and Peak-experiences*. Columbus: Ohio State University Press.

McCarthy, E.J. (1975) *Basic Marketing: A Managerial Approach*. Homewood, IL: Irwin.

McPherson, G. (2006) Public memories and private tastes: The shifting definition of museums and their visitors in the UK. *Museum Management and Curatorship*, Vol. 21, pp. 44–57.

Mehrabian, A. and Russell, J.A. (1974) *An Approach to Environmental Psychology*. Cambridge, MA: MIT Press.

Meroni, A. and Sangiorgi, D. (2011) *Design for Services*. London: Gower.

Merrifield, A. (1993) Place and space: A lefebvrian reconciliation. *Transactions of the Institute of British Geographers*, Vol. 18(4), pp. 516–531.

Mikunda, C. (2007) *Brand Lands, Hot Spots and Cool Spaces: Welcome to the Third Place and the Total Marketing Experience*. London: Kogan Page.

Mitchell, G. (1986) *Design in the High Street*. London: The Architectural Press.

Moore, C.M. and Doherty, A. (2007) The international flagship store of luxury fashion retailers. In Hines, T. and Bruce, M. (eds.) *Fashion Marketing*. Oxford: Butterworth-Heinemann, pp. 277–286.

Moore, C.M., Fernie, J. and Burt, S. (2000) Brands without boundaries: The internationalisation of the designer retailer's brand. *European Journal of Marketing*, Vol. 34(8), pp. 919–937.

Murray, C. (2001) *Making Sense of Place: New Approaches to Place Marketing*. Bounds Green: Comedia.

Nobbs, K. (2014) Dwelling time: On examining experience economy and the third space in fashion. VESTOJ: *The Journal of Sartorial Matters* (Volume 5 – On Slowness). London: London College of Fashion.

Nobbs, K., Moore, C.M. and Sheridan, M. (2012) The flagship format within the luxury fashion market. *International Journal of Retail & Distribution Management*, Vol. 40(12), pp. 920–934.

Oldenburg, R. (1999) *The Great Good Place: Cafes, Coffee Shops, Bookstores, Bars, Hair Salons and Other Hangouts at the Heart of a Community*. New York, NY: Marlowe & Company.

Pantano, E. (2010) New technologies and retailing: Trends and directions. *Journal of Retailing and Consumer Services*, Vol. 17(3), pp. 171–172.

Pantano, E. and Naccarato, G. (2010) Entertainment in retailing: The influences of advanced technologies. *Journal of Retailing and Consumer Services*, Vol. 17(3), pp. 200–204.

Pedroni, M. (2011) *Sellers of experience: The new face of fashion retail*. [Internet]. Available from http://www.inter-disciplinary.net/wp-content/uploads/2011/08/pedronifapaper.pdf. Accessed 13 December 2015.

Pine, B. and Gilmore, J. (1999) *The Experience Economy: Work is Theatre and Every Business a Stage*. Boston, MA: Harvard Business School Press.

Piotrowicz, W. and Cuthbertson, R. (2013) Introduction to the special issue: Information technology in retail: Towards omnichannel retailing. *International Journal of Electronic Commerce*, Vol. 18(4), pp. 5–16.

Plunkett, D. and Reid, O. (2012) *Detail in Contemporary Retail Design*. London: Laurence King.

Pomodoro, S. (2013) Temporary retail in fashion system: An exploratory study. *Journal of Fashion Marketing & Management*, Vol. 17(3), pp. 341–352.

Ponsonby-McCabe, S. and Boyle, E. (2006) Understanding brands as experiential spaces: Axiological implications for marketing strategists. *Journal of Strategic Marketing*, Vol. 14(2), 175–189.

Relph, E. (1976) *Place and Placelessness*. London: Pion Ltd.

Renko, S. and Ficko, D. (2010) New logistics technologies in improving customer value in retailing service. *Journal of Retailing and Consumer Services*, Vol. 17(3), pp. 216–223.

Rentschler, R. and Potter, B. (1996) Accountability versus artistic development: The case for non-profit museums and performing arts organizations. *Accounting, Auditing & Accountability Journal*, Vol. 9(5), pp. 100–113.

Riewoldt, O. (2002) *Brandscaping: Worlds of Experience in Retail Design*. London: Momenta.

Rosenbaum, M.S. (2009) Restorative servicescapes: Restoring directed attention in 3rd places. *Journal of Service Management*, Vol. 20(2), pp. 173–191.

Rumsey, A. (26 May, 2015) *Extreme engagement – Elevated engagement*, WGSN.

Sachdeva, I. and Goel, S. (2015) Retail store environment and customer experience: A paradigm. *Journal of Fashion Marketing and Management*, Vol. 19(3), pp. 290–298.

Saunter, L. (15 Dec, 2014) *Eight ways retail is capitalising on culture*, WGSN.

Saunter, L. (5 Jul, 2015a) *Hybrid lifestyle stores – Retail update*, WGSN.

Saunter, L. (3 Oct, 2015b) *Flexible store design: New concepts*, WGSN.

Schmitt, B. (1999) Experiential marketing. *Journal of Marketing Management*, Vol. 15(1–3), pp. 53–67.

Schmitt, B. (2003) *Customer Experience Management: A Revolutionary Approach to Connecting with Your Customers*. Hoboken: John Wiley & Sons, Inc.

Seaford, B.C., Culp, R.C. and Brooks, B.W. (2012) Starbucks: Maintaining a clear position. *Journal of the International Academy for Case Studies*, Vol. 18(3), pp. 39–57.

Seamon, D. (1979) *A Geography of the Lifeworld: Movement, Rest, and Encounter*. New York, NY: St. Martin's Press.

Sherry, J.F. Jr. (1998) The soul of the company store: Nike Town Chicago and the emplaced brandscape. In Sherry, J.F. Jr. (ed.) *Servicescapes: The Concept of Place in Contemporary Markets*. Chicago, IL: American Marketing Association, pp. 109–146.

Sherry, J.F., Kozinets, R.V. and Borghini, S. (2007) Agents in paradise: Experiential co-creation through emplacement, ritualization and community. In Carú, A. and Cova, B. (eds.) *Consuming Experience*. Abingdon: Routledge, pp. 17–33.

Skandrani, H., Mouelhi, N.B.D. and Malek, F. (2011) Effect of store atmospherics on employees' reactions. *International Journal of Retail & Distribution Management*, Vol. 39(1), pp. 51–67.

Skenasy, L. (2007) Starbucks is still the third place to be – Even if it's let itself go. *Advertising Age*, 78(12), p. 11.

Spena, T.R., Carida, A., Colurico, M. and Melia, M. (2012) Store experience and co-creation: The case of the temporary shop. *International Journal of Retail & Distribution Management*, Vol. 40(1), pp. 21–40.

Spire. (2013) *Pop-up store: Taking the retail world by storm*. Spire Research and Consulting Ltd. [Internet]. Available from http://www.spireresearch.com/spire-journal/yr2013/q1/pop-up-stores-taking-the-retail-world-by-storm/. Accessed 13 December 2015.

Story. (2015) Website banner. Available from http://thisisstory.com. Accessed 13 December 2015.

Surchi, M. (2011) The temporary store: A new marketing tool for fashion brands. *Journal of Fashion Marketing & Management*, Vol. 15(2), pp. 257–270.

Thomson, R. (1 May, 2014) Selfridges' fragrance lab takes shoppers on a perfume journey. *Retail Week*.

Townsend, S. (15 May, 2014) Property: Station retail. *Drapers*.

Turley, L.W. and Milliman, R.E. (2000) Atmospheric effects on shopping behaviour: A review of the experiential evidence. *Journal of Business Research*, Vol. 49(2), pp. 193–211.

Uggla, H. (2006) The corporate brand association base: A conceptual model for the creation of inclusive brand architecture. *European Journal of Marketing*, Vol. 40(7/8), pp. 785–802.

Verhoef, P.C., Lemon, K.N., Parasuraman, A., Roggeveen, A., Tsiros, M. and Schlesinger, L.A. (2009) Customer experience creation: Determinants, dynamics and management strategies. *Journal of Retailing*, Vol. 85(1), pp. 31–41.

von Borries, V.F. (2003) Niketown Berlin: The city as a brand experience. *Advances in Art, Urban Futures*, Vol. 3, pp. 75–86.

Warby Parker. (2015) Available from https://www.warbyparker.com. Accessed 3 December 2015.

Watson, H. (2007) Seoul's interior landscapes. *Architectural Journal*, Vol. 77, pp. 114–119.

Weller, S. (2013) Consuming the city: Public fashion festivals and the participatory economies of urban spaces in Melbourne, Australia. *Urban Studies*, Vol. 50(14), pp. 2853–2868.

Wellman, B. and Haythornthwaite, C.A. (2002) *The Internet in Everyday Life*. Malden, MA: Blackwell Publishing.

White, K. and White, F. (1996) *Display and Visual Merchandising*. Westwood, NJ: St. Francis Press.

Zeithaml, V.A., Bitner, M.-J. and Gremler, D.D. (2009) *Services Marketing: Integrating Customer Focus across the Firm* (5th ed.). London: McGraw-Hill.

Zeithaml, V.A., Parasuraman, A. and Berry, L.L. (1985) Problems and strategies in services marketing. *Journal of Marketing*, Vol. 49(Spring), pp. 33–46.

Zieleniec, A. (2007) *Space and Social Theory*. London: Sage.

Zimmerman, A. (2012) Can retailers halt 'showrooming?' *The Wall Street Journal*. Available from http://www.wsj.com/articles/SB10001424052702304587704577334370670243032. Accessed 13 December 2015.

6 From clicks-and-bricks to online-to-offline

The evolving e-tail/retail space as immersive media in Hong Kong and mainland China

Tommy Tse and Tsang Ling Tung

Introduction

When Harry Gordon Selfridge first opened his eponymous department store on Oxford Street in 1909, London's retailing industry was revolutionized. Selfridge 'literally changed everything about the way Londoners shopped' (Woodhead, 2007, p. 1) with its artistic shop windows, inventive in-store promotions, glitzy fashion shows and other entertainment, as well as premium customer services and facilities that mesmerized every elite consumer. In the adventurous American retailer's vision, shopping was at once a visual and tactile, gratifying and pleasurable experience that could be best relished in 'a moment of private self-indulgence and enjoyment' (Woodhead, 2007, p. 34).

However, in the late twentieth century, due to the unprecedented growth and changes in retailing services and consumption around the world triggered by the irreversible force of globalization, post-industrialization, urbanization, transnational mobility and money flows, branding and marketing, information and communications technology and so forth, rather than just a corner of the street, we witnessed the 'malling' of a large portion of urban space and gradual standardization of cityscapes in rapidly developing consumer societies, particularly in China and East Asia, from multi-story shopping malls, flagship stores and concept boutiques to guerrilla pop-up shops. Meanwhile, more and more consumers are becoming addicted to online surfing and shopping, and marketers and retailers tend to explore the online sphere, building their brands and selling their merchandises, leading to the rapid 'malling' of virtual space.

Does such a metamorphosis guarantee everlasting growth in sales and further perpetuation of consumerism in our society and culture? On the one hand, the emergence of online shopping and reliance on global travellers' and tourists' impulse (or price-conscious) consumption in global cities have created new challenges for brands and retailers improvising strategies to sell and impress the clienteles through their physical (also virtual) shops, no matter how enthralling they may be; on the other, they are striving to adapt to/ experiment with new modes of brand and design communication. There are simply too many ways to consumption, from communication channels and promotional strategies to product variety, that dazzle and distract consumers in each and every nanosecond.

As we place all these as the backdrop of branding and retailing practices, several key questions emerge: *is retail design still significant* amid the new opportunities and challenges? What are the alleged changes and actual practices in the contemporary retail industry and retail design as a tool of brand communication that we – whether as a researcher, practitioner or even just an ordinary consumer – have to attend to? What are their immediate implications and divergent effects to consumers, culture and society? More radically speaking, for instance, can the evolving virtual shopping experience and its potential synchronization with 3D printing technology – that is, to 'prosume' a piece of recyclable/ reprintable luxury fashion online with just a click and within a couple of minutes when one has an 'omnipotent' 3D printer at home – completely substitute and eradicate the offline one in the foreseeable future (Leopold, 2015; Lindgren, 2013)?

In this chapter, based on an interdisciplinary theoretical approach and recent empirical research in Hong Kong and Shanghai, we attempt to address the above questions, and the discussions will focus on the retail market conditions and their social, cultural and economic significance in the two locales within the East Asian market, providing insights to a wide range of audiences who are concerned about the future of the retail industry, as well as briefly discussing the impact of evolving retail designs, dictated by market trends, on the creative liberties of the designers.

Significance of retail space for branding and marketing

Rather than merely being an interface for facilitating economic exchange, retail space plays a significant role in brand building and marketing. Filled with symbolic meanings and subliminal clues associated with the brand imagery, the store environment represents an alchemistic blend between colour, decoration, lighting, material, music and scents for stimulating different human senses. 'In this environment the products will be presented in a manner directly related to the needs, preferences, aspirations, lifestyle and attitudes towards fashion or consumer target' (Favero and Alvarez, 2013, p. 27). Such representation aims to create a direct connection between the products and the needs, preferences, aspirations, lifestyle and attitudes towards fashion or consumer target (Sackrider et al., 2009). Both industry and academic researchers in retail design are concerned with how retail space offers brand experiences and communicates meanings to consumers. Showing the advantages of seasonal products offered at their best can be one of the primary objectives of tailored store designs and the rationale for regularly renewing them (Sackrider et al., 2009).

The architectural design, façade and glass windows of a retail store help visualize and accentuate a brand's essence, to evoke synaesthesia of target customers and pedestrians within the increasingly cluttered shopping environment (Favero and Alvarez, 2013). The iconic, colossal and cutting-edge flagship stores opened in cosmopolitan cities – particularly in the luxury, fashion and lifestyle sectors – present the ultimate form of this sensory experience to further bewitch their loyal consumers: a fully fledged product collection delicately displayed, equipped with innovative and experimental fixtures, and additional premium services offered in an ample, museum-like space altogether facilitate in consumers' minds a silent dialogue with the fashion designer's creative thoughts. Luxury brands such as Louis Vuitton, Christian Dior, Celine and Chanel have triumphantly transmitted the aesthetic visions of their creative directors to their clients *vis-à-vis* flagship stores, enhancing their acceptance and appreciation of the brand identity (Dion and Arnould, 2011; Tse and Wright, 2014). These flagship stores, especially those located in spaces in landmark buildings or historic structures, often stand out as tourist destinations to draw non-traditional customers' attentions (Nobbs et al., 2012). Archetypes are found in Hong Kong at Heritage 1881 (the former Marine Police Headquarters Compound), the Landmark, the International Finance Centre Mall and Harbour City; in Taipei at Taipei 101; and in China at Beijing's Sanitun Village and Parkview Green Fangcaodi, and Shanghai's Jing An Kerry Centre, Plaza 66 and Shanghai IFC Mall (Tse, 2015). The strategy enables the brand to make the right statement, in the right locations, and to the right customers, the HNWI (High Net Worth Individuals), trendsetters and affluent tourists (Nobbs et al., 2012).

A flagship store showcases the brand story to the consumer and utilizes all tools available to highlight the brand statement and philosophy (Crewe, 2015). Contemporary retail spaces are particularly striking in that for luxury brands, increasingly it is through processes of 'dematerialization, commodity fetishism and the elevation of the retail store and commodity aesthetic' that 'value is created and manifested as codes of meaning enshrined in commodities' (Crewe, 2015, p. 8). The store's role in brand communications embraces 'a market entry method', 'a conduit to market relationships', 'the focus of marketing communications' and 'the material embodiment and social context of a brand's identity' (Manlow and Nobbs, 2013, p. 51). The on-going exhibitions inside the flagship store also craft a 'third space' to showcase the brand's heritage, provenance and luxury status to its customers (Nobbs et al., 2012), whose rational understanding and emotional identification with the brand are further strengthened. However, the increasingly commercialized artistic ambience instilled in the retail space may put the elite brand status and heritage at risk (Manlow and Nobbs, 2013). Meanwhile, a second wave of digital revolution in the last decade has also transformed the consumer culture, shopping behaviours and patterns radically worldwide (Masten and Plowman, 2003); luxury and fashion brands are now hastening to translate their flagship concepts to the 'digi-tail' sphere with varied levels of sophistication and intricacy.

Emergence of virtual retail space/ 'e-tail' space

In order to survive in the contemporary digital world, being able to distribute and sell their products via online channels has become more common for traditional retailers. Instead of simply uploading images and technical information of the products onto the corporate-owned or multi-label e-commerce platforms, retailers have started to integrate into their apps relationship and networking features, using social news feeds, the (micro)blog feeds, inboxes and customization tools to leverage the brand personality: H&M, French Connection and ASOS provide some vivid examples (Lea-Greenwood, 2013; Magrath and McCormick, 2013; Tse, 2015). In China, online fashion retailing is no new phenomenon. With an estimated amount of 500 million users, WeChat – a hybrid platform of Facebook, Twitter and Instagram in China owned by Tencent – has greatly replaced Sina Microblog for fashion branding and engaging potential customers. From independent local designers to international labels like Burberry and Jimmy Choo, fashion retailing in China is experiencing an age of digitalization.

The nexus of hyperlinks and shopping processes in the cyber world creates a new focus on the virtual retail space, or 'e-tail' space, where a thorough understanding and careful design of consumers' virtual experience is needed, exactly as it is in the physical retail space. For example, if branding videos are successfully utilized on a website, they can effectively enhance a brand's personality as well as provide entertainment to the viewers (Abdinnour-Helm et al., 2005). Where brands experiment with the use of avatars in human–computer interfaces, an online customer can be ushered in and assisted by a virtual salesperson in the virtual retail platform through product searches and shopping tasks; this is an effective tool to enhance the online shopping experience and communication between the consumer and the brand. Such use of avatars increases consumers' intention to shop in an online store environment and builds a sense of credibility, trust, loyalty and satisfaction with the source (Keeling et al., 2010). Other innovative ideas include Tesco's trial of a virtual fitting-room via Facebook in 2012 through which consumers can create an avatar of their simulated body measurements for testing outfits before purchasing the items online (Barnett, 2012). Similarly, fashion labels like Hugo Boss, Superdry and Adidas use a virtual fitting room operated by Fits.me providing new virtual shopping experiences for the customer (Fits.me, 2013). By comparison, retailers in both Hong Kong and mainland China are still in an early stage of adopting these new tools in branding and selling their products to local customers.

Resembling the shop window of a physical store, the brand name and logo displayed in the virtual shopping process influences the consumer's response to brand identification and market differentiation (Magrath and McCormick, 2013). It does so by drawing attention to both the brand of the website/e-commerce platform, the virtual retail store, and its brand values, lifestyle and personality. Elements include consistent and recognizable typography, colours and symbols, design layout and aesthetics, and even size and shape of menu buttons. Combined with videos, animations, and images, this virtual ambience 'heighten(s) the user's perception of the online store in terms of safety, convenience and enjoyability' (Magrath and McCormick, 2013, pp. 104–107). These aspects are particularly valid among young consumers in Hong Kong (Yip et al., 2012) and sophisticated consumers of mainland China (Wang, 2012), affecting their sense of trust and willingness to shop in the online marketplace. Enhanced by rapid economic growth, East Asia's uplift in purchasing power associates higher social status with the price and product in society's eyes; therefore, luxury brands in consumers' eyes represent prestige and lifestyle (Shukla, 2015).

Global luxury and fashion retail business and Chinese consumers

Over the past two decades, the number of global luxury consumers has more than tripled, counting from about US$90 million consumers in 1995 to US$330 million in late 2013 (D'Arpizio, 2014). In 2013, the luxury market in mainland China was worth US$18.9 billion (Unger, 2014). In 2014, the global personal luxury goods market has further increased 3 per cent (4 per cent without considering currency effects) and reached 224 billion Euros (equivalent to roughly 245 billion US dollars) in revenue at a retail equivalent value (Bain and Company, 2015). Chinese consumers, who make up over 30 per cent of global luxury spend, now provide the key momentum for sustaining the luxury industry worldwide (Bain and Company, 2015). Behind the seemingly prosperous figures, the retail industry is now facing a radical change to the entire economic model of revenue and profitability. The traditional model of business collaboration between retailers and suppliers is collapsing; the continued growth of geographical mobility of consumers and rise of 'm-commerce' and 'e-tail' industry have gradually slowed down the boom in consumer spending and triggered new consumption patterns (Stephens, 2015). Notably, Chinese consumers spend abroad more than three times what they spend locally, due to their a greater sensitivity to prices (Bain and Company, 2015; D'Arpizio et al., 2014).

Xi Jinping's anti-corruption campaign to discourage extravagant spending by government officials in late 2012, slower economic growth in China, and the rise of pro-democracy protests in Hong Kong in late 2014 have unnerved mainland consumers; and the local fashion and luxury retail industry performance has suffered (Unger, 2014). Wealthy Chinese make fewer trips to Hong Kong amidst a backlash by local citizens' 'desinicized' sentiments (Roberts, 2015). The aggressive expansion of global luxury brands' retail networks over the past decade has now suddenly become a financial and unrewarding burden. As Chinese consumers contribute to the largest portion of online luxury sales (Unger, 2014) so luxury brands have been forced to reconsider their geographical footprint. In Hong Kong, rental costs for luxury companies is anticipated to drop 20 per cent (Roberts, 2015), while, in mainland China, competition from the booming e-commerce market and an oversupply of mall space have also led China's major retailer and biggest private property developer Dalian Wanda to restructure its business model and close down many of its retail stores to cut costs (Turns to e-commerce . . . , 2015).

From the global e-commerce to China's m-commerce

Buying online is an emerging global trend; global e-commerce increased by 19 per cent in 2013 alone, and it is predicted that at least 30 per cent of the total retail economy will be transacted online by 2025 (Stephens, 2015). Following this trend, China's e-commerce is thriving with 80 per cent of e-commerce in China controlled by Alibaba's portals (From Bazaar to Bonanza, 2014). The scale of its operations is evident in the sales volumes handled by two of its portals that together, in 2013, amounted to 1.1 trillion yuan (equivalent to roughly 170 billion US dollars), more than eBay and Amazon combined (The Alibaba phenomenon, 2013). By 2020, China's e-commerce market is forecast to be bigger than the existing markets in America, Britain, Japan, Germany and France combined (The Alibaba phenomenon, 2013). With advice from leading technology companies Tencent and Baidu, China's shopping mall giant Dalian Wanda will make its first venture in e-commerce to expand its enterprise into the increasingly digital marketplace (Turns to e-commerce . . . , 2015).

In a 2015 survey of Chinese consumers' shopping behaviour, 45 per cent of respondents reported that they shopped online at least once a week, and a similar percentage claimed they use smartphones to make transactions, highlighting the mobile phone as a key platform for online retailing in China. Consumers in third-tier and fourth-tier cities were particularly keen on online shopping as they have fewer physical stores and malls (Turns to e-commerce . . . , 2015). In the first quarter of 2015, China's mobile commerce market grew by 168 per cent, contributing 47.8 per cent to the entire e-commerce market, and, at this current growth rate, mobile e-commerce is promising to surpass desktop sales by the end of that year (iResearch 2015; as cited in Turns to e-commerce . . . , 2015).

Among all mobile shopping channels, social media is the most favoured; over 70 per cent of Chinese respondents shop with social media, the highest percentage in Asia. The online messaging app WeChat enormously facilitates this trend through its convenient shopping options, and its counterpart Alibaba is catching up fast in developing its own social media platform in cooperation with Weibo, with the launch of the messaging app 'Laiwang'. These are important developments for Generation Z online shoppers in particular, born in the mid-1990s and thereafter, as they have a stronger trust in online information, enthusiasm for social media, and an urge to search for a sense of differentiation (Turns to e-commerce . . . , 2015).

Beneath the flourishing surface lie a number of problems and other insecurities facing Chinese e-commerce. Early in 2015, Alibaba was sued by Kering, the company behind luxury brands such as Gucci and Bottega Veneta, for encouraging and earning profits from selling counterfeit goods (Kuchler, 2015). Observers also have doubts about the ignominious way in which Alipay, a free third-party online transaction system, was spun out from its parent company (The Alibaba phenomenon, 2013). However, with the developed marketplace model, it is not an easy task to control product quality, since responsibility for the products lies with third-party sellers. Once product quality becomes an issue, the marketplace finds itself squeezed between a rock and a hard place, as it attracts blame both from customers and from the brands trading on the site (Khurana, n.d.).

Shopping experience: Offline versus online

While the power of online shopping and its gradual replacement of offline shopping experience are commonly predicted, brick and mortar stores still offer an irreplaceable three-dimensional shopping experience for customers. These developments have considerable implications for retail branding and design. Ballantine et al. (2015) argue that when customers enter a store their sensory experiences are not independent of each other: they do not experience the music in isolation; they do not smell the scent without seeing the colours as well; they do not walk on the floor-covering without feeling the ambient temperature. The typical customer experiences degrees of stimuli as an on-going, integrated experience. Petermans et al. (2013) put forward the notion of the 'holistic nature' of in-store customer experience, and they argue that this holism not only includes tangible architecture design of the space but also, more importantly, includes 'the intangible or atmospheric aspects', such as the choice of music and the arrangement of colour. In addition to this, customers in Hong Kong and China even lay particular stress on the 'personalized shopping experiences' in a physical store, which provide them with 'convenient, interactive and unprecedented choice' (Groeber, 2015).

Stores facilitate social interaction. When making shopping decisions online, consumers' relative lack of social interaction can lead to incomplete knowledge of information, a more fragmented experience, and consequently the increased risk and uncertainty they feel (Mull et al., 2015). However, the development of Web 2.0 technology and open-graph capabilities has to some extent redressed this problem. They enable companies to interact with consumers online more directly and with higher immediacy; in a broader sense, it has seen the enhancement of the socialization between companies and consumers (Mull et al., 2015). Moreover, consumers' increased perception of socialness may not be with other 'real' people; it can be achieved through the use of avatars (Wang and Fodness, 2010) and more specifically through 'a positive association between an individual's perception of social presence, trust, and web site loyalty for online retailers utilizing avatars' (Gefen and Straub, 2004).

The distinction between two motivations of shopping, for fun (hedonic) and for needs (utilitarian) contributes to different brand experiences and design priorities. It has been observed that when consumers shop for fun, they immerse themselves in the deal-hunting and are less mindful of money and time. Interactivity, through the manipulation of images such as zoom or rotation, is believed to be one the key benefits that information technology (IT) has brought to online marketing (McCormick and Livett, 2012). Therefore, higher levels of IT enhance the consumer's sense of empowerment, which has a positive effect on both the perceived ease of use and usefulness of a website, and online product viewing contributes to enhancing such pragmatic experience and e-loyalty from a consumer (Hernández et al., 2009). The design of, and content in, fashion retailers' websites – such as blogs, styling tips, online magazines and social networking sites – can emphasise their fashion consciousness to the consumer. Retailers at all levels, such as high-end pure-play e-tailer Net-a-Porter and multichannel high-street retailer Topshop, design their sites to make products and fashion information accessible online. These features stimulate emotions and induce feelings of excitement amongst online shoppers (McCormick and Livett, 2012), which constitutes an important component of consumers' entire shopping experience.

It has been found that consumers' criteria for choosing web sites are primarily composed of *merchandise*, the provision of appealing products that suit their tastes; *assurance* found in issues of privacy protection, and transaction safety; *the guarantee for returns and refunds*; and *functions*, including timely assistance when consumers search for, view and compare products, and also easy and fast mobile purchases (Groß, 2015). Likewise, Kurkovsky and Harihar (2006) have noted that the key to successful interactive shopping systems rests in consumers' acceptance of the interface. In the long run, if radio, television and print media are to constitute a tailored cross-media integration, then a technological convergence can be expected in the near future, enabling consumers to make mobile purchases instantly when browsing magazines or newspapers via scanning QR-codes on mobile phone camera (Groß, 2015).

When consumers shop for needs, prices become their primary concern, and they actively search for efficient money allocation. In this scenario, online shopping is vastly more advantaged than offline shopping as 'price comparisons are much faster and easier *online*' (Scarpi et al., 2014, p. 265). Consumers tend to be less argumentative with price and 'have fewer expectations of finding a lower price' in physical stores, as offline shopping environment is characterized by 'greater maturity' (Scarpi et al., 2014, pp. 265). However, when shopping online, price consciousness plays a significant role as both utilitarianism and hedonism influence the consumers' virtual shopping journey, eliciting a greater consciousness of price (Scarpi et al., 2014). Notably, as both Chiu et al. (2011) and Slåtten et al. (2009) have pointed out, 'customers shopping for fun are more likely to be loyal to a brick-and-mortar store than to an online store', because physical stores provide them with layers of excitement and fun that virtual stores lack and thus positively induce their 'intentional loyalty' for physical retailing (Scarpi et al., 2014, pp. 266).

In Asian contexts, the atmosphere of brick-and-mortar stores plays a vital role. A study on young consumers' shopping habits in Hong Kong reveals that 'hard' (cognitive) and 'soft' (affective) attributes of stores are interwoven in their appeal to young consumers (Yip et al., 2012). This study has shown that apart from hard attributes such as quality and location, consumers lay much emphasis on their experience during the shopping journey. This is particularly the case during 'unfocused shopping', shopping for fun with no specific aim, when 'superior interior design or a comfortable environment can reinforce the worth of a product or service' (Yip et al., 2012, p. 14). Similar findings also exist in studies on China, as Wong and Yu (2003, p. 61) argue: 'a positive and pleasant shopping experience is likely to lead to repeat visits, loyalty, and even free advertising'. As Yip et al. (2012, p. 14) conclude, a much-loved store means more than a place to turn to when in need for clothing, food or cosmetics; it is a 'supplier of a good shopping experience' and a process involving 'both rational and emotional, cognitive and affective'.

The revolution in physical retail space

The inherent sensorial and experiential quality of physical stores equips them with the potential to become powerful media carriers, whose 'retailers can articulate their brand story, excite consumers about products and then funnel their purchase to any number of channels, devices and distributors' (Stephens, 2015). Being both a media outlet and a sales agent, physical stores are increasingly winning favour for a new breed of experiential retailers to maximize consumers' shopping experience of all categories. Aligning with this global phenomenon, 'the store in essence will become an immersive and experiential advertisement for the products it represents and a direct portal to the entire universe of distribution channels available' (Stephens, 2015). Facilitated by technologies such as facial recognition, video analytics, and mobile ID tracking, lived experiences can be transferred onto living websites, which enable retailers to keep track of the types of customers, their frequency of visits, their favoured sections in the store, their final purchase and even their comments afterwards (Stephens, 2015). Winter (2014) termed this scenario as the 'new high-tech mirror', in which consumers no longer physically try clothes on; the mirror holds their details from a digital scan of their body. The mechanism behind the virtual wardrobe is the motion-capture camera that produces realistic 3D images of customers, giving people virtual experience of how an item of clothing, handbag, or accessory could be matched, by capturing motion-picture it also allows immediate identification of customers' size and body shape (Winter, 2014).

Consumers are empowered by visuality and affective affordance to assume a new role as active interpreters rather than passive receivers of prescribed sales messages (Crewe, 2015). In other words, consumers are initiated as 'inevitable scopophilic participants', 'engaged interpreters' and finally 'fashionable interlopers' in the grandiose fashion display (Potvin, 2009, p. 10). Therefore, aestheticism constitutes a new analytical category in the research on interactive service work, and complements 'emotions in research on emotional labour' as the significance of their physical appearance is increasingly recognized (Hamermesh and Biddle, 1994; Spiess and Waring, 2005; Warhurst and Nickson, 2007; Witz et al., 2003). As Pettinger (2004, p. 180) argues: 'the clothing worn by workers is part of the performance of an organisation's brand image, and workers' bodies are part of how the brand is communicated'. Therefore, it can be anticipated that stores with proper physical appearance policies as well as clothing polices are more likely to 'comprehensively regulate the overall appearance of staff', and it can also be assumed that 'the existence of a physical appearance policy was indicative of at least a basic strategy to employ and deploy aesthetic labour' (Hall and Van den Broek, 2011, p. 92). As Yang (2010) puts it: 'consumers perceive m-services as value-added while shopping in store', which, in turn, can improve their overall shopping experience (Karaatli et al., 2010).

Users' requests for specific product attributes can be processed by decision support systems (DSS), which provide a body of background information that are to guide consumers' decision-making (Groß, 2015). That is to say, there are various possibilities for consumers to search for and to obtain desired information. For example, through a mobile phone camera they might either retrieve data by scanning product barcodes or QR-codes (Kawamura et al., 2008; Van der Heijden, 2006; Van der Heijden and Sørensen, 2005). An alternative m-shopping assistant solution is MRS (Mobile Recommender System), or recommendation agent system, which aims at providing consumers with meaningful recommendations that might be of their interest (Walter et al., 2012). Consumers can retrieve a matrix of data about products, services, offers or vendor web sites in recommendation lists, which are generated as the combination of user-data from mobile devices, their browsing behaviour, and existing channels including television, catalogues and the Internet, and consumption behaviour (Groß, 2015).

In a similar manner, navigation systems accelerate the course for users to reach a desired destination, and they have the flexibility to be 'located either inside or outside of a brick-and-mortar shop' (Groß, 2015, p. 229). As Hou and Chen (2011) observe, 'mobile navigation systems can greatly reduce shopping route distance by up to one third', thus vastly saving time for shopping. Not least, mobile tracking systems are also used to record consumers' shopping movements and relations, providing retailers with insights into consumers' shopping. This technology is particularly useful to 'optimize the pathway in the points of sale by boosting the customer's decision to purchase on impulse' (Groß, 2015, p. 229).

Qualitative research of fashion meanings and brand values in Hong Kong and Shanghai

To explain the relationship between retail branding and store design, it is important to uncover the actual process of generating fashion meanings and communicating brand values. Consequently, this chapter draws on a combination of qualitative research methods, in-depth interviews, participant observation and visual research to collect data from fashion industry professionals, including journalists, business development and marketing executives, digital media specialists and retailers in Hong Kong and Shanghai. In particular it is informed by participant observation in a renowned Shanghai-based luxury fashion e-commerce company Glamorous Fashion (the company and staff names have been anonymised). Modes of collaboration were observed among the editorial team, interactive/information technology (IT) team, graphic design team, media team, marketing team and sales team. This enabled the organizational structure and operational patterns of e-commerce business to be analysed in the context of retail design. In addition, visual research was conducted in key shopping areas in the two locales, and informal conversations were undertaken with various fashion industry participants about their experience and views towards brand communication, (online) retail design and (online) retail industry development.

The dying/death of physical retail industry?

Amid the popular discourse of the 'dying/death of physical retail industry', Glamorous Fashion (GF), one of the top-three luxury e-commerce platforms founded in mainland China, offers novel insights and empirical data for understanding the actual conditions and changes of luxury fashion retail industry and consumer behaviours in China in the past five years. As Cindy, Media Manager of GF, revealed, '[GF] is the largest luxury e-commerce website in Shanghai and the third largest in China'. Founded in 2008 by a then thirty-year-old Chinese entrepreneur who studied abroad and previously worked in the digital marketing team of a global advertising agency, the online retailing company is positioned as 'your personal virtual stylist'; its internally agreed marketing objectives indicate that the online multi-label luxury retail store mainly targets the new generation of consumers in China: the white-collars resided in various second-tier and third-tier cities who do not necessarily have the opportunity (and time) to purchase luxury or 'semi-luxury' goods (Lipovetsky, 2007) abroad and in physical retail stores in their own towns. The availability of mobile technology, Internet access and business-to-consumer (b-to-c) e-commerce platforms provides these potential shoppers convenience to shop online while they are at the office or on the way home after work and to receive their orders within two working days, while at the same time nurturing their online shopping habits. On GF's various e-commerce platforms, official online retail website, its own mobile app retail store and other affiliated ones in other popular mobile app shops in China, the refined images of a variety of luxury and lifestyle products for both genders were displayed and categorized neatly along the webpage, from brand-name T-shirts to coats, hoodies to dresses, footwear, homeware, jewellery, accessories, and even 'luxury food and beverages'; GF carries Western fashion labels including Armani, Alexander McQueen, Burberry, Coach, Dolce & Gabbana, Fendi, Gucci, Hermes, MCM, Michael Kors, Miu Miu, Prada, Stella McCartney Valentino, Versace, Vivienne Westwood and Zatchels, and the 'GF special prices' listed range from a few hundred to 35,000 RMB.

Interestingly, the Editorial Director of GF's custom e-magazine *FashionZine*, who previously worked as the Fashion Director of an international fashion title in Hong Kong, confessed that in reality it is much easier to sell fashion and lifestyle products online to male customers: 'many Chinese female customers still prefer trying out clothes and footwear, mixing and matching them in person whereas the male ones don't usually care' – which recalls the unique services and experiences offered by offline retail stores that are still (temporarily) unavailable and unattainable online. Speaking about the visual merchandizing missions in an online retail store, Jenson, Graphic Design of GF for over three years, revealed that the company's major target audiences consist of the less educated yet affluent population in the mainland, who may still like the most prestigious luxury brands such as Louis Vuitton, Gucci, Dior, Burberry and Prada, but are developing more interest in buying the up-and-coming semi-luxury brands such as Carven, Coach, MCM and Tory Burch: 'that is why the [visual and textual] content and design on our website and in our costume e-magazine are very simple and straightforward.' GF is indeed not exactly a fashion media company, and some of its staff, notably in Graphic Design and the IT team, perceive it as 'just a website for online retailing'. However in Jay's (founder of GF) and Tammy's vision, its affiliated *FashionZine* has a mission to reposition GF and revolutionize the luxury e-commerce business/industry in the long run. It will build GF as a 'Taobao in the luxury sector', Taobao being a large online marketplace where China Internet merchants and users sell and purchase all sorts of products and services, well-known as 'China's eBay'. The aim is to create an authentic and credible online retail brand that gathers quality sellers and potential buyers in one interactive, user-driven platform; minimizes the extra costs for sales promotion and product storage; ensures that the online retail platform has minimum or no faked product transactions; and educates Chinese consumers about, and redefines, luxury fashion, as well as why it can be approachable in their everyday lives.

In practice, the marketing team did not impose very strict and consistent rules in writing feeds, as long as they highlighted GF's luxury products as 'practical', 'approachable' and 'inexpensive and appealing', echoing the ideas of 'new luxury' and 'masstige', the compound of 'mass' and 'prestige' to describe the luxury for masses (Silverstein and Fiske, 2003; Von Maltzahn, 2015), in encoding fashion meanings (Silverstein and Fiske, 2003; Truong et al., 2009). Creative write-ups on 'How to dress fashionably' and 'What are the most fashionable items for this season?' were occasionally disseminated, yet the more direct and factual descriptions of product attributes and discounted offers were still much preferred and more frequently publicized via GF's Sina Microblog account to its 50,000-plus online subscribers.

According to GF's Google Analytics data, its monthly turnover exceeded 7 million RMB in May 2014, but based on experience the sales volume would be much bigger during the two annual 'high seasons' – Chinese New Year and the company's anniversary. Seasonal and festive discounts, e-coupons and virtual money (or 'virtual red packets') offered through emails, SMSs, instant messengers (e.g. WeChat) and microblogging sites (e.g. Sina Microblog) were given to draw potential customers' attention and stimulate their consumption through the cyberspace. The interactive online environment has also enabled a more aggressive and active pull strategy: two feeds per weekday and one feed on Saturday and Sunday, regularly disseminating emotive and lively statements and related visuals to its followers through the official GF Sina Microblog account, for branding as well as driving traffic/virtual visitors to the online retail store.

To strategically expand GF's online retail business and market penetration in China, collaboration with other established online/mobile app shopping malls (comprising JD.com, Tmall.com, Yougou.com and Micro Mall/WeChat Mall), search engines (online.sh.cn) and famous KOLs (that is, 'key opinion leaders', including local celebrities, famed fashion journalists and also popular fashion and ordinary bloggers in this case) is vital. The GF marketing team also adopts an integrated social media system named Kong Ming Social to monitor its various social media accounts, automatically adding new users in order to trigger them subscribing to GF's accounts and enlarging its audience base. 'You know, [distributing through appropriate] "channel[s]" is the key for whatever retail business in China nowadays,' Tammy repeatedly emphasized. Unexpectedly, quite a few co-workers in GF mentioned their perceived difficulty of maintaining the company's sustainable business growth in a long run due to several reasons: the volume of merchandise they acquired through direct collaboration with international luxury brands' merchandizing and business development teams was relatively small; profit margin per unit sales was relatively low; and offering competitive prices is perceived as a crucial factor to win over online customers.

To compete against the seasoned and tasteful introduction by shop staff/personal stylists, glittering interior decoration and aesthetically pleasing window displays in the traditional physical retail space, Tammy advocated the importance of *FashionZine* as not just auxiliary content but the key to GF's long-term prestige and triumph:

> [GF] is not only a retailing place, but also a platform for fashion. Why do we need to invest money in producing an e-magazine? Because we want our customers to gain more knowledge about fashion in addition to purchasing products via our webpage. [. . .] The other [Chinese] online retail stores temporarily do not have this direction. [. . .] So I guess the future trend in China, even the world, should be the combination of these two aspects. As a matter of fact, the business model of websites writing about fashion [online fashion media], from a commercial perspective, is not that profitable as they can no longer lure a lot of fashion brands to advertise there. On the other hand, if the website only sells products . . . for some rational buyers, why do they need to visit that particular website if they want to buy things? It is important for the online retail store to share more contents about fashion, people may therefore see the things they want to buy, or gain a sense of what is more popular recently from the website.

In one GF weekly internal meeting, editorial and marketing teams' colleagues respectively shared their views towards the webpage design messaging styles of successful Western websites (e.g. DealMoon.com) in general and other competitive online retail stores they regularly monitor and follow (e.g. Net-A-Porter.com, ASOS.com, My-wardrobe. com, Shopthemag.com, Zhenpin.com [珍品网], Ihaveu.com [优众网]). Vivienne (Head of Marketing at GF) and Tammy commented on the recent market research findings provided by the marketing team, such as their regular monitoring of likes and comments by netizens upon the promotional posts and feeds of GF and its competitors. They also suggested, in the process of analyzing the competitors' webpage designs, we should pay attention not simply to their visual presentation from our subjective aesthetic viewpoints but also to the percentage/distribution patterns of content in different webpage sections, the amount of discounts they offer (and for how long), the way they present their products' special offers textually (copywriting analysis), the architecture and user-friendliness of various hyperlinks created, etc. A GF marketing executive's prolonged negotiation with IT colleague Jamie was explained as a discussion of whether they should use the terms 'marketing price'/'discounted price' or 'GF price'/'campaign price' for a sales promotion message. On another occasion, the boss of GF ran from his room to Jamie's seat in the open office area, angrily pointing at his own iPhone's screen and scolding the IT staff publicly for their insensibility of adding a touchscreen button too close to an existing one on the first click-through page of GF's mobile app platform: 'Do you really know how to use smartphone apps? How tiny are your fingers to be able to click these two "tiny" buttons separately?'

For visual communication, several graphic designers and marketing team members said they used to do fashion/product photography themselves for creating unique and consistent GF images all the time, as the online retailing environment becomes more competitive and evolves so rapidly. In order to keep their brand/virtual store image fresh and timely every week, and due to a limited promotional budget, they had no choice but to handily use available images of Caucasian models online to create online banners and promotional visuals. Quite often this practice creates problems of aesthetic inconsistency and copyright infringement.

The issues of trust and authenticity continue to create a major hurdle for developing luxury and fashion online retail businesses in China. In GF's case, from time to time there were customers calling its hotline, persistently asking about how they could make sure that GF's products (or even their product certificates) were not faked, even though the company has already officially received a testimony of website safety issued by the government for its online platform. In brief, although the physical retail industry may be facing problems of various sorts due to the changing economic model of revenue and profitability (Stephens, 2015), the ubiquity of information and communications technology, and gradual saturation of luxury fashion sales in emerging markets, it may still be too naive to believe that the online retail industry in its current form can entirely replace the physical one with a totally different set of rules, hurdles and challenges. The role of physical retail stores as points of sales and one-way communication channels may evolve into 'living websites' and 'interactive media', scrutinizing consumer behaviours even more comprehensively and precisely through facial recognition, video analytics, mobile ID tracking, beacon technology, radio frequency identification and so forth (Stephens, 2015). A potential symbiotic relationship between virtual and physical stores can be built through innovative O-to-O ('online-to-offline' and 'offline-to-online') strategies.

A second insight into the state of the physical retail industry is provided by the successful online brand Net-a-Porter. A luxury e-commerce business, Net-a-Porter was founded by former journalist Natalie Massenet in London in 2000 and was designed in the style of a fashion magazine. It launched its Asia-Pacific business in 2012 after its integration with Shouke. Originally acquired by Swiss luxury conglomerate Richemont Group, the company was acquired by Yoox in the first quarter of 2015 in an all-share deal, which has made the Italian online fashion retailer an industry leader in the global online luxury market. Miffy, Marketing Officer at Net-A-Porter China, claimed that the British fashion e-tailer considered itself an 'IT' company at the core, being at the forefront of fashion as well as technology to generate an immersive experience for its clientele in buying products or even just consuming fashion news. Carrying a multitude of brands from extreme luxury to street fashion, rather than simply displaying photos of different merchandise on its online platform, Net-a-Porter always found a common thread passing through a myriad of products to communicate its brand values and endow its virtual designs with a compelling spirit:

> For the last two months, all of our advertising campaigns, our social media activations have been centered around what we called 'the heroines'. The hero, the woman hero of our times. It is about saluting these heroines, and sort of alluding to what sort of inspiration they provided for our generation, women. So that's the central theme. And we have created and showcased a product list that sort of matches the theme . . . and these themes are usually universal truths about women . . . we usually try to find these sorts of interest points that speak to our audience . . . tap into the actual sort of human nature . . . the deep insights of our consumers or what excites, motivates and inspires them. [. . .] I believe that the idea doesn't start from a jacket or a pair of shoes, it starts as a universal truth.

The birth of Net-a-Porter was triggered by the evolution of online technologies from Web 1.0, where only flat data could be transmitted and there were very limited interactions between users and the sites, and brand-generated sites. Miffy believed the new generation of consumers does not undertake fashion research on brand sites anymore; they are getting much smarter, more used to browsing information through their social networks facilitated by Web 2.0 technologies, where interactive data are allowed and interactions between users and sites freely flow. It is of the utmost importance for fashion brands to be 'social' and inject the fashion styles they sell into the consumers' daily behaviours, directly driving them to revenue-generating platforms.

In the context of China, a brand's localized communication and retailing strategies and relating to local consumers have become more important in the era of social media and mobile technology. For example, the newly created 'Double-Eleven' festival (11 November, 'Singles' Day' in mainland China) and the Chinese New Year have become a new opportunity for online retailers in recent years (see Figure 6.1) – discounts were offered, and billions of RMB of online sales could be generated in a single day. These new phenomena, including the Singles' Day Sale (created single-handedly by Alibaba/ TaoBao) and Digital CNY Red Packets Campaign (popularized by instant messenger WeChat by Tencent China), have also allured major brands such as Nike and Levi's to take part.

'One of Net-a-Porter's strongest selling points', as Miffy asserted, 'is providing top-notch fashion content for consumers on a weekly basis, which are followed, imitated and by many luxury and fashion e-retailers around the world'. Being a mixture of an e-commerce and a fashion media company, Net-a-Porter publishes a weekly digital magazine recommending trendy items that have already been curated by professional buying teams and personal shoppers. With an easy click, consumers can make an online purchase and keep up with the fad. Another rather innovative print magazine was also published in 2014 – a 'shoppable' magazine (see Figure 6.2) where a consumer can effortlessly scan the page with the NAP Shopping App.

Upon a customer doing so, direct links to the e-commerce platform pop up instantly, and the styles that a consumer sees in the physical magazine are ready for purchase. Instead

Figure 6.1 Taobao's 'Singles' Day' promotional campaign in China and Taiwan

Source: Taobao, 2013

Figure 6.2 Net-a-Porter's 'shoppable' magazine: online shopping at a click of a button

Source: Net-a-Porter 2015

of replicating the exact shopping experience in a physical store, a 'ceremony of purchase' is being created and offered by the British e-tailer in the delivery process:

> It is that our iconic, branded blackbox with a black bowtie when we deliver the merchandizes . . . the experience doesn't just stop after they pay online. So we put a lot of attention and we put a lot of time in ensuring that their entire purchase journey is the best one possible. So when consumers get these items in the mail or delivered, they can feel that a lot of care and attention has been put into their orders . . . our operation team also makes sure that each package is meticulously wrapped.

Nonetheless, seasoned fashion e-tailers like Net-a-Porter still face operational hurdles in actual practice, such as the payment methods and delivery/courier options and duration.

The irreplaceable values of physical retail space?

The Bluebell Group – a renowned retailer and distributor headquartered in Hong Kong, of multiple luxury fashion and lifestyle products across eight Asian countries since 1954 – also shows a unique vision of retail business, marketing and branding amid the new challenges to traditional retail industry. In both the individual interview and his talk entitled 'The rebirth of bricks-and-mortar' at the Retail Marketing Hong Kong Conference held in mid-April 2015 (Retail Marketing, 2015), Anson Shum, Marketing and Communication Director (Greater China) of the Bluebell Group, highlighted his optimism in the values of physical retail space and advocated that it still can hardly be replaced by online retailing's offerings. By rethinking about what customers really want, Shum analogized retail industry to the global music and film industries – the rise of digital piracy and the fall of CD/tickets sales since the start of twenty-first century had almost killed the two sectors, yet it does not mean that their products have lost their lustre and that people no longer listen to music or watch movies; apart from strategically tapping into the online sphere promoting their stars and products, both industries started investing more on creating and improving the theatrical and lively *total experience* to retain their target consumers' interest, from the live music performance of One Direction and Justin Timberlake (whose global tours combined grossed revenue was close to US$500 million and sold over 5 million tickets in 2014) to screening the spectacular Avatar (the highest-grossing movie of all time) in a 3D cinema, which are not (yet) utterly replicable in the online world.

Inspired by the idea of 'experience economy' (Pine and Gilmore, 1999), marketers still have strong faith in turning brick-and-mortar into a 'performance stage', an entertaining and unforgettable showground to enhance the experience of all senses. Meanwhile, Shum also believed that a through-the-line 'click-and-mortar' model, whether for marketing communication or retail, is the future of luxury, fashion and lifestyle retail industry. He narrated a twenty-year-old story of his visiting the French luxury bakery and sweets brand Ladurée's shop in Saint-Germain, Paris, as a teenager, and he was immediately drawn by its colourful shop windows, sweet scent and long queue outside the delicate, inviting entrance. Two decades later, his marketing team still puts high emphasis on creating such Parisian luxury experience in its physical Ladurée stores in Hong Kong, Taipei and mainland China, and at the same time adopting social media strategies. Over fifty famed Chinese celebrities, fashionistas, socialites, journalists and bloggers posted selfies with the colourful gift packs on their Facebook/Sina Microblogs/WeChat accounts, and collaborations with other fashion houses, including Nina Ricci and Lanvin and illustrators, brought in streams of local customers and tourists to the 'sweet tooth mecca' (see Figure 6.3). According to the marketer, it was proven to be a huge economic success in all three regions, and the idea of 'luxury food' has become a new trend around the world.

Nike Inc., a well-acclaimed American multinational corporation engaging in design and production of sporting outfits showcases a very distinctive, technologically advanced and thematic-based retail design, fuelled in part by its awe-inspiring advertising campaigns. In an interview with Betty (pseudonym), former Strategist at Wieden + Kennedy servicing Nike China, she outlines Nike's intricate process of creating successful commercial/ad campaigns through long-tenured partnership with advertising agencies. By formulating a comprehensive creative brief that coupled with intelligence ideas from the middleperson/advertising agencies, Nike is able to entrench its fashion in a very concrete manner and disseminate it through above-the-line promotional techniques and thematic elements in the retail design.

In order to stand out from competitors' retail spaces, Nike emphasizes a futuristic retail experience that intertwines physical space with digital experiences (see Figure 6.4), and this notion is epitomized in the construction of a premium retail space entitled NikeLab (Nike Inc., 2014a). Operating in both Shanghai and Hong Kong and incorporating social media platforms, NikeLab provides 'consumers with unique expressions of Nike's leading innovations with an experience that bridges brick-and-mortar retail, online commerce, and digital engagement' (Nike Inc., 2014a). As a hub of creativity, NikeLab not only offers personalized products through its customer-tailored service of 'NIKEiD', but also facilitates an interactive shopping experience that is in stark comparison to shopping in archaic and formulaic layouts. By merging the desirability of physical retail and digital

Figure 6.3 Local customers and tourists queued up at Ladurée's store in Harbour City, Hong Kong

Source: Bluebell Group 2014

Figure 6.3 (Continued)

Figure 6.4 Nike's 'futuristic' point-of-sale displays in Shanghai
Source: Tse, 2015

involvement, Nike's retail space elicits a 'best of both worlds' shopping experience for its consumers.

Apart from technological convergence, Nike's meticulously designed creative hubs also form a space enriched with symbolic meanings to an array of audiences. Jason, an experienced Retail Marketing and Digital Communication Manager of Capitaland Mall Asia, praised Nike's multifarious usages of its retail stores as a functional, transformational and diverse space for hosting various activities, such as events formulated by Nike Training Club, Kicks Lounge, etc.

Referring to the recently opened iAPM Shanghai Nike Women flagship store, Jason points to this particular retail space as not a mere extension/reinforcement of its current advertising campaigns but a landscape infused with connotations of sports lovers. Essentially, the Nike Women store in iAPM elicits a 'third place', where informal free public gatherings take place to facilitate people 'to develop friendships, enjoy conversations, and enjoy being part of a larger spatial community' (Oldenburg, 1999). Women sports lovers, such as members of Nike+ Training Club, perceive iAPM as the mecca of athletic training, as it provides with them a common area to congregate and enjoy athletic pursuits instilled in the group training experiences (Nike Inc., 2014b).

Imbued with a matrix of symbolic meanings targeting different consumers/audience, NikeLab and iAPM show Nike's ambition in venturing in the click-and-mortar trend of

Figure 6.5 Nike's 'glocalized' point-of-sales materials (POSM)
Source: Tse, 2015

China market. In an age where the discourse of digital primacy over physical retail stores has permeated mass consumption, Nike is still able to revitalize its brick-and-mortar retail space through the enhancement of interactive technology and creative branding.

However, NikeLab and iAPM are not unique to China but components in Nike's global marketing plans and branding communications strategies. In terms of Nike's uniqueness of brick-and-mortar retail spaces in China, the degree of localization, embedded in the 'glocalization process', has very much dissipated as there is a strict adherence to the uniformed and globalized branding and marketing strategies. The media campaign, branding communications, and retail display are to a large extent subject to the cooperate guidelines provided by Nike's headquarters in the United States, thereby possessing very limited room for localized innovation and creation (see Figure 6.5).

In other words, as the Chinese market is just one component of Nike's global entrepreneurship, it is obligated to align with the company's internal consistency. In terms of autonomy, advertisers and marketers in China are more likely to be just translating the prescribed slogan and re-shooting promotion materials with Chinese athletes and actors, instead of interpreting and decoding the brand's meaning in the particular social and cultural context. Consequently, resemblances can easily be found between the advertisements featuring the US idolized American basketball team and China's hero athlete Liu Xiang, in which there are no conspicuous differences in terms of its symbolic/cultural meanings that can be fully discerned. This phenomenon does not exist in China alone; to some degree it is Pan-Asian and, 'Euro-American culture continues to determine what is fashionable, and the global fashion companies, especially the successful ones, project their choice to the Asia-Pacific region through their marketing communications' (Tse, 2015, p. 263). Consequently, although Asian fashion is involved in the complicated negotiations with their head offices, it is not yet able to define Asian styles, thereby possessing little autonomy in anchoring its own fashion in the tide of globalization and limited to a very superficial level of participation in the global fashion stage (Tse, 2015, p. 263).

Developing both online and offline retail space

Epitomized by two adorable, rabbit-like illustrated icons Nai Nai and Vee Vee to present a sense of naiveté and purity, Naivee – a renowned Chinese smart-casual womenswear fashion label officially founded in 1999 and now with twenty-six franchised physical stores and special shop counters in Shanghai, over two hundred point-of-sales in China and a well-constructed e-commerce platform in mainland China – has narrated a successful through-the-line brand retail story to the researcher during an interview in 2014.

Sarah, Managing Director at Naivee, introduced the integrated marketing strategy adopted by her fast-growing company while demonstrating its innovative online platforms in her office's desktop. An emphasis was put on targeting clearly segmented upper-middle markets through holistic channels, and having its branding, marketing, promotion and retailing strategies well synchronized with each other with the support of seamless information and communications technology. 'All these [strategies] manifest a strong and clearly coordinated theme and business concept, which is rather original [in China]'. Every season, Naivee launches its new collection through a live-broadcast fashion show, with its products immediately available for online sale:

> [consumers are] watching the [fashion] show [online], and ordering [the new products] at once creates a very good experience for consumers. The synergy I just mentioned means, when a consumer scans the [Naivee fashion show's] QR code with her WeChat account's QR code scanner, the hyperlinks of respective pieces will be sent to her chronologically according to the fashion show rundown, and then she can place the order immediately [through TenPay or WeChat Wallet].

Meanwhile, Niu has claimed that their physical retail stores are indeed crucial to their commercial success. Instead of offering different forms of price-cut and discounts, Naivee focused on maintaining its perceived brand value by upgrading the customer experience. The 'intelligentized' in-store settings include interactive displays of product information and brand stories to deliver a 'modern sensuality' to its customers. Based on the researcher's observation of the brand's physical franchised stores in Shanghai, however, he could not locate any impressive interactive in-store display or identify any significant difference from other typical fashion stores.

Conclusion and implications for retail design

Based on the preceding case studies – Glamorous Fashion, Net-a-Porter, the Bluebell Group, Nike Inc. and Naivee in Hong Kong and Shanghai – three notable features emerge that epitomise current trends and point to future directions of the retail industry and retail design in East Asia.

First, although rapidly evolving in line with the global technological trend, e-commerce in East Asia is still at a nascent stage of development, in terms of the lack of 'authenticity' and consumer's trust towards these online platforms. The discourse around how online retail can shake physical retail's fundamental status is somehow overrated. It is true that click-and-mortar retail poses thorny challenges in profitability, operational mode and branding strategy to its counterparts; yet brick-and-mortar retail spaces still attract consumers by renovating themselves with symbolic meanings and interactivity, comprising Bluebell's 'experience economy' marketing strategy, Naivee's space of 'modern sensuality' and Nike's futuristic and interactive interior design. Physical retail space has been proven extremely successful in delicate commodity retailing as it renders consumers a 'total experience' that provokes their tactile and olfactory senses with the feeling of authenticity. Therefore, companies are not likely to completely surrender their physical retail spaces, even though they actively experiment with online platforms in hopes to elicit immersive shopping experiences.

Second, Asian markets do not enjoy equal status in glocalization, in which the embedded power dynamics are very much dominated by the West. This can be further manifested in the extensive emphasis that headquarters put on 'globalization', while the uniqueness in each locale often falls into oblivion (Tse, 2015). The elements of localization entrenched in the glocalized brand communications and marketing strategies adhere to the guidelines set by the head office of multinational enterprises, allowing limited room for genuine localized creative responses.

In some senses, rather than stimulating novel local marketing plans and branding strategies, glocalization prescribes retail strategies and reiterates the company's internal consistency. Therefore, although branding and retail design are thriving in East Asia, they consist of mainly one-way communication and 'top-down' imposition. In this light, even though Nike's use of innovative physical spaces have successfully attracted regular consumers and consolidate brick-and-mortar retail's instrumental status, they are still considered as mechanical components of Nike's global marketing strategy, rather than the unique contrivance devised by Asian marketers. Comparatively, Ladurée's mesmerizing visual merchandizing display and integration with its social media promotion demonstrates an excellent example of glocalized online-to-offline strategy.

Lastly, it can be anticipated that the future of the retail industry is to be predicated on the strategic click-and-mortar model. In elaboration, single existence of either will not suffice to sustain a brand, due to the fact that technological developments such as mobile navigation systems and immersive trans-media platforms will enhance the hybridity of physical and virtual spaces. Therefore, cross-platforms epitomized by Net-a-Porter's 'shoppable magazines' and GF's collaboration with multiple online channels and social media will become the future and evolving trends of fashion retailing. In the specific context of China, where a variety of social media platforms and online payment systems continue to grow steadily and increasingly permeate people's daily lives, localized cross-platform shopping channels are expected to become a dominant market presence in the near future.

The previous sections extensively discussed the impact of retail design, coupled with consumers' reactions, on companies' marketing and branding strategies. They illustrated how targeted consumers' needs and preferences exert considerable influences on brands' localization strategies, as well as the different levels of adoption for glocalized aesthetics. However, one aspect, which has not been examined in detail, is how do designers internally conceive their own retail designs? In other words, what are the evolving retail/e-tail designs' implications for designers?

As consumers still hold a relatively reserved attitude towards e-commerce due to 'authenticity' concerns, brick-and-mortar stores will continue to serve as an important component of retailing with enhanced focus on providing 'immersive experience' that evokes consumers' multiple senses, as evident from the above case studies on Bluebell Group (Ladurée) and Nike. Apart from a traditional demonstration of brand image and product display, technologies within the retail space, such as facial recognition and mobile analytics, are being increasingly emphasized to attract consumers, making their shopping experience more coordinated and integrated. To further illustrate the dynamics embedded within offline-to-online marketing integration, a recent example can be seen from Tommy Hilfiger's adoption of 3D goggles in physical stores, allowing consumers to remotely watch its launch show of the autumn collection (Rosenfeld, 2015), which resonates with our discussion on Nike's innovative use of its physical spaces. Online-to-offline marketing integration is also a viable factor in refining/re-shaping the 'total package' of consumers' shopping experiences, as shown in the juxtaposing examples elicited from Ladurée and Naivee. Ladurée is able to seamlessly connect its social media promotional campaigns with its visually enthralling merchandising display, while Naivee is unable to replicate the same success in its physical stores (with its rather traditional and simplistic in-store setting).

Nonetheless, the two examples point to a question that should not be ignored: it seems that only those 'masstige' brands are active in adopting new technologies. In essence, the affordability of cutting-edge technology has not yet reached to an extent where it has become a must for all retail designers. Therefore, the budget of physical retail design and construction is not likely to increase phenomenally for the entire industry; it is still an experimentally optional venture. As Bäckström and Johansson's study (2006) suggests, facilitative layout, comfortable personnel and a satisfactory selection of products are still major constituents of consumers' in-store experiences, showcasing that the addition of digital technologies to physical stores/retail designs are not imperative and considered as 'must have' elements in capturing the attention of consumers.

Even so, the evolution of retail design has far more obvious implications on click-and-mortar designers. As showcased by the vast experience of designers at Glamorous Fashion, the design process includes more than simply displaying product images and describing their features. To make this virtual space really captivating, e-tail designers can experiment with interactive technologies such as using avatars to illustrate the features, and producing augmented values by highlighting the resources and craftsmanship embedded in the products. Furthermore, as the case of Net-a-Porter illustrates, this platform is adaptive to the local market, in which designers' work involves aptly incorporating local elements into the platform instead of a literal translation of the Westernized versions/layouts produced by the respective headquarters of the companies.

However, predicated on the combination of qualitative research methods conducted with GF and Net-a-Porter, the perception is that e-tail designers are required to adapt their creativity to the rapid changing cycles of fashion. Consequently, the designers' creative liberties are constrained by the fast pace of change, coupled with other practical reasons such as the restrictions imposed by budgeting and human resources. In the future, in order for companies such as GF and Net-a-Porter to continue to differentiate themselves (not just from a pricing point of view) and to thrive as an e-tail space within these limitations, there should be a centralized focus on integrating the sales messages with that of their respective online fashion media platforms/online magazines. The aim should be to capture the attention of its target consumers by seamlessly synchronizing/engendering a more consistent presentation of fashion meanings and brand images, building it as a prestigious virtual point-of-sale.

Ultimately, considering both scenarios, it can be seen that as the accessibility of technology advances, the future of the retail industry resides in the integration of 'click' and 'mortar' space. It is observed that fashion companies still prioritize the authentic shopping experiences of its consumers within a retail space, as demonstrated by their tendency to remodel their respective shopping environments through incorporating additional digital technologies, such as 'high tech' mirrors for enhanced 'shopping immersion'. As a result, designers of both spaces are called upon to collaborate, their creativity positioned in a constant dialogue with consumers' preference and choices that are specific to each local market.

References

Abdinnour-Helm, S.F., Chaparro, B.S. and Farmer, S.M. (2005). Using the End-User Computing Satisfaction (EUCS) instrument to measure satisfaction with a web site. *Decision Sciences*, 36(2), pp. 341–364.

The Alibaba phenomenon. (2013). *The Economist* [online]. Available at: http://www.economist.com/news/leaders/21573981-chinas-e-commerce-giant-could-generate-enormous-wealthprovided-countrys-rulers-leave-it [Accessed 10 October 2015].

Bäckström, K. and Johansson, U. (2006). Creating and consuming experiences in retail store environments: Comparing retailer and consumer perspectives. *Journal of Retailing and Consumer Services*, 13(6), pp. 417–430.

Bain & Company. (2015). *Global luxury goods market expected to sustain steady momentum with 2–4 percent real growth in 2015* [online]. Available at: http://www.bain.com/about/press/press-releases/spring-2015-worldwide-luxury-goods-update-press-release.aspx [Accessed June 30 2015].

Ballantine, P.W., Parsons, A. and Comeskey, K. (2015). A conceptual model of the holistic effects of atmospheric cues in fashion retailing. *International Journal of Retail & Distribution Management*, 43(6), pp. 503–517.

Barnett, L. (2012). Online clothes-shopping: Is an avatar the answer? *The Guardian* [online] 29 February. Available at: http://www.theguardian.com/fashion/shortcuts/2012/feb/29/online-clothes-shopping-avatar [Accessed 30 June 2015].

Chiu, H.C., Hsieh, Y.C., Roan, J., Tseng, K.J. and Hsieh, J.K. (2011). The challenge for multichannel services: Cross-channel free-riding behavior. *Electronic Commerce Research and Applications*, 10(2), pp. 268–277.

Crewe, L. (2015). Placing fashion: Art, space, display and the building of luxury fashion markets through retail design. *Progress in Human Geography*, 40(4), pp. 511–529.

D'Arpizio, C. (2014). *Luxury goods worldwide market study winter 2014*. Available at: http://www.bain.com/publications/articles/luxury-goods-worldwide-market-study-winter-2014.aspx [Accessed 30 June 2015].

D'Arpizio, C., Levato, F., Zito, D. and de Montgolfier, J. (2014). *Luxury goods worldwide market study fall-winter 2014: The rise of the borderless consumer*. Available at: http://www.bain.com/publications/articles/luxury-goods-worldwide-market-study-december-2014.aspx [Accessed 01 July 2015].

Dion, D. and Arnould, E. (2011). Retail luxury strategy: Assembling charisma through art and magic. *Journal of Retailing*, 87(4), pp. 502–520.

Favero, M.B. and Alvarez, F.J. (2013). Integrated communication in retail fashion: A study of integration between advertising and communication at the point of sale. *Journal of Arts and Humanities*, 2(2), pp. 25–37.

Fits.me. (2013). *Fits.me signs five new retailers and brands*. Available at: http://fits.me/fits-me-signs-five-new-retailers-and-brands/ [Accessed 01 July 2015].

From Bazaar to Bonanza (2014). *The Economist* [online]. Available at: http://www.economist.com/news/business/21601869-chinas-e-commerce-giant-has-just-revealed-details-its-long-awaited-flotation-america-it [Accessed 25 October 2016].

Gefen, D. and Straub, D.W. (2004). Consumer trust in B2C e-Commerce and the importance of social presence: Experiments in e-Products and e-Services. *Omega*, 32(6), pp. 407–424.

Groeber, B. (2015). Take a look into the future of retail stores. *China Daily Asia* [online] 17 February. Available at: http://www.chinadailyasia.com/opinion/2015-02/17/content_15229054.html [Accessed 03 July 2015].

Groß, M. (2015). Mobile shopping: A classification framework and literature review. *International Journal of Retail & Distribution Management*, 43(3), pp. 221–241.

Hall, R. and van den Broek, D. (2011). Aestheticising retail workers: Orientations of aesthetic labour in Australian fashion retail. *Economic and Industrial Democracy*, 33(1), pp. 85–102.

Hamermesh, D.S. and Biddle, J.E. (1994). Beauty and the labour market. *The American Economic Review*, 84(5), pp. 1174–1194.

Hernández, B., Jiménez, J. and Martín, M.J. (2009). Key website factors in e-business strategy. *International Journal of Information Management*, 29(5), pp. 362–371.

Hou, J.-L. and Chen, T.-G. (2011). An RFID-based shopping service system for retailers. *Advanced Engineering Informatics*, 25(1), pp. 103–115.

Karaatli, G., Ma, J. and Suntornpithug, N. (2010). Investigating mobile services' impact on consumer shopping experience and consumer decision-making. *International Journal of Mobile Marketing*, 5(2), pp. 75–86.

Kawamura, T., Nagano, S., Inaba, M. and Mizoguchi, Y. (2008). WOM Scouter: Mobile service for reputation extraction from weblogs. *International Journal of Metadata, Semantics and Ontologies*, 3(2), pp. 132–141.

Keeling, K., McGoldrick, P. and Beatty, S. (2010). Avatars as salespeople: Communication style, trust, and intentions. *Journal of Business Research*, 63(8), pp. 793–800.

Khurana, A. (n.d.) The Retail Industry Is Turning Into a Virtual Marketplace. *Ecommerce.about.com*. Retrieved from http://ecommerce.about.com/od/ecommerce-trends-and-issues/virtual-marketplace.

Kuchler, H. (2015, May 17). Kering sues Alibaba over sales of counterfeit goods. *Financial Times*. Retrieved from http://www.ft.com/cms/s/0/f305b826-fca9-11e4-800d-00144feabdc0.html#axzz4HxoDICIm.

Kurkovsky, S. and Harihar, K. (2006). Using ubiquitous computing in interactive mobile marketing. *Personal and Ubiquitous Computing*, 10(4), pp. 227–240.

Lea-Greenwood, G. (2013). *Fashion marketing communications*. Hoboken: John Wiley & Sons.

Leopold, C. (2015). Fashion designer makes entire collection using small 3D printers. *Digital Journal* [online] 27 July. Available at: http://www.digitaljournal.com/life/lifestyle/fashion-designer-makes-entire-collection-using-small-3d-printers/article/439487 [Accessed 19 August 2015].

Lindgren, T. (2013). Fashion system Shanghai: The advent of a new gatekeeper. In J.L. Foltyn and R. Fisher (Ed.), *Proceedings of 5th Global Conference: Fashion – Exploring Critical Issues*. Oxford: Inter-Disciplinary.Net, pp. 1–8.

Lipovetsky, G. (2007). Modern and postmodern luxury. In: J. Teunissen and J. Brandt (Ed.), *Fashion & accessories*. Arnhem: Terra Press, pp. 28–41.

Magrath, V. and McCormick, H. (2013). Branding design elements of mobile fashion retail apps. *Journal of Fashion Marketing and Management: An International Journal*, 17(1), pp. 98–114.

Manlow, V. and Nobbs, K. (2013). Form and function of luxury flagships: An international exploratory study of the meaning of the flagship store for managers and customers. *Journal of Fashion Marketing and Management: An International Journal*, 17(1), pp. 49–64.

Masten, D.L. and Plowman, T.M. (2003). Digital ethnography: The next wave in understanding the consumer experience. *Design Management Journal (Former Series)*, 14(2), pp. 75–81.

McCormick, H. and Livett, C. (2012). Analysing the influence of the presentation of fashion garments on young consumers' online behaviour. *Journal of Fashion Marketing and Management: An International Journal*, 16(1), pp. 21–41.

Mull, I., Wyss, J., Moon, E. and Lee, S.E. (2015). An exploratory study of using 3D avatars as online salespeople: The effect of avatar type on credibility, homophily, attractiveness and intention to interact. *Journal of Fashion Marketing and Management*, 19(2), pp. 154–168.

Nike, Inc. (2014a). *Nike presents NikeLab*. Available at: http://news.nike.com/news/nike-presents-nikelab [Accessed 25 August 2015].

Nike, Inc. (2014b). *Nike women's-only store with premium on-site sports experience opens in Shanghai*. Available at: http://news.nike.com/news/nike-women-s-only-store-with-premium-on-site-sports-experience-opens-in-shanghai [Accessed 25 August 2015].

Nobbs, K., Moore, C.M. and Sheridan, M. (2012). The flagship format within the luxury fashion market. *International Journal of Retail & Distribution Management*, 40(12), pp. 920–934.

Oldenburg, R. (1999). *The great good place*. New York: Marlowe & Company.

Petermans, A., Janssens, W. and Van Cleempoel, K. (2013). A holistic framework for conceptualizing customer experiences in retail environments. *International Journal of Design*, 7(2), pp. 1–18.

Pettinger, L. (2004). Brand culture and branded workers: Service work and aesthetic labour in fashion retail. *Consumption Markets & Culture*, 7(2), pp. 165–184.

Pine, J.B. and Gilmore, J.H. (1999). *The experience economy*. Boston: Harvard Business School Press.

Potvin, J. (2009). *The places and spaces of fashion, 1800–2007*. London: Routledge.

Retail Marketing. (2015). *Marketing magazine* [online]. Available at: http://www.marketing-interactive.com/retail-marketing/hk/ [Accessed 10 October 2015].

Roberts, A. (2015). *Burberry demand lower Hong Kong rents as market Wilts Bloomberg business* [online] (Last updated 10.05 PM on 28th July 2015). Available at: http://www.businessoffashion.com/articles/news-analysis/gucci-burberry-demand-lower-hong-kong-rents-as-market-wilts [Accessed on 12 October 2015].

Rosenfeld, L. (2015). *Tommy Hilfiger makes virtual reality a part of the shopping experience* in Tech Times October 20. Available at: http://www.techtimes.com/articles/97500/20151020/tommy-hilfiger-makes-virtua l-reality-a-part-of-the-shopping-experience.htm

Sackrider, F., Guidé, G. and Hervé, D. (2009). Entre vitrinas: distribuição e visual merchandising na moda. *São Paulo: Editora Senac São Paulo*.

Scarpi, D., Pizzi, G. and Visentin, M. (2014). Shopping for fun or shopping to buy: Is it different online and offline? *Journal of Retailing and Consumer Services*, 21(3), pp. 258–267.

Shukla, P. (2015). *A closer look at luxury consumption in Asia: Luxury society* [online]. Available at: http://luxurysociety.com/articles/2015/07/a-closer-look-at-luxury-consumption-in-asia [Accessed 25 August 2015].

Silverstein, J.M. and Fiske, N. (2003). *Luxury for the masses: Harvard business review* [online]. Available at: https://hbr.org/2003/04/luxury-for-the-masses

Slåtten, T., Mehmetoglu, M., Svensson, G. and Sværi, S. (2009). Atmospheric experiences that emotionally touch customers: a case study from a winter park. *Managing Service Quality: An International Journal*, 19(6), 721–746.

Spiess, L. and Waring, P. (2005). Aesthetic labour, cost minimisation and the labour process in the Asia Pacific airline industry. *Employee Relations*, 27(2), pp. 193–207.

Stephens, D. (2015). *The future of retail is the end of wholesale: The business of fashion* [online]. Available at: http://www.businessoffashion.com/articles/opinion/future-retail-end-wholesale [Accessed 26 August 2015].

Taobao. (2013). *Taobao's "Singles' Day" promotional campaign in China and Taiwan*. Retrieved from https://anntw.com/articles/20131110-_5ae.

Truong, Y., McColl, R. and Kitchen, P.J. (2009). New luxury brand positioning and the emergence of masstige brands. *Journal of Brand Management*, 16(5), pp. 375–382.

Tse, H.L.T. (2015). An ethnographic study of glocal fashion communication in Hong Kong and Greater China. *International Journal of Fashion Studies*, 2(2), pp. 245–266.

Tse, H.L.T. and Wright, L.T. (2014). Luxury brands and deriving fashion meanings in a media context in Hong Kong. In G. Atwal & D. Bryson (Eds.), *Luxury Brands In Emerging Markets* (pp. 155–164). Hampshire: Palgrave Macmillan.

Turns to e-commerce as brick-and-mortar retail slows. (2015) *Jing Daily, Dalian Wanda*. [online] 17 August. Available at: http://jingdaily.us1.list-manage.com/track/click?u=555a04b48e1f20aecf5db4d6 1&id=f671a1d6d1&e=31e04bb349 [Accessed 10 October 2015].

Unger, B. (2014, December 13). Exclusively for everybody. *The Economist*. Retrieved from http://www.economist.com/news/special-report/21635761-modern-luxury-industry-rests-paradoxbut-thriving-nonetheless-says-brook.

Van der Heijden, H. (2006). Mobile decision support for in-store purchase decisions. *Decision Support Systems*, 42(2), pp. 656–663.

Van der Heijden, H. and Sørensen, L.S. (2005). Observations on the use of mobile decision aids for consumer decision making. *International Journal of Management and Decision Making*, 6(1), pp. 5–15.

Von Maltzahn, C.F. (2015). *The long way home: Luxury and its discontents*. Paper presented to Fashion Tales 2015. Università Cattolica del Sacro Cuore, Milan, 18–20 June.

Walter, F.E., Battiston, S., Yildirim, M. and Schweitzer, F. (2012). Moving recommender systems from online commerce to retail stores. *Information Systems and e-Business Management*, 10(3), pp. 367–393.

Wang, H.H. (2012). *Five new trends of Chinese consumers: Forbes* [online]. Available at: http://www.forbes.com/sites/helenwang/2012/12/17/five-new-trends-of-chinese-consumers/

Wang, L.C. and Fodness, D. (2010). Can avatars enhance consumer trust and emotion in online retail sales? *International Journal of Electronic Marketing and Retailing*, 3(4), pp. 341–362.

Warhurst, C. and Nickson, D. (2007). Employee experience of aesthetic labour in retail and hospitality. *Work, Employment and Society*, 21(1), pp. 103–120.

Winter, K. (2014, May 21). Every woman's new best friend? Hyper-realistic new virtual mirror lets you to try on clothes at the flick of the wrist and instantly share the images online. *Daily Mail Online*. Retrieved from http://www.dailymail.co.uk/femail/article-2635055/Every-womans-new-best-friend-Hyper-realistic-new-virtual-mirror-lets-try-clothes-flick-wrist.html.

Witz, A., Warhurst, C. and Nickson, D. (2003). The labour of aesthetics and the aesthetics of organization. *Organization*, 10(1), pp. 33–54.

Wong, G.K. and Yu, L. (2003). Consumers' perception of store image of joint venture shopping centres: First-tier versus second-tier cities in China. *Journal of Retailing and Consumer Services*, 10(2), pp. 61–70.

Woodhead, L. (2007). *Shopping, seduction & Mr Selfridge*. London: Profile 2007.

Yang, K. (2010). Determinants of US consumer mobile shopping services adoption: Implications for designing mobile shopping services. *Journal of Consumer Marketing*, 27(3), pp. 262–270.

Yip, T.C., Chan, K. and Poon, E. (2012). Attributes of young consumers' favorite retail shops: A qualitative study. *Journal of Consumer Marketing*, 29(7), pp. 545–552.

7 Heritage, adaptive reuse and regeneration in retail design

Bie Plevoets and Koenraad Van Cleempoel

Working with existing buildings for continued use has become increasingly important in contemporary architectural practice. The reasons for this are multiple, ranging from the need for sustainable development patterns, the current economic climate's need for less costly physical architecture and an ever-increasing awareness of the benefits of retaining our architectural heritage. All of this adds to the importance of what can be called 'adaptive reuse'. Although a widely accepted definition of 'adaptive reuse' seems to be lacking (for an overview, see Plevoets, 2014; Plevoets and Van Cleempoel, 2013), it implies (partly) changing the function and programme of a building, as well as physically adapting the building to new needs and requirements. The term may refer to altering buildings with heritage value – protected or not protected – or to 'ordinary' buildings without historical or architectural value. In what follows, we focus on adaptive reuse of heritage buildings (both protected and non-protected), although several arguments are also applicable to the general building stock.

In historic city centres, adaptive reuse of the existing buildings for retail and other commercial functions is a frequently occurring practice. However, seen from the point-of-view of the retail sector, dealing with historical buildings is not an easy task. Usually there are many stakeholders involved in retail-reuse projects, all with different interests: (governmental) agencies involved in conservation are primarily interested in the preservation of the heritage values of the building, while investors are mainly interested in the revenues of the project. However, reusing heritage for retail can also be an opportunity for both sectors.

In this chapter we elaborate on the challenges and opportunities of using and reusing heritage for retail. We do so through three concepts that underlie today's retail design theory and practise, but which are at the same time at the core of contemporary discussions related to heritage preservation: identity, authenticity, and sustainability. For each concept, we illustrate our argument with examples from practice and relevant literature.

Heritage and identity

Europe's urban and rural landscapes are strongly shaped and characterised by its historical architecture. This physical condition includes countless heritage sites that, in a way, have shaped Europe's identity. Different perhaps than in most other continents, the European landscape has grown historically, building upon structures and sites that have been passed on from one generation to another for centuries, adapting the landscape and its structures and sites to changing social, economic, cultural or political circumstances, and people's needs and desires. This process occurred spontaneously, mostly because of practical and economic reasons – reuse was cheaper and faster than new constructions – and was not directly intended as an act of conservation of cultural heritage. But, nevertheless, this process has created a strong sense of cultural and historical continuity. Based on that, the notion of 'heritage conservation' has been developed in Europe, mainly from the nineteenth century onwards; and also during the twentieth century Europe continued to play a major role in the development of concepts that underlay the theory and practice of heritage conservation worldwide (Choay, 1992; Jokilehto, 1999). In the Burra Charter, conservation is described as 'the processes of looking after a place so as to retain its cultural significance' (ICOMOS Australia, 2013, article 1). Up to the 1990s, the interpretation of 'cultural significance' was limited to tangible aspects – the authentic material evidence – and, as such, the process of conservation allowed only limited change to the building. Since the last decades, however, intangible aspects such as narratives, rituals and uses are considered important heritage values and part of the cultural significance of a place. This resulted in a broadening concept of conservation, which may include

> retention or reintroduction of a use; retention of associations and meanings; maintenance, preservation, restoration, reconstruction, adaptation and interpretation; and [the practice of conservation] will commonly include a combination of more than one of these. Conservation may also include retention of the contribution that related places and related objects make to the cultural significance of a place.
>
> (ICOMOS Australia, 2013, article 14)

Today, the European-built environment has been largely defined by this 'conservational' approach, and new development projects unavoidably have to deal with the present historic fabric. Retailers for instance have no choice but to deal with the existing (historic) context: single shops on primary locations in historical city centres are usually located in historical buildings, while shopping centres and other types of large-scale retail development projects are often located in existing sites which lost their original use (such as former industrial sites) or in which architecture has to be adapted to the existing (historic) context (English Heritage et al., 2005). There are, however, two approaches of dealing with heritage conservation and reuse: on the one hand, there is a problem-based approach in which the historic fabric is seen as a limitation towards the implementation of contemporary retail design; on the other hand there is an opportunity-based approach, in which heritage is used as a way to construct a particular retail branding, or to evoke a unique customer experience.

Within the problem-based approach, the retailer considers the typology and characteristics of the given heritage building or site as a limitation for the implementation of the retail design. In many (European) countries, the practise of conservation is strongly controlled by the government and specific agencies such as English Heritage in United Kingdom, the Commission nationale des monuments historiques in France, or the Agency Immovable Heritage in Flanders. These agencies oversee all works on protected buildings and sites in order to preserve its cultural significance. In practice, this usually results in restrictions towards physical adaptation of the building – for example, as to the creation of store windows and attachment of publicity on the façade of the building, or as to horizontal and vertical circulation and the use of certain materials and finishings in the interior.

In many historical centres, however, commercial development and the process of retail-reuse is already going on for decades. In the past, restriction towards adaptation of the existing fabric was often limited to the exterior of the building – the façade – and as a result the interior structure and interior features have become invaluable from a heritage-point-of-view. Therefore, façadism – the process of demolishing a building but leaving its façade intact for the purpose of a new structure in, around, or behind it (Richards, 1994) – became a frequently occurring practice. Although this approach is in general not supported by conservation policies today, in historical centres where pressure for development becomes stronger, this practice still occurs frequently and is often allowed by local urban planning departments.

Besides a problem-based approach, there is also an opportunity-based approach towards heritage, which considers heritage as a valuable asset, a capital of irreplaceable cultural, social, environmental and economic value (CHCfE Consortium, 2015). Starting from that assumption, some retailers use the historic building in which they are located – its tangible aspects, but also its intangible aspects such as narratives and atmosphere – as a differentiation strategy. In today's society, the purpose of consumption is not merely anymore to satisfy needs or wants but also to construct a social identity (Ogle et al., 2004). Besides the product at sale, an important factor for retail branding is the physical retail environment and the design of the retail space (Kent, 2007). Michel Van Tongeren puts it this way:

> A store environment is the ideal medium for communicating the values of a retail brand with great precision. The consumer can see, experience, touch and smell it; he has chosen to be there at that moment and is therefore highly receptive to it. Which is very different than watching a remote commercial in your own cluttered living room.
>
> (2003)

When consumers visit a store, they immediately make an association between the products sold in the store, their price, the store's 'tone of voice' and ambience, and the retailer's presence and identity. As a result, the retail environment and retail branding cannot be disconnected from one another (Van Tongeren, 2003, 2004). Still, the particular relationship between historic architecture – heritage – and retail design has received only limited attention by scholars so far. Kirby and Kent (2010a) examined the link between retail store architecture and the communication of brand identity through case studies of four food superstores in the UK. They found four strategies, which may be applied to communicate brand identity. However, they did not include reuse of historic buildings as a means for retail branding. In another study Kirby and Kent (2010b) recognize reuse of historic buildings as a means for place branding. Warnaby (2009) investigates the potential for historical architecture to contribute to the experience enjoyed by the retail users of towns and cities, but he finds that, very often, the retail design of the interior and exterior of the store does not incorporate the historic characteristics and features of the surrounding historic fabric; as such, seen from the ground floor, there is little that differentiates these historic districts from similar retail areas elsewhere. Starting from a similar observation, Saglar Onay (2013) studied a number of case studies of antique buildings in Florence of which the ground floor is transformed into a shop. She finds that most problems arise on technical aspects (integrating technical installations such as heating and lighting in an existing historic building) and on aspects of brand identity (incorporating the historical atmosphere of the host space in the retail branding).

Hyllegard et al. (2006) explored the relationship between consumers' identities and their responses to retail design at the Recreational Equipment Incorporated (REI) flagship store in Denver. Although the store was located in a former industrial building, the research's primary focus was on aspects of sustainability and not on historical features. Also Rubessi (2010) has analysed different case studies of retail design in historical buildings within the framework of ecological design. Maclaran and Brown (2005) studied consumer experience in the case study of Powerscourt Townhouse Center, a shopping centre located in a historic building. Their study demonstrated that prioritising commercialization over preservation of the *genius loci* – the spirit of the place – is detrimental to the consumer experience. Building further on that, we analyse how reusing the historic fabric may be an added value for the retailer in the context of retail branding. Therefore, we recognize two different levels on which heritage can make a possible contribution towards retail branding: first, on the level of the individual store located in a historic building; and, second, on an urban level, regenerating larger historical sites or districts into retail areas.

The historic building as a component in constructing a store identity

Instead of focussing on its limitations, some retailers perceive a historical building as a valuable asset and a way to construct a particular store identity. Being located in a historical building may render the offerings more 'authentic' and evoke an emotional experience from the customer. Some brands intentionally look for historical buildings for locating their store.

An example of such a brand is Apple. Indeed, as a brand, Apple has been very successful in constructing a strong identity. Its flagship stores – the so-called Apple Stores – are an important feature in this. Instead of a traditional retail space oriented towards selling goods, Apple Stores are organised as public spaces where people can see, touch and learn about Apple products; the stores are conceived as places for strolling and where people can meet; they are always centrally located in city centres (Gallo, 2012). Whereas in the United States, where Apple Stores were usually built as new constructions incorporating very advanced construction techniques and materials, in Europe the stores are often located in historical buildings; examples are Covent Garden (London) in a former industrial building, The Hague in a nineteenth-century shopping arcade, Opera in Paris in a former bank, and Amsterdam and Kurfürstendamm Berlin, both in a neoclassical listed building. In each of these stores, Apple applied a similar design strategy, which is to restore the historical façade of the building as well as preserve the remaining historical features in the building's interior. However, the newly integrated elements such as staircases, furniture and signing are the same as in any other Apple Store. As such, all stores retain a very characterizing and easily recognizable image.

Another brand that has intentionally looked for unique, existing buildings to locate its stores is the avant-garde fashion line Comme des Garçons. Comme des Garçons is widely credited to have invented the concept of 'guerrilla' or 'pop-up' stores. Guerrilla stores are stores that pop up unannounced, move into an empty building in a large city, transform the space into a trendy store and then disappear again after a few months; different from flagship stores, they are usually off the main shopping street (Dowdy, 2008). The first guerrilla store by Comme des Garçons opened in 2004 in Berlin. In the following years, temporary shops were opened in exocentric, but vibrant, cities such as Krakow, Warsaw, Athens, Cologne, The Hague and Beirut. Unlike the Apple Stores, each of the Comme des Garçons guerrilla stores have an absolutely unique outlook. Rather than disguising a building's former use, they often play it up; they are not 'designed' but rather seemingly

Figure 7.1 Apple Store Opera, Paris

Source: wikicommons, made by Cristian Bortes, free from copyright

thrown together by art students or some such (Dowdy, 2008; Van Cleempoel, 2008). On the guerrilla store website, Comme des Garçons describe their concept as follows:

1   The guerrilla store will last no more than one year in any given location
2   The concept for interior design will be largely equal to the existing space
3   The location will be chosen according to its atmosphere, historical connection, geographical situation away from established commercial areas or some other interesting feature
4   The merchandise will be a mix of all seasons, new and old, clothing and accessories, existing or especially created, from Comme des Garçons' brands and eventually other brands as well
5   The partners will take responsibility for the lease and Comme des Garçons will support the store with the merchandise on a sale or return basis

(Comme des Garçons guerilla store, 2005)

Their store in Cologne (2005–2006) was located in a former butcher's shop – Neffgen – a family-run company established in the 1950s. The atmosphere of the former butcher's shop was completely preserved; even the original name was not removed from the façade. The original butcher's shop fixtures and fittings were used to hang the clothes. In 2008, when the concept of guerrilla stores had been taken over by many other retailers and brands, Comme des Garçons terminated their guerrilla store concept.

The historic district as a retail area: Branding the city

The cultural and physical character of our towns and cities has always been influenced by the commercial activity they accommodated (English Heritage et al., 2005). But the nature of shopping and trading has changed radically in the course of time and consequently influenced the physical retail environment: e.g. demand for bigger shop units, rise of chain stores at the expense of the independent retailer, need for vehicle access for shoppers and servicing and demand for greater security (English Historic Towns Forum, 2008). These requirements present considerable challenges to historic towns. Jokilehto (1985) illustrates the tension between retail development and authentic preservation of historic fabric with the example of the historic town of Lübeck, which could not be accepted to the World Heritage List because too much of its fabric has been lost due to – among other reasons – uncontrolled commercial development. He concludes that in order to avoid unnecessary pressure for change and destruction, it is important to plan the type and scale of commercial and other activities for historic towns in a way that these can be absorbed by the historic structure, with respect for its identity.

But reusing historic buildings for retail may advance the viability of historic centres and as such may stimulate urban regeneration. Kirby and Kent (2010b) state that reuse of the city's architectural heritage can act as part of the city's image and its city branding. They explain that the purpose of city branding is to promote a city for certain activities and in some cases sell parts of the city for living, consuming and productive activities. An often-applied strategy is to orientate the city branding towards reworking, repackaging and re-presenting historical and existing cultural qualities of the city. Murzyn-Kupisz (2013) studied the impact of private commercial investment in historic monuments, and she found that restoration and reuse of heritage buildings proves a crucial impulse to start

Figure 7.2 Comme des Garçons, Cologne (2005–2006)

Source: Kira Bunse, 2005

and inspire regeneration of the village or town centre, and contributes to its 'image' or 'branding'.

An example of a city that differentiates itself through heritage is Łódź, a former industrial city in the centre of Poland, where many industrial sites became abandoned after the textile industry fell down in the 1980s. As the city largely developed through its industries, the city lacked a pre-industrial past. Łódź did not have earlier monuments, and, after the collapse of its industries, the city also needed a revitalisation of its buildings stock and redefinition of its identity (Sowinska-Heim, 2013). In 2006, one of the largest former factories in the city was transformed into a mix of shopping, hospitality, leisure and cultural functions. The project, called Manufaktura, includes the restoration of existing buildings – mainly applying the concept of façadism – as well as new constructions. As there has been a lack of well-organized public space in the centre of Łódź, major attention was given to the creation of a central square. In the years following the opening of the project, other initiatives of adaptive reuse of industrial sites by private investors have been realized in the city centre. Today, Manufaktura strongly contributes to upgrade the image of Łódź within Poland and beyond. The city also explodes this newly created image as a 'brand' for Łódź (Wycichowska, 2008), as a way to attract new investors, tourists and inhabitants. However, as argued by Julia Sowinska-Heim (2013), the project is primarily a commercial project that tells only a positive past; the newly created image is completely artificial and does not correspond in any way with the 'authentic' atmosphere of the nineteenth-century textile factory it refers to.

Authenticity versus Disneyfication

Since the adoption of the World Heritage Convention in 1972, authenticity is used as a way of evaluating the preservation and adaptation of heritage sites (Starn, 2002; Stovel, 2007). Semantically, the word 'authentic' refers to the Greek *authentikòs* (*autòs*, 'myself, the same') and the Latin *auctor* (an originator, authority), and thus to 'original' as opposed to 'copy', 'real' as opposed to 'pretended', 'genuine' as opposed to 'counterfeit' (Jokilehto, 1999). Being authentic is having authority – being trustworthy, credible, convincing, real, genuine or original (Webster, 1986).

The last decennium, authenticity also has become an important marketing strategy in diverse economic sectors such as (heritage) tourism, hospitality, leisure and retail. As competing in today's global market is becoming increasingly difficult since customers often perceive products and services as homogeneous, retailers try to be seen by customers as being original, trustworthy or 'authentic' (Petermans and Van Cleempoel, 2009; Pine and Gilmore, 2007). Locating one's store in a historic building can be a way for retailers to render their store and/or product as being authentic (Plevoets et al., 2010). An example of a historical retail building typology that has received increased interest by retailers and consumers in the context of authenticity is the arcade or *passage*. In different European towns, examples of this building type that date back to the nineteenth century still exist and regained popularity the last two decades as places for shopping and strolling around. In the Galleries Saint-Hubert in Brussels, for example, Belgian retailers and brands occupy several of the stores because they want to present their 'traditional' and 'local' products in this particular 'authentic' retail setting; examples are chocolatier Neuhaus or Delvaux leatherwear. In the Galleria Vittorio Emanuele II in Milan, many Italian fashion brands such as Prada and Versace occupy central locations in the arcade (Plevoets and Van Cleempoel, 2011).

The meaning of authenticity, however, is understood differently within the context of heritage conservation as in marketing and retailing. In the field of heritage conservation, authenticity of a building or site is linked to the values attributed to it. Although the interpretation of these values may differ based on the cultural context in which they are evaluated and may evolve over time, the concept of authenticity is considered to be a 'scientific' and 'objective' criterion for protection, conservation and restoration of heritage (e.g. ICOMOS, 1–6 November 1994; UNESCO, 2008). Contrarily, in the field of marketing, the concept of authenticity is equally linked to values but on a very personal, intuitive and subjective level; offering an authentic customer experience implies appealing to customers' senses, emotions and values with the aim to create personal, intuitive relationships with the specific brand or retailer (Petermans, 2012). In the field of marketing, authenticity is also being used as a true 'means' that retailers employ with the aim to try to differentiate their brand from competitors. However, as the experience of authenticity is personal and subjective, Pine and Gilmore (2007) state that in order to render a brand as authentic, the values communicated by that brand should be consistent on all different levels: its products, services, relationships and (retail) places.

Several studies have explored why and when customers perceive products as 'authentic' versus 'fake' (e.g. Lin and Wang, 2012; Lunardo and Guerinet, 2007; Starr, 2011). However, only a limited number of studies have analysed the authentic experience in relation to the retail space (Maclaran and Brown, 2005; Peñaloza, 2001). In what follows we illustrate different 'degrees' of authenticity and how they can be applied in retail design.

Authenticity: The staged, the faked, the hyperreal, and the simulacrum

Based on these diverging interpretations of the concept, what is considered an 'authentic experience' from a consumer's point-of-view may be seen as inauthentic from a conservator's perspective and vice versa. MacCannell (1973) introduced the term 'staged authenticity' – by other authors later referred to as 'fake authenticity' (e.g. Pine and Gilmore, 2007) – in the context of heritage tourism to appoint to experiences that are arranged in order to give tourists the impression to being able to interact with native people. MacCannell (1973) explains, though, that 'true authenticity' versus 'staged authenticity' are two poles of a continuum, that many nuances and interpretations may exist, and that, besides tourist settings, his theory also could be applied to other domains of social life. Following MacCannell's idea, several authors have developed a classification of authentic experiences in different contexts (e.g. Grayson and Martinec, 2004; Pine and Gilmore, 2007; Plevoets et al., 2010; Timothy and Boyd, 2003).

The differentiation between the 'fake' and the 'real', however, is much older than MacCannell's work, as it can be traced back to Plato's Theory of Ideas which distinguished the true (metaphysical) object and its image, the original and the copy, the model and the simulacrum, the authentic and the inauthentic. Plato's distinction moves between two sorts of images: on the one hand, iconic copies (well-founded images of the Idea, endowed with resemblance, 'modelled' in the Idea itself); and on the other hand, phantasmatic simulacra (insinuations, subversions, which are made without passing through the Idea) (Deleuze, 1983).

The theory on simulacra has been applied by Baudrillard within his critique on consumer society. In contrast with Plato, Baudrillard does not believe in objective reality or truth but only in the individual interpretation of it (Lepers, 2009). According to Baudrillard, we live in the era of simulation, inaugurated by a liquidation of all referentials: the model of the real has no origin or real anymore. It is no longer a question of imitation, or duplication, or even parody. He describes this 'decay of the real' in four steps:

> Whereas representation attempts to absorb simulation by interpreting it a false representation, simulation envelops the whole edifice of representation as itself a simulacrum. Such would be the successive phases of the image:
>
> * It is the reflection of a profound reality
> * It masks and perverts a profound reality
> * It masks the absence of a profound reality
> * It bears no relation to any reality whatever: it is its own pure simulacrum
>
> (Baudrillard, 1994)

In Baudrillard's view, this final phase is supposed to supersede all others; where in the first phase there is still a 'real' to refer to, in the final phase simulation no longer copies anything and reality is replaced by nostalgia which is the plethora of truth, of secondary objectivity, and authenticity (Hegarty, 2004).

Baudrillard argues that in the era of nostalgia, reality is replaced by hyperreality. He refers to Disneyland, among many other examples, as a perfect model of the hyperreal. In the first place, Disneyland is an imaginary world, which ensures the success of the operation, but it is also a social microcosm, a miniaturized pleasure of real America. Disneyland is presented as imaginary in order to make us believe that the rest is real (Baudrillard, 1994). The term 'Disneyfication' – sometimes also called 'Disneyization' – came into use to describe hyperreal places created to transform cultural capital in economic capital (Harris, 2004), and has been applied in heritage tourism and retail design. Characteristic to 'Disneyficated' places or sites is the fact that they are 'themed' around one particular narrative, instead of presenting its various layers or narratives (Bryman, 2004).

An example of such a Disneyficated 'heritage site' is Bataviastad, an outlet shopping village in the Netherlands, created as a theme park around the shipyard of the seventeenth-century vessel 'Batavia'. The design of Bataviastad is conceived as a reconstructed fortified town; aesthetically the village is a pastiche of historicised architectural elements inspired partly on Marken Island and partly on colonial architecture from the Caribbean where the original ship Batavia used to sail to (Groenendijk and Vollaard, 2006). Next to the fashion outlet there is the Batavia Yard Museum where visitors can go on-board on the 'authentic reconstruction' of the ship Batavia (Bataviastad, 2015). Although Bataviastad is definitely 'inauthentic' or 'fake' from a heritage point-of-view, it might nonetheless generate an authentic customer experience as the notion of authenticity in that sense is not objective but personal and individual. Indeed, even if consumers do know that the visited site is only an 'imagined', 'simulated' or 'Disneyfied' world, as shown by Grayson and Martinec (2004), this does not necessarily render their experience less authentic.

The simulacrum as an aemulatio of the original: An opportunity for retail design?

In his article 'Plato and the Simulacrum', Deleuze takes the theory on simulacra even further than Baudrillard (Deleuze, 1983). He starts from a similar definition of simulacrum as Baudrillard, but he undermines the very distinction between copy and model. In Deleuze's view, the simulacrum is not a degraded copy; rather it contains a positive power which negates both original and copy, both model and reproduction; the simulation is a process that produces the real. Deleuze describes the era of simulation as the 'overthrow of Platonism', which means to raise up simulacra, to assert their rights over icons or copies.

In the context of heritage conservation and restoration, the term simulacrum has often been used to point to restoration works that are not based on solid evidence but that rely on an impression or an idea of the original architecture or style (e.g. Brilliant, 2011; Hodges, 2009; Labadi, 2010; Mack, 2011; Scott, 2008; Theodoraki et al., 2009). A heavily criticized project in that sense is Viollet-le-Duc's restoration and reconstruction of the fortification of Carcassonne as it would be based on assumptions of the architect rather than on scientifically obtained evidence (e.g. Brilliant, 2011). However, in the book *Heritage and Globalisation*, Labadi (2010) states that, based on the definition given by Baudrillard, in practice all works of restoration are in fact a simulacrum; historic buildings, sites and towns are hardly ever 'frozen' in time but are subject to their social, economic and political context. As such it is impossible to bring back the building to its original condition. Hodges (2009) adds to that that artefacts restored or reconstructed as a 'simulacrum of an imagined former state', although not being authentic in a material way, have the potential of showing other aspects of authenticity such as, for example, craftsmanship. His approach corresponds to Deleuze's approach of the simulacrum holding a positive power in contemporary society.

In his book *On Altering Architecture*, Fred Scott (2008) pleads for a break regarding the taboo of copying that currently exists in relation to heritage conservation. He argues that in other art forms such as music and painting, copying has long been considered a serious activity; like the composer or the painter, the designer may find a source of sustained inspiration through the act of 'copying'. Throughout history, and during the Renaissance period in particular, imitation or copying of both nature and the Old Masters was highly valued in the fields of literature and art, and the particular relationship between the model and the copy has been subject of much philosophical and artistic debate. Building further on Scott's concept of copying and improving as a valuable strategy for adaptive reuse, we have introduced the concept of *aemulatio* (Plevoets and Van Cleempoel, 2014). *Aemulatio* is a concept from Renaissance art theory to refer to a particular type of copying that has been used in literature and visual arts and that aims at improving its model, rather than duplicating or interpreting it. In the context of adaptive reuse, we have used this term to describe projects that do not merely reconstruct or 'copy' the original features of the building but that instead try to surpass the original aesthetically as well as functionally, and as such create an *aemulatio* of the original host space.

An example of such a project is The Hague's Raad Van State (*Council of State*) by design office Merkx+Girod. Instead of restoring the original interior of the building or introducing a contemporary interior, the new interior attempts to *surpass* the original aesthetically as well as functionally, and as such creates an *aemulatio* of its model. The Empire style of the ballroom inspired the designers to find contemporary solutions to evoke the same luxurious and sophisticated atmosphere. The chandeliers, as with all other lighting fixtures, are customized for this room; they are composed of glass beads, some of which contain small slices of gold in order to produce a brilliant light. The columns in *stucco antico*, the gold leaf on the *stucco* of the ceiling, and the preservation of the symmetrically placed mirrors in the room all contribute to the brilliant atmosphere. Several of these features were created in collaboration with artists and craftspeople.

This approach, however, is new to the field of adaptive reuse and conservation, and examples of projects that create an aemulatio through the process of adaptive reuse are scarce and usually linked to cultural programmes. But the concept might hold a lot of potential for the retail design discipline as it aims to preserve the buildings' 'atmosphere' rather than their material features, and as such is strongly directed towards an 'authentic experience' of the host space on an individual level.

Sustainable retail design

In Europe, the process of adaptive reuse is closely linked to heritage preservation and revitalisation of historical centres. However, besides a method for dealing with heritage buildings, adaptive reuse is also a valuable instrument for sustainable development. In that sense, adaptive reuse becomes a discipline of interest not only in a European context but also in a global perspective. As demolition and construction are by far the largest producers of waste – in the UK, 24 per cent of the total waste material (Clark, 2008) – reducing waste is vital for creating environmentally responsible buildings and interiors. Reusing existing buildings is intrinsically respectful towards the environment because the amount of resources needed for reuse is far less than those needed for new constructions. Moreover, when the existing building is historically or architecturally significant, it provides a link to our cultural and collective memory (Brooker and Stone, 2008). As adaptive reuse is considered highly sustainable – environmentally and socially – a first step towards sustainable retail design is reusing an abandoned historic building.

What is sustainable design?

The word 'sustainable' refers to the Latin *sustinere* (*tenere*, 'to hold'; and *sus*, 'up'), or sustainable means 'to be maintained', 'endured' (Webster, 1986). Today, sustainability has often been approached as being ecologically responsible or 'being green' (Cassidy et al., 2003; Public Architecture, 2010; USGBC, 2010; Yudelson, 2009). Douglas (2006), however, makes a distinction between 'sustainable construction' and 'sustainable development'. Sustainable construction is concerned with minimizing construction waste and pollution, saving energy, increasing the use of recycled and locally produced materials and relying less on toxic chemicals. Sustainable development deals with urban, regional and local issues such as development densities, (public) transport and land-use. It includes social planning issues such as creating workplaces and housing near each other to reduce waste and minimize transport problems. In an ideal situation, 'sustainable design' covers both approaches – it implies sustainable construction including efforts for being green, taking into account sustainable development aspects such as urban planning and regional identity.

However, the definition adopted by the Brundtland Report that sustainable development 'implies meeting the needs of the present without compromising the ability of future generations' (United Nations, 1987, p. 1) covers a much broader interpretation of the term including social and economic issues. In *The Philosophy of Sustainable Design*, McLennan (2004) says:

> A lot of buildings and building products get designated green or sustainable because they contain a few features that lower their environmental impact to some degree. Sustainable design is not about features. . . . [Instead] Sustainable Design is a design philosophy that seeks to maximize the quality of the built environment, while minimizing or eliminating negative impact in the natural environment.

He argues that as the word 'sustainable' means 'to be maintained', it does not necessarily imply the need to change the way wherein we relate to the natural world. He believes that instead of 'sustainable design', 'restorative design' would better cover its meaning. In that sense, the most sustainable buildings are those that have been designed decades, or even centuries, ago, but which are still in use today without having encountered major alterations to their physical structure.

Manzini (2012) takes the discussion even a step further. He argues that only through a radical social innovation can we move towards a more sustainable society. Where design has in the past been part of the problem – mass-produced products that were intended for rapid consumption – it might become part of the solution as design holds the power to change the way in which people live and interact with their surroundings. Sustainable design in that sense could be a catalyst for changing the actions of different social actors in a more sustainable direction.

The tension between sustainable design and retail design

Reducing waste is vital for creating environmentally responsible buildings and interiors. Even more than architecture, interior architecture (and, in particular, retail design) is often seen as temporary as it anticipates current fashion and personal taste. Indeed, many interiors have a very short lifespan, ranging from a few days for scenografic installations to a few years for retail, to one or two decades for domestic interiors (Douglas, 2006). As a consequence, there is a strong tension between interior architecture and sustainable design (Tucker, 2015). In the retail sector, this tension seems to be most striking; retail is easily associated with patterns of mass consumption and increased ecological footprint as a larger share of the world's environmental problem is caused by individual and aggregate increases in human consumption (Maté, 2013; Schaefer and Crane, 2005). On a product level, efforts have been made towards the use of environmentally responsible materials for producing and packaging of products at sale (Cha, 2001; Maté, 2013), but, to stay competitive and appealing to customers, many retail interiors are being updated on a regular basis. This rapid change of interiors, however, produces tons of construction waste.

In order to reduce construction materials, and consequently the proportion of waste, retailers and retail designers started to work with reused materials to furnish, or even to construct, their stores. An example is the Third Wave Kiosk on the coastline of Torquay, Australia. The kiosk is not located in a retail area but needed to be integrated in the landscape of the coastline. Therefore, the designers Hobba Architects chose a material with a strong patina for the construction of the kiosk – recycled sheet piles typically used for seawall, bridge and pier construction – so that it seems to merge with the surrounding landscape. But also the guerilla stores by Comme des Garçons (see the discussion earlier in this chapter) are an example in this respect, as they usually add almost nothing to the existing building, except for some reclaimed materials from second-hand shops or garbage dumps.

Using recycled or reclaimed waste materials for retail design will not be sufficient to make the retail (design) sector truly sustainable. In a recent publication, Tucker (2015) pleas for a stronger link between interior architecture and sustainable design, whereby it should be self-evident for designers to get inspired by the genius loci of a particular architectural space at a particular location, and work generously with the present situation. In her view, history can inform and inspire designers in what they do today.

The last decade, several rating systems have been developed in order to evaluate the design of buildings and interiors as to their performance on sustainability. Today, the two leading certification systems are Leadership in Energy and Environmental Design (LEED), with 72,000 certified buildings, and Building Research Establishment Environmental

Figure 7.3 Third Wave Kiosk, Torquay

Assessment Method (BREEAM), with 425,000 certificated buildings (BREEAM, 2015; Green Building Council, 2015). Both have developed a certification system for new constructions as well as for the redesign of existing buildings in order to help a growing number of owners and tenants in defining strategies for acting sustainable. Both systems developed a quantitative analysis to attach a score to a particular project.

In 2010, 'LEED for Retail certification system' was introduced to address the unique challenges faced by the retail industry. Within LEED, there are in fact two – slightly – different certification systems specifically focussing on Retail: one for New Construction and another for Commercial Interiors. Both present six categories to measure how environmentally friendly a retail building or interior is (USGBC, 2010):

1   sustainable sites
2   water efficiency
3   energy and atmosphere
4   materials and resources
5   indoor environmental quality
6   innovation in design

Each category is again subdivided in a number of credits with an attached score. The total sum of credits in each category gives a score. BREEAM does not have a certification system for retail programmes in particular but thus also differentiates between 'BREEAM In-Use' for assessing the renovation of existing buildings and 'BREEAM New Construction' (BREEAM, 2013). The rating system and analysed categories are very similar to the LEED certifications.

For the LEED system, building reuse is only mentioned in one category of both lists (materials and resources). In the 'Commercial Interior' list, it accounts for 1 credit out of 110 credits in total; in the 'New Construction' it is mentioned twice for a maximum of 4 credits out of 110 (USGBC, 2010). We believe, however, that this is too limited and that adaptive reuse can contribute stronger to sustainable retail design, not only in an ecological way but also in an economic and sociological way by including aspects such as community involvement, social employment programmes, and expected and actual lifetime of the building and its interior.

Adaptive reuse as a strategy for sustainable design

Although these certification systems are very useful in stimulating sustainable design, Alan Durning (1999) explains that the only efficient measure for creating an environmentally friendly society would be a shift towards what he calls 'post-consumer lifestyle'. Herewith, he means that we have enough material comforts, but we should try to make them last longer. His idea is not only relevant on product level, but also with regards to the physical environment. Except for the recycling of scrapped materials and products, adaptive reuse of existing buildings is another way to work on such a 'post-consumer lifestyle'.

One of the most famous and iconic examples of adaptive reuse of a heritage building for retail is probably the bookshop Dominicanen in Maastricht (The Netherlands) – fomerly Selexyz Dominicanen. The project, which involved the transformation of a Medieval Gothic church into a bookshop, was widely published in national and international press and was even proclaimed as the 'most beautiful bookshop in the world' by the Guardian in 2008 (Dodson, 2008). The bookshop opened in 2006, and, up to now, only very limited changes have been made to its retail design. In contrast with the traditional notion of retail design being very fashionable and rapidly out-dated, in this particular case there seems no need to change the store's interior as the iconic design of the building has become part of the retailer's image or branding.

English Heritage takes the idea of adaptive reuse of heritage as a strategy for sustainable design even one step further. They state:

> The re-use and adaptation of heritage assets is at the heart of sustainable development. Not only does re-use lessen the amount of energy expended on new development, but heritage can be used to boost local economies, attract investment, highlight local distinctiveness and add value to property in an area.
>
> (English Heritage et al., 2004)

The above-described case of Manufaktura in Łódź is a clear example of the commercial reuse of heritage that generated a boost for local economy and development. Yet historic buildings often perform poorly in terms of energy efficiency and, as such, are not invariably beneficial in ecological terms. This causes particular technical challenges to architects, interior architects and engineers dealing with adaptive reuse, which has led to the development of extended theories and studies on technical aspects of adaptive reuse.

Generosity and sustainable design: An intrinsic relationship

Contrary to the project of Manufaktura that involved major remodelling works on existing buildings and several new constructions on the site, the ultimate sustainable interiors are those that have survived the course of time and remained unchanged since their creation. One example is Adolf Loos's (1870–1933) design in 1910–13 for Knize, one of the world's leading labels for stylish menswear at the time, in Vienna (Austria). The storefront is rather narrow and is made from black Swedish granite with an entrance door and display window worked in fine cherry wood. The actual store is surprisingly spatial, with an extension on the first floor. Characteristic interior features are the dark oak panelling, the glass display cases, a brick fireplace, oriental carpets, and English leather armchairs. The Knize store is preserved in its original state and is still used today. In addition to this first store, Loos also designed stores for Knize in Karlsbad (1921), Berlin (1927), and Paris (1927–28), but they were not preserved (Sarnitz, 2003).

The example of Knize, however, is a rather unique one. Usually these kinds of interiors change as well as the people that use them. Nevertheless, some buildings enjoy the intrinsic ability to easily host functions other than the ones for which they were originally built. Such buildings can be reused, without the need for major adaptation works. The term 'host space', introduced by Brooker and Stone (2004) and later adopted by Scott (2008), refers to the generous quality of a given building, which is open to 'host' new functions and users. Such 'generous buildings' are exemplary for sustainable design and do exist within the field of retail design. The above-described nineteenth-century shopping arcades that are still in use today are a clear example. Another example is the former Chemiserie Niguet in Brussels (Belgium), designed by the art nouveau architect Paul Hankar (1858–1901) in the late nineteenth century. Today, the store is used by Daniel Ost, a floral artist and sculptor. He had the building restored in all its details, not only the façade and the shop front but also the interior features (Heymans, 2006). Nature as inspiration is one of the main characteristics of art nouveau, which resulted in curved lines and flower and plant decoration; as such, the historic architecture and interior fits perfectly with the creations of Daniel Ost.

As designers – planner, architect or interior architect – we should try to create buildings and places that have generosity as an intrinsic characteristic, not only related to the field of retail design, but all fields of contemporary design practice.

Conclusion

Retailers have often applied a problem-based approach in dealing with heritage buildings. However, an opportunity-based approach holds much potential for different types of retailers and retail designers – from small independent shops to large shopping centres or flagship stores by international brands.

One of the primary goals of heritage preservation is to transfer the identity of a particular place or community to the next generations. The buildings that we have inherited from the generations before us are indeed endowed with tangible (e.g. materials, typologies, crafts) and intangible references (e.g. narratives, and atmospheres) of our collective, and sometimes also personal, memory. As a retailer, working with heritage might in that sense be an opportunity to establish a brand or store identity that merges with a particular building or site. This can be performed in a general sense, such as in the case of Apple Stores, whereby the historical structure and façade of a building is reused and incorporated into one's retail design. But it can also be in a very specific way, such as in the case of the guerrilla stores of Comme des Garçons, which often reuse the complete host setting 'as found' and seem to add no 'retail design' at all. Furthermore, next to the level of the single building, reusing heritage for retail can also contribute to the branding of the city as a whole, as for example in Łódz (Poland). For towns or regions without a historical centre, a heritage setting is sometimes staged or faked in order to create an 'authentic customer experience'. Examples within the field of leisure design are theme parks or themed restaurants; examples from retail design are retail outlet centres. This strategy of 'faking' a historical setting for commercial interests was first applied outside of Europe, in the United States and later in Asia, but is now occasionally applied in a European context as well. Indeed, a 'hyperreal' heritage setting does not bring on the same difficulties and limitations as a 'real' heritage setting.

Where since the 1990s retail design has been focused on offering memorable, 'spectacular' experiences to customers, in the last decade there has been a shift towards experiences that are less spectacular at first sight but that are instead deeper, more 'authentic'. As such, authenticity seems to have become the new benchmark for branding and retail design. Working with heritage, and heritage buildings in particular, is an excellent opportunity to create or strengthen an 'authentic' retail image. However, as authenticity in retail design is very often borrowed or constructed, the offered experience is often 'staged' or 'fake'. The risk for Disneyfication of the heritage site, but also of the retail image and branding, is high because often only one (positive) narrative about the site and its history is told. Outlet centres, such as Bataviastad, are an extreme example in that sense as they are often built up as theme parks, but the borders between the authentic and the fake are becoming more and more blurred, not only in the retail sector but also in the heritage sector. This, however, should not necessarily be seen as a negative evolution. The Renaissance concept of *aemulatio* shows that copying, or improving the existing, can be considered a valuable strategy for dealing with heritage buildings. Although most examples of this approach towards adaptive reuse of heritage exist in the cultural sector, we believe that the concept of *aemulatio* can be an opportunity for the retail sector as well, as this approach is focused on experiencing the building. Contrary to Disneyfication that usually tells and highlights only one narrative or heritage layer, *aemulatio* is multi-layered and may incorporate different values and layers of the heritage building or site.

Sustainability is today a very important issue in all aspects of design, and society at large. There are good individual examples of retail design that are increasingly sustainable from an ecological point of view, but there remains a strong tension between sustainability and retail design. This can be explained to a large extent via the presence of a consumer society in many Western countries, and the enormous waste of materials and goods that is brought about with the construction of many rapidly altering retail design projects that are present in the retail market via retailers' and designers' efforts to answer a particular call from large proportions of today's consumer public. On the level of retail design, we believe that we should move towards retail designs that are less temporal and that can be used for a longer time span. We therefore introduced the concept of generosity in (re) design of buildings and interiors. Examples of such 'generous' retail designs are conserved today in contemporary used nineteenth-century shopping arcades, department stores and boutiques. Their quality of design, materials, construction and atmosphere seems to be timeless and (re)usable for many different generations and purposes. Such design, that has this quality of generosity, may be an inspiration for contemporary retailers and retail designers not to make fashionable and quickly renewable retail designs but instead to strive to create stores and interiors that surpass the passage of time and remain interesting for retailers and consumers for the next several generations.

References

Bataviastad. (2015). *Bataviastad Fashion Outlet* [Online]. Available: http://www.bataviastad.nl/ [Accessed 7 November 2015].

Baudrillard, J. (1994). *Simulacra and Simulation*. Ann Arbor: The University of Michigan. Originally published as Simulacres et Simulation (Edition Galilee, 1981).

BREEAM. (2013). *BREEAM In-Use* [Online]. Available: http://www.breeam.org/page.jsp?id=360 [Accessed 7 November 2015].

BREEAM. (2015). Available: http://www.breeam.com/ [Accessed 7 November 2015].

Brilliant, R. (2011). Authenticity and alienation. *In:* Brilliant, R. & Kinney, D. (eds.) *Reuse Value: Spolia and Appropriation in Art and Architecture from Constantine to Sherrie Levine*. Surrey: Ashgate Publishing Limited.

Brooker, G. & Stone, S. (2004). *Re-readings: Interior Architecture and the Design Principles of Remodelling Existing Buildings*. London: RIBA Enterprises.

Brooker, G. & Stone, S. (2008). *Context + Environment*. Lausanne: AVA Publishing SA.

Bryman, A. (2004). *The Disneyization of Society*. Thousand Oaks: Sage.

Cassidy, R., Wright, G., Flynn, L., Barista, D., Zissman, M., Richards, M., Popp, D., Nigh, L. & James, B. (2003). White Paper on Sustainability. *Building Design and Construction,* November 2003. Available: http://archive.epa.gov/greenbuilding/web/pdf/bdcwhitepaperr2.pdf [Accessed 7 November 2015].

Cha, T. (2001). Ecologically correct. *In:* Chung, C.J., Inaba, J., Koolhaas, R. & Leong, S.T. (eds.) *Harvard Design School Guide to Shopping*. Köln: Taschen.

CHCfE Consortium. (2015). Cultural Heritage Counts for Europe. *Krakow*. Available: http://www.encatc.org/culturalheritagecountsforeurope/outcomes/ [Accessed 7 November 2015].

Choay, F. (1992). *L'allégorie du patrimoine*. Paris: Seuil.

Clark, K. (2008). Only connect – sustainable development and cultural heritage. *In:* Fairclough, G., Harrison, R., Schofield, J. & Jameson, J.H. (eds.) *The Heritage Reader*. London and New York: Routledge.

Comme des Garçons guerilla store. (2005). *Info.* Available: http://www.guerrilla-store-cologne.com/thestore/# [Accessed 7 November 2015].

Deleuze, G. (1983). Plato and the Simulacrum. *October,* 27(Winter 1983), pp. 45–56.

Dodson, S. (2008). Top Shelves. *The Guardian.* Available: http://www.theguardian.com/books/2008/jan/11/bestukbookshops [Accessed 7 November 2015].

Douglas, J. (2006). *Building Adaptation.* Oxford: Elsevier.

Dowdy, C. (2008). *One-Off Independent Retail Design.* London: Laurence King Publishing.

English Heritage, English Historic Towns Forum & Planning Advisory Service. (2005). *Retail Development in Historic Areas.* London: English Heritage.

English Heritage, RICS, British Property Federation & Drivers Jonas. (2004). *Heritage Works: The Use of Historic Buildings in Regeneration. A Toolkit of Good Practice.* London: English Heritage.

English Historic Towns Forum. (2008). *Focus on Retail.* Bristol: English Historic Towns Forum.

Gallo, C. (2012). *The Apple Experience: Secrets to Building Insanely Great Customer Loyalty, McGraw Hill Professional.* New York: McGraw Hill.

Grayson, K. & Martinec, R. (2004). Consumer perceptions of iconicity and indexicality and their influence on assessment of authentic market offerings. *Journal of Consumer Research,* 31(September), pp. 296–312.

Green Building Council. (2015). *This is Leed.* Available: http://leed.usgbc.org/leed.html?gclid=CPjw8pT5_cgCFSgXwwodyYoCQA [Accessed 7 November 2015].

Groenendijk, P. & Vollaard, P. (2006). *Architectuurgids Nederland 1900–2000.* Rotterdam: 010 Publishers.

Harris, D. (2004). *Key Concepts in Leisure Studies.* London: Sage.

Hegarty, P. (2004). *Jean Baudrillard Live Theory.* London and New York: Continuum.

Heymans, V. (2006). Een nieuw pak voor de oude hemdenwinkel. *Monumenten, Landschappen & Archeologie,* 25/4(juli-augustus), pp. 10–26.

Hodges, M. (2009). Disciplining memory: Heritage tourism and the temporalisation of the built environment in rural France. *International Journal of Heritage Studies,* 15(1), pp. 76–99.

Hyllegard, K.H., Ogle, J.P. & Dunbar, B. (2006). The influence of consumer identity on perceptions of store atmospherics and store patronage at a spectacular and sustainable retail site. *Clothing and Textiles Research Journal,* 24, pp. 316–334.

ICOMOS. (1994). *The Nara Document on Authenticity in Relation to the World Heritage Convention.* Nara: ICOMOS.

ICOMOS Australia. (2013). *Burra Charter.* Available: www.icomos.org/australia/burra.html [Accessed 7 November 2015].

Jokilehto, J. (1985). Authenticity in restauration principles and practices. *Bulletin of the Association for Preservation Technology,* 17(3/4), pp. 5–11.

Jokilehto, J. (1999). *A History of Architectural Conservation,* 4. Oxford: Elsevier.

Kent, T. (2007). Creative space: Design and the retail environment. *International Journal of Retail & Distribution Management,* 35(9), pp. 734–745.

Kira Bunse. (2005). Guerrilla store Comme des Garçons, Cologne, 2005 (C) Kira Bunse.

Kirby, A. & Kent, T. (2010a). Architecture as brand: Store design and brand identity. *Journal of Product & Brand Management,* 19(6), pp. 432–439.

Kirby, A. & Kent, T. (2010b). The local icon: Re-use of buildings in place marketing. *Journal of Town and City Management,* 1(1), pp. 80–91.

Labadi, S. (2010). World heritage, authenticity and post-authenticity. *In:* Labadi, S. & Long, C. (eds.) *Heritage and Globalisation.* New York: Routledge.

Lepers, P. (2009). *Baudrillard: Leven na de orgie.* Kampen: Klement/Pelckmans.

Lin, C. & Wang, W. (2012). Effects of authenticity perception, hedonics, and perceived value on ceramic souvenir-repurchasing intention. *Journal of Travel & Tourism Marketing,* 29(8), pp. 779–795.

Lunardo, R. & Guerinet, R. (2007). The Influence of Label on Wine Consumption: Its Effects on Young Consumers' Perception of Authenticity and Purchasing Behavior. In the Proceedings of the 105th EAAE Seminar, *International Marketing and Trade of Quality Food Products,* pp. 69–84. Bologna, Italy, March 8–10.

MacCannell, D. (1973). Staged authenticity: Arrangements of social space in tourist settings. *The American Journal of Sociology,* 79(3), pp. 589–603.

Mack, G. (2011). *Restoration, Renovation, Reconstruction, Simulation . . . Jacques Herzog on the Strategic Role of the Armory in Herzog & de Meuron's Approach to Architecture* [Online]. Available: http://www.herzogdemeuron.com/index/projects/complete-works/276–300/293-park-avenue-armory/FOCUS/conversation-1.html [Accessed 13 August 2013].

Maclaran, P. & Brown, S. (2005). The center cannot hold: Consuming the utopian marketplace. *Journal of Consumer Research,* 32(2), pp. 311–323.

Manzini, E. (2012). The scenari of a multi-local society: Creative communities, active networks, and enabling solutions. *In:* Chapman, J. & Gant, N. (eds.) *Designers, Visionaries and Other Stories: A Collection of Sustainable Design Essays.* London: Earthscan.

Maté, K. (2013). Remediating shopping centres for sustainability. *In:* Cairns, G. (ed.) *Reinventing Architecture and Interiors: A Socio-political View on Building Adaptation.* London: Libri Publishers.

McLennan, J.F. (2004). *The Philosophy of Sustainable Design.* Kansas City: Ecotone LLC.

Murzyn-Kupisz, M. (2013). The socio-economic impact of built heritage projects conducted by private investors. *Journal of Cultural Heritage,* 14(2), pp. 156–162.

Ogle, J.P., Hyllegard, K.H. & Dunbar, B. (2004). Predicting patronage behaviors in a sustainable retail environment: Adding retail characteristics and consumer lifestyle orientation to the belief-attitude-behavior intention model. *Environment and Behavior,* 36(5), pp. 717–741.

Peñaloza, L. (2001). Consuming the American West: Animating cultural meaning and memory at a stock show and rodeo. *Journal of Consumer Research,* 28(3), pp. 369–398.

Petermans, A. (2012). *Retail Design in the Experience Economy: Conceptualizing and 'Measuring' Customer Experiences in Retail Environments.* Doctoral thesis, Hasselt University & PHL University College.

Petermans, A. & Van Cleempoel, K. (2009). Retail design and the experience economy: Where are we (going)? *Journal of Design Principles and Practises,* 3(1), pp. 171–182.

Pine, B. & Gilmore, J. (2007). *Authenticity: What Consumers Really Want.* Boston: Harvard Business School Press.

Plevoets, B. (2014). *Retail-Reuse: An Interior View on Adaptive Reuse of Buildings.* Doctoral thesis, Universiteit Hasselt.

Plevoets, B., Petermans, A. & Van Cleempoel, K. (2010). Developing a theoretical framework for understanding (staged) authentic retail concepts in relation to the current experience economy. *In:* Durling, D., Bousbaci, R., Chen, L., Gauthier, P., Poldma, T., Roworth-Strokes, S. & Stolterman, E. (eds.) *Proceedings DRS2010.* Montreal, Canada, July 7–9: DRS2010.

Plevoets, B. & Van Cleempoel, K. (2011). Assessing authenticity of nineteenth century shopping passages. *Journal of Cultural Heritage Management and Sustainable Development,* 1(2), pp. 135–156.

Plevoets, B., & Van Cleempoel, K. (2013). Adaptive reuse as an emerging discipline: An historic survey. *In:* Cairns, G. (ed.) *Reinventing Architecture and Interiors: A Socio-political View on Building Adaptation.* London: Libri Publishers.

Plevoets, B. & Van Cleempoel, K. (2014). Aemulatio and the Interior approach of adaptive reuse. *Interiors: Design, Architecture, Culture,* 5(1), pp. 71–88.

Public Architecture. (2010). *Design for Reuse Primer.* Available: http://www.publicarchitecture.org/reuse/pdf/Primer-Online.pdf [Accessed 7 November 2015].

Richards, J. (1994). *Façadism.* London: Routledge.

Rubessi, C. (2010). Sustainable practice in retail design: New functions between matter and space. *IDEA Journal,* 2010 (Interior Ecologies), pp. 78–79.

Saglar Onay, N. (2013). Commercial use of antique interiors: Dialectics of the contemporary and the conservative. *International Journal of Academic Research,* 5(4), pp. 161–168.

Sarnitz, A. (2003). *Adolf Loos, 1870–1933: Architect, Cultural Critic, Dandy.* Cologne: Taschen.

Schaefer, A. & Crane, A. (2005). Addressing sustainability and consumption. *Journal of Marcromarketing,* 25(1), pp. 76–92.

Scott, F. (2008). *On Altering Architecture.* London: Routledge.

Sowinska-Heim, J. (2013). Conversions and Redefinitions – Architecture and Identity of a Place. *Art Inquiry: Recherches sur les Arts,* 15(24), pp. 191–205.

Starn, R. (2002). Authenticity and historic preservation: Towards an authentic history. *History of the Human Sciences,* 15(1), pp. 1–16.

Starr, R. (2011). *The Certification of Authenticity: Effects on Product Perception.* Doctoral thesis, University of Auckland.

Stovel, H. (2007). Effective use of authenticity and integrity as world heritage qualifying conditions. *City & Time,* 2(3), pp. 21–36.

Theodoraki, A., Theodoraki-Patsi, J. & Theodoraki, P. (2009). Restoration, reconstruction and simulacra: Comparative evaluation between matera and santorini. *In:* IAPS-CSBE & HOUSING Networks (ed.) *Revitalising Built Environments, Requalifying Old Places for New Uses*, 12–16 October 2009, Istanbul.

Timothy, D. J. & Boyd, S. W. (2003). *Heritage Tourism.* Harlow: Pearson Education.

Tucker, L. (2015). The relationship between historic preservation and sustainability in interior design. *In:* Thompson, J. & Blossom, N. (eds.) *The Handbook of Interior Design.* West Sussex: Wiley.

UNESCO. (2008). Operational guidelines for the implementation of the world heritage convention. Paris: UNESCO World Heritage Centre.

United Nations. (1987). Report of the World Commission on Environment and Development. Available: http://www.un-documents.net/wced-ocf.htm [Accessed 7 November 2015].

USGBC. (2010). *Practical Strategies.* Available: http://www.usgbc.org/Docs/Archive/General/Docs7760.pdf [Accessed 7 November 2015].

Van Cleempoel, K. (2008). The relationship between contemporary art and retail design. *In*: Peressut, L., Forino, I., Postiglione, G., & Scullica, F. (eds.) *Places and Themes of Interior.* Milan: Interiors Studies Franco Angeli.

Van Tongeren, M. (2003). *Retail Branding.* Amsterdam: Bis Publishers.

Van Tongeren, M. (2004). Retail branding. *In:* Christiaans, H. & Van Amerongen, R. (eds.) *Retail & Interior Design.* Rotterdam: Episode Publishers.

Warnaby, G. (2009). Look up! Retailing, historic architecture and city centre distinctiveness. *Cities,* 26(5), pp. 287–292.

Webster, N. (1986). Authentic. *In:* Gove, P. (ed.) *Webster's Third New International Dictionary.* Springfield, MA: Merriam-Webster.

Wycichowska, B. (2008). A New "Heart" of Lodz. A Project Worthy of the 21st Century. *Czasoposme Techniczne Wydawnictwo Politechniki Krakowskiej.*

Yudelson, J. (2009). *Sustainable Retail Development: New Success Strategies.* Dordrecht: Springer.

8 Evaluating retail design

Martin Knox

Introduction

This chapter asks the questions 'what is good retail design?' and 'in what ways do factors influence retail design and designers that challenge our perception of what is "good"?' The context in which we view retail design, in particular the changing times and the changing nature of the retail environment, is considered alongside the influences on that context. The chapter discusses the opportunities for, and responsibilities of, the retail designer and highlights the ways in which retail design can be evaluated against an ever-changing context. The aim is to challenge thinking about design rather than provide prescriptive answers to the questions raised; it recognises that there is no 'one way' to undertake retail design, and the questions posed throughout this chapter invite further exploration.

Change is the only constant

The past thirty years have seen dramatic and profound change in the way designers think and the world works. These have and continue to influence what retail design is and how it is done. Change is the only constant, and, when we evaluate retail design, what is going on in the world must always must be borne in mind in the designer's creative process. For example, the field of retail design in the 2000s includes websites and online shopping portals, while in the 1980s the World Wide Web did not exist and there was no concept of its impact on retailing.

At the outset, it is important to emphasise the influence of the world surrounding retail design. A fundamental undercurrent to the discipline is that designers are dealing with the future, so the way things are done now and the way things have been historically done will not work in the future. One of the challenges, and the incredible opportunity, of retail design is not just to stay ahead of the game but also to create it. Evaluating retail design, and determining what is 'good' design, also has its challenges, not least because it has to be placed in the context of its time. What was a brilliant design concept in the past may not be successful today. For example, the Next Group started a whole new trend in how retail spaces were thought about and designed in the 1980s. Retailing became about beautiful spaces, aspiration, brand and buying into a style. Retail design was all about aesthetics and being fashionable. The 1980s also saw the start of the consumer credit boom in the UK, which made aspirational shopping more accessible to a broad range of consumers.

Next retail group – revolution in retail design

Next launched in 1982. It appeared in a retail landscape that was homogenised, dull and unimaginative. George Davies, its founder and visionary, had a very simple premise: to create and present high-fashion women's wear in ways that the customer could build outfits; selling a wardrobe rather than a garment.

My involvement began in 1984 when George asked me to design the first ever Next Christmas theme and the first ever Next sale, then on to design a lingerie shop and many other projects. A couple of years later he asked me to set up a graphic design department for the rapidly expanding group. I and my team of ten were responsible for much of how the brand communicated itself across its many companies and sub-brands.

George hired non-experts. He loved creative people with ideas, and part of his genius was to allow us to explore and experiment. He trusted us to take risks and to take responsibility. We did not know how to do retail; we did not know what the rules were. And, anyway, those following the rules were our competitors on the high street and dull, dull, dull. The eighties was the decade of design, and we were the first to bring it into the mainstream in ways that were engaging, accessible and empowering for our customers. Next was a phenomenon that changed the face of British high-street fashion.

This period of affluence can be contrasted with the credit crunch of 2008 and its continuing impact in the next decade. Suddenly 'value' had a different meaning; no longer just cheap, bargains became badges of honour, and conspicuous consumption was no longer desirable; rather, it became increasingly socially unacceptable. Provenance and source became as important as price and 'hand-crafted' and crafting offered a whole new retailing opportunity. Digital technology too shifted the parameters of retail design. The emergence of mobile Internet access and apps meant shopping could be done on the move, prices compared, goods ordered from the best-value purveyor. Retail design has had to embrace graphic design, web design, app design as well as the physical shop floor, and all these different portals to the customer have to appear congruent and seamless. The experience of a brand has to be consistent across every route to market, be that a store, a website or many and various social media platforms.

The consumer's relationship with products and brands is no longer as stable as it was. Brands can be purchased in order to identify status in society or community, and less certainly individual identity. However, branding itself is changing, in recognition of personalised and customized product becoming more desired and increasingly easier to deliver. New techniques and technologies in manufacturing allow brands to order smaller quantities as well as being able to respond very quickly to the changing requirements of their markets

Disruption comes at us from all angles. Events and innovations can have a transformative effect – for example, the 9/11 terrorist attack in 2001 when the world was suddenly faced with a new type of threat and the economic crisis of 2008 which influence continued to be felt into 2015. The Internet enables everybody and, increasingly, everything to be connected all the time. We have access to immeasurable volumes of information and knowledge. A further aspect of disruption is evident in technological change. 3D printing will change the way we perceive and interact with products. Developments in the technology of storing energy are becoming more refined and accessible. The generation of energy is rapidly becoming less reliant on fossil fuels and methods harmful to the environment. Artificial intelligence and quantum computing are about to break into mainstream use and have the potential for us to question our very humanity. More generally, awareness of the impact humanity is having on the environment and the world's finite resources have led to new sustainability agenda.

The lines between offline and online retail are becoming increasingly blurred. Across these channels, the consumer has more control than ever before over decision-making and buying. It is certain that a hybrid, omnichannel future holds challenges of which we have no conception. In this scenario, creativity is paramount to develop solutions to those challenges, and the retail designer must be sensitive to this. Our design outputs must allow for these shifts. What retail design was, what it is and what it will become is in a state of constant change: the impact and effect on its outcomes is becoming greater and, to some extent, more profound in its range. As retail designers both creating and evaluating design, we have to be able to adapt and flow with change, and be the creators and manifestors of change too. In times of change, new ideas and new ways of thinking are required. The designer has to be aware of and prepare for disruption in the form of game changers, the people or things that suddenly change the course of design. Social media, for example, has been a game changer in communications; neither Facebook nor Twitter existed before 2004, but now they are primary communication channels for businesses as well as individuals. These changes will come with increasing regularity and impact all aspects of how we perceive ourselves and go about our lives and our relationships, of how we view and acknowledge products and how we reach them.

And, yet, it may be interesting to note the retail industry is, counter-intuitively, averse to change. That thing that sold well last year returns next year; best sellers are desperately held on to until such time as the next one appears. There is little allowance for innovation, for experimentation, for doing something new to transform the business model. This fear of change arises because we are always fearful of the new and untested, especially where budgets and margins are at stake. It is deemed much safer to repeat something that has worked in the past, even, and sometimes especially, if it was successful for a competitor, than to risk the budget on something innovative and experimental that we do not know for sure will work for us. George Davies took a radical step in designing Next in the 1980s at a time when the clothing retail sector was relatively undifferentiated. It was a simple concept, based on merchandising womenswear as outfits rather than products. It was hugely successful, copied and then defined the new normal. Now the norm is again to merchandise clothing by product type. This pattern of change raises questions about when the time is ripe for another new and radical concept, and who will be brave enough to challenge the status quo.

It is in this environment that designers must work their alchemy. It is up to the designer to take 'base metal and turn it into gold', to take a perceived need, transform it into a concept and turn that into something practical, something beautiful and a catalyst for change. There is a responsibility to balance the needs and fears, usually historical or short term, of their clients. Designers have to fit the client needs with the wants of the market, the customer and the changing landscapes in which the customers live their lives, being mindful of the potentials and opportunities delivered by change. They have to think about the culture of the client, what it is that they do and how are they received in the marketplace. They have to be aware of the zeitgeist, the feeling of the times and what they predict the feeling of the population to be in the future. They have to think about the cultures of the communities in which their clients have to sell products and services. Thus, designers' knowledge and critical reflection in thinking about a design problem has to be much deeper and broader than the project's aesthetics. It is against this backdrop that the designer decides what is and is not 'good' design.

Consideration of change, clients, communities, needs and wants can dramatically influence what is considered to be 'good' design. Good design has to be founded in the conditions of the present time but geared to the future, and the designer has to have the ability to encourage clients to open their thinking and create or further develop their vision. Influences from the zeitgeist as well as cultural sources will always inform design. It is up to the designers to avoid being influenced by current trends, and to design for the future; they seek to create lasting solutions that can be evolved in line with need. Fashion and trend are becoming increasingly anachronistic; time and rapid change allows less space for both. Consumers now have the ability via the Internet to buy anything, at any time, from anywhere. They no longer have to buy clothes seasonally, to have been sure to have bought swimwear in the summer for a winter sun holiday. They can buy wall tiles direct from the manufacturer in Italy, Bush Flower remedies from Australia and all manner of handcrafted items from anywhere in the world via specialist websites and portals. This is creating a new form of stability in a shopping climate where the consumer is now in control of what is bought and when. Retail brands therefore have to convey a reason to shop with them that goes beyond the products they offer.

Part of the challenge for creating good retail design is for the designer to have empathy for the customer, to *actively* become the customer. The designer's personal experience of retail, both good and bad, is the same as that of the customer. Good design will satisfy very different needs and requirements, clearly creating distinctive environments, say, for a grocer compared to that of a supermarket or sports shop. They have to be able to fully adapt to any situation; indeed, they must revel and rejoice in change in what is the designer's playground. And, for all, designers must create an environment that can adapt quickly, and that all channels open to retail have to offer a conducive environment. That environment, in all its manifestations, has to be able to evolve with the rapidly changing and shifting requirements of the marketplace.

The opportunity for retail designers

From a designer perspective, there is great joy in designing for retail. There is a fascination in absorbing every aspect of how an organization conceives, perceives and delivers its product. The retailing environment extends across distribution and communication channels: physical (offline) and virtual (online), through many media. The relationship between all these has to be considered. There are many routes to market open now to brands, and these contribute to and must support each other. The retail designer explores those routes and creates for all of them, while being mindful of their potential to create new opportunities. Skill sets have to extend from the conception of a physical environment to the online experience and the communication of a retail offer. Retail can best be described as the delivery medium or mechanism. Its mission is primarily about communication: the communication of a brand, its spirit and personality, compelling and truthful reasons for engagement, product benefit, provenance and meaning. The product itself becomes less important because consumers are likely to have formed an earlier awareness of, and expectation around, it.

The retail designer is at the very start of a process and sees the project all the way to completion and its further evolution. The process can be described and defined in a series of stages as:

1   **Awareness** – the designers must make themselves acutely aware of the needs of their clients, the customers, and the landscape or climate.
2   **Response** – taking the knowledge from stage one, the designers consider how their clients might develop better and/or new ways to deliver their offers in a retail environment. Designing and presenting very outline concept thoughts. It is critical that at this stage no final designs are shown. It should be up to the creative to encourage and guide their clients to be active contributors to the creative process. In so doing, the clients have a perception of ownership right from the beginning.
3   **Development** – the concepts are turned into designs that will work practically through to implementation. This phase will naturally go through many iterations as the concept develops and is tested.
4   **Specification** – the designs are used to prepare specifications for manufacture and implementation.
5   **Implementation** – work with the contractors to ensure their deep understanding of the requirements and ensuring that they interpret them within their means and abilities and within the budget.
6   **Management** – oversee and guide implementation.
7   **Launch** – support and guide the clients in all aspects of opening and promoting their new retail identity.
8   **Monitor** – work closely with the clients to monitor the success of their new environments and to help with their evolution.

Obviously, the clients will have their own thoughts on how they want to work with their designers, and it is for the designers to negotiate with and honour their clients' needs.

Designers have the opportunity to help organisations to discover and deliver their truth: their values, what they stand for, what they do, whom they really do it for. Many organisations will talk in terms of their customer demographics, but the psychographics, values and styles of their customers are far more important. Customers' buying decisions are grounded in their values and what is important to them, not whether they fit into a particular demographic. They buy from organisations that share and fulfil their values. So the skill of the retail designer is to question, listen and discover the deeper values and motivations of the client organisation and then express and frame these through their design work so that the end customers can recognise themselves in this retail environment.

Retail design is distinguished by its many and diverse stakeholders. Designers have to be able to closely relate to them and to take them all into account in both creating and evaluating design. The implications are that the retail designer is obliged to be multidisciplinary. The process requires an openness to be creative across graphic design, interior design, marketing, promotions, service design, ergonomics, customer flow, merchandise layout, organisational development and operations, cultural development and brand design and development. At the same time the designer needs to be able to translate these aspects into the various online and offline channels and other routes to market.

The starting point of the design project is an understanding of the clients' organisation, culture and operations. In delivering an expression of the clients, the work has to reflect the designer's knowledge of who they are and what they stand for. The next stage is to

- **Client** – this could be the person who commissions the project, the organisation they represent, the board of directors; it could be one person or many stakeholders.

- **Staff** – retail is a low-paid and demanding occupation; the customer-facing people within the industry are its greatest ambassadors, and the human face of their client often gets forgotten. Consider them within the brief and give them a culture and an environment designed to make their lives more fulfilled, and your client will have a highly effective and engaged work force.

- **Media** – however that manifests, those who tell others about their organization must be respected and included in some way.

- **Customers** – customers might form a single, easily identifiable group, though they are more likely to be diverse in their needs.

- **Suppliers** – making it easy for the supplier to have a relationship with both their client and the customer.

Figure 8.1 Retail design stakeholders

consider the service design, ergonomics, customer flow and merchandise layout. Walking in the end-users' shoes, the designer must understand their experience of this space. The ideas sketched by the designer, combined with the requirements asked for by the clients, may have to address comfort, safety, ease of navigation, and user friendliness. If the customers cannot find the product they are looking for or the environment does not feel comfortable to them, they will not linger and they will not return. At this point there must be a consideration of what the customer needs, wants and values in this space. The design of the interior, the web pages, the graphics, branding and marketing communications all follow to demonstrate to the customers that the company shares their values, will look after them and will fulfil their needs and desires. This has to be delivered with confidence and conviction. It also has to be true. The end-customers will determine if they have conveyed a truth or if they have mislead them with unrealistic promises that are not actually delivered.

This is a discipline that can offer only a partial training. Most retail designers now start from a background of interior design, architecture and increasingly from less closely related disciplines. The author himself comes from a fine-art background, which enabled him to take a completely open and boundless approach to what can be done. Indeed, a fine-art background accounts for some of the best retail designers for whom 'I don't know and have no interest in what can't be done' is a reasonable maxim. There are few other formal qualifications in retail design in the UK, other than the National Design Academy, which offers a Foundation Degree in Retail Design via online learning. The most common route is from an interior design qualification and followed by specialisation in retail design. Architects moving into retail design will have a more detailed training and interest in structure and construction. Whichever route designers take, theoretical study will only take them so far. The remaining qualities will arise from curiosity, passions, interests, awareness of the world, openness to new thinking, creativity, inventiveness, empathy and knowledge. And these will be dependent on being able to collaborate with specialists in many fields.

The power and responsibility of the retail designer

All professional designers have great power. Through creative thought and expression, artists, writers, musicians but also retail designers have the ability to affect the way people feel about themselves and the world around them. With that power and with those abilities comes the responsibility to produce work that works at many levels for their clients. Designers have to acknowledge and take responsibility for creativity beyond the purely aesthetic, to acknowledge and honour its skills, its crafts and its power and use them well and in positive ways.

The imperative to follow these precepts was brought on by the emergence of new consumers who are aware, self-actualizing, connected, increasingly responsible, vociferous, questioning and looking to be able to place their trust and see it honoured. The imperative naturally extends to the designers, to honour their power – not least because designers are, themselves, representative of these new consumers. We are all aware of when we are being manipulated and are, increasingly, discerning. Consumers refuse to be coerced, bullied or patronised by design any more. Many consumers have turned away from the superficial and seek greater meaning in all aspects of life and those things that they are prepared to allow into their lives. Consumers are increasingly interested in the authenticity and the provenance of those products and services that they buy, in meanings.

The responsibility of the designers is to acknowledge the desires and expectations of their clients and their clients' customers and to honour their trust; and this opens up enormous opportunity and potential. As stated above, we are living in a world of rapid and profound change, and change throws up challenges of which our cultures have neither a history nor an experience. The designer has the abilities to investigate and deliver new ways to resolve the new challenges.

It is no longer good enough simply to make something functional and beautiful, although these are a fundamental part of the design project. Designers have to move beyond problems of space and place; they have to be sociologists, anthropologists and psychologists in an understanding of how customers make decisions and how they are influenced by both the world around them and their own intuition, energy and feelings. An interest in, and an understanding of, human thought and behaviour will help determine what becomes effective design. Without empathy toward fundamental human needs, the designer will only deliver the superficial. Brands have historically *sold at* their customers and in so doing, perhaps, lost touch with their own humanity as well as their customers.

The designers now have to consider aspects of need known and unknown, way beyond their formal training, and to bring their creative minds to the fore. In many ways a designer is an alchemist, bringing together a number of ideas, thoughts and disciplines, the needs and wants of a variety of audiences, the moods and influences of the time, fashions and trends where applicable, and costs, budgets and economics, to create a piece of retail design gold. The result will be the environment best suited to the delivery of their client's brand, products and services. And while this may mean shop design, it will invariably also take in other channels and routes to market.

This integrated approach is underpinned by the honest appraisal and delivery of the ethos and values of their client. The task is to work out how to use them to gain and maintain the trust of the customer, and the mechanisms and devices available to them to achieve these aims. They will become the guardian of their client's brand through the process, and this means that they will be required to illustrate and articulate to their client exactly what *the client's* responsibilities will be in order to succeed.

Designers have an obligation to consider and be fully mindful of the impact and effect their work will have on all those who come into contact with it. This work can have an effect on the business and culture of the client's organisation far beyond the shop fitting (see the case study of Poundland). Designers will have to work with what their client's brand is and what it offers. If that conflicts with the common defining spirit, mood and sets of perceptions of the zeitgeist, then it is up to the designers as the 'guides' to advise and help their clients to find ways of bringing their products and services in line. However, the designers must be prepared to walk away from the project if their clients' motives are unsound or corrupt; then they have an obligation to not assist. Good retail design is about 'delivering good, honest, meaningful stuff to a discerning, mindful consumer', and if that is not at the heart of the designers thinking, then they are not designers; they are cyphers who will not succeed for their clients.

Increasingly, the role of the retail design is one of orchestrator and conductor. The designers communicate the concept to their client, who could be a single person (such as the marketing director) or the entire board. Designers work in partnership with the client to refine and develop the idea into something that will operationally and practically work. It is up to them to make the designs easy and affordable to implement, and those who will be responsible for implementation fully understand and engage with the project. The designs are a starting point to offer thoughts on how clients might evolve and develop their routes to market. The designers must oversee and guide the making to ensure that the outcome remains true to the concept and to the client need. They monitor and report progress. Overseeing the opening/launch, they go on to appraise and advise on how the whole can be evolved and easily refreshed. The power of the retail designers is that this role can be as much or as little as they want it to be. Indeed, care must also be given to just how much involvement the client thinks is needed. Designers can simply make beautiful, functional designs to a client's brief, or they can change cultures and leave a legacy that reaches much deeper than the fixtures and fittings. The choice is that of the designer.

Poundland: How retail design can be a catalyst for cultural change

My team and I completely rebranded and repositioned British retailer Poundland. What we did had a profound effect on the culture of the organization, from how the stores were perceived to how the directors viewed their business. It became the catalyst for massive expansion, going from eighty stores to over five hundred.

Researching Poundland was a joy. Here was a brand where the greatest aspect of the purchasing process, price, was not an issue. If you had a pound, you could buy something. I discovered them selling the most unusual and sometimes extraordinary products amongst the mundane. On one occasion I found a two-pack of ceramic garden gnomes, for only a pound. Looking at the box, I was astounded to discover that they came from a factory in what is now the Czech Republic. It was actually the very same place where production originated in the mid-nineteenth century.

My first meeting with the board of this company was interesting. They did not really know their purpose or their customers. I was invited into the board room – a dull and scruffy space with a very large, scratched and stained table, around which there were eight people. There was a faulty light flickering in the ceiling and a pile of old cardboard boxes stacked against one wall. The members of the board of management were grey-faced and unkempt. And I talked to them about respect. My overall impression of their stores was that of no respect: for their product, for their brand, for their customers and for themselves. In fact, their very boardroom and they themselves reflected this. They even had their brand identity inlaid in the floor at the entrance of every shop. People were coming into their stores and walking on their brand – another example of little self-respect.

We designed a new identity, new ways of merchandising and categorizing merchandise, new shop fits, new customer flow and new queue management systems. We re-addressed every aspect of how they presented and delivered their product as well as how they communicated themselves. We opened twelve stores for them at an average cost of £120,000. The figure that they gave me at the start, as an illustration of the cost of fitting the stores, was £160,000. I discovered, much later, that their actual figure was closer to £180,000. We showed their board that design could save enormous amounts of cash whilst delivering something very special, appropriate and game changing.

After completing the first twelve stores, I went back into their head office to hand over the roll-out program to them. Led into the boardroom, I was immediately struck by a change. The lights were all working, and there were fresh flowers on the very clean and polished boardroom table. There was a sideboard with fresh coffee and pastries for us to help ourselves to. Most striking were the people around the table – the same eight from a year before. They were fresh faced, well dressed, bright eyed and very enthusiastic. Transformed.

Every aspect of the organization was affected and positively transformed as a result of our work. We had delivered a highly effective and economic retail identity. And, *much* more, we had given the organization respect for itself and its customers. Poundland went on to open many more stores and by 2015 were trading in about 1,000 stores with the ambition to grow to 1,400 in the following years.

The influence of government policy

Government policy can influence retail design in that it contributes to the climate in which retailers operate; it influences the mood of the times, and what is deemed to be its priorities. Governments have an active role in defining and zoning retail locations, plans for buildings, and regulating the sale of products – for example, cigarettes, which in the UK and elsewhere can no longer be displayed. In these ways, policies provide a framework for development that may also limit the scope of design projects.

One major concern has been the health of retailing and its place in the social and economic fabric of the country. In the UK, the government has committed resources into regenerating central shopping areas, defined by the High Street, following high-profile reviews and reports. The Department for Communities and Local Government report (2013) noted:

> The successful high streets of the future will be where people live, use services, and spend their leisure time, including in an evening economy, as well as shop. Even the nature of retail on the high street is changing, with successful retailers mixing and matching online shopping with traditional shopping. The key to success and securing the long term future of the High Street, therefore, is for communities to strike the right balance between traditional retail and other uses for high street property – include markets and pop up shops, housing, community and social uses and entertainment and cultural activities. It will take creativity and imagination to enable high streets to adapt to this new environment.

This may open up new opportunities for the creative and imaginative retail designer to get involved in designing not just retail spaces but also communities and in creating the shopping street of the future.

A second way government policy can create opportunities for retail design is through devolution of autonomy and responsibility to regions. With regions and cities gaining more autonomy, it becomes more important for retailers to have local relevance and community connections, not simply imposing a one-size fits all for its outlets. This creates the challenge of maintaining brand identity, style and economies of scale nationally, or even internationally, across a number of stores, while also making each store relevant and attractive to its local catchment area. Ted Baker has addressed this issue with an ingredient list of retail parts that its team can pick from to use in its stores and adding local references. For example, in Nottingham, the Ted Baker store includes references to Robin Hood with murals of forest scenes and an arrow sticking out of a concrete column as if fired into it by the famous outlaw.

A third aspect of policy concerns housing. An emphasis on starter and affordable homes in particular areas can alter their demographics, and audience groups may change across locations. The retailers need to make sure their catchment area can maintain a store for future years where new stores are planned, which returns to their knowledge and respect for their customers. Buildings may have twenty-year leases, and there is the potential to change the shop fit four or five times within that time frame. The flexibility to adapt a store to a changing local customer profile may be required. At the time of writing, availability of space is high whilst landlords, with continually high rents and prohibitive terms, and local authorities, with high local rates, are making it economically very difficult to trade. Landlords have high expectations of returns on investment that do not necessarily reflect changing consumer patterns. In the UK, this is a great challenge to property owners who historically have become complacent about growth and the consistency of returns on their investment. City centres are changing, becoming more diverse with leisure, residential and social provision included in the mix. Retail is no longer the dominant aspect of city-centre life. And the landlords either are beginning to diversify themselves or are becoming far more active and imaginative in the management and successful usage of their properties. Too many shops and shopping malls present retail designers with new problems: to conceptualise alternative uses for the space, devise new formats and more generally their sustainability.

The influence of the media

Designers need to question what and who the media are. Traditional media is losing its position as the primary source of information and influence as increasingly the general public is more in control of what gets shared and read. Individuals are breaking stories on social media. Mainstream media is no longer the influence it was before the Internet arrived.

Mainstream media is in the business of popularising and often sensationalising thoughts and events. And clients are influenced. For example, there is still a push from mainstream women's media for 'youth is good and ageing is not'. This is in direct competition with the requirements of a growing demographic and, potentially, very lucrative market. It is also contrary to the spirit and mood of the buying public. They are increasingly being turned off by the media and making otherwise informed choices. Designers need to be mindful and have confidence to advise and guide their clients where they see the clients missing opportunities and being overly influenced by an increasingly powerless populist media.

At the same time, retail designers have to be aware of a negative press in both mainstream media and, possibly more importantly, social media. There was the saying that today's news is tomorrow's fish-and-chip paper; however, sharing on social media now has a more far-reaching effect and longevity than the daily news, and a disgruntled customer can do more damage on Twitter.

'Good' retail design

Good retail design is not simply about the aesthetic, a lovely looking store. It delivers something different every time a customer visits the store. That may be manifested through the use of hidden devices that the customer may not spot first or even on a second visit: small touches and details that, outwardly superfluous, enhance the experience – for example, the use of fragrances, lighting and sounds to create specific and particular ambience. Giving attention to more human customer service, not trying to contrive an experience but making it feel natural and timeless. The airlines are very good at this level of attention; essentially they all have an identical product but find ways of differentiating and making their travellers' journey a little different and memorable each time they travel. It facilitates a relationship between a brand and its customer.

Fun and challenge take precedence over good taste; it is better to create something that makes a statement and becomes recognized. Some people may not like it, but a store or brand that has a stance is far more engaging than a bland offer designed for a mass audience that no longer exists. Designers finding that they speak more with clients about finding and delivering the core values of the brand, not trying or contriving to do anything and to consider how they would feel and what makes them happy and content. While the retail industry has historically tried to identify with and target a mass market, the result is too often evident in a sanitised, standardised presentation contrived to attract everyone. Arguably, Marks and Spencer fell into this trap in the 1990s and up through the 2000s, losing sight of who its customers were and trying to appeal to everyone, with the notable exception of its M&S food halls. Good design delivers something special to a market intimately associated with and allied to the brand, its values and its ethos – and to those of its customer.

In this respect, design is turning to curation. A curated environment illustrates an affinity with a select group of potential customers in its attention to detail. A contrived and manufactured design is deemed less authentic. A curated offer is about considered choice. Curated retail ensures focused shopping and product relevance; it provides a customer with choices that will be most interesting depending on previous shopping choices, interactions and set preferences. All too often, particularly with supermarkets, consumers are bombarded by and ultimately disabled by too much choice. Curation extends through the design process and means the bringing together of diverse and eclectic elements to deliver something new and relevant to its audience. It has been taken from museums and art galleries where specific narratives are considered and delivered. It is not simply about displaying stuff and expecting people to buy; it is about delivering a choice considered in the interest of the customer.

Change and the contexts of change introduced at the start of this chapter have a continuing influence on notions of good retail design. What were deemed as low-end businesses are taking on the bright, clean, smart, fashionable image that was once the preserve of the high-end market. Primark, for example, has developed these elements into its shopping experience. The luxury and high-end markets are increasingly taking an anti-design stance by offering interesting challenges to their customers. Dover Street Market, a multilevel fashion retail and concept store created by Rei Kawakubo of Japanese fashion label Comme des Garçons, uses old sheds as cash desks, portaloos as fitting rooms and found objects for shop fittings for its £500 shirts. This is a great example of anti-design as design, or another form of design that demonstrates how design has to become less about contrivance and more about using methods that more profoundly engage.

Who decides what is good retail design is dependent on the industry sector and its design approach. There is much pressure on the practitioner from the design industry to follow trends and to stay with what is currently fashionable, acceptable and the style of the times. Ultimately, however, it must be the end user that decides, because if it works they come back, and if it does not they will not. The designers should look to their validation from the customers' response and from their happy clients. And as indicated above, good design can be anti-design in context.

In the author's experience, the following are usually evident in a piece of design work that stands out as good retail design:

- The designer's love for and awareness of change.

- The designer's respect for and understanding of a discerning customer.

- The designer was a good guide for their client. (The client relied on and trusted the designer to deliver something that satisfied their various needs as well as helped them to expand their thinking).

- The designer's ability to visualize and present ideas.

- The designer's awareness - of the world, of the zeitgeist of the time, the context of the project and of his/her self.

- The designer's ability to engage all the senses: sight, sound, touch, smell and feelings.

- The designer's ability to get to know about their client: what motivated them, what they and their organisation's values and ethos were, what their positioning was (i.e. who they are, what they are, why they are and for whom).

- The designer's curiosity: there is no single way to do something, and the designer's openness and willingness to explore shows through.

- Collaboration: the designer's ability to work (collaborate) with others of diverse experience and from other disciplines.

- The designer's empathy with their client, the end customer, collaborators and the project itself.

- The designer was inventive, creative, confident and clearly loved their work.

The questions that any evaluation should ask are:

Does it work – for the client and for their customer?

Does it do what the client wants?
Does it satisfy needs beyond what the client wants?
Does it feel right?
Is it beautiful?
Do people happily shop it and come back?
Does it deliver something new?
Is its effect greater than its purpose?

Figure 8.2 Elements of retail design

Ways of evaluating retail design

In this section we will consider evaluating design through the retail journey; through the senses; through the impact on environment, locality and community; through cost versus benefit; and through shopper experience.

The design process might be considered as a customer journey. Every aspect of the customer experience has to be considered and catered for by the designer. The journey follows a number of subtle phases. These exist for any transaction process, be it in a physical, offline environment or a virtual online environment. It might be worth visiting a number of retail outlets, both online and offline, and consciously walking through this customer journey. The following challenges should always be in the mind of designers: the first encounter that brings the retailer into the consciousness of their potential customer; the creation of a cohesive experience where every aspect supports the requirements of the client; the spirit of their brand; and the customer's decision to engage.

> **Phase one** represents the approach, walking up to a store, clicking onto a website, coming up in conversation. The customer is drawn by activity from everywhere, all of which is designed to attract attention. The retail designer has to acquire a share of that attention without simply adding to the noise. This requires thoughts about distance branding or messaging and elements that will subtly enter the consciousness from a distance. These are devices that are visible from distance and at the approach, both on the street and online, that help to set the scene, attract attention and engage interest and curiosity.

As the customer approaches the retailer, attention needs to be directed towards the window/home page, to the product and brand message. This is a critical point and is evident in every retail sector. GAP in the early 2000s had a very strong, and successful, single product promotional message: supermarkets have relied on a multitude of product price promotions. Paul Smith attracts using gentle wit and humour; their approach is to do it on a small intimate scale so that the viewer does not get the joke until their nose is virtually pressed to the glass or curious enough online. Supermarkets achieve it by pumping the smell of bread baking into their entrance lobbies and lighting fruit and vegetables to make them appear *super* fresh. The window/home page is becoming less a showcase and more a promise of what is within – an abstract of a potential experience.

> **Phase two** is the transition from outside to inside. It is fine to have a fantastic window or home page, but, if this does not lead the viewer into the store, it fails its purpose. If there is a great window but no well-defined entrance or attractive point of access, the same applies. Designers have to create ways to welcome and include their potential customer at this point and implement devices that will motivate the viewer to cross the threshold into the shop. This is a critical stage: the point at which the viewers become potential customers because of the degree at which they are committed to entering. The process is critically time bound, as decisions take only seconds or split seconds.
>
> **Phase three** brings the customers into the store and gives them a dilemma about what to do next. Consideration needs to be given to creating an area where the potential customer can orientate him/herself. Many retailers use this space to aggressively present us with product. This acts as both a barrier and a challenge.

Suddenly, our commitment to enter is exploited: we become exploited and com-promised, and instantly we may be offended and repulsed.

The imperative in this phase is to allow a space around the entrance where the potential customer can comfortably step into the store and take time to survey, acclimatise and appraise. The length of this process is now critical. For the customers to orientate themselves, they need to feel comfortable and unhurried; designers allow for three to eight seconds. The implications of potential customers hovering around the entrance before they decide to take the next step of their 'journey' need to be assessed. The levels of information at this point should be integrated with some of them overt on entering, some leading to points of greater information, some designed to intrigue, and some hidden waiting to be discovered. There is a balance to be achieved between the visual and experiential, and between the brand, the product and the promotion. The designer must assess how the balance should be altered through the customer journey.

Phase four has the customers committed to entering and beginning to shop or browse. The designer has to consider the elements that draw them in and around the store in ways most conducive to them finding something they may want and that allow them to feel relaxed and unpressured. The design challenge is to find ways the retailers can acknowledge their potential customers without directly selling to them.

Phase five – environmental concerns. The store now has to engage with a *real* potential customer. The environment must offer a safe, easy-to-navigate place that gives the customer best access to products. The designer must consider the ease with which the customer may choose a product, view it and take it off a shelf and must consider the needs of any non-customers accompanying the customer.

Phase six. This is when the customer needs the most detailed information. The designer must consider ways that the customer can clearly identify the product, its provenance, what it costs, how it is used and what its purpose is. We have to be mindful of expressing, in the opinion of the brand, why the customer might want or need it. And with all of this, the designer must make it easy to find help that they are able to trust.

Phase seven. The store now has a customer. Consider the total experience and the extent to which it is comfortable, fun, interesting, easy, challenging and special. This should make the customer feel honoured, and honour is an underused word, but, if we consider this question, we are far more likely to keep this customer and build loyalty: honour develops trust, which develops loyalty.

Phase eight. The transaction. Now that the customers have made their choice, the retailers must decide if they want them to linger, or to pay and leave as soon as possible. As soon as the customers are ready to pay, they need to consider how quickly they want to leave. The retailers may want to create a deeper relationship with their customers, and should consider whether the customers want to enter into a deeper relationship with the brand.

Designers and consumers are shifting in their awareness, perceptions and expectations. It is not that they are buying any more, so much as why they are buying and consuming, and it is the 'why' of a product and experience that creates community and belonging. So if the retailer/brand wants to create something more than a straightforward retail/consumer relationship, the transaction process will require greater consideration.

Phase nine – the exit. Customers expect to have some form of welcome when they arrive, be it explicit or implied. They also have a need to have an elegant and dignified exit. The design of the store and the product may be presented to give something positive on exit. Some stores mawkishly have the words 'thank you for shopping at . . .' above the exit; this is a tired concept and somewhat patronising.

The retail designer has many aspects to consider and evaluate through this process:

- The physical environment of lighting, materials, layout, style, product placement and visual merchandising. The virtual environment has to match the physical as much as possible. The brand and client personality, the placement of brand cues and messaging all must be consistent, so common threads and links must be considered.
- Safety and ease of access: the ergonomics of the experience have to be considered; making it comfortable to access all areas and product, and making the environment safe.
- The feel: design has to work with all the senses – sight, sound, touch, smell as well as a felt sense. How the design feels to the customers is crucial to their experience of it.

Evaluating design through the senses

Consumers perceive and process everything through their senses. In a variety of shops, what you see, hear, smell, touch and feel is noticeable. In order for the customers to have a full experience, we designers must present our clients products utilising all of our senses. Designers are mostly used to working with the visual, creating a space that is aesthetically pleasing to the eye, and they use colour to denote different emotions and energies – for example, blue to calm, red to excite. Colours influence how consumers view the personality of the brand or the desirability of the product. They use different materials and textures to create different visual effects. One of the most important tools in the designer's kit is lighting. It can make a drab product sparkle or turn it into a beautiful product. Lighting can also be used to trick, so must be used honestly.

Sound is becoming a much more recognized component of good design, and can improve or disrupt workplace productivity. It can be contrasted with noise, which is most complained about in open-plan offices. Sound can enhance the shopping experience or make the whole ambience of the place feel wrong. Much more than playing some piped music, sonic branding is a whole area of design that needs to be considered. Smell is another sense that can bombard us and is often overlooked in the design process. How does a shop smell? It might be the chemicals used to finish off the garments which create an assault on the customers' noses or might be the smell of freshly baked bread or sugary patisserie that beckons them to come in. Smells evoke memories and emotions even more strongly than visual cues. Abercrombie & Fitch, for example, regularly sprays its own fragrance in stores to engage the nose and convey a lifestyle 'packed with confidence and a bold, masculine attitude'. The approach, it believes, helps shoppers to associate with the smell, generating enhanced brand identification and loyalty. Supermarkets use the aroma of fresh bread pumped through the entrance hall to evoke comfort and a sense of belonging. Fortnum and Mason's menswear department smells of old leather and cedar wood. It is comforting and comfortable, familiar and invigorating. When evaluating design, remember to use your nose.

Touch, even without actually touching something, is often combined with the visual cue. If something looks like it will feel warm or cold, that will likely influence the customer's perception of it. Wood and wool are usually warm to the touch; metals, cold.

Consider how the use of materials creates sensations or perceptions through touch. Temperature contributes to the sensory environment; it is important that a store is pleasantly warm – a little too chilly or stiflingly hot and our customer will be repelled. Different times of year dictate the required temperature. A perennial is winter. We enter a physical store wrapped up for the cold and very quickly become uncomfortable because the shop is warm. I cannot think of any shop that makes secure coat pegs available for customers.

Consumers' perceptions and sensory information all add up to a feeling or sensation. What is seen, heard, touched, smelled and experienced will culminate in a feeling that is pleasant or unpleasant, a sense of it being right or wrong. This feeling is what ultimately makes the decision for the customer, 'I like this place, I'll come back', or 'This place feels wrong, I'll go somewhere else'. Increasingly there is also an energy or an intuition that we tap into as consumers. Sometimes we cannot even explain why something feels right or wrong; it just does. Spaces and places have energies too. They have the energy of the designer, the client and the people working in them. An example of this is the case study on cancer research, and how that may be a catalyst for change.

Cancer research: How retail design is about a feel and a sense of place and may be a catalyst for change

In 2004, I was commissioned to design a brand new retail business for Cancer Research UK. The concept and its implementation were multi-faceted. (This was much more than a charity shop). We presented great products in an engaging and inclusive environment. The environment enabled customers to find out about the charity in ways that were designed to tap in to natural curiosity. The shops developed community and became focal centres for volunteers and interested individuals. They provided a route to information. The culture of the charity was positively impacted. Every one of the thirty shops looked the same and had the same products, merchandising, promotions, layout, music, etc. However, each shop felt different when the customer crossed its threshold. They had the personality of the people running them. Macclesfield was run by Eddie, a fun and highly enthusiastic lady. . . . That is what her shop felt like, full of fun and buzzing with energy. Leslie ran a shop in Northwich; she was calm and very caring . . . and that is what you felt on entering her store.

When I delivered the first stages of concepts to the board, I wanted to present, visually, what the shops would feel like. My presentation comprised a set of visuals that conveyed how the shops would feel: far less the look and much more the sense of place and experience that we wanted the visitor to have. When we opened the first shop in Hammersmith London, I was really happy when the marketing director came up to me, smiling, and said, 'You know what, Martin, this feels exactly as you showed us at that first presentation'.

The intention from the outset was for this to be an experience for the customer that was exactly what they wanted it to be. It was for them to choose for themselves what its meaning was.

At the outset, I wanted an outcome that the client did not brief me on. The culture within the charity was not good. I set an intention that this commission, WISHES, would act as a positive virus within the culture of the organization. And, some months after we opened the first shops, I was in conversation with one of the directors, and he let slip with the comment, 'You know what, Martin, something odd has happened here since we launched WISHES. My people seem happier somehow, the atmosphere at head office feels lighter'.

Evaluating design through the impact on environment, locality and community

Designers have a responsibility to be conscious and mindful of the greater effect of what they do. Physical stores as well as the virtual ones have profound effects on their locale. The environmental impact of a physical store and its shopping area can be great. It is a responsibility of designers to consider the local and community impact of their client's business. How can they ease the environmental burden, enhance community and make a better place around where they exist?

Enlightened retailers are becoming aware that they can consider the 'What else and what more' in order to enhance their offer and at the same time make their wider environment and community a better place. There is a growing need for corporate businesses to take responsibility for their societal and environmental impacts. Their fortunes can change overnight, and, if they do not take responsibility for their presence, they will struggle and in some cases fail. The year 2015 saw a steep and rapid decline in the value of Tesco. A retail brand universally reviled, though regularly shopped at and outwardly very successful. Its working methods and business practices became revealed and shown to be dysfunctional and destructive. Its share price plummeted. Its market share dropped dramatically. Its decline from grace highlighted dysfunctional aspects of its industry, and a chain reaction began to take place. At the time of writing, this chain reaction is gaining momentum, and the whole landscape of supermarket retailing is in crisis.

Retail design has impermanence in its spirit. It is likely to change every three to five years, even sooner given the rapid changes the world is experiencing, with a revamp or a whole new refit. It may be iconic in its time and for its audience, but rarely is it iconic for a lifetime. For example, Dover Street Market in 2015 might be considered as iconic. It breaks all the rules, sells opulence in an anti-opulent environment; it is exclusive and yet excludes no one; all are welcomed. In five years' time, its presentation may be totally different. By contrast, a building can be iconic for a lifetime and beyond. The Guggenheim Museum, Bilbao, designed by Canadian architect Frank Geary, is a building that changed the nature, and uplifted the culture, of a struggling industrial city in northern Spain and has become an icon of its generation. The building dramatically contrasts with its surroundings whilst also being in harmony with them. It became a catalyst for a positive shift in the economic fortunes of the city. Bilbao suddenly became a place to visit, and tourism became part of its economy, replacing the heavy industry that had gone.

Evaluating design as cost versus benefit

Retail design is often considered expensive, and yet it is quite feasible for a retail designer to save the client considerable amounts of money on a project. In the case of Poundland, for example, by judicious design and purchasing, we saved the client around £60,000 per shop fit on what it had previously been spending.

A format where this is something of an anomaly is the flagship store. Flagship stores have long been loss leaders for brands, and it is debatable as to how necessary they will be to brands in the future. Brands' retail investment soared in the 1990s and early 2000s, with projects becoming increasingly elaborate and expensive in the quest to gain awareness and brand loyalty. Brands may justify the financial burden of a flagship as a necessary part of their marketing and promotion activity, suggesting that the lasting impact of a flagship visit can be far stronger than advertising campaign exposure. They see the flagship as bringing their universe to life, making a statement and creating theatre to excite and entice, which online shopping is struggling to do, by its nature not being able to give a physically embracing experience. However, as technology develops, it is able to give increasingly intimate and personal experiences and will continue to do so.

Evaluating design by shopper experience

Evaluating shopper experience is an entire field of research with specialist companies and university departments, all trialling methods and technologies that just might hold the answer to what makes the customer buy. Retailers are always seeking that particular objective. There are a number of limitations in evaluating retail design through such methodologies. Retail design is only one small element of what makes a brand or product successful. The client has to be served by the '7Rs', to have the right product or brand, the right ethos and sets of values, with the right message for the right audience at the right time, in the right place with the right value to the customer. Retail design can work magic, but it cannot work miracles where the other elements are not in place. The clients also have a responsibility to fulfil their obligation to their customers, giving them what they want, when and where they want it, through all the tools at their disposal, not only through retail design.

Conclusion

Designers are facilitators, curators and guides, perhaps more so now than simply the creators of spaces. They have to be able to interpret the culture of their clients and deliver that through a vastly wide gamut of media/routes to market. As well as how those are communicated, the designer has to consider the ways by which the message or promise is received, adopted and embedded. There also has to be consideration towards the impact that these customer portals have on the client culture and on the locale or environment in which the client operates.

Design as a career is so wide ranging, and that is what makes it such an exciting and powerful opportunity. It is now the responsibility of the 'creative' to take ownership of the power they have to effect the way people feel about themselves and the world we live in. From a designer perspective, the meek will no longer inherit the earth – it will be the creatives! Go out now and create a better world.

Reference

Department for Communities and Local Government (2013) *The Future of High Streets, Progress since the Portas Review*. Available at: https://www.gov.uk/government/uploads/system/uploads/attachment_data/file/211536/Future_of_High_Street_-_Progress_Since_the_Portas_Review_-revised.pdf. Accessed 12th December 2015.

9 Communication and stakeholders

Tiiu Poldma

Introduction

This chapter explores retail design in terms of formal and informal communication modes that entice consumer spending. Issues explored include the role of consumers in the designed retail store, the context of stakeholders and designers creating the complete retail experience together using tacit knowledge, and the influence of online shopping and how this influences consumer choices. Shopping and the retail environment are rapidly changing as informal social activities and communication modes, marketing and advertising strategies further influence customer decisions and choices. People decide to shop, have a coffee, socialize and engage together in the various forms of retail experiences that they have, and both communication and social activity form the basis of many choices made in retail and retail design. We will explore these concepts in this chapter. Not only is communication a fundamental way for retailers to reach out to consumers; it also influences how stores are conceived and designed, how advertising and branding are marketed to potential customers and how decision-making occurs on various levels and by various stakeholders. Designers play a fundamental role in both communicating with retailers and in creating shopping environments that communicate the end goals of the retailer's brand. Designers also take conceptual ideas and work with stakeholders to transform the retail brand into the reality of the retail environment, whether this is virtual or the real physical store design. Stakeholders and their relationship with designers will also be explored by examining how clients and designers use communicative tools such as co-creation and co-design to develop retail store concepts and make meaning of design decisions. These all form part of the tools used as an aesthetic catalyst to generate design ideas and create tangible and viable retail solutions, often with these more tacit forms of knowledge.

Two case studies are examined to explore how both formal and informal communication modes are applied. The case studies show a retailing clothing store design and a clothing retail website promoting a solution for water in one part of the world using a retail approach in another part of the world. In the first example of the store design, both formal and informal modes of communication inform decision-making. A particular form of conversational meaning making (Vaikla-Poldma, 2003; Poldma, 2010, 2014) occurs between client and designer through the designing of the concept for the store, which frames the co-creation and co-design of the store and its evolution from an idea towards a completed product. In the second example of the website, informal modes of retail are used to benefit a humanitarian need in a different part of the world, as retail goes beyond selling to encompass problem-solving from an engineering perspective.

Retail design, traditional commercial trade, the concept of 'selling' and communication and changing consumer buying patterns

Approaches to retail design have transformed substantially in just the past twenty years as buying patterns and ways of shopping have changed, and been changed, by technological advancements and also by consumers whose needs and tastes are constantly morphing. In the traditional retail design of physical stores of the past fifty years, the consumer and the owner-retailer were essentially the lone stakeholders as the users and clients respectively. Conversely, in today's retail environment, the shopper has become a savvy online consumer with changing tastes that are both affected by and influenced by virtual online possibilities that challenge traditional shopping patterns and retail store experiences of the past. People from diverse age groups, social situations and cultures continuously search for enriching and meaningful shopping experiences as they are enticed by goods and services both online and in the new and dynamic retail shopping environment in every part of the world. Stakeholders are multiple, ranging from the traditional retailer to complex marketing and communication strategists, each creating both online and physical retail experiences locally and worldwide. And while online shopping increases the need for retailers to become more innovative in how they communicate to attract sales, conversely the new technological world and urbanization are also changing social patterns of people both as consumers and as participants in social life. People still want to communicate and find social participation increasingly in urban places. Shopping malls, stores, cafes and restaurants have become gathering places for those who are aging. This in part is changing the way that retailing is done and subsequently how the physical store and retail experience are conceived.

A brief historical perspective: Commerce, retail and communication

To add a perspective on how communication modes currently influence retail experiences, a situating of historic context is presented to understand how and why communication has become such an embedded part of how retail design works. Communication modes have long existed in the very way that retail has emerged in Western society particularly. While mercantile trade has existed for centuries, 'commercialism' in its current form began about 1300 A.D. in Europe where attitudes to merchants were those of negative connotations such as 'disapproval of the "best" elements in society' (Lower, 1978, p. 126). With the change towards a technological and increasingly urban society in Europe towards the end of the nineteenth century, the added notions of progress and hard work took hold as people gained freedom from feudal systems and forged domesticity and with that became consumers. Material progress has been a concept in Western civilization for about three hundred years and has recently accelerated at a pace not known previously in history. Wright (2004, p. 3) notes that

> most people in the Western cultural tradition still believe in the Victorian ideal of progress, a belief succinctly defined by the historian Sidney Pollard as the assumption about a pattern of change exists in the history of mankind . . . that it consists of irreversible changes in one direction only, and that this direction is towards improvement.

Retail emerged at this time as a means of allowing the newly created consumer in a new technologically advancing society to be able to acquire things in ways never before seen in history, and moved society from a traditional agricultural and rural one towards an urban and consumer-oriented one. As the twentieth century approached, and as domestic life burgeoned within this new technologically progressive society, shopping and buying goods accelerated to what became known as the retail industry, with retail design broadening to include creating concepts of retailing, retail design, merchandising, advertising and new and various forms of selling to consumers that have morphed over the past century and a half (Malnar & Vodvarka, 1992; Wright, 2004).

Changing retail approaches in store designing

Retail design accelerates from the earliest country store and initial order catalogues in North America to full flagship store shopping from the 1950s onwards and during the baby boom era in North America. Retail exploded during this time through the early 1990s with both store types and store designs emerging as a fully developed specialty of interior design and architecture. Emerging retail merchandising types include flagship retail stores, various types of boutiques, specialty stores, and chain stores.

Each store type and approach taps into consumer needs, and each with increasingly sophisticated advertising, sales strategies and ways to attract consumers. Retail design became sophisticated in that the more standardized store plans of the mid-century gave way to a variety and alternative ways to design retail stores. Stores became tied to a specific design approach, whether it was the unstructured and rough interior of the big-box store or the fully detailed and higher-end boutique; each store type developed its brand accordingly to suit consumer needs, demands and price points. Certain understood retail strategies included price points suiting designed store styles, from upscale higher-end products shown off in megastore designs to low budget 'non-design' unfinished warehouses for 'no name' and low-cost retail approaches.

The emergence of visual merchandising and online shopping as communication strategies

Emerging approaches to retail design in the early 1990s honed the concept of visual merchandising and store displays (Barr & Broudy, 1990; Pegler, 2006), wherein retail design became a sophisticated means of commerce. Communication modes at this time thus incorporated the visual display as a means of enticing customers into the store. However, at this time, retail design still relied almost exclusively on the physical store designs to bring in customers to buy products. As Pegler (2006) notes changes in retailing in both the 1970s and the 1990s:

> During most of the 20th century, most people in the US shopped in department stores, large specialty stores and in small mom-and-pop stores that were usually geared toward the local neighborhood trade . . . it was the late 60s and early 70s that ushered in the 'boutique' phenomenon; and specialized shops-within-a-shop that began to show up in major department stores . . . the 1990s has witnessed the growth of a new phenomenon: the superstore or big box store . . . (and) the vendor shop . . . miniatures of the designers' or band names own retail stores . . . for the buying public. Visual merchandising and display more than just attracts them – it keeps them in the store.
>
> (Pegler, 2006, p. 297)

Communication modes thus were essentially visual and linked to both the store display and the subsequent store design itself, each one enticing and then encouraging the consumers to enter and purchase goods or services, and hopefully more than they might have intended. Boutique and mega-stores each developed heightened approaches to specifically target certain types of consumers. Window displays and store designs in the 1980s targeted markets very specifically using their particular store designs as communication modes.

The advent of online shopping and changing communication modes

And while the mail-order catalogue remained strong in some sectors, eventually this retreated as online shopping began to take hold, beginning in 1994. The advent of online shopping began to change the nature of the retail environment as the nature of the shopping experience itself began to change along with how consumers could tap into buying without having to go to a physical store. According to Griffin and Collins (2007), 'the catalog concept has evolved further with the development of interactive shopping media' (p. 177).

With this new way of buying, in the past twenty years or so, spatial design of physical stores has undergone transformational change as well. Branding and the spatial ambiance increasingly began to take precedence alongside consumer-driven experiences. As I noted in 2009:

> With globalization, consumer desires are becoming ever more immediate, and physical retail spaces compete with virtual stores . . . this acceleration of goods acquisition allows for consumers to tap into their needs for sensual and exotic products and services through brands that have become easily accessible.
>
> (Poldma, 2009, p. 171)

Branding the environment as reflective of the retail experience emerged in the 2000s with the heightening of consumer tastes and as the virtual online retail experience began to take hold. First, physical stores expanded and changed as big-box stores emerged to attract a new type of consumer, and while they first competed with online shopping this rapidly changed with both online and physical-store shopping providing consumers multiple shopping experiences. Second, brand marketing emerged as a major tool for various people to sell products, and the concept of 'multi-category design' emerged to suit the expanding need of consumers for certain products produced by designers themselves, whether in fashion or in design and architecture, all to promote a 'lifestyle concept' (Griffin & Collins, 2007, pp. 165–166).

Visual merchandising as an emerging formal and informal communication mode

Third, visual merchandising became a sophisticated approach as a way of combining formal and informal communications modes. Visual merchandising is a heightened form of communication that uses a combination of visual story display, retailing, and advertising to emphasize the ways that merchandise is displayed and 'branded' to the public. This is done by the dominance of various factors such as color, location and coordination of merchandise, price, brand, end use etc. (Pegler, 2006). Each choice recalls the communication of both formal and informal messages to the buyer – the design and placement of merchandise in the interior of the store is detailed to entice and attract shoppers for what they may need and to go beyond to entice them for things that they may not even want. In essence, retail design thus becomes communication, in terms of both communicating for purchase and communicating more subliminal messages that appeal to various needs and desires as these are connected to acquiring things (Pegler, 2006).

The concept of the idea of point of purchase became the complete means by which a product was promoted. As notes Pegler (2006):

> 'Point of purchase' has become in recent times a complete and convoluted industry. It is display, fixturing, store design, and advertising all in one. It is the total image fabrication of a product; the attraction to the product as well as the provider of the product to the selling floor (p. 311) . . . 'used to be synonymous with impulse shopping' (p. 311) and can be '. . . permanent, semi-permanent, temporary or promotional'.
>
> (p. 314)

Store designs reflected these new approaches, and designers provided retailers with designs that pushed these ideas even further (Barr & Broudy, 1990). In the last twenty years, retail design has also been transformed by globalization, wherein the branding of the retail object and spatial ambiance have become essential elements of communication (Poldma, 2009). The informal communication of the store as an entertainment place took hold as

> ambiance and lifestyle in both virtual and physical retail environments is what sells, as lifestyles are created and fostered through the acquisition of goods. . . . [T]he space transcends the retail aspect and becomes a meeting place, where emotions are manipulated into a positive experience, enticing the customer to buy even more.
>
> (Poldma, 2009, p. 171)

Consumer buying patterns, types and stakeholders

With these various techniques in mind, the evolution has also occurred with the consumer and the types of stakeholders involved, as current buying patterns have become entrenched in individual desires and needs. For instance, the sheer volume and diversity of available merchandise in the North American retail market suggests a full range of choice. And yet, for example, gender preferences in shopping remain more or less the same since the 1990s – males tend to prefer buying for need, while women buy on impulse as much as need, and these patterns occur both in online and in physical-store shopping. Furthermore, buying patterns range from age to gender to type of consumer, and this complicates the retail landscape. Retail markets are thus responding by providing every range of product sold in every way possible – from online to physical presence to several versions of shopping in between.

Types of consumer appeal

Types of consumer appeal have broadened to include people from all ages and stages of life. While in the fifties and sixties most shopping was done by families in domesticated situations (Malnar & Vodvarka, 1992), today there are as many types of consumers as there are ways to shop. From children to youth and from aging baby boomers to older shoppers, there are multiple types of consumers, and each one requires a branded approach to reach the target market. In essence, stores

> have become seductive places that aim to attract customers over time. This means enticing people into the store and providing an experience that they will appreciate and return therefore buying more goods in the process. Retailers are increasingly making store design 'an adventure', a seductive place where people would want to shop . . . the store creates a backdrop with its design, where form, color, lighting and texture all integrate to transform the brand into a fascinating sensory experience, promoting the product to the fullest.
>
> (Poldma, 2009, p. 171)

For example, in the United States, consumers are multiple, as Generation X, Generation Y and millennials join aging pre-Depression baby boomers and diverse cultural contexts in the composition of the retail consumer. Globally, marketing to the different generations and cultural backgrounds of the consumer is varied as each generation has its own particular needs, desires and tastes. When location and cultural background are added to the mix, the specific aims and goals of communication are then honed to the particular group or groups targeted (Gur u, 1984; Williams & Page, 2011). New disciplines have emerged in marketing and psychology sectors as private industry and marketing agencies vie for the consumers' dollar and work to appeal to heightened consumer sense and the type of shopping experience that they need, require and desire.

Formal and informal communication modes: Cool-hunting, advertising and store design

Current forms of formal and informal communication use aspects of these earlier ways of attracting customers and include formal approaches using advertising and promotion, and informal approaches such as word-of-mouth and cool-hunting.

Informal modes of communication in retail design: Cool-hunting

Informal communication modes include the word-of-mouth and online communication tools used to entice people to products and services. These informal modes are consumer-based in that through word of mouth and subliminal messages in media and online the consumer is enticed to buy for a perceived need or desire. Informal modes of communication include (but are not limited to) online methods and scoping methods. Examples of new ways of shopping go beyond online experiences and are reflective of shopper needs and desires. Online methods promoted by social media allow customers to express their views on products and services, and provide vehicles for word-of-mouth engagement of products or services. Other informal modes seek to glean consumer reactions and desires, such as cool-hunting.

Cool-hunting is a term that originates from fashion and the means to find and forecast the next trend, and then entice consumers to buy that product. It is used in marketing and retailing to find the next best trend (Pedroni, 2012). Firms and individuals are hired to find out what branding might work for markets, which is done in-house or by firms hired to scope out what consumers want or desire. Data is usually collected using ethnographic methods. In particular these methods are used for scoping out the desires of the youth population, a demographic sometimes seen as unpredictable (Gloor & Cooper, 2007). This approach has really exploded in the past few years, as retailers and interested consumers look for the latest trends and promote lifestyle choices based on these trends.

Street fashion and ethical practices

Related to these concepts is the role of the everyday (Steeves, 2006) and the influence of celebrities on fashion choices and consumer decision-making. Designers are often encouraged to follow trends and then set them through innovation. Celebrities capture style or create it, often drawing from influences in the moment. Street fashion, for example, often takes its cues from the underground and from issues that face people in their everyday lives or issues that people want to expose in society. Fashion during the punk era or when rap first emerged, for example, influenced underground consumer buying choices first, and then migrated to more mainstream fashion as people saw and accepted these new trends. The experiences of people as drivers of fashion or as consumers of fashion communicates the 'questioning of traditions and rules' (Featherstone, 1991, in Damhorst et al., 2006, p. 76). Ethics is also an element of consideration here, as consumers may question 'the ethics of global apparel production systems and consumers in economically advantaged countries. . . . [C]ontroversy abounds about the hiring of poor people around the world to sew garments for incredibly low pay' (Damhorst et al., 2006, p. 77).

Formal modes of communication

Formal modes of communication include advertising and the physical retail store design. These reflect the brand and provide the framework for the retail experience, in that communication in retail aims at the consumer formally using advertising and promotion to sell the product or service using the design of the retail concept brand. This is practical and practice-based, in that retail designs rely on the practical application of how understanding human behavior and buying patterns are translated into tangible physical designs to both predict and promote retail designs and products as they are put into commercial marketplaces. Advertising and physical store design are currently the most common formal modes of retail design and the retail experience, and these are used in tandem with visual merchandising methods to various degrees.

Brandscaping has become pre-eminent, as advertising and branding meld together to create a retail environment ever more enticing to consumers. Media plays an increasing subliminal role in supporting certain brands and giving exposure to certain trends (Damhorst et al., 2006, p. 108). Related concepts include 'retailment'; 'the term "retailment" has been coined to describe the use of multiple activities in the retail environment to create hybrid retail concepts' (Poldma, 2009, p. 171).

With the increase in online shopping, one would think that stores would be empty. I was recently walking the streets of Chicago, and the proliferation of shops, cafes and bakeries was astounding. There were throngs of people walking and shopping regardless of the time of day. At every corner there were bakery-cafes and shops mixed in with the larger retailers, hotels and businesses. People were shopping, yes, but what was notable was the throng of people congregating together, shopping, then having a coffee, all consumers and all engaging in social activity. The formal modes of communication were evident in the advertising and branding images vying for the attention of the shopper, and then enticing the shopper into the store and the designs of the stores themselves.

There is speculation among retailers that, in the future, less footprint area will be required by stores as people increasingly refer online to their choices and needs and may only come to the store to validate or to see for themselves a product. However, until everyone is online and people no longer feel the need for tactile touching and trying out potential products, it is an open question as to when this might occur. Other factors also contribute to communicating the shopping experience, which we will discuss next.

The psychology of buying

To be able to use formal and informal modes of communication requires understanding the psyche of the buyer. While originally retail design essentially was targeted at selling the most for the highest price possible, these goals are diversifying as retailers search for the most cost-effective way to reach consumers while also targeting their desires and needs through understanding consumer behavior and psyche while also satisfying the need for sales. New research and emerging literature expands beyond consumer sales as the primary goal of retail design and visual merchandising. Various issues include understanding the psychology and perceptions of buying, the changing patterns of buying in light of virtual online abilities, understanding current market trends and predicting consumer behavior, targeting age groups and identifying their needs, and considering changing buying patterns, consumer perceptions and behavior. Various techniques are used by specialists hired by retailers, such as experts in behavior, psychology, anthropology, marketing and business, all exploring how to delve deeper into the customer psyche and predict buying trends.

As stores became meccas of customer enticement in the latter part of the twentieth century, designers employed subliminal techniques such as impulse and destination purchasing as specific ingrained methods used in the planning and design elements chosen for a particular interior retail space, as a way to entice customers into a store, and then to lead them towards destination items, often far into the store. Once there, the design plan and spatial organization then guided customers back towards the point of purchase area, each moment enticing with impulse buying items, even as they pay for their goods (Barr & Broudy, 1990). This form of enticement begins even before the store design, in branding exposure and advertising promoting products to consumers 24-7. Fashion trends and trend forecasting are used to predict consumer desires (Damhorst et al., 2006), while advertising and brand recognition further entice people to buy products, or new ones of the same thing, even if they do not need them.

Shopping with added social and ethical value

Perceptions of buying have recently been changing with the advent of shopping becoming increasingly both a social activity and an ethical one. The additional value of shopping both as a social activity and as an ethical decision adds new dimensions to the perceptions of buying. First, people are congregating more and more often together to shop, to have a coffee together or just to meet at the local shopping center or mall. This social activity has supplanted similar communal activities that occurred in the markets and community centers of the past. People get together for group activities such as walking together in the mall or to have a coffee together within a community-type atmosphere that more often than not happens within the shopping center or the commercial downtown complex.

Second, the ethical values we use as consumers for making decisions are influencing what purposes we buy for and what causes people might support when making purchases. Our values are increasingly influencing our choices as we support causes or identify with certain products for various personal, social or cultural reasons. How people spend money may also include making sustainable and ethical choices to make a difference in the world. These social, ethical and cultural values have become goals for some consumers who are making buying decisions.

Shopping as both a social experience and a form of social communication

Shopping has always been a form of social communication and social experience. Shopping as an experience is a mode of social endeavor, regardless of age or stage of life, cultural location and urban place; however, the ways we socialize and come together are very different today than from the ways that we engaged in social activity in the markets, agoras or traditional shopping centers of the past century (Kepron, 2014). Social activity provides various opportunities for communication depending on differing needs of people, whether it is youth searching for the newest trend and hanging out together, or older people going to the shopping complex for social activity and social participation. We can also choose not to socialize by using electronic check-outs in the store and not speaking to a soul. Even if they are not necessarily socializing, people still like to congregate in places such as shopping malls, cafes and restaurants.

The need for social activity and the need for communication are changing how we use retail spaces such as cafes, shops and malls in urban places as meeting spaces now more than ever before. Activities that used to be segregated – in that we would shop for goods at a grocery store or have lunch or dinner in a restaurant – have long become merged and transformed as dynamic experiences that are happening all together in a time/space continuum. We buy and consume regularly in places where we also do business 24-7, while we engage with colleagues or friends around the world from the comfort of our local café as we are online. Designing has become engaged with the notion of the 'collapse of time', in that global transnational movements have collapsed time into space, and with it transformed how we have experiences, and consequently how we design retail environments. Time has collapsed into space as space changes to account for dynamic activities we engage in, and interior environments capture these dynamics in increasingly diverse ways (Poldma & Wesolkowska, 2005). Designing for 'the collapse of time' means thinking about spaces from a phenomenological perspective, and accounting for people's experiences in real time and for how designed spaces respond to these experiences. Lived experience and the social construction of space are morphed by technology, and interior spaces are no longer singular environments experienced over a long period of time, as was the case before global communication. This means that spaces are places intrinsically tied to lived experience and that this varies from person to context to place (Duncan & Ley, 1993; Vaikla-Poldma, 2003; Poldma & Wesolkowska, 2005). In a similar manner, Lefebvre suggests that

> social space is inhabited by a variety of conceptual objects, natural and social, including the virtual networks and technologies . . . that facilitate the exchange of information and goods. Place as a practices space is tightly linked to the mobility of the individual within the space and his interactivity within it.
>
> (Lefebvre in Poldma & Wesolkowksa, 2005, p. 56)

Consequently, spaces are multiple-activity places, and the people's use of space is defined not by the space but rather by their activities and personal priorities.

Shopping as a form of social participation and inclusion

Shopping has become a means for those who are aging or for people with disabilities to find meaningful social engagement. The shopping environment has also become a way for people with various abilities to congregate in shopping malls and at cafes and to socially engage together. New forms of social congregation are emerging particularly with older populations in places where the retail mall has also become a destination for people to find a sense of community and to combat a sense of isolation. The aging consumer is not 'elderly' and has specific needs different from the youthful or mid-age consumer (Kearney, 2013). For people who are aging, going to the mall or meeting downtown and shopping together are an easy and attractive way to remain socially active.

For persons with disabilities this has been shown to provide a means of social engagement as well as a means to fight stigma and social isolation. Shopping and malls provide much-needed public spaces for people who may not have the economic means to pay for entertainment, or for those who seek a destination for daily life activities, and for still others in many parts of the world, providing a reprieve from the mundane of the everyday. Social aspects of retail experiences, while neither formal nor informal modes of communication, are a form of communication that provides a different way for consumers to engage in the retail experience nevertheless, and, in particular for aging populations in many countries, that provides people with places to go to avoid loneliness and isolation.

Retail communication modes as forms of identity

Currently, retail design is faced with changing and dynamic situations that temporalize the retail concept into what is here and now. People take hold of local commercial retail environments as a means to their identity and find meaning in the social aspects that these stores and businesses provide. For example, when hurricane Katrina wreaked havoc on New Orleans in 2005, many neighborhoods were severely damaged in poorer marginal communities. With no retail malls or stores nearby, seeing a crumbling community, one resident decided to take it upon himself to create a community environment using the retail store, a first in the neighborhood. What has also become a community place and a social gathering place in a once devastated area has become both a retail establishment and a beacon of hope (Hartman, 2015). Not only communicating but also serving a social and community need, this retail store provides all this and more. The construction of a sense of place and identity became embedded in these actions as well. By appealing to the community and a need for a sense of self, the retailer in New Orleans provides what people both want and need: a place to congregate and a place to buy and feel a sense of self, of community and of identity. This is all part of our lived experiences, and the retailer taps into these needs from a very fundamental perspective of survival of the community. Other examples include shops for women's shelters and selling products to support local community groups, each one providing the means for struggling communities to both create a sense of identity and provide a place to socialize and congregate (Rothschild, 1999).

At the other extreme are shops and malls, amusement parks and recreational spaces, each competing for the consumer dollar with sophisticated branding and marketing to promote a certain lifestyle. Informal and formal modes of communication communicate a lifestyle and brand beyond the acquisition of goods and into the realm of lived fantasies. An example in North America is Disneyworld and Disneyland. This is a cultural icon, and a cultural phenomenon, communicating a way of life and an identity that is carefully crafted and cultivated. As H. Peter Steeves (2006) notes, both 'being and meaning' are found in the way that brand-name identity is cultivated.

Visiting Disneyland, we become Disney tourists. We live in society with Disneyland, and 'Disney is responsible for constructing part of our cultural identity . . . in terms of the creation of a self and a community within the confines of the park' (Steeves, 2006, p. 164).

Steeves elaborates on how this occurs and suggests that, in North America, personal tastes are imbued with corporate identities, and even '[t]he clothes we wear have long been known to say who and what we are' (2006, p. 167). So while we may ignore these messages, they nevertheless exist in society for those for whom these messages have meaning.

The social construction of space and place

Store designs, as with the designs of corporate spaces or institutions, reflect the identities and attitudes of a culture or of a society. Social communication in interior spaces is in part manifested through the identities and branding that are promoted, and through how the spaces then are both designed and also socially constructed. Similarly, the social construction of spaces and places are governed by the identities that designers and stakeholders wish the retail spaces to promote. In the past, spaces were created to provide services for some and not for others (Poldma, 2009, pp. 232–234). This basic idea still remains, as retailers appeal to certain target groups, and omit others.

However, as dynamic aspects of technology and use of space change, the identity and personal experiences become augmented, and social construction of spaces takes on new and different meanings, from unisex to cultural to social or ethical meanings, depending on the purpose for the retail environment created. Social norms are also changing and depending on the culture within which retailing occurs, and these impact on how retailing is done.

Emerging issues in stakeholder relationships in the design of retail spaces: Co-creation, co-design and lived experiences

In terms of interior spaces and both virtual and physical spaces of retail, interior design and client-user tacit knowledge is a valuable asset in designing retail spaces. Stakeholders in retail design have expanded to include potential buyers who are used by large-scale corporate retailers to gauge consumer trends and needs/desires, while smaller retailers use designers as the point of contact to understand future trends and possibilities.

Consumers in the physical store are still vital to retail success. While more people opt for online shopping, the reality is that people still go to stores to shop, and retailers understand that physical formal modes of communication such as advertising and the physical store must be accompanied by the more informal communication modes that are now available. Perception of value plays a large role in the consumer willingness to buy (Ullakonoja, 2011), while altruistic purpose will also motivate shopping, if the consumers believe that they will contribute to something more than a retail purchase. These are forms of tacit knowledge that contribute to how retailers glean the pulse of consumers and try to predict what they will want to buy.

Kepron (2014) suggests that shifting consumer experiences and needs dictate more acute responses by a team of people. New stakeholders now include marketing experts, sales managers, designers, store owners and managers, buyers, developers and other stakeholders who all contribute to the making of the retail experience. And yet, at the fundamental level, Kepron also suggests that

> what customers will really want will be for products and services to be imbued with utility and significance. The design – of products, services and entire experiences – will become a critical factor in making entire shopping places relevant in a world of ubiquitous access and abundant choice.

> (p. 16)

What is of value to one consumer is something entirely else for another consumer. While some enjoy online shopping, others still prefer seeing the product, while still others use both informal and formal communication modes. People will review advertising online, speak to experts or friends, and then may purchase directly online or only after validating their ideas with the tactile experience in the store. Certain products require the tactile experience, while others do not, and the consumer makes these decisions now, unlike in the past when the retailer made these decisions of what consumers would buy and how.

The role of stakeholders creating that experience thus becomes two-fold. First, multiple needs and shopping experiences require that those stakeholders involved in the retail design process come together and create the virtual and physical means for that experience to occur for the right type (or types) of consumers for a given product or product-experience. Second, while all stakeholders will try to understand the type of desired consumer experience, essential to that experience is both utility and significance for the consumers, and how the design and communication modes of the retail concept speak to them as potential customers.

The role of co-creation, co-design and meaning making in retail experience development

Both co-creation and co-design are usually used as tools in the development of designed products and retail concepts. Co-creation and co-design require that all participants work together in developing new products and services, and collaboratively participate together in the retail development. Co-creation strategies include involving consumers in product and service decision-making. Large corporations use co-creation strategies to organize target markets and consider how their product can provide the best value for their consumer needs. Smaller retailers rely on word-of-mouth and use co-creation strategies by testing ideas on their clients.

Co-designing is a similar approach and has emerged from participatory research strategies used by researchers when considerations of user experiences are crucial to a product or service success for the users themselves (Sanders & Stappers, 2008). This involves using strategies that involve the persons for whom the product or service is created. Designers work together with the users and various stakeholders to develop design program needs and briefs, concepts and implementation of the ideas into the designed retail environment.

In terms of store designs themselves, these can be both virtual online stores and/or real, physical store designs. In interiors, the role of the store design remains one of reflecting the retail concept or brand desired and providing a certain desire for the shopper that is reflected in the other aspects of the branding as a complete retail package. Interior design thinking is used to elicit design concepts and ideas and to transform potential ideas and branding concepts into the reality of the retail concept implemented in a physical interior space. The means to making meaning includes the stakeholders working together to understand what is required or desired, translating consumer needs and desires, predicting consumer patterns, aligning clients to these, and linking the marketing and physical product sales through design thinking and, ultimately, designed interior spaces, products and packaging.

Co-creation, co-design and the role of phenomenological experience

In particular, it is the conversations that designers have with users that are framed within a particular form of aesthetic conversational meaning-making (Poldma, 2010) between clients and designers that is a valuable and necessary part of the retail design experience. Interior designers collaborate together with clients and the various stakeholders involved in a retailing project as the prime means for understanding the types of contexts and experiences needed for a particular retail approach, and from which spatial designs are created to support branding and intentions (Vaikla-Poldma, 2003; Poldma, 2011). This is predicated on a phenomenological approach, wherein the 'real, lived experiences' of both stakeholder and user are understood by the designer in real time (Vaikla-Poldma, 2003). In this type of design approach, designers work together with corporate clients, retailers and the various stakeholders, all of whom create the retail experience, the branding, and ultimately, the store design itself. When engaging with users and stakeholders, 'we make our aesthetic design decisions considering the ways that people live in and appropriate space, integrating their activities in changing and dynamic acts that are experienced in everyday living' (Poldma, 2009, p. 233). Both the act of shopping and the act of designing the shopping experience are phenomenological when they are experienced in real time and in the act of the experience itself. A consumer will use cues perceived from both the formal aesthetics of the retail design and the word-of-mouth of fellow consumers to make decisions in the experience of shopping.

In terms of the designer and the retailer, they co-design experiences together to create the experiences that consumers will have. The designers in this approach temporarily step into the shoes of all concerned stakeholders to subjectively understand what is needed to best communicate the intentions of the participant-stakeholders for the intended design concept. They then return back to the role of the designer who puts together the concepts to accurately reflect the co-participant ideas in a co-creation/co-design approach, and incorporating the pragmatic needs and technical contextual requirements to objectively create the spatial design to reflect qualities desired and the required technical elements that make the store functional and aesthetic.

This approach is phenomenological, in that the persons who are involved are actualizing the design concept through their real, lived experiences in real time. These experiences form the groundwork for the designs that ensue. The designer then interprets these experiences into tangible designs for the physical space. Depending on the scope and size of the project, the designer may work intimately with a lone retailer or develop ideas with entire teams of marketing experts, sales managers, store owners and managers, buyers, developers, project management specialists, architects and engineers, and the consumers who will use the products and/or services.

The design and location of stores themselves are a result of multiple stakeholders who determine the best possible combination of these elements in the decisions made to design and locate a store in a particular place. In terms of specific ways that stakeholders and designers interact, the co-creation and meaning making that occurs and the subsequent design of stores and restaurants also includes conversations and interactions that work through both bottom-line financial issues and more tacit issues such as the store identity and the way that this will be transformed into a tangible reality of the store design itself. People are fickle, and their tastes and desires change often. Designers or retailers alone no longer dictate the retail approach, as both clients and consumers are stakeholders with subjective needs. This is tacit knowledge that needs to be captured by designers and translated into a workable and successful retail design, and this remains one of the foundations of retail design as a spatially designed place for products and services.

With these various ideas and considerations in mind, we will now explore the communicative strategies of two case studies, one a formal retail store design and the second one a website that sells clothing for hydrating the world. In the first example, we will look at how co-creation and co-design both occur within the framework of the design of a small clothing franchise. The first case study is an example of a retailer revitalizing a brand using both formal and informal communication modes, while the second example uses informal communication modes and retailing for creating solutions to water problems halfway around the world from the location of the retail website.

KC clothing company: A case study about client–stakeholder relationships and strategies for retail design

The first case study example shows how these ideas are put into practice in the creation of a new store concept. KC clothing is a high-quality clothing retailer, and, as they say on their website, 'KC Clothing Company creates a bridge between casual and contemporary with high quality, lifestyle clothing targeted at fashion aware and quality-conscious men and women' (retrieved from http://confedcourtmall.com/store-directory/stores-alphabetically/kc-clothing).

This clothing store was an existing clothing retailer that had a solid foundation of return clients but wanted to change locations, update the store and image and expand its branding and image to integrate its emerging sense of the marketplace where it is located to tap into the desires and needs of its customers. Using a co-creation and co-design approach, the interior designer worked directly with the owner to develop a concept for the retail store. The store needed to reflect the local ambiance with a contemporary freshness that would be reflected in both the virtual advertisement communication and the physical space. Using visual sketches, materials and conversation, the stakeholders used design thinking and meaning making to translate a leased space into a retail concept that would capture the essence of what the retailer wanted and what is reflected in its customer needs and desires.

Working together, the designer and client developed ideas and brainstormed on what would be able to represent what the client wanted. First, ideas were exchanged about different ways to represent the store branding needed. Then initial rough ideas were developed of the store design in sketch form and with all the contextual elements considered, including potential branding graphics, materials, color, merchandising techniques, lighting and support services. In Figure 9.1 we see how the designer explores potential ideas with the design process using the loosely organized ideas and material suggestions that are then

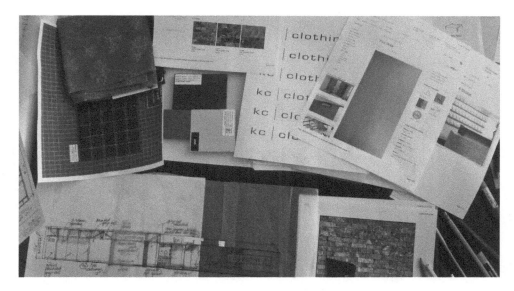

Figure 9.1 An example of the desk during a preliminary work session
Source: Poldma, 2011

discussed through a series of conversations. Figure 9.1 shows the working desk of the co-creation and co-design as it happened initially. The designer and client developed the emergence of the design/branding concept, done both with online and actual visual tools.

Through a series of intense conversations, meaning was made about how to create a brand, an atmosphere, a way to connect with consumers, and an expression of these qualities using design elements to create the store image that reflected the brand. The client and designer each arrived at the table with some ideas in mind and used visual images, materials and sketches to express what each stakeholder was thinking would be great to develop the store design. Using conversation meaning making, the meaning was made through the examination of the store design in organizing the store itself, through the elements of displaying and through creating an image of lifestyle reflecting the goals of the owner who had a close relationship with client needs and desires to create a product reflective of both the urban place and the store itself.

Once the preliminary ideas were sorted out and the ones to be used emerged from the back-and-forth conversations, the designer presented the final concept to the client for approval. At this point other stakeholders were brought in to help to orchestrate the concept transfer from ideas into solutions. Both the designer and the client worked with various stakeholders to ensure that the ideas would be translated into the tangible reality desired. Figure 9.2 shows the evolution towards a materialization of the visual elements of the store in terms of details and materials as proposed.

Again, these required fine-tuning as the store design and final choices began to take shape. Branding and graphic communication are fundamental to the store concept development alongside virtual advertising mechanisms. This was then translated into the development of the advertising, the logo and the various components needed for advertising, marketing and the merchandise selection and store implementation. The client consulted

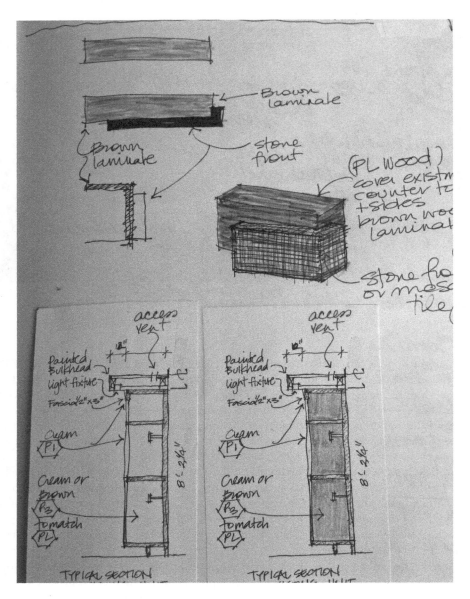

Figure 9.2 Preliminary sketches and material concepts of the proposed store

Source: Poldma, 2011

with the various stakeholders in the process regularly to glean the most attractive way to develop the lifestyle the client wanted to convey for potential and existing customers who bought the clothing as a reflection of both lifestyle and brand.

Completed and successful, the retailer uses online media to perpetuate the image and continually reflect the quality of the product and services that are provided. Formal communication occurs through advertising and the physical location, while informal

Figure 9.3 The final store design implemented
Source: Poldma, 2011; Courtesy: K. MacKenzie

communication continues with online word-of-mouth tools such as Facebook and Twitter and various local activities.

Hydrated world: A case study about devising an engineered humanitarian solution using an online shopping experience

In this second example, a branding approach is used to solve a severe crisis in the world. Through word-of-mouth, I was made aware of this clothing company that my nephew was developing. As a traditional interior designer of retail spaces, I was drawn to the approach of solving a world problem using a retail website as the catalyst.

Using a 'virtual store' approach and connected to lifestyle, two partners from a mechanical engineering background developed a way to solve water issues in places where water is in scarce supply, and using found local materials and simple concepts to empower local people to develop their own water source in various places where water is scarce. To be able to sponsor the creation of the filters they designed, they began a retail clothing 'store' virtually online, to raise funds to support the development of the water filter solution and to use the retail website that sells clothing. The company makes a commitment that every item sold will provide clean water to those in countries where this is not possible. Hydrated World began as a 'Kickstarter' project, with the partners identifying a clear goal: 'Every item purchased provides someone in a developing nation with 500 litres of clean drinking water each year for 25+ years' (retrieved from https://www.kickstarter.com/projects/1822576907/hydrated-world).

The partner-owner-engineers have devised a way to provide that clean water and use media, advertising and retail shopping to engage consumers in shopping while contributing

HYDRATED WORLD

THE APPAREL COMPANY WITH A MISSION TO ELIMINATE THE
WATER CRISIS.

Every item purchased provides someone with access to 500 L of safe water/year for 25 years.

We're working with grass roots teams to create sustainable water in the developing world.

Figure 9.4a Hydrated World X logo

Source: Hydrated World; Courtesy: Mack Saunders and Spencer Kelly (February 2015)

SAFEWATER
+PROJECT

We work with the African based Safe Water Project. The Safe Water Project launches locally owned and operated social businesses in South Sudan. The project teams are trained to build and test the biosand filters to ensure the recipients are protected from contaminants in the water. Every water project we work on ensures that 100% of the project cost is used in the African economy. Every water project not only saves lives, but also helps with development, employment, health and sustainability of villages in Africa. The bio-filters do not require any chemicals or replacement parts to operate, providing a source of safe water for up to 30 years.

Figure 9.4b Safe Water Project logo

Source: Courtesy of Monolith (September 2014)

to a growing world humanitarian need. In this instance there is no physical store, yet, when online, the potential customer is enticed by a youth lifestyle and style that is attractive, and to clothing that is both chic and functional. Figure 9.4 shows an example of part of the web site, demonstrating the branding and the ways that the company communicates with potential customers:

According to Aleksander, 'To date, Hydrated World has sponsored over 50 biosand filters, helping over 500 people and providing over 1,000,000 liters of safe water each year.'

Discussion

In the example of Hydrated World, the online project uses retail as a means of raising both funds and awareness of a dire humanitarian need. Not only is design the catalyst for a necessary and useful solution, the concept developed is supported by retail as a means to raise funds through the sale of clothing that is marketed to a lifestyle type; the sales provide the means to provide the water to places where it is needed, and also provide the people who need it with the tools to get the water they need. Online shopping can thus offer solutions to world and humanitarian situations when the products sold work towards providing solutions to real urban or rural human problems, in this case providing clean water to communities in need.

In the case study KC Clothing, we witness an active transformation of a brand that currently uses online advertising and social community to provide high-quality products to its customers. Success is reflected both in the advertising and marketing of the brand and in the way the store design and image reflects the lifestyle being provided by the clothing that is presented. Both the beauty and quality of the local environment and the high-quality brand come through in the simple integration of formal and informal communication modes.

As we have seen with the case study of the clothing retailer, the merging of online and physical retail store environment captures for the owner the essence of the lifestyle brand that they use to sell a quality product.

Both formal and informal modes of communication inform the ways that retail design has emerged as a way of reflecting consumer desires, experiences and needs. Store designs and online shopping both are vehicles to engage consumers, and each product tailors its target market using various formal and informal tools.

Conclusion

For retailing, retailers and retail designers, communication is essential in relaying the value of the product and the retail experience. Whether it is the creation of the retail concept with the branding and identity, or the ways that people shop in virtual and real stores, design can influence consumer purchasing and the shopping experience itself. Communication is a part of the design process from the moment the client and designer speak and work together, and through the development of the brand and concept both as communicative tools. Communication is fundamental for the implementation of the design and the ability of the design to convey the product/service to the consumer using the various tools described in this chapter. Formal and informal communication modes are continuing to change as quickly as the available tools change. Ultimately we have seen how both virtual and real forms of stores work for their intended purpose, and how both formal and informal communication modes can be used to elicit perceptions and meanings for consumers and sell quality and lifestyle choices to potential buyers.

Social and ethical considerations continue to become issues to consider in retail and retail design as well. As the baby boomer age group becomes older, they are already demanding different products and services than their predecessors, and consumer patterns will continue to change. Implications for design and designers include understanding these dynamics, how these issues affect consumer choices, and how valuable the role of communication is for enticing shoppers and developing brand loyalty through their application of the design process. Ultimately, what will drive retail in the future will depend on the type of society people want to live in and how what they buy will provide the means for that society to sustain itself. Community and ethics are playing a larger role in how retailing is done in certain sectors, as consumers look for both utility and a response to their desires.

Acknowledgements

KC Clothing Company, Charlottetown, PEI, owner Kim MacKenzie
  Hydrated World, Waterloo, Ontario, Canada, partners Aleksander Poldma and Spencer Kelly

References

Barr, V. and Broudy, C. (1990). *Designing to Sell: A Complete Guide to Retail Store Planning and Design*, Second Edition. London: McGraw-Hill.

Damhorst, M.L., Miller-Spillman, K.A. and Michelman, S.O. (2006). *The Meanings of Dress*, Second Edition. New York: Fairchild Publications, Inc.

Duncan, J. and Ley, D. (Eds.). (1993). *Place/Culture/Representation*. London and New York: Routledge. Frontline program 'The Merchants of Cool' November 2002. Retrieved from http://www.pbs.org/wgbh/pages/frontline/shows/cool/.

Featherstone, M. (1991). *Consumer culture and postmodernism*. London: Sage.

Gloor, P.A. and Cooper, S.M. (2007). *Coolhunting: Chasing Down the Next Big Thing*. AMACOM Div. American Management Association. ISBN 0-8144-7386-5.

Griffin, J. and Collins, P. (2007). *Wear Your Chair: When Fashion Meets Interior Design*. New York: Fairchild Publications, Inc.

Gurău, C. (1984). A life-style analysis of consumer loyalty profile: Comparing Generation X and millennial consumers. *Journal of Consumer Marketing*, 29(2), pp. 103–113.

Hartman, S. (2015). *Ten Years After Katrina, Man Looks to Revive Lower Ninth Ward*. CBS News. Retrieved from http://www.cbsnews.com/news/katrina-new-orleans-ten-years-after-hurricane-beacon-of-hope-emerges-in-lower-ninth-ward/

Hydrated World Kickstarter project. (n.d.). Retrieved from https://www.kickstarter.com/projects/1822576907/hydrated-world

Hydrated World Website (n.d.) Retrieved from www.hydratedworld.com

Kearney, A.T. (2013). *Understanding the Needs of the Aging Consumer*. Consumer Goods Forum, 19 pages. Retrieved from https://www.atkearney.com/documents/10192/682603/Understanding+the+Needs+and+Consequences+of+the+Aging+Consumer.pdf/6c25ffa3–0999–4b5c-8ff1-afdca0744fdc

Kepron, D. (2014). *Retail (r) Evolution*. Cincinnati, OH: ST Books.

Lower, A.R.M. (1978). *A Pattern for History*. Toronto: McLelland & Stewart.

Malnar, J.M. and Vodvarka, F. (1992). *The Interior Dimension: A Theoretical Approach to Enclosed Space*. New York: Van Nostrand Reinhold.

Pedroni, M. (2012). From Fashion Forecasting to Coolhunting: Prevision Models in Fashion and in Cultural Production. In Berry, J. (Ed.), *Fashion Capital: Style Economies, Sites and Cultures*. Oxford: Interdisciplinary Press, pp. 97–113.

Pegler, M.M. (2006). *Visual Merchandising and Store Design*. New York: Fairchild Publications Inc.

Poldma, T. (2009). *Taking Up Space: Exploring the Design Process*. New York: Fairchild Publications.

Poldma, T. (2010). Aesthetic meaning - making as Design Thinking: Communicating within the Design Process. In Uber, T. (Ed.) In the proceedings of the IDEC International Conference, March.

Poldma, T. (2011). Transforming interior spaces: Enriching subjective experiences through design research. *Journal of Research Practice*, 6(2), Article M13.

Poldma, T. and Wesolkowska, M. (2005). «Globalization and Changing Conceptions of Time – Space: A Paradigm Shift for Interior Design?» In – Form 5, University of Nebraska, Lincoln, Nebraska, USA.

Rothschild, J. (1999). *Design and Feminism: Re-visioning Spaces, Places and Everyday Things*. New Brunswick, NJ: Rutgers University Press.

Sanders, E. and Stappers, P.J. (2008). Co-creation and the new landscapes of design. *Co-design*, 4(1), pp. 5–18. Retrieved from http://www.maketools.com/articles-papers/CoCreation_Sanders_Stappers_08_preprint.pdf

Steeves, H.P. (2006). *The Things Themselves: Phenomenology and the Return to the Everyday.* Albany, NY: State University of New York Press.

Ullakonoja, J. (2011). *The Effects of Retail Design on Consumer Perceived value.* Master thesis, Department of Marketing. Aalto, Finland: Aalto University, School of Economics.

Vaikla-Poldma, T. (2003). *An investigation of learning and teaching processes in an interior design class: An interpretive and contextual inquiry.* Unpublished doctoral dissertation, McGill University, Montreal, Canada.

Williams, K.C. and Page, R.A. (2011). Marketing to the generations. *Journal of Behavioural Studies in Business,* 3, 1–17. Retrieved from http://www.aabri.com/manuscripts/10575.pdf

Wright, R. (2004). *A Short History of Progress.* Toronto: House of Anansi Press, Inc.

10 Online retail design

Delia Vazquez and Anthony Kent

Introduction

For store-based retailers, the rapid growth of information gathering and shopping on the Internet has become a major challenge. It has radically changed the entire value chain from the manufacturer to the end consumer, and it has facilitated the compression of spatial distances, time and knowledge (Carnoy and Castells 2001). During the 1990s, retailers began using the web to communicate with customers, business partners, and investors. New forms of networks and connections contributed to the emergence of e-commerce and access to information, services and products. It enabled and accelerated mediation between suppliers and customers, and contributed to the development of more personal relationships between the brand and consumer. In this, the digital revolution fundamentally changed the balance of power between producers to consumers, empowering consumers through access to knowledge, services and products.

In undertaking these changes, the importance of website design and its interface with users was recognised from an early stage (Hanna 1997). The site, framed by the PC screen, could 'stage' performances to encourage repeat attendance by audiences (Moon 1999). Its design facilitated collection of personal data and personalised marketing. Technological advances increased online capabilities, and their acceptance by consumers led to new communication and distribution paradigms across physical and digital media. Multichannel and omnichannel retailing strategies aimed to integrate brand communication, experiences and merchandise (Verhoef et al. 2015). Throughout these developments, design has taken a central role by communicating the retail brand to consumers across all their digital devices, from desktop to mobile. Moreover, online retail design itself has evolved as new possibilities for interaction and engagement have emerged. Their dimensions and their fit with e-commerce form the central theme of this chapter.

Online retailing

The growth of e-commerce has made significant inroads into the traditional world of store-based retailing. While many of these retailers have extended their operations online, start-up entrants such as Net-a-Porter and ASOS have recorded significant success without, or with very limited, physical store presence. For these retailers the product assortment is the primary driver rather than the retailing format itself (Korgaonkar et al. 2006); the entire store environment has had to be recreated on a screen. The retail designer's ability to appeal to all senses of the shopper through a complex combination of ambient, structural, social, and aesthetic elements has, over time, been reduced to a predominantly visual appeal (Eroglu et al. 2001). However, a greater diversity of online environments, media and software presents new opportunities for design and its future direction. These are evident in four modes of online retailing: 'pureplay' online sites, portals, mobile devices and integrated omnichannel sites.

Pureplay retailers

A pureplay retailer exists only online in contrast to bricks-and-clicks stores, which have physical store presence and online presence (Pan et al. 2002). With this format, it is easier to search and compare products and brands than in physical stores (Grewal et al. 2004). Costs are minimised due to the absence of store acquisition and operational costs, and there is more flexibility on pricing and order fulfilments (Agatz et al. 2008). For some sectors, pureplays will achieve a dominant market share – for example, in online luxury retailing (Verdict 2014). In this context, Net-a-Porter has been notably successful by marketing a range of luxury fashion brands in one business (Wiseman 2010). It has three website offerings: net-a-porter.com, mrporter.com and theoutnet.com, catering to women, men and those with mid-luxury incomes (Mintel 2014a). The company enhances hedonic shopping behaviour online through additional features such as fashion editorial content and advice. All three websites produce e-magazines and were the first to sell augmented reality glasses (McCormick and Livett 2012; Mintel 2014a). It also offers a number of premium website functions including a Net-a-Porter 'Live' feature, providing 'as it happens' data on product sales, which allows customers to see others' buying behaviour at the same time as them (Helmers et al. 2015). Net-a-Porter has an international rather than domestic presence; but this highlights a limitation in its site design and communications as it caters to fewer languages than its competitors Yoox or the Outnet (Guercini and Runfola 2015).

Portals

Online retailing comprises both stand-alone sites and portals, which consolidate different businesses. While portals created significant interest in the early years of the Internet, Amazon emerged as the most dominant player. The company has been highly innovative in expanding its portfolio from its origins as a bookseller. Its web services continue to increase, and the business continues to rapidly diversify from e-books to fashion apparel, and to provide a sales platform for other companies. Its well-designed website and effective links have effectively increased its performance (eConsultancy 2015). It offers product recommendations and, through unique algorithms, is able to personalise the store for each customer. The ease of the company's one-click-to-purchase approach is particularly attractive in assisting consumers with convenience shopping and repeat purchases (Bellman et al. 1999) and allowing them to make side-by-side comparisons of products whilst they shop (Currim et al. 2015). The click-through and conversion rates are evident in its advertising effectiveness (Linden et al. 2003). It further differentiates its operation through a fast delivery service, Amazon Prime, for both domestic and international orders, and with Amazon lockers that allow consumers to pick up goods in convenient locations (Mintel 2014a). This has led to the company's development as a leader in online retailing, and a dominant and expansive position in its field (Grewal et al. 2004).

Mobile devices

The online retail channel has been extended through the use of mobile devices, in particular smartphones, to provide almost unlimited access and availability (Brynjolfsson and Milgrom 2013). Successful shopping in this medium addresses three dimensions: connectivity to the

Internet, the device itself, and its content through websites and applications. Apps have demonstrated their importance through their ubiquitous availability, their personalising and interactive features, and their high level of user engagement. For fashion retailers, apps provide content, but also social networking capabilities that allow users to engage and socially interact with friends and other users. These developments bring commercial advantages, as online personalisation has been shown to have a positive effect on purchase intentions (Lee and Park 2009). Mobile communication also facilitates convergence between physical and digital environments; it can be used as an online medium in-store to supplement or replace the material environment.

Mobile commerce enables retailers to use different strategies to integrate consumers' experience. It offers a unique marketing capability to send push notifications and relevant geo-specific content to consumers, as well as an individualised shopping experience. It enhances service quality through the benefits of contactless payment, including the reduction of queues at cash desks. Mobile technologies in various ways allow retailers to communicate directly with consumers, through RFID devices and in-store Wi-Fi, while they can facilitate click-and-collect, allowing customers to purchase online and collect items in-store. However, mobile devices present their own design challenges in scaling websites from large to small screens, their utility on smaller devices and issues of accessibility and speed. Their content design in particular can be defined in three ways: as a mobile website, replicating the retailer's online or desktop website, but viewed via a mobile device; as a web application where the retailer's online or desktop website is optimised for viewing on a mobile device; and as a mobile application, which has content designed specifically for use on a mobile device taking into account the format and functionality of the mobile device (Magrath and McCormick 2013). These different modes fundamentally determine the possibilities and parameters for design.

Omnichannel

Omnichannel retailing requires a company's channels to be aligned to present a single face to the customer as well as a consistent way of doing business (Carroll and Guzman 2014; Frazer and Stiehler 2014). Channels are viewed as complementing rather than competing against each other (Blazquez 2014) and provide new sources of differentiation by combining the advantages of physical stores with the information-rich experience of online shopping (Rigby 2011). The challenge of channel integration is as much operational as branded, so retailers have to provide smooth transitions between different channels, which customers can use simultaneously. In this context, all channels are interchangeable.

Omnichannel accessibility requires branding and touchpoint consistency across the channels. This has significant implications for website design, which should reflect brand values evident in the physical forms of the store and printed media such as catalogues, as well as physical and non-physical forms of marketing communication. However, it may be manifested in a number of different forms, such as blogger-exposure and message, and product placement. Online retail branding should recognise this complex environment and the need to project the retail brand in conjunction with host or other third-party requirements. It can exploit the potential of social media by establishing an online brand community, one that is specialised and not geographically bound, based on a structured set of social relations among followers of a brand (Phan et al. 2011).

However, omnichannel retailing is not without its disadvantages. Consumers may engage in 'showrooming' behaviour, whereby shoppers browse in-store, but choose to buy online. This can lead to high cost implications in managing physical stores (Rapp et al. 2015), and could also be found vice versa with 'webrooming' behaviour (Verhoef et al. 2007). While cross-channel integration may 'improve consumers' trust, increase their loyalty, boost their conversion rate, and create greater opportunities to cross-sell' (Cao and Li 2015: 212), if a retailer is more prominent on one channel than another, then this may have impact on sales growth. Employing in-store technologies such as virtual mirrors and a greater product assortment online may help to decrease free-riding cross-channel behaviour (Heitz-Spahn 2013; Pantano and Viassone 2015). Nevertheless, if consumers are more familiar with shopping on a retailer's particular channel, they may be hesitant to move away from it (Cao and Li 2015). Thus, retailers should recognise there should be a balance between operating on all channels and minimising costs on channels that may not be frequented.

The rise in omnichannel retailing has highlighted consumer interest in shopping in all types of retail outlets. This has motivated pureplay retailers to seek out alternative strategies to compete effectively (Agatz et al. 2008) and leading e-tailers such as ASOS to attempt cross-channel integration. For example, ASOS introduced its magazine app, which serves a functional purpose alongside its transactional app (Baker 2012). One key to success is to feature niche or exclusive product categories and to source products not widely available with a primary 'focus on cost and efficiency'. These requirements contribute to a greater emphasis on a customer-centric approach (Brynjolfsson and Milgrom 2013).

Contexts of online retail design

The online retail design environment has developed through three interlinked trajectories: changes in technologies and consumption and the growth of interactive, experiential sites.

Technological change

The establishment of the World Wide Web in 1991 provided the first global hypertext environment. The Graphical User Interface (GUI) introduced graphics, icons and images that simplified computer-user interactions. Text-based websites rapidly gave way to more visual and moving images. Authoring software such as Dreamweaver enabled companies and personal computer users to design their own web pages. In the retail industry, rapid developments in computers and software created new opportunities for designers. Web 2.0 technologies subsequently increased levels of user interaction through blogs, wikis and social networking (Constantinides and Fountain 2008). These improvements made the web more dynamic and interconnected through simplified information sharing.

The next development from Web 2.0 to Web 3.0 was facilitated by the use of mobile devices, advances in broadband connectivity, and faster wireless networks (Interactions 2013). More powerful processors and greater data storage capacity was combined with miniaturisation to open up new design options. Larger and clearer screens relative to the size of the device, a greater diversity of functions and uses, and the convenience of tablet devices extended their online commercial reach.

The evolution of Web 3.0 defined the age of the 'intelligent web' and the exchange of information from user to machine through the semantic web, data mining, and intelligent recommendations (Markoff 2006). These attributes increased user convenience by refining information and providing more specific results. Additionally, with Web 4.0 consumers were able to access apps running on smart mobile devices to utilise user interface interactions and location (Interactions 2013). A higher level of interactivity was achieved through two-way communication to create a personalised, user environment (Merrilees and Fry 2003). Web 3.0 enabled a digital understanding of consumers through their searches, comments, likes and browsing history. Overall, Web 3.0 has created a more seamless experience as mobiles, tablets, tablets and mobile hybrids have emerged from the original desktop PC to influence consumer usage.

Changes in consumption

The early commercial development of the Internet was based on new communication and distribution channels but, due to unrealistic expectations of its technologies, largely failed to deliver a satisfactory customer experience. Slow connection speeds, under-performing websites, and restricted user-business interactivity limited the growth of 'click'-based retailing. Early functions focused on marketing communications and the presentation of, and information about, products and retailers. From the early 2000s, consumers increasingly began to demand more immediate gratification from their digital devices, to conduct faster searches, and to connect with likeminded users as a loose affiliation of consumer tribes (Kaplan 2012; Malik et al. 2016). As Web 3.0 gained momentum, it was accompanied by a growth of trust in online sites and transactions, privacy and security of information, and the increased use of PayPal and other authenticating software (Leavitt 2010).

Online shopping behaviour was initially characterised by problems of acceptance and trust in the non-physical store and payments systems. Consumer switching behaviour between brands and channels and their loyalty subsequently stimulated interest in site design and navigation. Online consumption continued to change in respect of the utilisation of Internet-enabled devices and worldwide e-commerce transactions. It was estimated that by 2014, purchases conducted via mobile devices, such as smartphones and tablets, already accounted for nearly one third of global online retail sales (Wagner et al. 2015). As a result, consumers' shopping journey and decision-making processes have become less predictable as consumers adapt and adjust to the mix of retail content, communications and accessibility online and offline.

From communicative to experiential websites

The remote character of Internet communication and the flexibility of the form create contexts in which to experience time and space in different ways. Initial interest centred on computer-mediated communication and possibilities of messages that were disseminated immediately, without limitations of context, community sanctions and moral arbiters. The connectivity of the Internet generated new temporal and spatial demands, being available anywhere and at any time and responding immediately to communications in a global world. Technology made the distant and foreign become present and tangible (Shields 1996). In addition, electronic communication and the culture of the Internet in particular have provided better modes of interface through graphics and sensory interfaces which present a 'virtual reality'.

As Crewe (2013) demonstrates, immersive environments have the capacity to absorb the subject with unprecedented multidimensionality and present opportunities for design to communicate not only with the visual sense but with all the senses. From this perspective, virtual spaces can be understood to be as vibrant as physical ones. The divide between active and communicative humans as agents and as passive objects looks increasingly untenable. In this, the Internet has the capacity to remediate conventional representations such as stores, magazines and photographs, and to reanimate images over time and in space.

Online retail design functionality

Online retail design has to evaluate and accommodate a range of requirements and features. Understanding consumers and their potential use of the site creates initial propositions about its functionality. Second, they require attention to the provision of accurate and timely information about the brand and communication media with the brand but also other users. Consequently, commercial objectives merge with the principles of user-experience and interactivity to attract and maintain the consumer's interest.

The function of design for a commercial site is to move the consumer easily towards purchase with the minimum of irritation and loss of trust in the shopping process. For commercial functionality to exist, a site should respond to the user needs of individualisation, navigability and reciprocity, which allow two-way information exchange between the site and users and synchronicity, which provides real-time feedback. These elements all need to be simultaneously present (Huang 2003) and increasingly have to accommodate dynamic and visual elements (Hausman and Siekpe 2009). Content presentation in particular has changed with the exponential growth of Snapchat, Instagram, blogging and vlogging (Mintel 2014a; Warner et al. 2015). The design response has been to accelerate their use within web designs, resulting in changes to the characteristics of the virtual 'store' environment.

Site functionality can be classified by two individual traits: high-task relevant and low-task relevant environments (Eroglu et al. 2001). A high-task-relevant environment is defined by all the site descriptors, textual or pictorial, that appear on the screen and provide relevant cues to facilitate and enable the consumer's shopping goal attainment. By contrast, a low-task-relevant environment demonstrates site information that is relatively inconsequential to the completion of the shopping task itself. Both are needed to generate atmospheric responsiveness, whereby the store's environmental qualities determine purchase intention.

High-task-relevant cues are driven by the demands of marketing and include price, delivery, merchandise descriptions, and delivery and return policies (Eroglu et al. 2001). These features contribute to user trust of the site through responsive design; for example, a men's clothing website based on clean pages, simple forms, and unnecessary distractions (eConsultancy 2014). In this way, the Dune shoe brand has made use of various UK and European product sizes (eConsultancy 2014). These features can be considered as utilitarian as they provide convenient access to product information which positively leads to revisit intention (Kim et al. 2015).

Colours, borders, background aesthetics, amount of white space, animation and sound relate to low task relevant cues (Eroglu et al. 2001). These subtle aids trigger positive memories and provide a pleasurable experience. However, achieving the combination of these effects can be frustrating to the consumer and have a detrimental impact on the revisiting behaviour and brand loyalty. For instance, animation can attract attention but can also be distracting; images can enhance the brand's identity, yet their presence may be annoying if the loading of the images delays the completion of the shopping task (Eroglu et al. 2001). Some consumers may also have heightened sensitivity to the website design in general, and this may be associated with an overall disenchantment with the external environment (Grossbart et al. 1990). While some websites need animation in order to be consistent with their brand identity (for instance, the proactive use of live chat), there is evidence that interaction with product presentation on a website may not cause a significant response for consumers familiar to the brand (eConsultancy 2014). Restricted interactivity can be more effective compared to fully interactive websites, in order to entice users to further explore the website, thus boosting online-offline conversion more effectively (Cheng et al. 2015). There is a balance to be achieved between designing for the consumer's valuable dwell-time on a page and for encouraging exploratory behaviour.

To facilitate desirable consumer behaviour, the functional dimensions can be differentiated as four sub-components (Aladwani 2006). The first component is the technical dimension, which refers to website characteristics such as security, ease of navigation, search facilities, site availability, valid links, personalisation or customisation, speed of page loading, interactivity and ease of access. The second component is the general content, which includes characteristics such as content usefulness, completeness, clarity, currency, conciseness and accuracy. The third component is specific content, which includes characteristics such as contact information, general company information, product and service details, consumer policies and customer support. The final component is appearance, which refers to characteristics such as attractiveness, organisation and consistent use of fonts, colours and multimedia. It is the integration of these components in the retail site that moves it from a typical step-process search function towards a more fluid process embedded in multi-media.

The search process, using different cues and content, is typically directed towards accessing information. It is an important construct in website quality (Éthier et al. 2006), and its richness is an essential variable in creating a high-quality site (Éthier et al. 2006; Park and Kim 2003). As the online channel is used to search for information and to compare products, it is essential for online retailers to ensure they provide enough detail to support shoppers in reaching informed purchase decisions (Pantano and Naccarato 2010). Examples may include fabric composition or country of origin, shipping and handling fees, or if the item is out-of-stock. Information on online checkout pages should be presented clearly and be easily available (Lohse and Spiller 2003). A high level of detailed product information corresponds to consumer satisfaction, as well as reducing risk when purchasing online. Measures of product information and service information quality (Park and Kim 2003) can include retailers' contact information, returns or exchange, and security and privacy information (Kim and Lennon 2010; Lohse and Spiller 1998). In these ways information availability can enhance utilitarian shopping behaviour (To et al. 2007) as can the organisation of the information. Different formats such as lists can influence search performance, depending on the shopping task, and therefore shopping behaviour (Hong et al. 2004).

Information not only about products but also about the retailer can influence users. Online retailers such as Monsoon also feature 'Who we are' and 'ethical trading' information, as the fashion retailer is a part of the Ethical Trading Initiative (www.monsoon. co.uk). This corporate level of information helps to improve the brand's credibility in its perceptions towards sustainability (Creyer 1997). Social elements can also be integrated within rich text and visually enhanced images, improving a retailer's social presence. This results in higher levels of 'perceived usefulness, trust and enjoyment of shopping websites, leading to more favourable consumer attitudes' (Hassanein and Head 2007: 689).

Online information extends to visual product presentation, as functional product viewing drives both utilitarian and hedonic behaviour (Lee et al. 2010). The absence of tactile input still remains a huge barrier in online shopping, increasing perceived risk; for example, consumers are unable to ascertain the correct size of clothing (Mintel 2014a; Peck and Childers 2003). This further emphasises the need for effective product presentation methods. By providing functions such as image enlargement and product rotation, consumers can obtain more knowledge about the product. Whether there is an optimum level of product information has been the subject of academic discussion (Jiang and Benbasat 2007). A high level of interactivity may require greater cognitive effort, which would have a negative impact on positive emotions and behavioural intent (Mosteller et al. 2014; Shih 1998).

Whilst some authors argue the importance of textual information over visual information (Kim and Lennon 2008) and vice versa, it is observable that both types of information are important for fashion retailers in helping to attract consumers to a webpage. While consumers possess different styles of processing (verbalisers vs. visualisers), both types of information have been shown to have an effect on mental imagery (Yoo and Kim 2014). Ultimately, information quality positively influences loyalty and purchase behaviours (Park and Kim 2003).

The ease with which consumers use the website, and their absorption, has led to consideration of the 'flow' concept, and websites designed so as to fully immerse consumers in a 'flow state' (Koufaris 2002; van Noort et al. 2012). Thus a functional retail site must provide the means for navigation. Shoppers need to locate themselves and move around the online store easily, and they feel less in control when a website is difficult to navigate or when links are missing or inactive (Eroglu et al. 2001). Navigational design may provide a similar function to the design of signage in brick-and-mortar stores, but its aim must be to enable the completion of a shopping task. Consequently the site requires an information architecture strategy to organise and label websites to support usability most visibly through the home page and its navigation bar (Frick and Eyler-Werve, 2014). Ease of navigation will be determined by the initial length of the site supported by navigation design patterns (NDPs) such as scrolling, tabs and menus (Eroglu et al. 2001). Its tools include sitemaps and search bars located at the bottom or top of the page, and these are found both on commercial and on social media websites, where Facebook, Flickr and Twitter house functional navigation tools such as search bars, alerts, simple drop-down menus, and buttons for sharing content (eConsultancy 2015). However, the transferability of navigation tools from one site to another is variable; in navigating on smartphones, scrolling seems to be unhelpful – for example, the scrolling of images is not apparent on Instagram. Thus, traditional patterns of menus and tabs remain effective for websites but not necessarily on other personal devices.

Online experience design

The functional but also experiential dimensions of retail websites are reflected in the changing processes and outputs of design. The designer's role in computer design was transformed, as past 'visualising and materialising skills were replaced by the requirement to create virtual or architectural systems and efficient, effective and pleasurable usability' (Sparke 2013:135). This required different approaches to systems and interface design, and additionally a need to understand people's emotional relationship with complex machines. Complex service systems also extended interactions into multiple functions, including person-to-person and technology-enhanced encounters, self-service and computational services, and multichannel, multi-device, location-based and context-aware services (Glushko 2010, cited in Keating et al. 2011).

Julier (2008) argues that computers impose a new format, a new structure and new organisation requirements on the designer. The rapid pace of change in the development of on-screen platforms, hardware and software left designers 'struggling to ascertain a critical discourse and language for it' (Julier 2008:170) while taking on the role of technological and cultural intermediaries. In this account, potential narrative situations are defined by search activities and the user's movement through virtual spaces, which move online sites towards a narrative dialogue (Parvinen et al. 2014). For Sparke (2013), this complex relationship prioritises the capacity of its practitioners to be able to create narratives and scenarios through the skills of illustrators, animators and film-makers. Designers have had to broker new developments in electronic media and have played a crucial role in shaping both content and new ways of working with collaborative networks. Increasingly projects have drawn on a wide range of design disciplines in flexible networks in which the synthesis of design processes, skills, methods and culture may be more important than predicted outcomes (Julier 2008).

The creation of online design collaborations has been accompanied by the continuing evolution of relationships with the end-user. The over-arching design implications to deliver experiential qualities are evident in user-experience and experience design approaches. The complexity of these relationships between designers, technologies and users is explained by Buchanan's (2001) new 'orders' of practice and research, which demonstrate the growing importance of interactivity in moving a focus on 'signs' (graphic and communication design), to 'objects' (product design), 'interactions' (interaction design) and finally 'systems' (environment and system design). Where technologies rapidly evolve and mature, they open up design processes and problem-solving capabilities based on what people need, rather than a succession of new features.

The concept of user-experience (UX) originated in human-centred design research in which users' needs and demands are accounted for throughout all phases of design (Nuutinen and Keinonen 2011). Snel (2013) explains that experience consists of three elements: something in the environment, which is experienced; the encounter between someone and something; and the effects experienced by someone. An online environment will define an experience because "an experience is always what it is because of a transaction taking place between an individual and what, at the time, constitutes his environment" (Dewey 1997, p. 43). In this context it was recognised as the 'cognitive state experienced during navigation' (Novak et al. 2000, p. 22), and this dynamic sense of experience extends to relationships with other people, places and objects. A customer has an experience every time they come into contact with a company or product, so designers need to facilitate the retailer's management of multiple experiential touchpoints and all the elements or cues that are part of the website. In achieving this aim, the two key components comprise the online setting of the website in which cues are created by design (Grove et al. 1992). The second concerns the online 'servicescape' and how the site determines the level of involvement of customers in the service delivery process (Bassi et al. 2013).

This interactivity distinguishes experience design from an instrumental approach in its support for users' hedonic needs, such as stimulation and self-expression, as well as pragmatic needs, products and services. The tradition of user-experience design aims at broader views of users' emotional, contextual and dynamically evolving needs, and the impact of users' previous experiences on new experiences (Nuutinen and Heikkinen 2013). Two approaches have been evident in its development, which have come to influence each other: 'user as subject' and a participatory 'user as partner'. They provide the opportunity to access expertise and participate in the informing, ideating and conceptualising activities of the early design phases (Sanders and Stappers 2008). In this holistic and temporal approach to user experience, the designer needs to account for repeat exposure to experiences and its effect on reducing excitement and memorability. The online site, and this has implications for the physical site too, should provide for unexpectedness, novelty and originality through an understanding of user experience at perceptual, emotional and cognitive levels (Lykke and Jantzen 2016).

These design approaches balance consumer research with the designer's imaginative envisioning of the future. They highlight the need for online retail design to accommodate interactions between the brand and consumer and the location of value creation outside the producer (Ind and Coates 2013). The co-creation of experiences generates value through participation and involvement within a sensory and emotional environment. Co-creation can also describe retailer and consumer collaboration on social e-shopping sites, where consumers use tools and social features to create and share content. Consequently it includes all consumer interactivity and experiences within e-store environments (Spena et al. 2012). It is a participative process where organisations are no longer the definers of value, but instead people and organisations generate and develop meanings together (Ind and Coates 2013).

In adapting online experience design to retailing, three main themes have been identified: product experience, customer support, and customer interface design (Bassi et al. 2013). Product experience can start well before the customer's interaction with the retailer's site, through the use of blogs, social networks and reviews (Kietzmann et al. 2011). Design of online shopping sites requires attention to both the anticipation of a purchase and post-purchase experience, as well as the location of the experience. As Jantzen (2013) proposes, there is a tension between the immediate but volatile present of experiencing, the past of prior experiences and the future of imminent experiences. Product experience should integrate product-related information about the brand and its features, with service-related information about post-purchase delivery, including tracking and returns procedures (Dadzie and Winston 2007). The way in which products are presented can generate mental imagery of post-purchase product use (Fiore et al. 2005). Search facilities extend the experience by providing convenient and time-efficient access to, but also engagement with, the retailer's products and services, including real-time help and advisory services. Previous viewing and purchasing behaviour can enable the retailer to make product and service recommendations (Chang and Nunez 2007). An online site has to overcome problems of hierarchical or filtered order of the product displays and the effect this has on customer perceptions of product variety and experience (Chang 2011). Consequently the design of the retail website has to have the flexibility to respond to new products, looks and styles and to allow retailers to rapidly adjust categories and promotions according to changes in the external environment.

The presentation of the product can compensate for the non-physicality of online retailing. To be experiential, a product must allow for active participation by users (Jantzen 2013), and its experiential value will depend both on the level of information and sensory appeal (Jeong et al. 2009). Low levels of experiential value are derived from basic images and higher levels from more precise product details and more complex settings for the images. This is reflected in fashion retailers' increasing use of websites for brand engagement to 'stimulate emotions and induce feelings of excitement' (McCormick and Livett 2012: 34). Image interactivity technology facilitates the alteration of a product's design, background, viewing angle or distance, which stimulate a pleasurable shopping experience (Fiore et al.

2005). With interactive visual presentation, for example, the ability to zoom into an image and to view it through 360° and 3D imagery, the consumer's sensory experience increases (Fiore et al. 2005; Yang and Wu 2009). As the level of complexity increases, an editorial strategy is required, led by an online editor-in-chief to manage the integration of images with brand narratives.

Static but increasingly dynamic product imagery, found in videos and other rich media content, further enhance the shopping experience (Kim and Forsythe 2010). In part, they provide online shoppers with detailed information but also allow them to interact with products and examine the product on screen, thereby increasing their enjoyment, promoting engagement and reducing risk. This is evident in the use of dynamic images to generate a sense of fantasy as the consumer browses clothing products and their settings (Fiore et al. 2005). They allow visual stories to be developed with the aim of engaging the viewer, and these may have a marginal commercial content. The integration of ambient music and sounds with images further enhances the site's atmospherics, gains attention and increases the memorability of the experience (Bassi et al. 2013). However, these dimensions are moderated by changes in consumer behaviour as shorter attention spans for video clips and site navigation itself will demand more impactful design compacted into smaller timeframes.

In practice, differences exist between retailers' product visualisation strategies, as not all online retailers will resort to the same combination of image interactivity functions. For example, ASOS now employs catwalk videos. Others such as Very use 360-degree views of the model (Mintel 2015). Some websites use virtual product experience (VPE) to give consumers a sensory satisfaction which they otherwise would have experienced in a store. An example of this is the Land Rover website, which uses video clips with visual and sound effects to represent cars in motion. The Samsung website allows users to hover their mouse over the image to view a 360° product (Cheng et al. 2015), while Hunter conveys colour contrast in its call to action buttons (eConsultancy 2014).

The quality of customer support has a significant impact on customer intentions, behaviours and attitudes towards an online brand (Ding et al. 2010). Support is provided through different media for immediacy, including FAQ sections and real-time contact through texting chat rooms embedded in the website, and by email and telephone. Support through social media allows for further customisation, community and relationship building with customers. Pre- and post-purchase customer support are important aspects to gain information about the products before purchasing, and for post-purchase delivery status, technical advice and returns services. The opportunities to design individual and personalised services are evident at ASOS, where customers can chat to a specialist stylist before making purchase decisions or post-purchase if they wish to return or exchange items (Bassi et al. 2013). Premier services, at an extra charge or based on size of order, offer further personalised delivery and support opportunities.

A further element of product experience and customer support concerns the globalised accessibility of a brand and its local reach. This requires a consideration of language adaptability, the desired local look and a feel for local cultures. Visual design that includes icons, symbols and other navigational tools can create a system for the viewer to structure information (Cyr and Trevor-Smith 2004). The design scheme may have to address different user cultures, and these features must be adopted in social networks, on the website and on customer service portals (Bassi et al. 2013).

As visual media supplement and replace textual interactivity, for example the integration of video and photography into online sites, they provide further challenges to the organisation and combining of design skills. Moreover, a narrow focus on the technical and visual has extended into social and cultural elements, thereby capturing many aspects of the system that are subject to coordinated design decisions (Murray 2011). In addressing individual and societal needs, designers should continue to explore different approaches, taking a longer term view that addresses larger scopes of inquiry (Sanders and Stappers 2008). These aspects lead to a broader consideration of interactivity and interface design.

Online retail design and interactivity

From an organisational perspective, interactivity aims to overcome the lack of face-to-face services in the processes of online shopping. For designers, the aim of interactivity may be to simply create a satisfying experience for the user (Murray 2011); its outputs encompass communications, customised information, image manipulation, and entertainment for the customer (Fiore et al. 2005). A design focus on customer interaction highlights two roles for the designer to promote the 'voice of the customer' and, defend the integrity of products from compromises that reduce value from the customers' and users' viewpoints (Topalian 2003). However interactivity, and the use of 'inter' as literally 'between' materials, things and people, can take different forms and influence different design approaches.

One form of interactivity focuses on interpersonal communication in online marketplaces that specifically increases through bi-directionality, timeliness, mutual control and responsiveness (Yadav and Varadarajan 2005). Early developments in computer-mediated communication defined four dimensions of engagement: individual from group communications as one-to-one or one-to-many, for example, blogs; many-to-one, found in retailer communications to customers; and many-to-many, in the form of discussion groups (Paulsen 1995). As advances in hardware, software and content fuel the ambitions and capabilities of users and retailers, so website design has to adapt to accommodate complex and dynamic mixes of communication media.

A second form of interactivity, user–machine interaction, has drawn on a systems perspective. Interaction design, with its origins in computer design, is by definition concerned with what users do and with user-testing in system design (Faiola et al. 2010). The location and spaces of the computer, website and content both create and mediate interactivity. These aspects distinguish users interaction with the computer itself from interaction with media, and how control of the medium influences the delivery of information. The implications of computer-mediated interaction are evident in the convergence of sensorial, experiential and emotional aspects in the virtual and material worlds (Yoo et al. 2010). These forms create different levels of interactivity with implications for site design. Low-level interactivity, drawing on earlier human–computer interaction theory, can be defined as feedback. At higher levels, online design can facilitate better consumer decision making, consumer relationship marketing and personalised marketing strategies (Yoo et al. 2010). In practice, while simplicity and intuition are guiding principles of interactivity, the complexity of integrating site navigation, social media, image, video and sound, checkout and support functions requires detailed planning through user stories and user task mapping (Frick and Eyler-Werve 2014).

The designer's place in facilitating interactivity in a retail context concerns not only communication between consumers and organisations but also its control. Different concepts and locations of control and ownership exist within designed retail environments. For the designer they raise issues of authorship – from designer as a creator to a selector of forms. The website and its links to other sites involve a 'dialogue of control and feedback between a user and a programme' (Julier 2008:179). Computer technology, through its repertoire of accessible web design software and techniques, can exercise control over design through its homogenizing effect, which contrasts with retail brands' focus on individualization and personal experiences. For the consumer in a co-created environment, awareness of retailer control over the website and, in particular, access to personal details can lead to problems with permission marketing and potentially a reduction in interactivity.

User–machine and particularly human–computer interactivity require interfaces as an external presence to an interactive device. While the definition of an interface has evolved (Bruinsma 2003), the customer interface remains an important element of success for online retailers, where customer satisfaction and loyalty are dependent on its quality (Bassi et al. 2013). However, achieving these objectives through different sized screens, websites and apps, presents visualization, content and navigational complications. These are evident, for example, in fashion retailers' online style guides and images and their compatibility with different devices. Further, the location of interfaces has become more complex, reflecting their diversity and ways of navigating through a shopping journey that increasingly blend physical and digital worlds. Print media and advertising signage can provide immediate online access through QR codes. Interfaces with mobile devices enabled by RFID can be attached to instore tags. Retail stores themselves create new interfaces through interactive look-up points, access to visual promotional and informational materials, and the integration of virtual environments. These dimensions provide considerable scope for experimentation by specialist retailers, including Harvey Nicholls, Karen Millen and Jimmy Choo. With virtual interfaces customers can browse the shop and look at shoes merchandised on shelves, dresses on racks and other accessories as though they were in a physical retail setting. The store itself can be re-conceptualised as a converged environment of online and offline worlds through different types of interactive surfaces, both those it owns and those of its customers. This diversity of interfaces provides new design opportunities as well as issues of control and ownership for designers, retailers and consumers.

Design and social media

Social media are an increasingly important part of online retailing (Turban et al. 2015) and embrace the three categories of social networking sites, content sharing sites, and blogs, including microblogs (Kaplan and Haenlein 2010). Fundamentally their purpose must be to enable participation (Miel and Faris 2008) and to share user-generated content. For organisations, the objectives of social media can be built around dimensions of engagement (consumer or company-led) and relationship-building to create excitement or intimacy as a listening and caring function (Kozinets et al. 2014).

Social networking to some degree mimics communication in the real world, existing online and connecting known and unknown users with common interests, thus giving rise to a new paradigm, social commerce (Ellahi and Bokhari 2013; Huang and Benyoucef 2015). For users, the most important features on social media websites have been shown to be friendliness, community presence, navigation, efficiency, privacy, entertainment and navigability. However, designing for the complexity and integration of social networking websites has to be balanced with speed and accessibility. Too many applications, such as java scripts, graphics, and video, can slow the site down with demonstrable negative effects on usage (Ellahi and Bokhari 2013).

While social networks have had a distinctive position in social media, the boundaries between user visits to these networks to socialise and shopping visits to e-commerce websites is breaking down through a need respectively to generate income and customer relationships. Thus, features on websites such as 'comment' buttons are vital to encourage reviews and electronic word of mouth (Huang and Benyoucef 2015). Product reviews and ratings add functionality for the consumer and more positive responses for the retailer (eConsultancy 2014). In this respect retailers and service providers such as Trip Advisor demonstrate a further example of online learning and convergence of site design for feedback and analysis.

The Web has increasingly enabled and encouraged the creation of user-generated content, beyond the social classification of content by tagging and folksonomy. Moreover from an organisational perspective, it has facilitated a new editorialisation of retail, blurring online and offline, magazine and store. Both user- and organisation-generated media have tended to use more visual images, pictures and videos rather than text, whilst allowing comments and editing on content (Phan et al. 2011). The online version of *Harrods* magazine demonstrates these extra digital and interactive features. Page-by-page scrolling reveals more content, including videos and interviews, access to a variety of fashion shoots, and various beauty tips. The content is available to be downloaded every month in conjunction with the release of each (physical) new issue of the magazine. The lead item on many pages is a bespoke video, made for the magazine from fashion shoots and using high-quality production. Besides these practices, Web design principles require webpage creators to trust and to involve their users, while enabling them to harness network effects and collective intelligence to create applications that improve as more people use them.

The design implications for social media content have focused on increased co-production and co-creation, as designers need to design image and text based storytelling opportunities for retail brands that can be visualised on different sizes of screen. Bloggers increasingly have a role in story-telling through text and visual imagery in vlogs combining the skills of make-up artist, editor, and live magazine; individual bloggers integrate content and narrative in one designed interface. Consequently, blogging contributes to a merged world in personalising, co-creating, reviewing and demonstrating materiality. It provides a story and a lifestyle setting that creates, innovates and makes real new lifestyles and possibilities of using products to create consumers ideal selves or possible selves (Wang et al. 2015).

Gamification, Virtual Reality and Augmented Reality

The hedonic and flow aspects of website design have been influenced by gamification and the application of game design principles for non-gaming design contexts (Robson et al. 2015). Hypertext writing was initially observed to mirror game design, where players focus not on the detail of the virtual world but rather on the outlines and geometry of objects (Fleming 1996). Deterding et al. (2011) suggest that design can change user experience in a different context and that gameful design – the practice of creating a gameful experience with a specific intention in mind – has a fit with gamefulness, the lived experience, and gameful interaction, the objects, tools and contexts that bring about the experience of gamefulness (Seaborn and Fel 2015). For consumers from the Y and Z generations, gamification and social media can define innovation take-up. More broadly, gamification with its focus on relationship building and reward informs the concept of retailer loyalty schemes. Thus, game design principles can be applied to retail design contexts to expand the potential of virtual retailing, where companies showcase their physical stores (Robson et al. 2015).

The success of other online 'realities' has been defined by their adaptability to technological and financial development, combined with consumer acceptance. The commercial application of the Second Life virtual world has declined, and for brands its presence provides low-end experiential and emotional value (Barnes et al. 2015). The business model appears to have been overtaken by subsequent opportunities that emerged for live and interactive video. However, Virtual Reality (VR) and Augmented Reality (AR) have the potential to merge the real and digital worlds in distinctive ways that impact online retail design. Virtual Reality can be seen as a world portrayed through a three-dimensional computerised interface that imitates the environment of the 'real world'. While gaming designers see 4D virtual reality with 3D gaming in response to brain movements and emotional states, marketers see the scope for this technology to be used in other contexts. Through a marketing lens, VR can create new environments for building brand equity through the use of experiential service interactions (Barnes et al. 2015). The scope for interactions is evident across the online retail industry, from Ben Sherman's virtual components such as folded clothes to a virtual Grocery Brand Instacart (Mintel 2014b).

By contrast, AR overlays one or more layers of digital content on the real world through an intermediary device, allowing access to both the virtual and the physical world. While VR needs more complex headwear to create credible immersive visual effects, AR can work with mobile devices. AR also provides an arena in which customers can immerse themselves in a virtual gaming world; for example, a camera connected to PlayStation 4 uses the controller's position to support AR games, and Xbox Kinect users can overlay clothes on their bodies to see themselves on their TV screen (Barnwell 2015). Future developments will see the merging of digital and physical worlds extended to social media applications, whether by new forms of collaboration or market consolidation, evident in Facebook's acquisition of Oculus Rift (Mintel 2014c).

The fashion experience: The Burberry store

The many aspects of online retail design and their convergence have been particularly evident in Burberry's development plans. Phan et al. (2011) explain the repositioning of Burberry as a pioneer in social media marketing through its social media strategy in the early 2000s. The company used Twitter effectively during its autumn and winter launch in 2011 by tweeting exclusive photographs of models from backstage before they hit the catwalk through Tweetwalk, held in their Regent Street flagship store, thus blurring the boundaries between store and livestreaming (Burberry plc 2015; Mintel 2011). Similarly they launched an App for iPad named 'Buy the Catwalk' for consumers to purchase the items from the catwalk instantly and seamlessly (Mintel 2011).

In luxury retailing, it may be argued that what is sold and how it is delivered to the customer are synonymous (Moore et al. 2010). Consumers engage in memorable experiences that provide them with satisfaction and may influence their purchasing behaviours. Retailers want these experiences to remain salient in the consumer's mind and therefore influence repatronage and consumer loyalty. (Dholakia et al. 2010). It may be argued that Burberry manages multichannel consumer behaviour without a direct and 'hard sell' approach as it enables the consumer the freedom to browse the shop (Dholakia et al. 2010).

Technology has facilitated the enrichment of consumer experiences and enabled Burberry to become a digital fashion leader (Mintel 2011). The company set the agenda for luxury brands at a time when the sector was highly sceptical of the benefits of the online channel and of social media in particular. With considerable foresight, Burberry aimed to develop its revenue streams, broaden its reach, and appeal to younger, affluent consumers (eConsultancy 2009). In so doing, the brand was shaped into a 'digitally-savvy international powerhouse' (Vogue 2015). As a demonstration of this position, the Burberry Brit store in Covent Garden was opened in 2011 with the aim of attracting a new younger consumer demographic through its features, a video wall, touch screens with life-size images of clothing, iPod docks and interactive iPads (Mintel 2011).

In the following year, Burberry opened its Regent Street store as an 'events and innovation hub' (Vogue 2012). It became clear that Burberry designed its retail space in the UK capital to specifically combine digital technologies such as virtual catwalks, in order to create a digital presence for their luxury millennial consumers. The use of social media was extended to a live stream 'In-Tweet' through their Twitter account (Burberry plc 2015), and in 2014 Burberry was the first luxury brand to sell products through Twitter Buy where users could buy directly through Twitter (Burberry plc 2015). 'Burberry Acoustic' extended the brand by using the Regent Street flagship store as a music venue. This use of the store in an innovative format blurs the lines between retailing clothes and a lifestyle to Burberry fans, extending beyond the selling of clothes alone (Mintel 2014b). The development of the sensory environment through music continued with the launch of its own iTunes and YouTube Music Channel, in which music is understood to be 'intrinsic to what we do'. Simultaneously it demonstrated its loyalty to both digital innovation and Apple (Mintel 2015).

As the fashion sector generally aims to generate high levels of visibility in capital cities, this move enabled Burberry to extend the boundaries from the physical to the online world (Mintel 2011). Burberry has effectively integrated its physical store with its digital presence, thus beginning the process of morphing retail stores into multichannel and omnichannel experiences. The company has innovated in the luxury sector by being an early adopter of integrated multichannel retail experiences. Ultimately, its strategy must ensure a balance between the positive benefits to the consumer, cost reductions for the company and the potentially negative effect on interactivity where staff may be replaced by machines (Grewal et al. 2009; Renko and Druzijanic 2014; Verhoef et al. 2009).

Conclusion

The trajectory of online retail design is one determined by the intersecting capabilities provided by communications technology, software, content and devices. From relatively static and information-driven sites, online retail design has been driven by the possibilities for interactivity and experience. These point to opportunities for merged consumer worlds, including mixed realities, Augmented and Virtual Realities, personalised services and geo-positioning to inform and extend consumer use and loyalty. These worlds present different challenges in the design of spatial, visual and sensory environments. The converged environment has elements that fuse and integrate into one seamless mobile interface that embraces the design of mobile devices, commerce, games and Virtual Reality, and their interconnectivity. Websites and apps will develop and exploit aspects of 3D design, such as avatars alongside the integration of locational (GPS) devices.

The Burberry case study demonstrates the opportunities for retailers to work across the boundaries of in-store and online environments, in order to create a distinctive design solution. The provision of in-store Wi-Fi has increased, and some stores offer touchscreens and tablets to provide information and product 'lookups'. In general, video screens show fashion collections, and apps for fashion retailers offer inspirational looks. In a future defined by this physical and digital interconnectivity, designers must balance shoppers' appreciation of functionality with more playful or communicative dimensions of multi-channel interaction. Devices and interactive software should save consumers time searching for products and services. Design must account for the consumers' preferences to be engaged, rather than marketed to, by the retailer. This will require the continual monitoring of the shifting world of social media, its communities, and individuals. In moments of space and time, users may want to use their mobile device as a sharing medium. In shared snapshots, image is everything, and the retailer provides the backdrop.

Technology trends point to the expansion of interactive shop windows and in-store communication that draw on the combination of GPS, near-field communications such as Apple iBeacon, and shopper smartphones. These will enable personalisation to be taken to a higher level with real-time offers, new product updates and post-purchase customer support. To support their brand, retailers will increasingly look at the adaptability of their customer relationships, so stories, images, videos and news – fashion blogs have been particularly successful – will continue to provide retail opportunities.

Trials of devices, content and contexts and advances in technologies and retailer know-how will define future developments in Virtual Reality. New devices will enable the design of more realistic immersive environments. Immersion is particularly interesting in its creation or re-creation of 3D environments, by helping to envisage lifestyle options for shoppers in their living spaces. They will create opportunities to re-visit retailers' shows, events and exhibitions, and for the retailer to extend the lifespan of selected promotions to individual customers. Embracing all these developments is Web 5.0 and with it the potential to develop a sensory dimension to existing online interactivity and new approaches to design. Future online applications will show how materials and equipment physically, sensually and emotionally interact with us and between themselves.

References

Agatz, N.A., Fleischmann, M., & Van Nunen, J.A. (2008) 'E-fulfilment and multi-channel distribution–A review'. *European Journal of Operational Research*, Vol. (187) Iss. 2, pp. 339–356.

Aladwani, A. (2006) 'An empirical test of the link between website quality and forward enterprise integration with web customers'. *Business Process Management Journal*, Vol. (12) Iss. 2, pp. 178–190.

Baker, R. (2012) 'Asos to launch weekly magazine app'. *Marketing Week*, 3 September [Online]. Available at: http://www.marketingweek.com/2012/09/03/asos-to-launch-weekly-magazine-app/ (Accessed: November 2015).

Barnes, S.J., Mattsson, J., & Hartley, N. (2015) 'Assessing the value of real-life brands in virtual worlds'. *Technological Forecasting & Social Change*, Vol. (92), pp. 12–24.

Barnwell, A. (2015) PS4 users eat your heart out — you can now try on clothes with your Xbox One. 13 December. Available at: http://www.digitaltrends.com/home/xbox-one-mall-app-virtual-fitting-room (Accessed: August 2106).

Bassi, N.S., Smart, P.A., & Ponsignon, F. (2013) 'Designing for flow in online apparel retail'. In the *Proceedings of the Cambridge Academic Design Management Conference 2013*. Cambridge: University of Cambridge.

Bellman, S., Lohse, G.L., & Johnson, E.J. (1999) 'Predictors of online buying behavior'. *Communications of the ACM*, Vol. (42) Iss. 12, pp. 32–38.

Blazquez, M. (2014) 'Fashion shopping in multichannel retail: The role of technology in enhancing the customer experience'. *International Journal of Electronic Commerce*, Vol. (18) Iss. 4, pp. 97–116.

Bruinsma, M. (2003) *Deep Sites*. London: Thames and Hudson.

Brynjolfsson, E., & Milgrom, P. (2013) Complementarity in Organisations, in *The Handbook for Organisation Economics*. Ed. Robert Gibbons and John Roberts. Princeton: Princeton University Press, pp. 11–55.

Buchanan, R. (2001) Designing research and the new learning. *Design Issues*, Vol. (17) Iss. 4, pp. 3–23.

Burberry plc (2015) *'Burberry to Premiere on Periscope with a Live Broadcast of Its "London in Los Angeles Show"'* Burberryplc.com [Online]. Available at: http://www.burberryplc.com/media_centre/press_releases/2015/burberry_to_premiere_on_periscope_with_a_live_broadcast_of_its_london_in_los_angeles_show (Accessed: November 2015).

Cao, L., & Li, L. (2015) 'The impact of cross-channel integration on retailers' sales growth'. *Journal of Retailing*, Vol. (91) Iss. 2, pp. 198–216.

Carnoy, M., & Castells, M. (2001) 'Globalisation, the knowledge society, and the network state: Poulanztas at the millennium'. *Global Networks*, Vol. (1) Iss. 1, pp. 1–18.

Carroll, D., & Guzman, I. (2014) The New Omni-Channel Approach to Serving Customers, Accenture, 2014, Pg. 4. Retrieved from: http://www.accenture.com/SiteCollectionDocuments/communications/accenture-new-omnichannel-approach-serving-customers.pdf.

Chang, C. (2011) 'The effect of the number of product subcategories on perceived variety and shopping experience in an online store'. *Journal of Interactive Marketing*, Vol. (25), pp. 159–168.

Chang, I.R., & Nunez, M.A. (2007) 'Improving web-catalog design for easy product search'. *INFORMS Journal on Computing*, Vol. (19), pp. 510–519.

Cheng, Y., Jiang, Z.J., & Benbasat, I. (2015) 'Enticing and engaging consumers via online product presentations: The effects of restricted interaction design'. *Journal of Management Information Systems*, Vol. (31) Iss. 4, pp. 213–242.

Constantinides, E., & Fountain, F.J. (2008) 'Web 2.0: Conceptual foundations and marketing issues'. *Journal of Direct Data and Digital Marketing Practice*, Vol. (9), pp. 231–234.

Crewe, L. (2013) 'When virtual and material worlds collide: Democratic fashion in the digital age'. *Environment and Planning A*, Vol. (45) Iss. 4, pp. 760–780.

Creyer, E.H. (1997) 'The influence of firm behavior on purchase intention: Do consumers really care about business ethics?'. *Journal of Consumer Marketing*, Vol. (14) Iss. 6, pp. 421–432.

Currim, I.S., Mintz, O., & Siddarth, S. (2015) 'Information accessed or information available? The impact on consumer preferences inferred at a durable product e-commerce website'. *Journal of Interactive Marketing*, Vol. (29), pp. 11–25.

Cyr, D., & Trevor-Smith, H. (2004) 'Localisation of web design: An empirical comparison of German, Japanese, and United States web site characteristics'. *Journal of the American Society for Information Science and Technology*, Vol. (55), pp. 1199–1208.

Dadzie, Kofi Q., & Winston, E. (2007) 'Consumer response to stock-out in the online supply chain'. *International Journal of Physical Distribution & Logistics Management*, Vol. (37), pp. 19–42.

Deterding, S., Dixon, D., Khaled, R., & Nacke, L. (2011) From game design elements to gamefulness: defining "gamification". *Proceedings of the 15th International Academic MindTrek Conference: Envisioning Future Media Environments*. New York NY: ACM.

Dewey, J. (1997) *Experience and Education*. New York: Touchstone.

Dholakia, U.M., Kahn, B.E., Reeves, R., Rindfleisch, A., Stewart, D., & Taylor, E. (2010) 'Consumer behaviour in a multichannel, multimedia retailing environment'. *Journal of Interactive Marketing*, Vol. (24) Iss. 2, pp. 86–95.

Ding, M., Ross, W.T., & Rao, V.R. (2010) 'Price as an indicator of quality: Implications for utility and demand functions'. *Journal of Retailing*, Vol. (86), pp. 69–84.

eConsultancy (2009) *'Cover Story: Burberry Joins Push Online by Luxury Brands'* Available at: https://econsultancy.com/nma-archive/47878-cover-story-burberry-joins-push-online-by-luxury-brands (Accessed: 19th December 2015).

eConsultancy (2014) *'Responsive Website Design'* Available at: https://econsultancy.com/blog/66081-responsive-web-design-15-of-the-best-sites-from-2014/ (Accessed: November 2015).

eConsultancy (2015) *'Net-A-Porter Launches Its Own Social Shopping Network: Review'* Available at: https://econsultancy.com/blog/66405-net-a-porter-launches-its-own-social-shopping-network-review/ (Accessed: November 2015).

Ellahi, A., & Bokhari, R.H. (2013) 'Key quality factors affecting users' perception of social networking websites'. *Journal of Retailing and Consumer Services*, Vol. (20), pp. 120–129.

Eroglu, S.A., Machleit, K.A., & Davis, L.M. (2001) 'Atmospheric qualities of online retailing: A conceptual model and implications'. *Journal of Business Research*, Vol. (54), pp. 177–184.

Éthier, J., Hadaya, P., Talbot, J., & Cadieux, J. (2006) 'B2C web site quality and emotions during online shopping episodes: An empirical study'. *Information & Management*, Vol. (43) Iss. 5, pp. 627–639.

Faiola, A., Davis, B.S., & Edwards, R. L. (2010) 'Extending knowledge domains for new media education: integrating interaction design theory and methods'. *New Media & Society*, Vol. (12,) Iss. 5, pp. 691–709.

Fiore, A., Kim, J., & Lee, H. (2005) 'Effect of image interactivity technology on consumer responses toward the online retailer'. *Journal of Interactive Marketing*, Vol. (19) Iss. 3, pp. 38–53.

Fleming, D. (1996) *Powerplay: Toys as Popular Culture*. Manchester, Manchester University Press.

Frazer, M., & Stiehler, B.E. (2014) Omnichannel retailing: The merging of the online and off-line environment. In the *Proceedings of the Global Conference on Business and Finance*, Vol. (9) Iss. 1, pp. 655–657.

Frick, T., & Eyler-Werve, K. (2014) *Return on Engagement: Content Strategy and Web Design Techniques for Digital Marketing*. Abingdon: Taylor & Francis.

Glushko, R. (2010) Seven Contexts for Service System Design, in *Handbook of Service Science*. Ed. P.P Maglio, C.A. Kieliszewski & J.C. Spohrer. New York: Springer, pp. 219–249.

Grewal, D., Iyer, G.R., & Levy, M. (2004) 'Internet retailing: Enablers, limiters and market consequences'. *Journal of Business Research*, Vol. (57) Iss. 7, pp. 703–713.

Grewal, D., Levy, M., & Kumar, V. (2009) 'Consumer experience management in retailing: An organising framework'. *Journal of Retailing*, Vol. (85) Iss. 1, pp. 1–14.

Grossbart, S., Hampton, R., Rammohan, B., & Lapidus, R.S. (1990) 'Environmental dispositions and consumer response to store atmospherics'. *Journal of Business Research*, Vol. (21), pp. 224–242.

Grove, S. J., Fisk, R. P., & Bitner, M. J. (1992) Dramatizing the Service Experience: A Managerial Approach, in *Advances in Services Marketing and Management*, Vol. (21). Ed. T. A. Swartz, D. E. Bowen & S. W. Brown. Greenwich, CT: JAI Press, pp. 91–121.

Guercini, S., & Runfola, A. (2015) Internationalisation through e-commerce: The case of multibrand luxury retailers in the fashion industry, in *International Marketing in the Fast Changing World (Advances in International Marketing)*, Vol. (26), Ed. B. Stöttinger, B.B. Schlegelmilch, & S. Zou. Bingley, UK: Emerald Group Publishing Limited, pp. 15–31.

Hanna, J. (1997) 'The rise of interactive marketing'. *Design Management Journal*, Vol. (8) Iss. 1, pp. 34–39.

Hassanein, K., & Head, M. (2007) 'Manipulating perceived social presence through the web interface and its impact on attitude towards online shopping'. *International Journal of Human-Computer Studies*, Vol. (65) Iss. 8, pp. 689–708.

Hausman, A.V., & Siekpe, J.S. (2009) 'The effect of web interface features on consumer online purchase intentions'. *Journal of Business Research*, Vol. (62) Iss. 1, pp. 5–13.

Heitz-Spahn, S. (2013) 'Cross-channel free-riding consumer behavior in a multichannel environment: An investigation of shopping motives, sociodemographics and product categories'. *Journal of Retailing and Consumer Services*, Vol. (20) Iss. 6, pp. 570–578.

Helmers, C., Krishnan, P., & Patnam, M. (2015) '*Attention and Saliency In Online Markets*' Available at: http://lacer.lacea.org/bitstream/handle/123456789/52355/lacea2015_attention_saliency_online_markets.pdf?sequence=1.

Hong, W., Thong, J.Y., & Tam, K.Y. (2004) 'The effects of information format and shopping task on consumers' online shopping behavior: A cognitive fit perspective'. *Journal of Management Information Systems*, Vol. (21) Iss. 3, pp. 149–184.

Huang, M.H. (2003) 'Designing website attributes to induce experiential encounters'. *Computers in Human Behaviour*, Vol. (19), pp. 425–442.

Huang, Z., & Benyoucef, M. (2015) 'User preferences of social features on social commerce websites: An empirical study'. *Technological Forecasting and Social Change*, Vol. (95), pp. 57–72.

Ind, N., & Coates, N. (2013) 'The meanings of co-creation'. *European Business Review*, Vol. (25) Iss. 1, pp. 86–95.

Interactions (2013) *'Web 3.0 Has Begun'* Interactions [Online] Available at: http://interactions.acm.org/archive/view/september-october-2013/web-3.0-has-begun (Accessed: November 2015).

Jantzen, C. (2013) Experiencing and experiences: a psychological framework, In *Handbook on the Experience Economy*. Ed. J. Sundbo, and F. Sorensen. Cheltenham: Edward Elgar, pp. 146–170.

Jeong, S.W., Fiore, A. M., Niehm, L. S., & Lorenz, F. O. (2009) 'The role of experiential value in online shopping: The impacts of product presentation on consumer responses towards an apparel web site.' *Internet Research*, Vol. (19) Iss. 1, pp. 105–124.

Jiang, Z., & Benbasat, I. (2007) 'The effects of presentation formats and task complexity on online consumers' product understanding'. *MIS Quarterly*, Vol. (31) Iss. 3, pp. 475–500.

Julier, G. (2008) *The Culture of Design*, 2nd edn. London, Sage Publishing.

Kaplan, A.M. (2012) 'If you love something, let it go mobile: Mobile marketing and mobile social media 4×4'. *Business Horizons*, Vol. (55) Iss. 2, pp. 129–139.

Kaplan, A.M., & Haenlein, M. (2010) 'Users of the world, unite! The challenges and opportunities of Social Media'. *Business Horizons*, Vol. (53) Iss. 1, pp. 59–68.

Keating, B., Fitzgerald, R., & Barrass, S. (2011) Designing Context-Specific Service Systems: Applying Pattern Design Principles to Service Design. In the *Proceedings of the 1st Cambridge Academic Design Management Conference*. September. Cambridge, University of Cambridge.

Kietzmann, J.H., Hermkens, K., McCarthy, I.P., & Silvestre, B.S. (2011) 'Social media? Get serious! Understanding the functional building blocks of social media'. *Business Horizons*, Vol. (54), pp. 241–251.

Kim, H., Choi, Y. J., & Lee, Y. (2015) 'Web atmospheric qualities in luxury fashion brand websites'. *Journal of Fashion Marketing and Management*, Vol (19), pp. 384–401.

Kim, H., & Lennon, S. (2008) 'The effects of visual and verbal information on attitudes and purchase intentions in internet shopping'. *Psychology & Marketing*, Vol. (25) Iss. 2, pp. 146–178.

Kim, H., & Lennon, S. J. (2010) 'E-atmosphere, emotional, cognitive, and behavioral responses'. *Journal of Fashion Marketing and Management: An International Journal*, Vol. (14) Iss. 3, pp. 412–428.

Kim, J., & Forsythe, S. (2010) 'Factors affecting adoption of product virtualisation technology for online consumer electronics shopping'. *International Journal of Retail & Distribution Management*, Vol. (38), pp. 190–204.

Korgaonkar, P., Silverblatt, R., & Girard, T. (2006) 'Online retailing, product classifications, and consumer preferences'. *Internet Research*, Vol. (16) Iss. 3, pp. 267–288.

Koufaris, M. (2002) 'Applying the technology acceptance model and flow theory to online consumer behavior'. *Information Systems Research*, Vol. (13) Iss. 2, pp. 205–223.

Kozinets, R., Dolbec, P.-Y., & Earley, A. (2014) Netnographic Analysis: Understanding Culture Through Social Media Data, in *The Sage Handbook of Qualitative Data Analysis*. Ed. U. Flick. London, Sage Publications, pp. 262–276.

Leavitt, N. (2010) 'Payment applications make e-commerce mobile'. *Computer*, Vol. (43) Iss. 12, pp. 19–22.

Lee, E. J., & Park, J.K. (2009) 'Online service personalisation for apparel shopping'. *Journal of Retailing and Consumer Services*, Vol. (16) Iss. 2, pp. 83–91.

Lee, H.-H., Kim, J., & Fiore, A.M. (2010) 'Affective and cognitive online shopping experience: Effects of image interactivity technology and experimenting with appearance'. *Clothing and Textiles Research Journal*, Vol. (28) Iss. 2, pp. 140–154.

Linden, G., Smith, B., & York, J. (2003) '*Amazon.com Recommendations Item to Item Filtering*'. Industry Report. IEEE Internet Computing. Available from http://ieeexplore.ieee.org/xpl/login.jsp?tp=&arnumber=1167344&url=http%3A%2F%2Fieeexplore.ieee.org%2Fxpls%2Fabs_all.jsp%3Farnumber%3D1167344.

Lohse, G.L., & Spiller, P. (1998) 'Electronic shopping'. *Communications of the ACM*, Vol. (41) Iss. 7, pp. 81–87.

Lohse, G.L., & Spiller, P. (2003) Internet retail store design: how the user interface influences traffic and sales, in *New Directions in Research on e-commerce*. Ed. C.W. Steinfield. West Lafayette, IN: Purdue University Press, pp. 32–63.

Lykke, M., & Jantzen, C. (2016) User Experience Dimensions: A systematic approach to experiential qualities for evaluating information interaction in museums, in *CHIIR. Proceedings of the ACM SIGIR Conference on Human Information Interaction and Retrieval*, Carrboro, NC.

Magrath, V., & McCormick, H. (2013) 'Marketing design elements of mobile fashion retail apps'. *Journal of Fashion Marketing and Management: An International Journal*, Vol. (17) Iss. 1, pp. 115–134.

Malik, A., Dhir, A., & Nieminen, M. (2016) 'Uses and gratifications of digital photo sharing on Facebook'. *Telematics and Informatics*, Vol. (33) Iss. 1, pp. 129–138.

Markoff, J. (2006) 'Entrepreneurs see a web guided by common sense'. *The New York Times* [Online]. Available at: http://www.nytimes.com/2006/11/12/business/12web.html?pagewanted=1&_r=0&ei (Accessed: November 2015).

McCormick, H., & Livett, C. (2012) 'Analysing the influence of the presentation of fashion garments on young consumers' online behaviour'. *Journal of Fashion Marketing and Management: An International Journal*, Vol. (16) Iss. 1, pp. 21–41.

Merrilees, B., & Fry, M. L. (2003) 'E-trust: The influence of perceived interactivity on e-retailing users'. *Marketing Intelligence & Planning*, Vol. (21) Iss. 2, pp. 123–128.

Miel, P., & Faris, R. (2008) 'News and information as digital media come of age'. *The Berkman Center for Internet & Society at Harvard University* [Online] Available at: http://cyber.law.harvard.edu/sites/cyber.law.harvard.edu/files/Overview_MR.pdf (Accessed: 15 August 2016).

Mintel (2011) *'Consumer Attitudes Towards Luxury Brands UK – November 2011'* Mintel [Online]. Available at: http://academic.mintel.com/display/600571/ (Accessed: November 2015).

Mintel (2014a) *'Fashion Online – UK – August 2014'* Mintel Oxygen, Available at: http://academic.mintel.com (Accessed: 02 May 2015).

Mintel (2014b) *'Blurring the Definition of a Clothing Retailer – 29th April 2014'* Mintel [Online]. Available at: http://academic.mintel.com/display/702655/?highlight#hit1 (Accessed: November 2015).

Mintel (2014c) *'Virtual Reality – enhancing the experience?'* [online]. Available at: http://academic.mintel.com/display/707731/?highlight [Accessed: 7 November 2014].

Mintel (2015) *'Burberry Launches Apple Music channel'* Mintel [Online]. Available at: http://academic.mintel.com/sinatra/oxygen_academic/display/id=749476?highlight#hit1 (Accessed: November 2015).

Moon, M. (1999) 'Branding in the networked economy'. *Design Management Journal*, Vol. (10) Iss. 2, pp. 61–70.

Moore, C., Doherty, A.M., & Doyle, S. (2010) 'Flagship stores as a market entry method: Perspectives from luxury fashion retailing'. *European Journal of Marketing*, Vol. (44) Iss. 1/2, pp. 139–161.

Mosteller, J., Donthu, N., & Eroglu, S. (2014) 'The fluent online shopping experience'. *Journal of Business Research*, Vol. (67) Iss. 11, pp. 2486–2493.

Murray, J.H. (2011) *Inventing the Medium: Principles of Interaction Design as Cultural Practice*. London: MIT Press.

Novak, T.P., Hoffman, D.L., & Yung, Y.-F. (2000) 'Measuring the customer experience in an online environment: A structural modeling approach'. *Marketing Science*, Vol. (19) Iss. 1, pp. 2–42.

Nuutinen, M., & Heikkinen, M. (2013) Evaluating the Levels of Design Management in User Experience-oriented Companies – Experiences from Finnish Metals and Engineering Industry. In the *Proceedings of the Cambridge Academic Design Management Conference*. Cambridge, University of Cambridge.

Nuutinen, M., & Keinonen, T. (2011) User Experience in Complex Systems: Crafting a Conceptual Framework. In the *Proceedings of the Cambridge Academic Design Management Conference*. Cambridge, University of Cambridge.

Pan, X., Shankar, V., & Ratchford, B.T. (2002) Price competition between pure play vs. bricks-and-clicks e-tailers: analytical model and empirical analysis. *Bricks-and-Clicks e-Tailers: Analytical Model and Empirical Analysis*.

Pantano, E., & Naccarato, G. (2010) 'Entertainment in retailing: The influences of advanced technologies'. *Journal of Retailing and Consumer Services*, Vol. (17) Iss. 3, pp. 200–204.

Pantano, E., & Viassone, M. (2015) 'Engaging consumers on new integrated multichannel retail settings: Challenges for retailers'. *Journal of Retailing and Consumer Services*, Vol. (25), pp. 106–114.

Park, C-H., & Kim, Y-G. (2003) 'Identifying key factors affecting consumer purchase behavior in an online shopping context'. *International Journal of Retail & Distribution Management*, Vol. (31) Iss. 1, pp. 16–29.

Parvinen, P., Oinas-Kukkonen, H., & Kaptein, M. (2014) 'E-selling: A new avenue of research for service design and online engagement'. *Electronic Commerce Research and Applications*, Vol. (14) Iss. 4, pp. 214–221.

Paulsen, M.F. (1995) *The Online Report on Pedagogical Techniques for Computer-Mediated Communication* [Online]. Available at http://emoderators.com/wp-content/uploads/cmcped.html (Accessed: 15 August 2016).

Peck, J., & Childers, T.L. (2003) 'To have and to hold: The influence of haptic information on product judgments'. *Journal of Marketing*, Vol. (67) Iss. 2, pp. 35–48.

Phan, M., Thomas, R., & Heine, K. (2011) 'Social media and luxury brand management: The case of Burberry'. *Journal of Global Fashion Marketing*, Vol. (2) Iss. 4, pp. 213–222.

Rapp, A., Baker, T.L., Bachrach, D.G., Ogilvie, J., & Beitelspacher, L.S. (2015) 'Perceived customer showrooming behavior and the effect on retail salesperson self-efficacy and performance'. *Journal of Retailing*, Vol. (91) Iss. 2, pp. 358–369.

Renko, S., & Druzijanic, M. (2014) 'Perceived usefulness of innovative technology in retailing: Consumers' and retailers' point of view'. *Journal of Retailing and Consumer Services*, Vol. (21) Iss. 5, pp. 835–843.

Rigby, D. (2011) 'The future of shopping: Successful companies will engage customers through "omnichannel" retailing: A mashup of digital and physical experiences'. *Harvard Business Review*, Vol. (89) Iss. 12, pp. 64–75.

Robson, K., Plangger, K., Kietzmann, J.H., McCarthy, I., & Pitt, L. (2015) 'Game on: Engaging customers and employees through gamification'. *Business Horizons*, Vol. (59), pp. 29–36.

Sanders, E.B.-N., & Stappers, P.J. (2008) 'Co-creation and the new landscapes of design'. *CoDesign*, Vol. (4) Iss. 1, pp. 5–18.

Seaborn, K., & Fel, D.I. (2015) 'Gamification in theory and action: A survey'. *International Journal of Human-Computer Studies*, Vol. (74) February, pp. 14–31.

Shields, R. (Ed.) (1996) *Cultures of Internet: Virtual Spaces, Real Histories, Living Bodies*. London, Sage.

Shih, C.F. (1998) 'Conceptualising consumer experiences in cyberspace'. *European Journal of Marketing*, Vol. (32) Iss. 7/8, pp. 655–663.

Snel, A. (2013) Experience as the DNA of a Changed Relationship Between Firms and Institutions and Individuals, in *The Handbook on the Experience Economy*. Ed. J. Sundbo and F. Sørensen. Cheltenham: Edward Elgar, pp. 122–145.

Sparke, P. (2013) *An Introduction to Design and Culture, 1900 to the Present*. London, Routledge.

Spena, T.R., Caridà, A., Colurcio, M., & Melia, M. (2012) 'Store experience and co-creation: The case of temporary shop'. *International Journal of Retail & Distribution Management*, Vol. (40) Iss. 1, pp. 21–40.

To, P., Liao, C., & Lin, T. (2007) 'Shopping Motivations on the Internet: A study based on utilitarian and hedonic value'. *Technovation*, pp. 774–787.

Topalian, A. (2003) 'Experienced reality: the digital era'. *European Journal of Marketing*, Vol. (37), pp. 1119–1132.

Turban, E., King, D., Lee, J.K., Liang, T.P., & Turban, D.C. (2015) *Electronic Commerce*. New York: Springer International Publishing.

Van Noort, G., Voorveld, H.A., & van Reijmersdal, E.A. (2012) 'Interactivity in brand web sites: Cognitive, affective, and behavioral responses explained by consumers' online flow experience'. *Journal of Interactive Marketing*, Vol. (26) Iss. 4, pp. 223–234.

Verdict Retail (2014) *Online Pureplays to Hold a 30% Share of Online Global Luxury Spend by 2020* [Online]. Available at http://www.verdictretail.com/online-pureplays-to-hold-a-30-share-of-online-global-luxury-spend-by-2020 (Accessed: November 2015).

Verhoef, P.C., Kannan, P.K., & Inman, J.J. (2015) 'From multi-channel retailing to omni-channel retailing: Introduction to the special issue on multi-channel retailing'. *Journal of Retailing*, Vol. (91) Iss. 2, pp. 174–181.

Verhoef, P.C., Lemon, K.N., Parasuraman, A., Roggeveen, A., Tsiros, M., & Schlesinger, L.A. (2009) 'Customer experience creation: Determinants, dynamics and management strategies'. *Journal of Retailing*, Vol. (85) Iss. 1, pp. 31–41.

Verhoef, P.C., Neslin, S.A., & Vroomen, B. (2007) 'Multichannel customer management: Understanding the research-shopper phenomenon'. *International Journal of Research in Marketing*, Vol. (24) Iss. 2, pp. 129–148.

Vogue (2012) Burberry Opens Regent Street Flagship. *Vogue.com* [Online]. Available at: http://www.vogue.co.uk/news/2012/09/13/burberry-regent-street-flagship-opens (Accessed: November 2015).

Vogue (2015) *Angela Ahrendts* [Online]. Available at: http://www.vogue.co.uk/person/angela-ahrendts (Accessed: November 2015).

Wagner, G., Schramm-Klein, H., & Steinmann, S. (2015) E-Tailing in a Connected Devices World: A Review and Research Agenda. In the *Proceedings of the European Association for Education and Research in Consumer Distribution Conference*. IGR-IAE University of Rennes 1.

Wang, S.J., Hsu, C.P., Huang, H.C., & Chen, C.L. (2015) 'How readers' perceived self-congruity and functional congruity affect bloggers' informational influence: Perceived interactivity as a moderator'. *Online Information Review*, Vol. (4), pp. 537–555.

Warner, C., Stone, L.G., & Knowles, A. (2015) *Building Native Computer Applications Using a Browser Platform*. Google Inc. U.S. Patent 8,990,710.

Wiseman, E. (2010) 'One-click wonder: The rise of Net-a-Porter'. *The Guardian*, 11 July [Online]. Available at: http://www.theguardian.com/lifeandstyle/2010/jul/11/natalie-massenet-net-a-porter-internet-fashion (Accessed: November 2015).

Yadav, M.S., & Varadarajan, R. (2005) 'Interactivity in the electronic marketplace: An exposition of the concept and implications for research'. *Journal of the Academy of Marketing Science*, Vol. (33), pp. 585–603.

Yang, H.E., & Wu, C.C. (2009) 'Effects of image interactivity technology adoption on e-shoppers' behavioural intentions with risk as moderator'. *Production Planning and Control*, Vol. (20) Iss. 4, pp. 370–382.

Yoo, J., & Kim, M. (2014) 'The effects of online product presentation on consumer responses: A mental imagery perspective'. *Journal of Business Research*, Vol. (67) Iss. 11, pp. 2464–2472.

Yoo, W.-S., Lee, Y., & Park, J. (2010) 'The role of interactivity in e-tailing: Creating value and increasing satisfaction'. *Journal of Retailing and Consumer Services*, Vol. (17) Iss. 2, pp. 89–96.

11 Globalisation and localisation

The high-end fashion retail perspective

Bhakti Sharma

Introduction

The term 'globalisation' is as polarising as it is confusing. There are as many definitions of the word available as there are opinions. Every industry has a personal take on the term.

By the late 1980s, 'international integration' was an acceptable synonym for globalisation as improvised by Resnick (1989) and originally developed by Davidson and Harrigan (1977), and Levitt (1980) and many others after that, including Hamel and Prahalad (1985). Medina and Duffy (1998) provide an extensive history of the definition. Resnick's definition was more process oriented, one that described globalisation as the phenomenon that allowed firms obtaining raw materials from one market with financial support from another and so on and so forth while selling the finished product in yet other national market. This act of making products worldwide in scope and application was further clarified in research by Medina and Duffy (1998), who defined globalisation as the process of adopting country and target-market dictated product standards – tangible and/or intangible attributes – from environments around the world to achieve a highly uniform product. Thus, in the words of Mertl (2013, p. 31), globalisation is 'the sum of all phenomena, which lead or refer to a status of permanent and unlimited possibilities of interaction between all cultures'.

But to discuss concepts of culture without local and native would be sacrilegious. An inherent part of globalisation is localisation. Localisation, according to Serkan (2009), is an international strategy used by companies to modify their products and services so that products have local features demanded by local consumers and are suitable to local laws and standards.

So far, I have introduced only two terms. Throw in terms such as 'glocalisation', 'standardisation', 'adaptation' and 'customisation', and you are no closer to solving this intellectual puzzle than where you were when you had first started.

Extensive research has been conducted on globalisation and related terms (Davidson and Harrigan, 1977; Hamel and Prahalad, 1985). Heery and Noon (2008) explained glocalisation as a business strategy which allows each of its national subsidiaries to operate as freestanding businesses that conform to the business and employment practices that prevail in the host country. Buzell in 1968 explained standardisation as the practice of offering identical product lines at identical prices, through identical distribution systems, supported by identical promotional programs, in several different countries. Adaptation is the strategy of developing new products by modifying or improving on the product innovations of others, and customisation is tailoring the product to the special and unique needs of the customer as defined by Bennett (1988).

Fast-fashion companies are epitomizing these terms. Zara, H&M and Topshop offer identical product lines in different countries at a lightning fast turnaround rate. Technological advancement and the ability to create a large number of styles in limited quantity in record speed – as exhibited by fast fashion brands such as Zara, Gap, H&M and ASOS – represent the homogenisation / McDonaldisation parameter of globalisation. High-end fashion brands are not within everyone's reach, and high-street brands offer affordable high-end fashion to masses globally with a compromised quality. Additionally, high-end brands and designers such as Karl Lagerfeld, Chanel, Balmain and Lanvin are partnering with fast-fashion brands for limited-time collections to make product available to the masses and to cut counterfeit products. As Tungate (2012, p. 32) notes, 'Luxury brands could show they knew how to talk street, the chain stores would benefit from the glitter, and there would be lots of free publicity for everyone'. While Tungate's statement about the designer-fast fashion brand appears accurate, his commentary on the end of 'slavish brand worship' (2012, p. 35) era requires further investigation.

Despite slowing economies, fast-fashion companies have posted increased profits and have thrived. Fast-fashion companies emphasize the democratisation of fashion in a global economy, providing everyone with an equal choice to fashion and access to designs of high fashion brands at a low price. They are often accused of copyright infringement and copying of styles and designs; these companies move quickly along with changing designs, bringing exclusivity to the mass market, until it is not exclusive anymore.

From design to advertising to distribution from a centralised facility, these companies have standardised the globalised market. A billboard of an ad campaign with a model on a white background in China would be no different from one in Sweden. Fast-fashion brands also have flagship stores much like the high-end brands. While flagship stores of high-end brands offer an exclusive experience that pleases the senses, the flagship stores for fast fashion offer exclusive products in terms of relevant and most recent designs. In Mikunda's (2006) definition, the flagship stores are defined as the principal store of a retail chain that carry a single brand of product, are owned by the manufacturer of the brand, and operated with the intention of building or reinforcing the image of the product rather than operating to sell a product.

The fast-fashion companies do not develop or dictate the style. It is the high-end brands that do that. And this chapter attempts to address these definers of fashion in a globalised setting.

While this chapter does not attempt to define globalisation and localisation again or provide the reader with a chronological history of the evolution of the terms and redefine 'homogenisation', 'hybridisation', standardisation and other related terms, it discusses the presence of high-end fashion brands in globalised retail settings. It also discusses the strategies that these brands are taking in a volatile and constantly changing retail market where the parameters of globalisation and localisation are changing every day. This chapter is also not about the economic impacts and assessments of global and local production and consumption. This chapter discusses the fine line that high-end luxury brands walk each day to make locals and natives adapt and buy globalised designs and what strategies the brands are implementing to penetrate the local market. It discusses the effect of globalisation on localisation, the inter-dependency, the contradictions and the co-existence, specifically in a luxury brand setting.

Luxury fashion brands

Business and marketing practices have learned how to co-exist in foreign lands since the times of the Silk Route. But because of globalisation – technological advancement, record speeds in manufacturing, international cultural exchanges – the boundaries of space and time have been compressed. As demonstrated by fast fashion brands, the turnaround time of designs into the market is very quick. This is true in every market of the brand globally. High-end fashion brands are also able to manufacture and sell their designs in an international market such as Taiwan at the same time as they are being sold in Paris. In earlier times prior to flagship stores, prior to brands entering global markets, the designs were available to a handful of ultra-rich clientele through trunk shows only. Technological advancement and market penetration has allowed brands to immerse in the fabric of the localised society. A holistic market immersion and the phenomenon of compression of time and space has only been made possible by globalisation in a localised setting. A flagship store in Tokyo not only may appear to be similar to the flagship store for the brand in Paris spatially, but it now has the ability to offer the same product line at parallel moments in time. Brands have entered global markets, they have localised their product and marketing strategies, their practices of conducting business have stood the test of time in the realm of adaptation, and the customs of the brands have been customised to the local cultures' religious and native belief system. Successful fast-fashion brands have mastered the art of translating business practices to propositions that are relevant in a local market.

One industry that is however pushing the boundaries of relevance is that of high-end fashion. The luxury fashion market is not one to just be relevant. The rebellious, privileged child of fashion, luxury retail and high-end brands are redefining the vows of the marriage between globalisation and localisation.

In an interview for the marketing news conducted by Levy (2010), Donna Sturgess, the founding partner and president of global marketing agency Buyology Inc., remarks that an important skill to achieve success in local markets is the skill of anticipation. She also comments on the anticipatory action-packed nature of the game of understanding the local market to use it for global benefit of the brand. The luxury fashion market has been playing this game of anticipation since the early 2000s. Not only have they been playing the game; this industry has been defining the rules of the game and changing the game every day.

The incipient nature of the globalisation and localisation in the luxury retail market creates a more speculative playing field for researchers . . . but most certainly a philosophical one. And that is where the magic happens. It is a rather invigorating time for the high-end fashion industry. While the business and marketing gurus have just finished defining trends in globalisation and all associated parameters, the fashion industry is already busy in challenging the rules and challenging time tested ideas such as 'change the product to adapt to the market'. While most brands understand the discernible behavioural, attitudinal, socio-economic behaviours of the market and are adapting their products and marketing to the local standards, the fashion industry is changing the makeup of the local values. While the common business practice is to build a relationship with the local using the strategies of market immersion, the high-end fashion industry is bringing new cultural themes to the local market and enriching the native experience. The luxury fashion industry is not one to change or one for change. It believes in cultural exchange. The high-end fashion industry believes in mutualistic growth. In the following section, the mutualistic and parasitic effect of the relationships that the fashion industry has developed with artists, architects and the cultural community is discussed.

The strategy

Sustaining the company while maintaining brand exclusivity and creating a legacy with their customers are the main international challenges faced by the ever-evolving world of luxury fashion retail. In a global market, high-end retailers have developed new functionalities, preserved existing methodologies, and reconfigured new strategies of providing their customers with an experience richer than retail. Design is at the heart of this universe. To this end of creating culture, fashion retailers have turned to various formulae, such as larger than life flagship stores, collaboration and research with star architects on the development of these stores, or partnerships with local artists to inspire a new collection or with theatre and film artists to create advertising campaigns – albeit to further retail. These strategies extend far and beyond the traditional entry market methods of brand image creation, generating ad content, and media dominance. The ideas adopted and introduced to the world by high-end fashion brands of employing cultural factors to segment global markets speak primarily to the customers' attitudes, lifestyle, and needs, and immerses the consumers at a cognitive, emotional and intuitive level – true to the theory proposed by Healy and Beverland (2007).

Researchers such as Pine and Gilmore (1999) and Klingmann (2007) have discussed theories such as 'retailment', 'experience-providers', 'experience economy' and 'business as a stage' in the literature for retail environment. Luxury retailers are constantly reinventing their branding to reflect their ever-changing values and to extend to an even more dynamic customer base. Experience economy as described by Kozinets et al. (2002) is engaging and entertaining experience that brands provide to the customer in addition to their product.

In 1988, Belk introduced the strategy of the brand's adoption of a local culture by developing the identity of the consumers through the association and collection of objects, events and experiences. Flagship stores attempt to form a connection with the consumers through a spatial association also known as brandscaping. In his book published in 2002, Otto Riewoldt defines the term as a three-dimensional design of brand settings that forges backdrops for experiences with a high entertainment value.

To anticipate – according to Sturgess' vision of future – is to build a sustaining relationship with the consumer, and, to this end, high-end fashion brands employ various visual and spatial unifiers such as advertising, names, logos, signage, magalogs (promotional catalog or sales brochures designed to resemble a high-quality magazine), annual reports, product design and packaging, brand characters, product placement, event marketing and sponsorships, websites and electronic media, retail stores, flagship stores, brand exhibitions, or brand cities. But in a world where brands are ubiquitous and users have an ever-evolving awareness of brands – a market where a retail store has a shelf life of six years – both the brand and the consumer are looking for an experience richer than retail, an experience affective at a visceral level. The six-year shelf life and a complete revamp are yet to be seen in a flagship store. High-end fashion flagship stores seem to have stood the test of time, and the original architecture of the stores has been around since inception.

And this is where design, art and architecture and the role of local artists and architects as generators of cultural capital cues in. A prime reason for creating a more experiential space in retail is the democratization of retail. As luxury goods are available more freely, the need to keep them exclusive is important – for instance, by creating flagship stores that sell limited products exclusive to the store. By using the intersection between art and fashion, luxury brands have created a mass market for luxury goods while keeping the products exclusive to the store selling them. This can be illustrated via a citation from Gasparina (2009, p. 43), who stated, 'It represents a continuing utopian theme in the avant-garde movement, an effort it "changes life itself"'.

Art, fashion, architecture, music, theatre, cinema and photography express ideas of personal, social, economic and cultural identity, and reflect the concerns of the user and the ambition of the age. They also are indicators of the prominent culture of a time, a common thread that connects these trades. While these trades are intrinsically different, it is the prominent visual culture that connects these trades and creates a symbiotic relationship between them as has been seen in numerous collaborations between fashion houses and architects. Fashion and its patronage of the arts and architecture create a cultural capital. Bourdieu (1984, p. 10) defined 'cultural capital as high cultural knowledge that ultimately redounds to the owner's financial and social advantage. Fluency and immersion of arts, architecture, music, dance, theater, cuisine represents capital because the knowledge can be turned in financial and social benefits'. The cultural capital generated as a result of collaborations between the brands and the native artists and designers is nothing short of iconic and a tale that history books will tell timelessly.

The motive

While the fashion brands are not modifying their products to suit the local market, they are most certainly partnering with local artists for a cultural exchange and a creation of a product line that is suited not only to the local market but that becomes the standard line for the brand worldwide. While designer-artist/architect collaboration has been seen historically with the Schiaparelli–Dali lobster dress, Rabanne-Future systems Selfridges façade, and Gucci-Grace of Monaco bag inspiration, Louis Vuitton's 2006 partnership with Yayoi Kusuma goes above and beyond a symbolic gesture. The collaboration was iconic and pertinent. Louis Vuitton changed its monogram to represent Kusuma's signature polka dots as homage to the artist, and the style reminiscent of pointillism was represented on bags, accessories, shoes and leather goods in addition to visual and storefront display and exhibits.

In addition, the exposure that the artist gets due to international exhibition and partnership with the brand is the patronage that an artist needs. The brands used this technique as a market entry method, but it certainly has stood the test of time. 'Local' culture or 'local' products might have historically non-local origin, but they become 'local' because they have been adapted in the place for a long time, and they are just more 'local' than new things brought by the recent global flows.

But there is more than meets the eye. There is a bigger motive for the collaboration between the artist and the brand than the mere creation of cultural capital. Localisation is not just a persuasion technique employed by global brands as a market entry method. It seems as if we have entered a dark age where brands are not trying to just sell their merchandise but have a bigger agenda instead – one in which old techniques of trunk shows and flagship stores have been superseded by the need to re-define a culture. Global brands are using localisation to their advantage not just to sell more merchandize but also to understand the vulnerabilities of a culture and to morph the culture so that it does not remain local and indigenous anymore and takes a more global form. The strategies employed by brands to change the appearance of a race is more than skin-deep in an industry where the patrons of Gucci are not any different in Japan as they are in Australia. They might be when the brand is using localisation as a market entry method. But after the morphing of culture has taken place, after the subversion has occurred, after the global brand slowly but surely has planted a stronghold in the economic and cultural makeup of a place, are the Japanese and the Australian patrons same in more than just their love for Gucci?

It has been suggested that brands act as social signals, gain their meaning from a cultural context, and can be invested with symbolism, which communicates social status, wealth and social group conformity (Lewis and Hawksley, 1990). This symbolic significance also invests the brand with a psychological importance, whereby brand ownership can be used as a vehicle for self-identification and expression (Schiffman and Kanuk, 1997; Tomlinson, 1990).

In the executive summary for a study for the UK fashion scene when fashion brands were beginning to employ market dominance strategies in 1985 – strategies very similar to the ones that the brands are employing in the new global markets – Fernie, Moore et al. (1997) suggest that a common market entry method at the time was that each of the brands received a 'free' plug in a national newspaper and the implied association with a particular niche in society – a niche that was for the elite few, not the masses. And this exclusivity is what mattered rather than the quality or nature of the product itself. If this exclusivity was ever to be diluted, then the appeal of the brand to the very wealthy and the superstars would diminish. Decades later, the high-end fashion brands stayed true to their word and did not make any cuts that would diminish or dilute their appeal or brand in the global market. The ancient wisdom of localisation tells us that for market immersion, brands must alter their product to the local market. When Louis Vuitton entered India, it did not alter or develop monogrammed saris instead of scarves. In markets such as India, high-end fashion brands have utilized the strategy of flagship stores to expand to new territories and markets. In doing so, they have enhanced customer loyalty, enriched the brand meaning, and created a cultural exchange while exploring synergies between physical, social and symbolic value of the global brand and the local society.

Subversion tactics and the good in globalisation

According to Leroy (2004), the crucial issue remains the relationship between an economic system, the individual and the social values society promotes – in other words, how responsible global capitalism is or can become. In economic and legal literature, subversion tactics to overthrow and modify the law in developing countries to develop a brand in a new territory is present. The case by Louis Vuitton for patenting the checkerboard pattern was dismissed when the court cited the pattern to be too commonplace to be owned by one brand. Subversion may also be referred to as corruption of a person's moral values and are on full display when global brands enter new markets. Transformation of an established social order takes place when high-end luxury brands incorporate previously untested methodologies of modifying the existing values and systems in place to enter and stay in a new market. Whether it is subversion of law or subversion of moral values, subversion takes place. But not all subversion is bad. In high-end retail, subversion tackles the delicate connection between globalisation and localisation.

Has the development of flagship stores and immersion in the market through sociocultural strategies, the subversion tactic of modifying a person's belief system, thus altered the culture of the place in the fashion industry? In high-end retail, are the traditional roles of globalisation and localisation reversed?

The answer to these questions may be in one subversion tactic of modifying the moral values while entering the market – the flagship store.

Flagship stores

Flagship stores are retail spectacles that serve the purpose of retailment, exclusive social interaction and creation of culture, all while providing an exclusive sales shrine for the customer.

In terms of location, flagship stores have historically been located at an existing city centre/prime location or in a historical neighbourhood such as the Champs-Élysées in Paris or at a brownfield site that has been revitalized, such as the impact that the Louis Vuitton flagship had on the Nagoya Sakae neighbourhood in Tokyo. In opening the flagship store at a brownfield site, the luxury brands are establishing new city centres and gentrifying the neighbourhoods and in the process improving the socio-economic conditions. The Louis Vuitton store in Nagoya Sakae was in a location that was previously isolated. When it opened in 1999, writes Magrou (2011), the architect Jun Aoki received little help from the heterogeneous contact of the site flanked by an open-air parking lot, and there were no elements offering tangible support of what was to become the emblem of a fashion house. In traditional theories, brand immersion was possible if brands placed their stores in established locations with maximum exposure. Integrating stores in new, non-established city centres or distressed neighbourhoods as has been seen in the Roppongi district in Japan as a market entry method was previously unheard of. The differences in digressing from traditional globalisation and localisation strategies by luxury fashion retailers have been expanded in Table 11.1.

The opening of flagship stores in new and previously unexplored neighbourhoods attracts new vendors as has been seen in the Louis Vuitton store in Nagoya Sakae and explained in a case study later in this chapter. In a traditional retail setting such as a mall, similar trade attracts other vendors to start competing businesses in the area. In the re-development or revitalization projects, a flagship store acts as a solid, iconic standalone anchor. If a big brand such as McDonald's were to open in a brownfield development, the chances of another McDonald's opening in that area are limited when compared to an Armani

Table 11.1 Comparison of laws of globalisation and localisation in tradition retail setting with the high-end fashion setting

Traditional laws of globalisation and localisation	*Globalisation and localisation as practiced by high-end fashion houses*
Standardise product	No change to product; collaboration with local artists is evident
Localise advertising	Advertising is standard globally
Stores in well-established city centres	Stores have been seen in brownfield sites, remote neighbourhoods; flagship stores have developed new and previously distressed neighbourhoods
Maximum product to reduce competition	Limited product for a limited time
Sell to niche target market only	Open to all; several floors reserved for VIP access
Enter a new market with old technology or product not current in developed markets	Same line of product available globally at the same time
Segmentation strategy (based upon the 'demand side of the market and represents a rational and more precise adjustment of product and marketing effort to consumer or user requirements' [Smith, 1956])	Product or marketing not adjusted; the local consumer and culture become part of the marketing strategy
Adaptation or subversion (local laws)	Neutral
Customisation of products due to economic disparity, beliefs and traditions	Local customs are used at special events and launch parties; local culture is celebrated

anchor flagship store being the driver for an Armani home flagship store. The flagship stores of the global brands act as an anchor for new businesses. This is one positive effect of the localisation of the global brand. Brands such as Prada and Louis Vuitton are also investing in developing the neighbourhood. The purchase of a Milanese heritage café Cova in 2014 by Louis Vuitton's parent company LVMH is a step toward the brand offering its customers high-quality places to meet friends and mingle during the shopping experience.

Most flagship stores also exhibit limited products for a brief period of time. In traditional globalisation strategies, brands would flood the market with their products to aim for market dominance by eliminating competition. If a customer was looking for a specific branded product, there may be different vendors that sell that particular product, but the more visible the brand, the higher the sales. However, in a flagship store the intent is reversed to portray only a specific product, a specific brand, and a specific flagship store to purchase that product . . . within a stipulated amount of time.

Flagship stores are glamorous, but they are not out of reach. The example of London and the exclusive quality of the stores for the niche few applies to flagship stores, but not without a few restrictions.

The main purpose of flagship stores is not retail. A space analysis conducted by Sharma (2014a) of high-end fashion stores including Louis Vuitton, Prada and Chanel in the relatively new market of Japan showed that in fact only 21 per cent of the entire flagship store footprint was used for retail purposes. What about the rest of the space? Sharma's analyses (2014b) demonstrated that 79 per cent was used for retailment, open to the public. Retailment concerns theatres, opera halls, restaurants by celebrity chefs, etc. and education about the brand, brands as purveyors of art and culture. Flagship stores aim to offer customers a venue to 'watch the opera' – why not grab a bite to eat, prepared by a celebrity chef, while you are there? These aspects are all part of the big retailment extravaganza called the flagship store of the high-end fashion brand that is open to one and all. And come to think of it, a few years ago . . . it could be located on a site that was a brownfield or not fit for human existence, let alone entertainment.

High-end fashion brands are playing a role in localisation of a different kind, one that involves the local artists, which put the local on the globe. Hamel and Prahalad (1994) defined strategic architecture as the imagined future that is built. Describing the importance of architecture as marketing tool, they suggest that in order to build strategic architecture, top management must have a point of view through which new benefits, or 'functionalities' will be offered. Not only do the creative directors of the high-end fashion brands work closely with architects to envision and develop these flagship stores together, several designer lines available exclusively at the flagship stores are developed in collaboration with local artists. Paul Thompson, the rector of London's Royal College of Art, points out in his interview to Swengley (2011) that commissioning avant-garde designers to work with them allows these brands to stress their heritage and contemporaneity in one breath. To this end, high-end fashion brands have indulged in artist collaborations in the fields of cinema, theatre, travel scholarships or culture themes set around equestrians or yacht sailing, just to name a few.

High-end luxury brands have not stopped at artist collaborations.

Putting the world of luxury to philanthropic use in new and emerging markets, brands have a shared similar vision on environmental and social causes as well. The market entry and brand launch events range from sponsorships and involvement with vintage car rallies, the America's Cup, limited edition handbags to benefit children, and limited edition products and books with proceeds going to charities around the world – another social thread that binds the brands together. As per Moore et al. (2010, p. 152), 'events such as launch parties, fashion shows and charity evenings are used to maintain interest in the brand, reward the loyalty of stockists, as well as to generate and nurture new business'.

3Ps of global marketing no more

Innovative market-entry methods, flagship stores in brownfield sites for gentrification of distressed neighbourhoods, limited product availability, glamour and the arts for the masses hardly fit the mould of accepted marketing practices in a global setting. In their paper about choosing between globalisation and localisation as a strategic thrust for international marketing effort, Ramarapu et al. (1999), identify the 3Ps of global marketing as place, people and product. The two strategies for companies entering new markets are to standardise or localize the 3Ps. According to their research, only a few products can be standardised, and adaptation is needed to win buyers.

If we compare the traditional 3Ps of marketing with the strategies used by high-end fashion houses, standardisation of products is not happening, and neither is the localisation of advertising taking place. The contrary is however true. As per Fernie et al. (1997), these fashion houses invariably adopt a brand identity based on brand values and images that have a global and universal appeal. This invariably involves the development of a standardized set-up and operating formula that controls the place of set-up, the location within the set-up area (normally off-centre), the shop fit, advertising and promotions. A comparison of traditional laws of globalisation and localisation with their application in a flagship setting is provided in Table 11.1.

Louis Vuitton: A case study

Through a study of literature, architectural drawings, published interviews and annual reports, the creation of cultural capital generated as a result of the interdisciplinary collaboration of fashion, art and architecture in new and emerging global markets by Louis Vuitton is discussed.

Since 2006, LV has been named the most valued luxury brand by two independent studies commissioned by Interbrand (2013) and WPP Plc. (2012).

In 2012, LV achieved double-digit revenue growth with a reported net profit of 1666.7 million Euros, and, to put the numbers in perspective, LV owns 185,000 square metres in over seventeen production facilities in Europe and the United States, and retail distribution sites all over the world in over 8,000 square metres of area.

True to the mission of the LVMH group to represent the most refined qualities of Western *Art de Vivre* around the world, LV became a legend in the art of travel by creating luggage, bags and accessories as innovative as they were elegant and practical especially through their monogram line, the Damier line for men, the Cuir Epi, Nomade and Taiga, and the monogram-embossed Empreinter.

But under the artistic direction of its former creative director Marc Jacobs, LV has led the avant-garde of fashion and is now active in other creative spheres such as arts, theatre, travel and architecture, which may be seen as a more refined art of branding in order to extend luxury fashion far beyond sales of goods. In an interview, Arnault (2013) points out that through patronage, Louis Vuitton wishes to give something back in the general interest to share their economic success with everyone. As fashion penetrates into the global psyche and culture, fashion – a business that depends on trends – should generate constant change as a core business priority (Golsorkhi, 2009). Increased market competition, heightened customer awareness, the need to create worldwide awareness and the need to stay new, fresh and relevant drives brands to interact with the customer at levels of personal values, art and culture, and philanthropy through various marketing and architectural strategies.

Entering the global market via flagship architecture and cultural patronage

In his foreword for the book for Louis Vuitton's architecture and interiors, renowned educator Mohsen Mostafavi (2011) emphasizes the close liaison between architecture and fashion. Architecture as the setting for selling the goods or the valorisation of fashion by providing minimalist spaces has created a new mass hysteria. But the development of mass hysteria and a building shell requires a star architect.

For entry into a new market such as Japan in 1996, LV tried a new spin on localisation. Instead of finding a previously established city centre, LV started by bringing a local star architect to develop a previously unknown site. Since then, Nagoya Sakae has become Tokyo's fashion centre. While once modernist architects rejected the idea of designing for commercial buildings, since 1998, when LV first partnered with Jun Aoki, LV has opened fourteen stores in Japan, seven of which have been designed by Aoki. The LV that boasts of an in-house architecture department did not work with signature architects in Japan, since they wanted to develop a language unique to LV. In collaborating with a relatively less established architect in 1998 in a market where architects did not want to design for commercial buildings, LV entered the Tokyo market on the basis of architectural creativity. LV was an established name at the time, and, while working with Aoki who was true to the Japanese minimalist aesthetic and preserved the timeless quality of the building on the exterior and interior at the Nagoya Sake store, LV was shifting its architectural mentality in the design of commercial buildings. The status of Jun Aoki as an avant-garde architect appeared to be important to LV in order to communicate a message to the architectural fraternity in Japan, thereby employing a local strategy to introduce a global brand. Was working with a designer who was not a star architect just a decision to develop an in-house design language true to LV, or was it a way of energizing the architectural fraternity and to portray that commercial buildings for global brands can be designed with local sensibilities? Was the conceptualisation of the LV store in the local market with an architect with modest star power and cultural capital at that time a means of the brand to exercise an authority that it would otherwise not have had? The impact of bringing a local architect who understood the market and the local architecture was an immersion technique applied by several high-end brands. Prada and Rem Koolhaas is another example of the brand's patronage of the artist and the architecture. The connection with local architects and artists creates a symbolic gesture that local customers recognize: local star architect becomes a visionary and strategist for the brand in the new market. As Ryan (2007, p. 8) notes, architecture becomes one of 'the most powerful symbols used by corporations to mediate identity and assert institutional interests in global markets'. The partnership with the local architect who becomes a cultural mouthpiece for the brand helps in communicating and introducing the global image of the brand in a local packaging to the new customers.

As Tungate points, 'luxury brands are in competition to see which of them can open the most immense, sense-scrambling spaces' (2012, p. 66). LV's parent company, LVMH, has committed itself to regenerating memorial sites and major monuments of history and culture including Château de Versailles, Palais Royal, Paris, and the birthplace of designer Christian Dior where temporary exhibitions about the life of the designer are held. In addition, LVMH has supported major art exhibitions around the world at new global markets including Hong Kong, Singapore, India and Taiwan, just to name a few.

The core of LV philosophy lies around travel and trunk-making. Louis Vuitton has created a travel series and sponsors the 'Journeys Awards' to independent filmmakers that create short movies on their travel experiences.

LV's strategy of store expansion, development of new flagship stores by commissioning local architects as a new market entry method, teamed with the group's mission of restoring, promoting and enriching the heritage are events that have high cultural and media impact and that open the fashion brand to a new market. The creative collaboration between the brand and the architect or the brand and the museum or other inter-disciplinary collaborations creates a renewed interest in the brand while obvious connections to the brand's conventional marketing initiatives remain minimized.

LV's initiatives in art, culture and architecture and the collaborations between the brand and star architects, amateur moviemakers, established corporate collaborations and avant-garde artists are a befitting example. Since the mid-1990s, LV has undertaken massive renovation and store expansion initiatives; has collaborated with over ninety artists, architects and fashion designers in new markets; has published several books on travel, art, architecture and fashion; and has opened two art spaces. As a result LV has reported double-digit growth in revenue since 2004. Since the opening of the first flagship store in 1999, LV has expanded twenty of their stores worldwide and still continues to do so. In Japan alone, since 1999, LV has opened fourteen stores. On the revenue growth and the increase in the stores, Igarashi (2009, p. 13) comments, 'the remarkable domestic sales results as well as Japan's dominance in the brand's total sales contributed to growth of flagship stores and artist collaborations'. The only thing the brand has done differently in the last decade is defying the theories of marketing and business practices in a global market.

'With the advent of modernity, public, and commercial institutions such as museums, city halls became the focus of change, but retail design was paid scant regard' (Igarashi, 2009, p. 14). But luxury retail brands have grown tremendously in the last two decades in global markets. From the flagship stores of the 2000s to the digital flagship stores and social media outreach of 2010–2013, retail brands are reaching out to the consumer, as they have never done before. But as is evident from LV stores, the flagship stores are becoming a prototype for their brand stores where by involving the native, they are making the local market adapt to a global standard. Also, what is evident from the multiple artist collaborations is that the portrayal of LV and other such brands as cultural ambassadors is here to stay. Commenting on customers viewing the contribution of companies as corporate citizens, Ricca (2013) points out that by promoting causes from education to art to architecture fulfils both business and cultural agendas for the locals.

By collaborating with other disciplines in a volatile market, brands are balancing short-term performance versus long-term prosperity in a global setting.

And if any of the above hypotheses are true, does that make the collaboration with local artists just another milestone in the evolution of luxury retail till the next trend comes around? Also, as the rapid growth of luxury brands in the global market continues to take place and as luxury brands compete for consumers' attention, is it not too long before that art and architecture intersection with fashion become ubiquitous and no longer unique? Business of fashion and trend-forecasting engine Millward Brown Optimor is predicting that LV is losing its ground as the most valuable luxury brand to close competitors Prada and Gucci, when the brand's value declined 12 per cent from 2012 to $22.7 billion in 2013 (Bloomberg, 2013).

But since luxury retail brands are forever evolving and ephemeral to the point of being volatile in nature, only time will tell if the marketing strategies of intersecting disciplines will stand the test of time. This opens avenues for future research and empirical data collection.

In the current scenario, luxury brands such as LV do provide a cultural and visual spectacle – an experience stage for the brands' users. Is it time that the laws of globalisation and localisation are revised and the rules that are being tested by companies such as LV become the norm?

Conclusion

While academic disciplines have played an important role in defining globalisation and localisation, the high-end fashion retail industry is challenging these definitions that have been previously accepted and applied to other industries. The visual spectacle of the design of flagship stores is more than the tip of the iceberg. The visual extravagance of flagship stores, the presence of high-end fashion brands in developing new neighbourhoods and improving the quality of life in historic neighbourhoods, and the creation of cultural capital are not mere gestures but more grandiose statements.

Flagship stores are a recent phenomenon, the first ones emerging in the early 2000s. Hence, very little literature, documentation and data are available on this subject matter. While brands wish to protect the 'trade secret' nature of the flagship store, it is important that researchers and designers study the heterogeneity of flagship stores and the spatial and functional boundaries that are being pushed. By analysing the marketing features of flagship stores and studying the impact of spatial organization and functionality of flagship stores in a globalised setting, a lot can be learned about the changing face of design and architecture – the duality of the space and the ability of a design to digress from the key function it is designed for such as retail in this case, maybe indicating a wave of the future. Taking the example of the flagship stores, what if the functionalities are reversed for other market sectors as well in a global setting? For instance, if flagship restaurants of famous chefs were to open in new markets and new cuisines were to be introduced globally with other offerings such as retail, ideologies and definitions of market sectors would be reversed. Additionally, the impact that brands and flagship stores are having on the socio-economic fabric of the new markets should be studied to identify future trends in business and design. Designers need to study further on the cognitive, intuitive, and visceral connections possible for users of space in the form of museums, theatres and opera houses that develop around retail locations – a strategy that high-end brands are implementing in new global markets.

Globalisation has been studied as a global phenomenon that affects different regions of the world in different ways. In high-end fashion retail, the same fervour for inaugurations in flagship stores is seen in Asia and in Australasia. Architecture enthusiasts visit the Apple glass box on Fifth Avenue, NYC, with the same glimmer in the eye as they approach the Guggenheim, a few buildings north of the Apple flagship. And Apple certainly does not disappoint: a building that has already changed the retail mind-set on its own – by patenting glass stairs just the way it patents its products, by forcing the customers to go to the basement of a retail location previously known as the problematic plaza, by developing a clutter-free technology store where wires are non-existent – and as if that was not enough, in 2011, Apple renovated the ninety-panel glass façade to a fifteen-panel seamless façade. High-end fashion brands use a consistent design sensibility for all their stores around the world with the exception of a visual spectacle. So the different effect on different regions of the world parameter of globalisation is being challenged by high-end fashion brands. The design, creativity and innovation of the brands is affecting the regions of the world in a consistent fashion, and this phenomenon can be applied to other areas and market sectors of design and architecture as well.

Prior to flagship stores, high-end fashion brands had a traditional retail strategy. Merchandise was placed in the store where the customers would shop and not necessarily visit the store for its architecture. If brands had to enter a new market, they would tend to seek out franchise owners or merge with a local company. The architecture of the store in a new market would conform to the local architecture, customs, laws and tradition. With the advent of the game-changing strategies of high-end retail brands of strong visual presence, reversing the methodologies of retail stores to become entertainment centres, and consistent awe-inspiring architecture by collaborating with star architects, global is becoming the new local. High-end fashion brands are not discarding local traditions. A tea-party ceremony in Japan or the patronage of a heritage café in Cova are signs that the brands are embracing the local. These design and architectural principles of the flagship stores and other strategies are undeviating from region to region around the globe. The visual spectacle is consistent, the partnership with the star architect is at the heart of the game changing rules; the flagship store as the entertainment centre and as the brand shrine is uniform. The flagship store provides a cosmos for the local to exist. The flagship store becomes the space to have the local experience in a global setting. And we will see the adaptation of the boundaries of globalisation that are being pushed by the high-end fashion brands by brands entering and existing in various regions around the global. We will see a more subtle infusion of the local in the form of art, architecture, music, theatre and culture within the brands.

The design needs to not adapt to the local. Globalisation does not dominate. Local does not cease to exist. In the new setting, globalisation and localisation co-exist.

References

Arnault, B. (2013). *RE: LVMH patronage, social, and cultural institution*. Available: http://www.lvmh.com/lvmh-patron-of-the-arts-and-social-solidarity [May 20, 2013].

Bennett, P. (1988). *Dictionary of marketing terms, American marketing*. Association, Chicago, IL.

Bloomberg (2013). *RE: Louis Vuitton loses ground as most valuable luxury brand*. Available: http://articles.economictimes.indiatimes.com/2013–05–22/news/39445307_1_prada-louis-vuitton-brand [May 23, 2–13].

Bourdieu, P. (1984). *Distinction: A social critique of the judgement of taste/ Pierre Bourdieu; translated by Richard Nice*. Cambridge: Harvard University Press.

Buzzell, R. (1968). Can you standardize multinational marketing? *Harvard Business Review*, 46, November–December, pp. 102–113.

Davidson, W. & Harrigan, R. (1977). Key decisions in international marketing: Introducing new products abroad. *International Executive*, 20, pp. 11–12.

Fernie, J., Moore, C., Lawrie, A. & Hallsworth, A. (1997). The internationalization of the high fashion brand: The case of central London. *Journal of Product & Brand Management*, 6, pp. 151–162.

Gasparina, J. (2009). 33 Colors. *In:* Castets, S. (Ed.), *Louis Vuitton: Art fashion and architecture*. New York: Rizzoli (pp. 42–48).

Golsorkhi, M. (2009). Introduction. *In:* Dietrich, L. (Ed.), *60 innovators shaping our future*. London: Thames and Hudson (pp. 208–239).

Hamel, G. & Prahalad, C. (1985). Do you really have a global strategy? *Harvard Business Review*, 63, July–August, pp. 139–148.

Hamel, G. & Prahalad, C.K. (1994). Competing for the future. *Harvard Business Review*, July–August, pp. 122–130.

Healy, M., Beverland, M., Oppewal, H. & Sands, S. (2007). Understanding retail experiences – The case for ethnography. *International Journal of Market Research*, 49(6), pp. 751–779.

Heery, E. & Noon, M. (2008). *A dictionary of human resource management*. New York: Oxford University Press. Available at http://oxfordreference.com/view/10.1093/acref/9780199298761.001.0001/acref-9780199298761 (Accessed 25 October 2016).

Igarashi, T. (2009). Learning from Louis Vuitton. In: Castets, S. (Ed.), *Louis Vuitton: Art, fashion, and architecture*. New York: Rizzoli (pp. 12–16).

Interbrand (2013). *RE: Best global brands of 2012*. Available: http://www.interbrand.com/en/best-global-brands/2012/Best-Global-Brands-2012-Brand-View.aspx [May 19, 2013].

Klingmann, A. (2007). *Brandscapes: Architecture in the experience economy*. Boston: Massachusetts Institute of Technology.

Kozinets, R.V., Sherry, J.F., Deberry-Spence, B., Duhachek, A., Nuttavuthisit, K. & Storm, D. (2002). Themed flagship brand stores in the new millennium: Theory, practice, prospects. *Journal of Retailing*, 78, pp. 17–29.

Leroy, D. (2004). The Challenge of Global Capitalism: The Perspective of Eastern Religions. In: Dunning, J. & Prince, O.W. (Eds.), *Making globalisation good: The moral challenges of global capitalism*. Oxford: Oxford University Press (pp. 232–252).

Levitt, T. (1980). Marketing success through differentiation – Of anything. *Harvard Business Review*, 58(3), pp. 92–102.

Levy, P. (2010). The state of globalisation and localisation. *Marketing News*, 4(11), pp. 17–18.

Lewis, B.R. & Hawksley, A. (1990). Gaining a competitive advantage in fashion. *International Journal of Retail and Distribution Management*, 18(4), pp. 37–43.

Magrou, R. (2011). London Bond Street. In: Edelmann, F., Luna, I., Magrou, R. & Mostafavi, M. (Eds.), *Louis Vuitton architecture and interiors*. Hong Kong: Rizzoli (p. 142).

Medina, J.F. & Duffy, M.F. (1998). Standardization vs. globalization: A new perspective of brand strategies. *Journal of Product & Brand Management*, 7(3), pp. 223–243.

Mertl, C. (2013). Globalizations, Globalities, Global Histories Some Theoretical Corner Stones. In: Strobl, P. & Kohler, M. (Eds.), *Phenomenon of globalization: A collection of interdisciplinary globalization research essays*. Frankfurt: PL Academic Research (p. 19).

Mikunda, C. (2006). *Flagship stores: Brand lands, hot spots cool spaces*. London: Kogan Page.

Moore, C.M., Doherty, A.M. & Doyle, S. (2010). Flagship stores as a market entry method: The perspective of luxury fashion retailing. *European Journal of Marketing*, 44(1/2), pp. 139–161.

Mostafavi, M. (2011). Louis Vuitton-Architecture, Fashion, and Fabrication. In: Edelmann, F., Luna, I., Magrou, R. & Mostafavi, M. (Eds.), *Louis Vuitton architecture and interiors*. New York: Rizzoli (pp. 242–245).

Pine, J.B. & Gilmore, J.H. (1999). *The experience economy: Work is theatre and every business a stage*. Boston: Harvard Business School Press.

Ramarapu, S., Timmerman, J.E. & Ramarapu, N. (1999). Choosing between globalization and localization as a strategic thrust for your international marketing effort. *Journal of Marketing Theory and Practice*, 7(2), pp. 97–105.

Resnick, B. (1989). The globalization of world financial markets. *Business Horizons*, 32(6), pp. 34–41.

Ricca, M. (2013). *What's in store for 2013: Luxury*. Interbrand. Available at https://issuu.com/interbrand/docs/iq-2013-whats_in_store_ (Accessed 10 August 2016).

Riewoldt, O. (2002). *Brandscaping: Worlds of experience in retail design*. Berlin: Birkhauser.

Ryan, N. (2007). Prada and the art of patronage. *Fashion Theory*, 11, pp. 7–24.

Schiffman, L. & Kanuk, L. (1997). *Consumer behavior*. Englewood: Prentice-Hall.

Serkan, Y. (2009). Localization. Encyclopedia of Business in Today's World. *SAGE Publications*, pp. 1024–1026. Available: http://dx.doi.org/10.4135/9781412964289.n586. [November 2015].

Sharma, B. (2014a). 21st century flagship store architecture in new luxury retail markets: A comparative study of Louis Vuitton, Prada, and Chanel flagship stores in Tokyo. *The International Journal of Design Management and Professional Practice*, 7(3), pp. 63–74.

Sharma, B. (2014b). Flagship stores: The new all-inclusive shoppingscape. *Lusofona Journal of Architecture and Education*, 8, pp. 695–709.

Smith, W.R. (1956) Product differentiation and market segmentation as alternative marketing strategies. *Journal of Marketing*, 21(1), pp. 3–8.

Swengley, N. (2011). *RE: Artists add lustre to luxury brands*. Available: http://www.theartnewspaper.com/articles/Artists-add-lustre-to-luxury-brands/25263 [December 10, 2012].

Tomlinson, A. (1990). *Consumption, identity and style: Marketing, meanings and the packaging of pleasure*. London: Routledge.

Tungate, M. (2012). *Fashion brands: Branding style from Armani to Zara*. London: Kogan Page.

WPP (2012). *Brand Z: top 100 most valuable brands 2013*. [pdf] New York: Millward Brown. Available at: http://www.millwardbrown.com/brandz/2013/Top100/Docs/2013_BrandZ_Top100_Report.pdf [Accessed 25 October 2016].

12 The future of retail and retail design

Henri Christiaans

Changing retail landscape and the bigger picture

The transformation in shopping and shopping behaviour over the last decade has been phenomenal. The growth in online shopping, the recessionary mind-set of consumers, and the rise of digital and social media has all led to a much more fragmented approach to shopping in terms of what, where, when, how and why people buy. Nowadays, shopping is not merely a local activity. In search of the exact product of their choice or for the lowest price, customers use the whole world as their shopping area. The online possibilities have broadened the horizon for retail in such a way that in the Western world they have partly substituted the brick-and-mortar stores. The percentage of empty spaces in shopping streets is still growing. However, a look at the global picture shows us that for the developing markets in the world, there is a window of opportunity for investment in physical retail, be it China and India or South America and Africa. And the big global retailers are taking that opportunity already. Together with closing stores, an even bigger number of physical stores are opening nationwide.

In order to predict the future of retail the global picture is one thing, but we also need a closer look at the retail development per sector. From food retail to fashion and from electronics to luxury brands, each of these sectors show different growth curves and a variety of formats and channels. Hence, because of global differences and differences per sector, an overall view of the retail market is hardly possible. Nonetheless, there are trends in society, which will have a profound influence on retail and retail design.

Before going into the expectations about the future of retail, we have to be aware that the transformation of retail is part of societal, technological, economic and ecological changes, each of which will strongly influence how our lives are going to be and how we will behave. Important global and local developments are the following:

- Urban population growth (with a young urban population with high potentials)
- Self-driving cars and their revolutionary impact on all aspects of mobility and transport, but also on the rise and fall of jobs and retail
- Increasing information flow and the role of all sorts of media
- The necessity of ecologically sustainable development

As Fitch (2012) used to stress, retail and society influence and change each other constantly and make certain shop concepts very popular, and others redundant. In other words, shops have to stay relevant in relation to our changing habits; retail brand loyalty is often fickle. Retailers therefore must have a heightened knowledge and appreciation of the contemporary way of life and the way to act within this context. And as consumers become ever more design literate, retailers in every sector realise that they must invest in design, not only to exceed consumers' expectations, but, in all cases, simply to meet them.

What are the trends in society in general, and how will they influence the retail world in the years to come? Let's have a look at these developments.

Online-offline

Over the past few years, physical retail was not able to compete with the personalization and convenience provided by online shopping. By monitoring piles of rich customer data, online retailers were at a huge advantage compared to the offline retailers, providing a superior experience for the consumer (Mehta, 2014). But we can observe a behaviour change. Shoppers show a clear tendency to swing back to offline stores. Immediate gratification when buying in a physical store is one of the main reasons for this change, let alone the increasing time people spend on shopping as a leisure activity. Shops respond to this development by experience-offering showrooms. In light of this, a recent study conducted by IBM (Klena & Puleri, 2013) indicated that in five years' time, buying locally (directly from the store) will supersede online purchasing. Besides, the physical and digital worlds are merging; the physical stores adopting the ease, convenience and excitement previously reserved for online shopping. However difficult the future shopping behaviour will be, the fact is that, in order to fulfil the future customers' needs, brick-and-mortar stores must undergo significant changes in the next sections, several relevant changes will be further explained.

At the same time, the e-market keeps growing as well, improving its services, such as same-day delivery to customers and reducing the interaction costs. In the larger cities, the market will mature, which is why e-commerce players will better serve the smaller cities and rural areas.

Omnichannelling

One speaks of a multichannel strategy when a brand operates multiple channels simultaneously but lacks a clear combination between them. A cross-channel strategy is in place when a brand promotes more than one channel (physical store, QR advertisements, help desk, webshop and so on) simultaneously and has established a clear structure between them; this allows customers to easily switch between the channels without needing to enter the information twice. 'Within an omnichannel operating model, customers are able to interact and transact across all channels and touch points of their preference interchangeably and simultaneously (in real-time)' (McKenzie, S. [2012], http://ecommerceconsulting. com, 2012, no page).

Today, the retail channels are relatively easy to identify: physical stores, webshops, applications or a combination of these. Technology, however, is blurring the lines between the different channels. Augmented reality apps are providing brands with the ability to offer virtual experiences at any place and at any time. As augmented reality increases in popularity, it constitutes a new tool for brands to compete with. Amazon has already developed a function for its app that recognizes products: simply framing an object within a device's viewfinder allows for the app to recognize the product. Within mere seconds, the user is presented with purchasing options for that particular object and/or similar objects available within the Amazon marketplace.

The new question for marketers thus becomes, 'When and where in the world are consumers when they are considering or in need of the things we sell?' (Stephens, 2013). Once that question is provided with a solid answer, one can start analysing the channels and media that can be used to 'get' to the consumer. According to Gary Schwartz, author of *The Impulse Economy* (2011), consumers' purchasing path has changed. With the mobile shopper, a purchase can occur without the path. Most consumers have already conducted thorough research on a product by the time they step into the store to buy it. Google refers to this as the 'zero moment of truth' (ZMOT) and has developed a model on this notion. With the mobile-first approaches, the use of beacons (see below) will increase, as well as cross-channel customer profiling, to bridge shoppers' online and offline worlds (Van Veelen, 2014).

Every expert in the area of shopping will agree that omnichannelling integration is a must-have. Physical and virtual environments will converge. Many of today's customers already expect retailers to provide consistency across touch-points, whether they are in a store, online, reading email, engaging with social media or using a mobile device. Retailers will face greater pressure to deliver products anywhere, at any time. To do this, they will expand their use of store inventory to fulfil online orders, move toward same day delivery from local stores and so on.

The channels will be used in a more selective and personalised way, meaning that retailers have clear data about the preferences of their customers regarding the types of products and services.

Omnichannel strategy for Scotch & Soda
Colin Jansen (designer), 2014

In a recent retail design project, an omnichannel strategy for the Dutch global fashion brand Scotch & Soda was developed. The main focus was the integration of the official Scotch & Soda stores and the online webstore. Integration of these channels has three main objectives:

1   Enhancing the brand experience consistently through the channels.
2   Using customer variables to create a more tailor made experience for each individual customer.
3   Supporting the customer in pre-purchase steps.

Additionally, the following two objectives are included:

4   Decreasing the amount of walked sales (on- and offline).
5   Lowering the threshold for online ordering.

For stimulating a local connection between brand and customer, the city DNA was used to create the store DNA, which is the bridge between the brand and a local in-store experience.

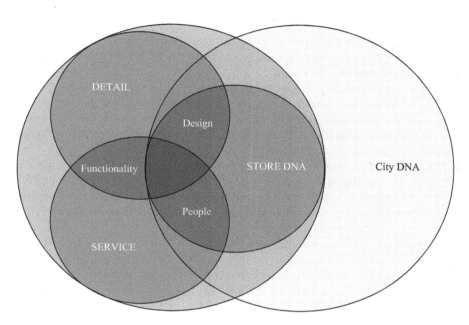

Figure 12.1 Development of an omnichannel strategy for a fashion brand
Source: Jansen, 2014

The store DNA entails concrete factors that define the in-store experience like the type of customers, the direct neighbourhood, the in-store staff, the interior etc. and is different for each store. Having different store DNA is in line with the brand's 'raison d'être', as it focuses on the individuality of each store and its location, and inspires customers by expressing this. Yet, as they function as local interpreters of the overarching brand, the stores are united in their diversity. This unity in diversity also plays in on the brand's exclusivity that customers appreciate: although the brand is growing, the individual and unique feel still holds on to the exclusivity.

Technology

In a 1997 article by Butter et al. in *McKinsey Quarterly*, a revolution in 'economic interactions' fuelled by technology was already predicted. With interactions, they addressed (p. 5) 'the searching, coordinating, and monitoring that people and firms do when they exchange goods, services, or ideas'. And that is exactly what retail is about. Over the years, most of those interactions are shaped by computing and communications technologies, whether we look at the way that goods are exchanged or that consumers are both supported and monitored. By technology the interactions have massively increased and will further increase in the future, be it via digital technology in and outside the store or via data analysis tools. But speculating on directions of this new technology is hard to do because of the enormous speed of developments. At least what can be predicted, according to some innovative retailers, is that the future of retail consists of two types of experiences (Van Veelen, 2014). The first embodies a fully animated experience, where outstanding brand representatives are supported by advanced technology in satisfying their customers. The second is a fully automated experience, guided by technologies that are supported by bright and highly trained individuals.

Companies will introduce shopping capabilities in other arenas, similar to the *Tesco Homeplus* virtual shopping experience in the Seoul subway system. As consumers continue to hunt for speed and convenience, retailers will seek opportunities that grant customers the ability to shop, pay and schedule delivery in unique environments, from parks and airports to bus stations and stadiums.

Technology in brick-and-mortar stores can be used in various ways: to trigger an in-store experience, to appeal to mobile users, to increase convenience for shoppers and employees, or to promote a retailer's brand. An overview of technological applications gives an impression of what is possible and in what direction future developments can go:

- Customers can use their smartphones to access information on products and pricing via NFC-enabled shelf-edge labels,[1] and scan and add items to their basket.
- Radio-frequency identification technology (RFID) connected to products which trigger related footage on nearby screens.
- Touch screens for customers used in different formats, such as a horizontal one in a table, in a kiosk, and as a screen on the wall. In a more rigorous way, there are small stores of big brands that use touch screens and kiosks to allow customers to order for delivery in the shop or at home. They provide access to their whole product range without the need for the same shop floor space of their usual stores.
- Another technology is the use of club card details by a customer to pick up a handset in the store and scan items to buy. Payment is automatic after the items are added to the trolley.
- Virtual mannequins are triggered by customers removing a hanger from the rail. They then will see models in their chosen garment.
- Hubs in the store that allow users to browse the catalogue or scan barcodes on items and explore product information. Customers can choose to order on the device and collect at a later date or have the product delivered.
- Mirrors that double as video screens. Or they are interactive, which allow users to try clothes on 'virtually', using a gesture based interface. Another type are motion-sensitive mirrors which display footage of models wearing products from the store as customers walk past them.
- Virtual reality and augmented reality shopping become common among the bigger retailers, making use of the simulated three-dimensional possibilities of virtually rotating and (dis)assembling of products that are still in a closed box.
- Special iPad apps are designed to help customers and sales assistants in store, allowing them to access the product catalogue, check stock and help with sizing issues. In those stores where this application is present, normally the staff is armed with these iPads.
- Point-of-sale (POS) devices enable staff to check out customers anywhere in their stores, in that way preventing boring queues for their customers.
- Robot technology, finally, has entered retail. Setting aside the applications for supplying, navigation and packaging of goods, robotics applied as support for customers in the store might become hot for retailing in the future. Some human-sized robots

are already on the market, leading customers to select the items they seek, and another rolling one that can use its one arm to pluck items from a shelf.

(Brewster, 2015)

Not all technologies mentioned are already widespread. In addition, the virtual applications which are meant to give a customer a near-physical experience are still lacking the same sensuality of trying on clothes and knowing if they fit the customer's body.

Finally, with all those technologies, there is a danger that the social function of shopping in a physical environment gets lost, be it a shopping street, a mall/department store or a local store in the neighbourhood. Retailers should also use technology to help staff in the store recognize and develop a relationship with each shopper.

Big data

The world is awash with information on such a scale that analysing, correlating and reinterpreting these data has become of vital economic value. Big data is all about extracting the meaningful, insightful and useful data that provides value to a customer.

> Big data refers to things one can do at a large scale that cannot be done at a smaller one, to extract new insights or create new forms of value, in ways that change markets, organizations, the relationship between citizens and governments, and more. But this is just the start. . . . [T]he new techniques for collecting and analysing huge bodies of data will help us make sense of our world in ways we are just starting to appreciate.
>
> (Mayer-Schönberger & Cukier, 2013, pp. 6–7)

Over the last decades new data-crunching technologies have come up, and nowadays data can cleverly and dynamically be reused for innovation and new services. The connectivity of big data has already been proven to be of significant value in areas such as healthcare, biology and also retail. It has become the raw material of business, a vital economic input used to create a new form of economic value.

As consumers, we profit on a daily basis from these technologies, whether we look for a hotel on our smartphone comparing price/quality/location data, or make a matched profile for dating. Digital platforms such as mobile apps and social networks make ample use of big data. Now more than ever, consumers use these platforms to take control of their shopping experience. For retailers, the use of big data has two sides. One is the opportunity to offer a high quality of customer experience by quickly responding via the right channels on the expectations of its customers. An advantage of this approach is that retailers can personalize these experiences by their knowledge about the customers' profiles. That is at the same time the other side of big data use: the opportunity for retailers to gather and analyse data from their customers. Retailers can combine data from web browsing patterns, social media, industry forecasts, existing customer records etc. to predict trends, prepare for demand, pinpoint customers, optimize pricing and promotions, and monitor real-time analytics and results. Coordinating the current and future multichannel shopping interaction requires entirely new data competencies for the retailer whose business now depends upon whether it can manage, integrate and understand this vast array of data coming at a non-stop pace (Shockley & Mercier, 2015).

In sum, big data application is a digital revolution which is almost unprecedented. For retail it represents a cultural shift in the way wherein retailers connect with consumers.

Location

Although retail sales of brick-and-mortar stores and online stores are growing towards each other, consumers clearly prefer shopping in physical stores, according to the A.T. Kearney Omnichannel Shopping Preferences Study (2014).

Therefore, where merchants place their stores plays an outsized role in determining whether their chains fly or flop (Thau, 2014). 'You can't do business in a brick-and-mortar store without the presence of customers, and proximity to customers is as elemental to a brick-and-mortar store as air, food and water are to each of us as human beings' (Mark Cohen,[2] in Thau, 2014). Retailers are now turning to big data to help them find the right location. Technology platforms for visualizing data in the form of maps is helping retailers fine tune how to pick a store location with the goal of driving more traffic and boosting sales.

On the negative side, over the last ten years retail vacancy has dramatically increased due to the economic recession and the increase in online shopping. In several countries, this has led to a slowdown in mall construction. In the United States, it is expected that within fifteen to twenty years as many as half of America's shopping malls will fail (Peterson, 2014).

Social media

Social media may still drive only a small share of total online retail sales, but its impact is becoming impossible to ignore. Social-driven retail sales and referral traffic are rising at a faster pace than all other online channels (Smith, 2015). According to the same author, the top five hundred retailers earned $3.3 billion from social shopping in 2014, up 26 per cent from 2013, as he quotes from the 'Internet Retailer's Social Media 500' – that is, as he says, well ahead of the roughly 16 per cent growth rate for the overall e-commerce market in the United States.

Over the last several years, brands have used social media to market their products, talk to customers and even make merchandising decisions; but in the coming years, we anticipate retailers to add 'selling' to the list of things they can do on social sites. Sites like Pinterest or Instagram already mimic an e-catalogue set-up, showcasing the products of a particular brand. Offering a buy button would attract consumers' attention and encourage on-the-spot buying.

Social media affects the way consumers perceive a retailer's brand, and retailers' marketing strategies make use of that (Shankar et al., 2011). On the one hand, social media allow consumers to connect with their favourite retailers online to stay informed about new developments; on the other hand, consumers will also inform their social communities on media such as Facebook about the perceived quality of the retailer and its products. Trust and loyalty will thus become more dependent on these media.

In that way social media have opened up a new level of dialogue between a business and its consumers, a trend that will become even stronger in the coming years.

Consumers

Consumers have more power than ever before in the shopping experience, and, as a result, companies will provide rich information optimized for every possible screen that consumers can use to interact with a retailer. Retailers will also integrate scanning and other tools to unlock content in the apps that consumers use. In the upcoming years, customers will shop around all the more, and more retailers will take broader steps toward transparency. In my view, there are several trends with regard to consumers which are worth highlighting:

- The power of tribes: powerful communities are being formed around brands and experiences – from runners and cross-fitters to foodies and gamers. More communities will be tied to brands and experiences as never before and will influence major buying decisions.
- New methodologies are required to understand shopper behaviour in the shopping environment, along with understanding the perceptions and needs of the key influencers in relevant shopping channels. This should help consumers by personalizing and contextualizing retailer interactions, while anticipating their needs in real-time.
- Personalization: while 'customization' was the keyword over the last decennia for manufacturers and retailers in offering products and services, the new paradigm is 'personalization', through

  - Personalized products and services (e.g., see miAdidas, iPhone)
  - Loyalty programs
  - Relationship of staff with the shopper
  - Personalized pricing

The flipside of personalization is that privacy will be at stake and should be addressed even though young generations seem hardly to be aware of this issue. And, if they are aware, they do not care.

Consumers' mind set

In order to compete with online shopping, the physical store is all the more a place where consumers can and will have real-time experiences with products or lifestyles.

In my view, one of the most interesting and relevant approaches to this matter comes from the Fitch company ('Shopping in the mind'). They believe that the process of simply finding something you need, today, or fantasizing about a purchase over several months, is governed by three universal twenty-first-century mind states: dreaming, exploring and locating.

Locating

In this mind state, the consumers are looking for a specific brand, product or service. They have a short attention span, are often replenishing their usual stock, or already know the specific product/model they are looking for. As consumers, we have done this for years, but, today, we have a few more online tools on hand to help the process.

Most retailers see 'locating' as their comfort zone and have built and evolved their stores around this 'locating' mind state: they have avoided putting up too many barriers, have made sure that the signage is at the right height and have kept the aisles clear, quite rightly making the shopping journey easy and pain free. So, they have considered all 'as it should be'. But it does not have to be just that; it can achieve more.

Exploring

In this state, the consumers are open-minded but have category-specific purchase intent. They have a longer attention span, may have a few options in mind but are open to suggestions and want to be inspired and informed in equal measure. The Internet can quickly grow loyalty in this area as the ability to compare and contrast a wide range of products is easy. However, a key component of the 'exploring' mind set is trial and being able to touch, feel and test drive products.

Dreaming

In this mind state, consumers are actively looking for new ideas and inspiration. They have undefined needs and wants and are skipping between categories and brands to find inspiration and the fulfilment of desires.

Whether daydreaming at one's desk or on the bus, one can be 'shopping in the mind' and have that desire or interest satiated in many ways.

These three mind states, which can occur at the same time or in different sequences – in-store, out of the store or online – offer the core tools for a designer.

Ecology

Society finds itself amidst a large transition. While this transition may cause an unstable society, it simultaneously introduces opportunities for radical change (Rotmans, 2012). Changes in science, politics, economy, art and culture have induced considerable scepticism. The modernization of the Netherlands (and Europe) for instance at the end of the nineteenth century is a good example of a previous transition phase. The modernization had radical effects on education, suffrage, healthcare and the social structure of the Netherlands. It was started in quest of a new type of society (Kemp et al., 1998). The current transition phase ultimately leads to a more sustainable society. As it is, consumers are spending money they do not have, and humankind is taking from the earth what can never be repaid. A total of 3 to 5 trillion dollars in natural capital vanishes every year, which constitutes more than the annual costs of the current financial crisis (Holtzman, 2012). This forms the foundation for an ecological crisis.

The growing need for a more sustainable world will have impact on the retail sector, in terms of both energy consumption, consumerism and ethical issues of honest labour. However, as we define sustainability in a wider context, also encompassing economic and social dimensions, the importance of retail as one of the biggest employers in the world should be considered as a sustainability aspect.

Retail design

Although retailing as commerce is timeless, Retail Design is one of the most challenging fields of design, embracing both disciplines of architecture and industrial design. The term 'retail design' encompasses all aspects of the design of the physical store as well as, in a technological sense, a virtual store: ranging from store frontage, fascia and signage, through to the internal elements of equipment, merchandising, display, lighting, in-store communications, point of sale and finishes. Retail design also involves 'an understanding not only of what will work aesthetically within the space, but how it will perform functionally and commercially, how it can be built to budget and meet the many regulations governing the use of a public space' (Pradhan, 2009, p. 374). Retail design is the touch point for responsibly developing and extending communications between brand and customer.

In the world of retail, consumer experience has become the primary issue; the consumer's journey through the shopping mall, the individual retail outlet or department store, the Internet store. This experience, whether physical or virtual, consists of many interdisciplinary connected elements (see Petermans et al., 2013), including the senses it addresses, the service concept, the visual merchandizing, the way of communicating in every aspect and the interior or the interactive design; all are touch points that, positively or negatively, will affect the shopping experience.

Retail design, therefore, is concerned with new ways of exploring and enhancing the experience of interaction with other individuals, with products and with the environment by blending design thinking and design techniques together with an understanding of human behaviour and modern technology. It is the retail designer's task to relate to and develop this experience through visual, spatial and communicative expression. Communication is the platform underlying and surrounding the spatial concept because this concept communicates the brand personality.

In designing a retail space, a holistic approach is needed because so many design elements – such as shape, materials, interior, finish, typography and composition – have to play together to form the brands' visual language. Through a compelling imagery and design style, the designer has to bring about an emotional connection between the brand and the consumer, thereby communicating the company's values and identity. Visual brand language is a key ingredient necessary to make an authentic and convincing brand strategy that can be applied uniquely and creatively in all forms of brand communications to both employees and customers. Successful design creates a memorable experience for the consumer, encouraging repeat business and boosting the company's economic health. It is a long-term creative solution that can be leveraged by an executive team to showcase the brand's unique personality (Brunner & Emery, 2009; Lockwood & Walton, 2008).

A core issue for any business active in the retail sector must always be an empathic understanding of the culture of shopping. Retail mirrors society: social, economic, political and sustainable retailing that attempts to be successful calls for appreciation of the way in which the global and local shopping cultures both shape and are shaped by their respective societies. By learning from the past, by a better understanding of the present, we will be able to better design for the future.

Within both food and non-food sectors, for example, it is apparent that even discounters such as Aldi and Lidl have made significant investment in retail design in recent years, adopting the visual language and signatures of middle and even high-end retailers. This has the effect of raising the bar even higher, to the extent that 'discount' is often now the norm.

Similarly, non-product sectors, such as financial services, have also found they need to follow suit. Banks have realised that selling intangible products such as investments and loans needs to be evidenced more tangibly by designing environments which are more closely related to stores than banking halls, making the process, from beginning to end, more familiar, and in turn adding perceived value in the way they communicate.

Formats of the future

Retail is known for its many different store formats. From shopping mall to kiosk and from department store to pop-up store, all these different formats do not have an eternal life. New formats will continue to show up, depending on a new context.

Because the retail designer is mainly responsible for the design of the format, it is interesting to reflect about the question how retail spaces and formats will look in the next twenty years.

A recent report by Deloitte Research (2011) stated that 'retailers need to re-define the store proposition and identify how they can best address the changing customer needs within the walls of the store' (p. 2). The store should breathe the brand, and it must be a place in which shoppers can do more than simply view and buy the products; a store will operate no longer as a storehouse but instead as an integral part of the multichannel experience. Deloitte Research observes five key difficulties for retailers in the marketplace:

- Consumer spending levels will remain weak, in particular for discretionary goods.
- Business costs will continue to rise, increasing not only the variable costs but the fixed central cost, as well.
- Technology will further evolve, and an increasing number of interactive devices is profoundly changing consumer shopping behaviour.
- Competition will be intensified through a shrinking market and an increasing number of players converging from other sectors or other countries.
- Retailers' sustainability agenda and policies will significantly contribute to commercial performance.

These challenges require retailers to re-evaluate and revise their store formats to face the future with a commercially sustainable proposition. To achieve this, retailers must possess a true understanding of changing consumer requirements (Van Veelen, 2014).

The design of retail spaces

Due to the many aforementioned changes in retail, the physical retail space will change as well. The interior will be different as a consequence of (1) the disappearance of the check-out, (2) virtual fitting rooms and aisles, which will supplement the physical world via consumers' phones and connected wearable devices, and (3) the access of information and special offers through augmented reality, which will allow consumers to move through a store or to see how they would look wearing something without trying it on.

On a local scale and culture, retail spaces might become more flexibly used, such as giving room to pop-up stores and other temporary solutions. However, this will not structurally change the retail landscape. Looking at the different formats, Van Veelen (2014) comes to the following observations based on his research in the Netherlands. His analysis is complemented with our own insights.

Flagship stores

We predict an increase in flagship stores in the near future, because these are the showrooms of the future. One of the main differences with regular stores is that flagship stores employ better-trained staff. The flagship stores maintain their focus on service and hospitality, a place that invites shoppers to spend more time there than in other stores. At flagship stores, experience is often prioritized above sales.

Complementary systems

This concerns formats that have evolved around cross-selling opportunities or other mutual benefits and/or target groups for both consumer brands and retailer labels. Popular retailers often allow small local labels or brands to place a shop-in-shop solution within their store. An important aspect is that there must be a clear mutual benefit for both parties. According to the consulting agency 'Strategy &', complementary systems are 'an opportunity for small brands to obtain prime store space before investing in long-running retail contracts, and they are an opportunity for the retailer to remain agile to pick up new trends and to keep the store fresh and exciting with revolving new assortment' (Kesteloo & Hoogenberg, 2013, p. 10). This may eventually lead to the rise of mega stores, whereby traditional retailers transform into market managers with a range of shop-in-shop formats, thereby forming an attractive place to shop.

Flexible formats

A well-known flexible format is the pop-up shop. This format was first used by retailers who were seeking alternatives for their long-term rental contracts. An interesting example is the 'Broodfiets' (bread bicycle) in Utrecht: the bike cycles through the city of Utrecht on a daily basis to offer fresh sandwiches and coffee to passers-by. Alternatively, a message can be left on its Facebook page, so that it can deliver the bread on location. The flexible format is also used by brands to create a marketing buzz for new launches, to trigger impulse buying or to conduct consumer testing. Their temporary character draws attention and induces feelings of unexpectedness amongst customers.

Virtual showrooms

Virtual showrooms are small or mid-sized formats that feature digital interaction via touch screens or other devices. Today, many retailers are using these digital tools to display their collection. It is particularly attractive for large retailers such as IKEA and various car brands, as this technique allows them to reach the urban areas in addition to their outlets at the city borders. Audi, for example, is planning to open twenty Audi City formats in the next few years. For customers, 'virtual showrooms provide the benefit of "experiencing" a product that is customized to their liking and needs (like a customized car, kitchen, or shoe)' (Kesteloo & Hoogenberg, 2013, p. 11).

The virtual showrooms are expected to grow rapidly in the city centres, as this is where retail space is most expensive.

Segment concepts

These are already spin-offs from larger chains, which focus on a specific segment – i.e. a particular segment of their product range, or a specific target audience.

Examples of segment stores are H&M, which launched its '& Other Stories' luxury concept, and in the Netherlands SuitSupply, a brand that recently launched an online female line (see box below).

A female line for SuitSupply
Imke van der Linden (designer), 2015

The brand targets businessmen and offers them both tailor-made suits and convection-sized casual apparel, through online and offline channels. In each brick-and-mortar store, a tailor is working in its in-store atelier. Despite this, the brand lacks a strong omni channelling system.

Recently, the brand started an online female tailor-made line. Since women tend to shop offline more than online, the designer's challenge was: 'How can the offline shopping experience be translated into an online shopping experience?'

The design proposal is a throughout online platform consisting of three different experiences: 'Personal Shopping', 'Tailor-Made' and 'Virtual Store'. Female consumers can shop in the regular online shop as well as in the virtual store. By doing so, needs and wishes of consumers with the three different states of mind – locating, exploring and dreaming (see earlier in this chapter) – are fulfilled. The virtual store translates the experience of shopping in brick-and-mortar stores into an online experience, where consumers search and browse through the store. They can place items they like in the virtual fitting room, in which they can enter their body measurements and then try the items on their personal mannequin.

When it comes to ordering the apparel, consumers are provided with the option to order a convection-sized item or to order a tailor-made item. In the last case, consumers first ask for a design kit, consisting of several fabric samples, measuring tape, and a product sample of a specific garment. After they receive the design kit, they go back to the online platform and create the tailor-made item, by selecting their preferred fabric, haberdasheries and adaptions and by entering their body measurements.

Additional to the experience of shopping in the virtual store is a subscription model which offers consumers to let a personal shopper shop for them. Consumers have to create an online profile and have to answer some questions about their needs and wants.

Pick-up and drop-off points

Pick-up and drop-off points allow customers to pick-up and/or drop-off products that they have purchased online or in the physical store. These can be either small local stores (e.g., Kiala points), high-traffic locations (railway or gas station), warehouses, local grocery stores or post boxes and lockers in the streets or in shopping malls. These are designed to surpass the limits of online shopping, the payment of shipping costs and the inconvenience of fixed delivery windows.

Mash-ups

In the future, the different store formats will not be easily categorized. Combinations of the different formats will appear: pop-up stores within complementary systems, a virtual showroom alongside a drop-off point, segment concepts on wheels, and many other combinations.

Shopping malls

Worldwide shopping malls are feeling the pinch as growth slows. They are showing signs of over-density and over-capacity. About 15 per cent of US malls will fail or be converted into non-retail space within the next ten years (Peterson, 2014). There are some examples where the original mall has been transformed into new retail formats. One of them is Bikini Berlin. The basic concept of Bikini Berlin is a unique combination of shopping, working, cinema, recreation, urban oasis and hotel. In the centre of the complex are sixteen Bikini Berlin Boxes for varying, short-term tenants. The boxes are modular systems. The minimalistic design of the boxes puts the attention on the products of the respective tenants. The rental rates are relatively low, so it is possible for young entrepreneurs or designers to show their products and ideas to the broader public.

Retail design as a discipline

Retail design is concerned with new ways of exploring and enhancing the experience of interaction with other individuals, with products and with the environment by blending design thinking and design techniques, together with an understanding of human behaviour and modern technology. In designing the space offline or online, the retail designer needs to keep a holistic view on the client's brief, reasoning from its brand's identity and trying to visualise the space as an expression of that identity, drawing upon the fields of interior design, communication design, product design, packaging design and visual merchandising.

The user-centric nature of retail design makes this new field important for retail development. A retail designer must have a strong understanding of the customer, the client's needs, so that with availability of new technology tools, designers are now helping marketers and retailers to create unique experiences that connect with customers on a deeper, emotional level.

Retail design can be seen as a discipline on its own. Due to the necessity of integrating several design disciplines with branding into a holistic vision, it is one of the most challenging and difficult design disciplines.

Notes

1 NFC (Near Field Communication) and RFID tags are programmed with any sort of information. They can be put in almost any product.
2 Quotation in the article. Mark Cohen is professor of marketing in the retailing studies department of Columbia University's business school, and former CEO of Bradlees and Sears, Canada.

References

Brewster, S. (2015). Robotics startups are coming to the retail aisle. *Fortune*, November 11, 2015. Available from: http://fortune.com/2015/11/11/robotics-retail/. [Accessed: 14 August 2015].

Brunner, R., and Emery, S. (2009). *Do you matter? How great design will make people love your company.* Upper Saddle River: FT Press.

Butter, P., Hall, T.W., Hanna, A.M., Mendonca, L., Auguste, B., Manyika, J., and Sahay, A. (1997). A revolution in interaction. *The McKinsey Quarterly*, Nr. 1 PDF, p. 5. Available from: http://www.mckinsey.com/insights/strategy/a_revolution_in_interaction.

Deloitte Research (2011). *The changing face of retail.* The store of the future: The new role of the store in a multichannel environment. Report. Available from: http://www.rasci.in/downloads/2011/The_Store_Future.pdf. [Accessed: 14 August 2015].

Fitch, R. (2012). *The ascent of shopping*. Inaugural lecture, Delft University of Technology.

Holtzman, D. (2012). *The new digital tipping point*. PricewaterhouseCoopers, Report. Available from: https://www.pwc.com/gx/en/banking-capital-markets/publications/assets/pdf/pwc-new-digital-tipping-point.pdf. [Accessed: 1 June 2015].

Jansen, C. (2014). *On- and offline retail channel integration strategy for Scotch & Soda, Ltd*. School of Industrial Design, Delft University of Technology, The Netherlands: Master Thesis.

Kearney, A.T. (2014). *On solid ground: Brick-and-Mortar is the foundation of omnichannel retailing: Omnichannel shopping preferences study*. Available from: https://www.atkearney.com/documents/10192/4683364/On+Solid+Ground.pdf/f96d82ce-e40c-450d-97bb-884b017f4cd7. [Accessed: 14 August 2015].

Kemp, J., Schot, J., and Hoogma, R. (1998). Regime shifts to sustainability through processes of niche formation: The approach of strategic niche management. *Technology Analysis and Strategic Management*, 10(2), 175–195.

Kesteloo, M., and Hoogenberg, M. (2013). *Footprint 2020: Offline retail in an online world*. Available from: www.strategyand.pwc.com. [Accessed: 14 November 2015].

Klena, K., and Puleri, J. (2013). *From transactions to relationships. Connecting with the transitioning shopper*. IBM Institute for Business Value, consulted via http://www-935.ibm.com/services/us/gbs/thoughtleadership/transitioningshopper/ (Accessed July 1, 2015).

Lockwood, T., and Walton, T. (2008). *Building design strategy*. New York: Allworth Press.

Mayer-Schönberger, V., and Cukier, K. (2013). *Big data: A revolution that will transform how we live, work, and think*. Boston: Houghton, Mifflin & Harcourt.

McKenzie, S. (2012). *Omni-channel retail: A term so confusing, even those doing it best don't know what it means*. Available from: http://ecommerceconsulting.com/2012/05/omni-channel-retail-a-term-so-confusing-even-those-doing-it-best-dont-know-what-it-means.html. [Accessed: March 2014].

Mehta, P. (2014). *Why the future of retail will blow your mind*. Available from: http://www.entrepreneur.com/article/234407. [Accessed: 20 August 2015].

Petermans, A., Janssens, W., and Van Cleempoel, K. (2013). A holistic framework for conceptualizing customer experiences in retail environments. *International Journal of Design*, 7(2), 1–18.

Peterson, H. (2014). America's shopping malls are dying a slow, ugly death. *Business Insider/Retail*. January 31, 2014. Available from: http://www.businessinsider.com/shopping-malls-are-going-extinct-2014–1. [Accessed: 1 June 2015].

Pradhan, S. (2009). *Retailing management: Text and cases*. New Delhi: Tata McGraw Hill Education Private Limited.

Rotmans, J. (2012). *In het oog van de orkaan*. Boxtel: Aeneas.

Schwartz, G. (2011). *The impulse economy: Understanding mobile shoppers and what makes them buy*. New York: Simon and Schuster.

Shankar, V., Inman, J., Mantrala, M., Kelley, J.E., and Rizley, R. (2011). Innovations in shopper marketing: Current insights and future research issues. *Journal of Retailing*, 87S(1), S29-S42.

Shockley, R., and Mercier, K. (2015). *Analytics: The real-world use of big data in retail*. Available from: http://www-935.ibm.com/services/us/gbs/thoughtleadership/big-data-retail/). [Accessed: 15 August 2015].

Smith, C. (2015). *It's time for retailers to start paying close attention to social media*. Available from: Business Insider. www.businessinsider.com/social-commerce-2015-report-2015–6. [Accessed: 20 August 2015].

Stephens, D. (2013). *The retail revival: reimagining business for the new age of consumerism*. Wiley: Ontario, Canada.

Thau, B. (2014). How big data helps chains like Starbucks pick store locations – An (unsung) key to retail success. *Forbes/Retail*, April 24, 2014. Available from: http://www.forbes.com/sites/barbarathau/2014/04/24/how-big-data-helps-retailers-like-starbucks-pick-store-locations-an-unsung-key-to-retail-success/ [Accessed: 1 June 2015].

Van Veelen, T. (2014). *The design of a future supermarket*. School of Industrial Design, Delft University of Technology, The Netherlands: Master Thesis.

Author biographies

Bethan Alexander is a passionate spokesperson, consultant and lecturer with a specific lens on maximising customer engagement through multi-sensorial fashion brand experiences. Having spent eighteen years working internationally with fashion brands including Converse, Elle and Kangol and establishing her own consultancy business, Brand Baker, Bethan now brings the same verve to her academic role. Within higher education, Bethan has held senior lecturing positions at London College of Fashion and University of East London and has guest lectured at more than ten global institutions. Bethan is a published author, international conference presenter and active researcher. Her research spans Multi-Sensory Fashion Retailing, Customer Brand Experiences Online and Offline and Innovative Retail Formats.

Filipe Campelo Xavier da Costa holds a PhD in Business Management from University of São Paulo, Brazil. He has a background in marketing research, consumer behaviour and user experience studies, and his research interests include retail design strategies, customer experience and food studies. He is a faculty member and a researcher of Design Graduate Program at Universidade do Vale do Rio dos Sinos (UNISINOS), Brazil.

Henri Christiaans is Chair Professor and Dean of the School of Design & Human Engineering (DHE), Ulsan National Institute of Science & Technology (UNIST), as well as invited professor at the School of Architecture of University Minho, Portugal. He holds a Master's Degree in Psychology and a PhD in Industrial Design Engineering. Henri was for many years associate professor at the TU Delft School of Industrial Design Engineering in the Netherlands, where he was head of the Master's specialization on Retail Design and the Master's Program Integrated Product Design. He conducts research and teaching in retail design, creativity in design, cognitive ergonomics and research methodology. In addition to the many papers published in reviewed journals and conference proceedings, he has published books about retail design, design thinking, innovation management and research methodology. Henri was and still is involved in the development and implementation of new design courses all over the world. For many years, he has been a design consultant working with companies in the Netherlands, Portugal, Croatia, Slovenia and countries in Africa. He was formerly editor-in-chief of the *Journal of Design Research* (www.inderscience.com/jdr).

Gabriel Gallina is an Architect and Urbanist, holds an MBA in Marketing from Fundação Getulio Vargas (FGV), Brazil, and is currently a Master's Degree candidate at Universidade do Vale do Rio dos Sinos (UNISINOS) Design Program, Brazil. His professional experience is related to retail projects and environmental graphic design. His research interests include retail design strategies, wayfinding and creative cities.

Marcelo Halpern is a Designer, holds a Master's degree in Design from Universidade do Vale do Rio dos Sinos (UNISINOS), and is a PhD candidate at Universidade Federal do Rio Grande do Sul (UFRGS) Design and Technology program in Brazil. Halpern is a faculty member at Escola Superior de Propaganda e Marketing (ESPM), where he teaches design and technology-related courses. Currently, he focuses his work and research on topics such as design for experience & emotion, and persuasive technologies.

Anthony Kent is Professor of Fashion Marketing at Nottingham Trent University. He completed a PhD from the University of the Arts London for his research into the locational contexts of fashion retail stores and their built environments and interior design. Previously he undertook a funded MBA, specialising in retail, and holds a BA (Hons.) in Modern History from the University of Oxford, where he received two awards. He has worked as a product planner for a footwear company and retail management in the Buying and Merchandising function. He is a Member of the Chartered Institute of Marketing, Fellow of the Royal Society of Arts and Fellow of the Higher Education Institute, and he is Chair of the Committee for the Marketing Special Interest Group of the British Academy of Management.

Martin Knox comes from a retail design background and is now utilizing the principles of that discipline and many other approaches to work with leaders and their organisations to help them find, articulate and deliver their truth. One of the instigators of next (the retail phenomenon), Martin learned that it was a positive benefit to not stick to historical rules when undertaking commissions and implementing new approaches and ways of delivering his clients organisations and their products. His clients have included: Next, Sainsbury's, Boots, BHS, The Post Office, M&S, Schuh, Cancer Research UK, Dixons, Help the Aged, Early Learning Centre, Start-Rite, Poundland, Magnet, Converse, Kangol . . . amongst others. Since the early 1980's Martin has been developing and delivering new thinking in Retail and Design Management including: Brand Identity, Brand Development, Brand Creation, Retail Consultancy, Market Intelligence, Senior Management Mentoring, Graduate and Post Graduate Lecturing.

Tsang Ling Tung is a Research Assistant in the Department of Sociology, the University of Hong Kong (HKU), and is currently engaged in a government-funded comparative analysis of fashion industries in China and South Korea. Tsang graduated with a BBA (Marketing) degree at HKU, pursues his interests in Sociology, and is now progressing along on his Master's Degree in Media, Culture and Creative Cities. His planned areas of specialization for future research include race and ethnicity, identity, masculinity and Asian sporting body. Tsang had versatile internship experiences with multinational companies, such as Nike, Estée Lauder, Shanghai Tang (Richemont) and Robert Walters.

Ann Petermans holds a PhD in Architecture and is affiliated to the Faculty of Architecture and Arts of Hasselt University (Belgium). Her PhD focused on the translation and investigation of the principles and practices of the 'experience economy' within the discipline of interior architecture in general, and retail design in particular. In her PhD, she investigated what 'experiences' in retail environments entail, and which research methodologies can be used to gain insight in experiences in retail stores. Since her PhD, her research scope on experience and wellbeing has widened to involve not only retail environments but diverse sorts of environments wherein people reside, live, work, function and aim 'to feel well'. Next to research on experience, well-being and happiness in architecture and interior architecture, Ann also teaches on these subjects in the Master's in Architecture and Interior Architecture at Hasselt University.

Bie Plevoets studied Interior Architecture at the PHL University College in Hasselt (BE) and Conservation of Monuments and Sites at the Raymond Lemaire International Centre for Conservation in Leuven (BE). In 2014, she obtained a PhD in architecture at Hasselt University; her thesis was entitled 'Retail-reuse: An interior view on adaptive reuse of buildings'. Her current research focuses on the theory of adaptive reuse and preservation of spirit of place. Besides research, she teaches courses on adaptive reuse in the Bachelor's and Master's of Interior Architecture and the Master's of Architecture at Hasselt University.

Tiiu Poldma is full professor, School of Design/Director of the FoCoLUM Lighting Lab, Faculty of Environmental Design, Université de Montréal, and regular researcher at the Centre for Interdisciplinary Research in Rehabilitation (CRIR). Tiiu has spent over thirty years as an award-winning interior designer of commercial and retail environments. Her principal research interests are in the complex contexts of commercial design/branding, institutional and residential design for vulnerable populations including children, the aged, persons with disabilities and humanitarian design initiatives in situated, project-based learning. Other research interests include the dynamics of theory/practice in interior design problem-solving, and developing arts-based, interpretive design research methodologies from participatory research perspectives.

Katelijn Quartier holds a PhD in interior architecture (topic retail design) and currently works at the Faculty of Architecture and Arts of Hasselt University, where she teaches retail design in theory and practice. In addition to teaching, she is researching what the store of tomorrow should look like and what the role of design plays in it. She has presented her work at various international conferences and she has published, among others, in *Powershop 2: New Retail Design* (Frame) and in the *Journal of Environmental Psychology*. In addition to her academic career, she runs her own retail design agency.

Bhakti Sharma is an Associate Professor and Chairperson at the Department of Interior Design, State University of New York at Buffalo, where she has taught courses in corporate and retail design, lighting design, thesis and research, and coordinated internships. She received a Master's of Science in Design degree with concentration in Facilities, Planning, and Management from Arizona State University in 2006, where her focus was the study of socio-economic impact on hospitality lighting. Originally from India, Sharma has a Bachelor's of Architecture degree from Punjab Technical University. She has worked on several large multi-use, corporate, retail and religious projects in Arizona and India. Her research focus is on corporate architecture and branding.

Tommy Tse is Assistant Professor in Department of Sociology, the University of Hong Kong, and specializes in fashion communication, luxury branding and media and cultural studies. His work has appeared in the *Asian Journal of Business Research*; *International Journal of Fashion Design, Technology and Education*; *Clothing Cultures*; *International Journal of Fashion Studies*; and *Luxury Brands in Emerging Markets*. Tse taught at Hong

Kong Baptist University and Hong Kong Design Institute, and has experience in advertising and marketing in several media companies and creative agencies; he also worked as a project-based copywriter for various global fashion brands for over six years.

Koenraad Van Cleempoel studied Art History in Louvain, Madrid and London. He obtained his PhD degree at the Warburg Institute. Since 2005, he has been engaged in establishing a research unit in interior architecture at Hasselt Universit. He has published on the relationship between art and science during the Renaissance, especially in the field of scientific instruments. Currently, he is engaged in the study of adaptive reuse of heritage sites in general and religious heritage in particular.

Delia Vazquez is Senior Lecturer in Retail Marketing at the University of Manchester. She spent five years working in Retail Management and Buying with the Co-operative Group, where she developed her retail design skills in marketing and the retail environment. She is currently founder and Programme Director of the International Fashion Retailing MSc at the University of Manchester. She has published forty-two publications since 1996 in Retail Design Management and Online Retailing fields. She was the first academic to teach Retail E-Commerce in the UK in 1998. She has supervised eight PhD students to completion on Online Retail and Online Retail Design subject fields. Her current research interests include Online Virtual Fit interfaces, Brain Computer Interaction, and Fashion aesthetics online.

Index

Note: Page numbers in italic indicate a figure or table on the corresponding page.